W9-ACG-086

Black
Imagination
and the
Middle Passage

The W.E.B. Du Bois Institute brings together leading scholars from around the world to explore a range of topics in the study of African and African American culture, literature, and history. The Institute series provides a publishing forum for outstanding work deriving from colloquia, research groups, and conferences sponsored by the Institute. Whether undertaken by individuals or collaborative groups, the books appearing in this series work to foster a stronger sense of national and international community and a better understanding of diasporic history.

Series Editors

Henry Louis Gates, Jr.
W.E.B. Du Bois Professor of Humanities
Harvard University

Richard Newman
Research Officer
The W.E.B. Du Bois Institute
Harvard University

The Open Sore of a Continent
A Personal Narrative of the Nigerian Crisis
Wole Soyinka

From Emerson to King
Democracy, Race and the Politics of Protest
Anita Haya Patterson

Primitivist Modernism
Black Culture and the Origins of Transatlantic Modernism
Sieglinde Lemke

The Burden of Memory, the Muse of Forgiveness
Wole Soyinka

Color by Fox
The Fox Network and the Revolution in
Black Television
Kristal Brent Zook

Black Imagination and the Middle Passage
Maria Diedrich
Henry Louis Gates, Jr.
Carl Pedersen

Black Imagination and the Middle Passage

• • • •

Edited by

MARIA DIEDRICH

HENRY LOUIS GATES, JR.

CARL PEDERSEN

New York   Oxford

Oxford University Press

1999

Oxford University Press

Oxford   New York
Athens   Auckland   Bangkok   Bogotá   Buenos Aires   Calcutta
Cape Town   Chennai   Dar es Salaam   Delhi   Florence   Hong Kong   Istanbul
Karachi   Kuala Lumpur   Madrid   Melbourne   Mexico City   Mumbai
Nairobi   Paris   São Paulo   Singapore   Taipei   Tokyo   Toronto   Warsaw

and associated companies in
Berlin   Ibadan

Copyright © 1999 by Oxford University Press, Inc.

Published by Oxford University Press, Inc.
198 Madison Avenue, New York, New York 10016

Oxford is a registered trademark of Oxford University Press

Library of Congress Cataloging-in-Publication Data
Black imagination and the middle passage / edited by Maria Diedrich,
Henry Louis Gates, Jr., Carl Pedersen.
p. cm.—(W.E.B. Du Bois Institute)
Includes Index.
ISBN 0-19-512640-8—ISBN 0-19-512641-6 (pbk.)
1. American literature—Afro-American authors—History and criticism.   2. Slave-trade
in literature.   3. Caribbean literature (English)—Black authors—History and criticism.
4. Afro-Americans—Intellectual life.   5. Afro-Americans in literature.   6. Slaves
in literature.   7. Blacks in literature.   8. Slave trade—History.
I. Diedrich, Maria.   II. Gates, Henry Louis.   III. Pedersen, Carl.
IV. Series: W.E.B. Du Bois Institute (Series)
PS153.N5B554   1999   98-24622
81.9'893073—dc21

1 3 5 7 9 8 6 4 2

Printed in the United States of America
on acid-free paper

Contents

Part III "In Africa, There Are No Niggers"

Contributors

Editors

MARIA DIEDRICH holds a Chair in American Studies and is director of the American Studies Program at the University of Münster, Germany. She is president of the Collegium for African American Research and a fellow at the W.E.B. Du Bois Institute for Afro-American Research at Harvard. Among her book publications are *Communism in the Communist Party of the United States between World Wars I and II* (1979), *Escape from Bondage: The American Slave Narrative between the Declaration of Independence and the Civil War* (1986) and *Love across Color Lines: Ottilie Assing and Frederick Douglass* (1999). Among others, she has coauthored and coedited *Protest, Rebellion, and Dissent within the Black Community* (1989; with Berndt Ostendorf), *The Black Columbiad: Defining Moments in African American Literature and Culture* (1994; with Werner Sollors) and *Mapping African America* (1999; with Carl Pedersen and Justine Tally).

HENRY LOUIS GATES, JR., teaches English at Harvard University, where he is W.E.B. Du Bois Professor of the Humanities, chairman of the Afro-American Studies Department and director of the W.E.B. Du Bois Institute for Afro-American Research. Among his numerous publications are *The Future of the Race* (1996; with Cornel West), *Loose Canons* (1992), *The Signifying Monkey* (1988), and *Figures in Black: Words, Signs, and the "Racial" Self*

(1987). He edited *Reading Black, Reading Feminist: A Critical Anthology* (1990), *The Classic Slave Narratives* (1987), *"Race," Writing, and Difference* (1986), and *Black Literature and Literary Theory* (1984). With Charles T. Davis he coedited *The Slave's Narrative* (1985), with K. A. Appiah the Amistad Literary Series, with Nellie McKay the *Norton Anthology of African American Literature* (1997). He is also general editor of the Schomburg Library of Nineteenth-Century Black Women Writers.

CARL PEDERSEN is associate professor of American Studies at Odense University, Denmark and the conference secretary of the Collegium for African American Research. He has been a research fellow at the Schomburg Center for Research in Black Culture (1993) and the W.E.B. Du Bois Institute for Afro-American Research (1996). He has coedited *Voices from the African American Experience* (1995; with Fran Hopenwasser) and *Mapping African America* (1999; with Maria Diedrich and Justine Tally). His essay "America's Others: The Uses of the Black Underclass and the New Immigrants" was published in *Social and Secure* (1996), edited by Hans Bak at al., and "Sea Change: The Middle Passage and the Transatlantic Imagination" in *The Black Columbiad* (1994), edited by Maria Diedrich and Werner Sollors.

Contributors

STEPHEN D. BEHRENDT is currently a research associate at the Du Bois Institute, Harvard University. He received his PhD in History at the University of Wisconsin-Madison in 1993. His thesis was entitled "The British Slave Trade, 1785–1807: Volume, Profitability and Mortality." He is author of several articles on the transatlantic slave trade, which have appeared in *History in Africa, Slavery and Abolition,* and other journals.

JESÙS BENITO and ANA MANZANAS teach American and English literature at the Universidad de Castilla-La Mancha, Spain. Apart from a number of articles on African American literature which have appeared in different journals, they have written a book on James Baldwin and Toni Morrison, entitled *La estética del recuerdo: La narrativa de James Baldwin y Toni Morrison* (1994). They have also coedited translations into Spanish of a selection of Olaudah Equiano's *The Interesting Narrative of the Life of Olaudah Equiano* (1994), W.E.B. Du Bois's *The Souls of Black Folk* (1995), and Martin Luther King's *Sermons and Speeches* (1997).

EVA BOESENBERG studied German, English, and Indology at Freiburg, Germany. Her dissertation focused on gender, orality, and literacy in Zora Neale Hurston, Alice Walker, and Toni Morrison. She has also written about Gloria Naylor and Ntozake Shange, as well as black male images in basketball. Assistant professor for American Studies at Martin-Luther-University Halle-Wittenberg, she is currently working on money and gender relations in the American novel.

MELBA JOYCE BOYD is a poet, educator, essayist, filmmaker, and biographer currently teaching at Wayne State University. Among her volumes of poetry are *Cat Eyes and Dead Wood* (1978), *Thirteen Frozen Flamingoes* (1984), *Song for Maya* (1983), and *The Inventory of Roses* (1989). Her biography of Frances E. W. Harper, *Discarded Legacy: Politics and Poetics in the Life of Frances E. W. Harper* came out in 1994. Her film, *The Black Unicorn: Dudley Randall and Broadside Press*, premiered in 1996. The poem included in this volume, "Transatlantic Passages Revisited, Tenerife" was written as a tribute to the CAAR conference.

LENE BRØNDUM received her MA from the University of Copenhagen; her master's thesis dealt with African American folk traditions in Toni Morrison's *Song of Solomon* and Ralph Ellison's *Invisible Man*. She taught American Studies at the University of Copenhagen and Roskilde University and is now teaching at a high school in Copenhagen. She has published an educational game of English grammar for high school students.

FRANÇOISE CHARRAS taught at the University of Paris VII for a number of years before becoming maître de conférences at the Université Paul Valéry of Montpellier where she currently teaches Afro-American and Caribbean literatures. She has published several articles and translations in the field of American Gothic fiction as well as articles on Toni Morrison and Paule Marshall.

HÉLÈNE CHRISTOL received her PhD from the University of Paris, Sorbonne, with a thesis on American writers and the Sacco-Vanzetti affair; it was published in 1984 by the University of Lille Press. She is now professor of American Studies and chairperson of the American Studies Program at the University of Provence, Aix-Marseille I, France, and the director of the Aix-based research group in American Studies, GRENA. She is the author of various publications on the American radical tradition and on aspects of African American culture and literature. Among her more recent articles are "Black Riots and 'Urban Guerilla' in the 1960s" in *Urban America in the Sixties* (1994) and "Reconstructing American History: Land and Genealogy in Naylor's *Mama Day*," in *The Black Columbiad* (1994), "Social and Political Transgressions in Gloria Naylor's Novels," in *La Transgression* (1996) and "Figures de l'authorité: Maîtres et esclaves dans *Kindred* d'Octavia Butler" in *Normes et Autorité*.

DAVID ELTIS is currently professor of history at Queen's University, Kingston, Ontario and a research associate of the University of Hull, England and the Du Bois Institute, Harvard University. He received his PhD from the University of Rochester in 1979 and is author of *Economic Growth and the Ending of the Transatlantic Slave Trade* (1987) and many articles on migration and the impact of the slave trade on Africa.

JAMES A. EMANUEL is a poet and scholar currently living in Paris. With Theodore L. Gross he coedited *Dark Symphony: Negro Literature in America* in 1968, and his critical study *Langston Hughes* came out in 1967. Among his collections of poetry are *The Treehouse and Other Poems* (1968), *Black Man Abroad* (1978), *The Chisel in the Dark* (1980), *The Broken Bowl* (1983), and *Deadly James and Other Poems* (1987); his collected poems were published in 1991 as *Whole Grain: Collected Poems, 1958–1989*. His poems have been widely anthologized, and published in journals all over the world. Emanuel wrote "The Middle Passage Blues" as a tribute to the CAAR conference in Tenerife.

M. GIULIA FABI received her PhD from the University of California-Berkeley and is currently assistant professor of American literature at the University of Rome. She has published articles on William Wells Brown, Frank J. Webb, Toni Morrison, Amelia E. Johnson, Frances Harper, Sutton E. Griggs, Henry James, Edward Bellamy, Pauline Hopkins, and African American feminist criticism. She is editor of an anthology of African American short stories and is currently completing a book on the trope of passing in early African American fiction.

GENEVIÈVE E. FABRE is professor at the Université Denis Diderot-Paris VII, where she has organized several international conferences on Hispanics and African Americans. She has authored books and essays on F. S. Fitzgerald, Joyce Carol Oates, James Agee, the Harlem Renaissance, and the theater of protest. She has edited two volumes of essays on Toni Morrison (one with Claudine Raynaud, 1992) and two volumes on ethnicity. She has also edited *History and Memory in African American Culture* (with Robert O'Meally, 1994), and *Feasts and Celebrations of American Ethnic Communities* (with Ramón Gutierréz, 1995) and a collection of essays (1997) on "the street" in North American ethnic neighborhoods. After writing on African American theater (*Drumbeats, Masks and Metaphor*, Harvard University Press, 1984), she is now preparing a book on African American commemorative and celebratory events, 1750–1875, and co-editing (with Michel Teith) books on the Harlem Renaissance and on Jean Toomer, and (with J. Heideking) on Festive Culture and National Identity in the United States, 1787–1900.

KATJA FÜLLBERG-STOLBERG is a research fellow for African and African American history at the Geisteswissenschaftliche Zentren e.V., Center for Modern Oriental Studies, Berlin, Germany. She is teaching African and African American history at Homboldt University, Berlin, and the University of Hannover. She did her PhD thesis on the impact of the Great Depression in Northern Nigeria (*Nordnigeria während der Weltwirtschaftskrise 1929–1939*, Centaurus Verlag, 1997). Her current research project is "The African American Appropriation of Africa. The Black American's Image of Africa between 'Civilizing Mission' and Pan-Africanism." Her articles on the Congo atrocities, on African American women missionaries in Central Africa, and "Afrocentrism" were published in Germany.

JOHANNA X. K. GARVEY holds a PhD in comparative literature from the University of California, Berkeley. She has taught at Rutgers University and New York University and is currently associate professor in English and was founding codirector of the Program in Black Studies: Africa and the Diaspora at Fairfield University. She has published articles on contemporary women writers of color, including Larsen, Petry, Marshall, Kincaid, Naylor, and Morrison, as well as James Joyce and V. Woolf. Her forthcoming book is *City Voyages: Gender and Reflexivity in the Modern Novel*.

FRITZ GYSIN is a professor of English and American literature at the University of Bern, Switzerland. He has written two books, *The Grotesque in American Negro Fiction* (1975) and *Model as Motif in Tristram Shandy* (1983), and has published articles on Sterling Brown, Joseph Conrad, Leon Forrest, Charles Johnson, Nathaniel Hawthorne, Langston Hughes, Nathaniel Mackey, George Schuyler, Jean Toomer, Mark Twain, John Edgar Wideman, and Sherley Anne Williams. He is working on a book about boundaries in African American fiction. He is a founding member of the Collegium for African American Research.

CYNTHIA S. HAMILTON is subject leader for American Studies at the Crewe and Alsager Faculty of Manchester Metropolitan University. Her work on the slave narrative and related genres has resulted in a number of conference contributions. An article on "Revisions, Rememories, and Exorcisms: Toni Morrison and the Slave Narrative" is to be published in the *Journal of American Studies*. A longer work is in progress: *The Finest Sentiments: Slavery and Popular Discourse in Ante-bellum America*.

CLAUDE JULIEN teaches American Studies at Université François Rabelais in Tours (France). He defended his doctoral dissertation "L'enfance et l'adolescence chez les romanciers afro-américains, 1853-1969" in 1981 (Université de Paris 8). He has contributed a number of articles on African American fiction and African American studies to various journals in Europe and the United States. His preferred approach to fiction is discursive analysis thanks to the tools of "sociocriticism." He is a co-founder of the Cercle d'Etudes Afro-Américaines (CEAA) based in the universities of Paris III, Tours and Paris VII.

CLARA JUNCKER, associate professor (1996), Center for American Studies at Odense University, Denmark, has lectured and published widely on African American studies on both sides of the Atlantic, including *Black Roses: Afro-American Women Writers* (1985). She has taught African American Literature at Tulane University, University of California, Los Angeles, the Copenhagen Business School, Aarhus University, and Odense University.

TOBE LEVIN holds a PhD in comparative literature from Cornell University. She is a lecturer in American Studies for the University of Maryland European Division and J.W.-Goethe Universität Frankfurt and has coedited a collection of essays on FGM, with Ingrid Braun and Angelika Schwarzbauer. *Materialien zur Unterstützung von Aktionsgruppen gegen Klitorisbeschneidung* (1979). Her articles have been published in European and American journals.

ROBERT H. MCCORMICK, JR., taught for six years at Harvard in the Department of Romance Languages and for history and literature. He is now an associate professor in literature at Franklin College in Lugano, Switzerland. Specializing in nineteenth-century French literature, especially Hugo and Zola, McCormick has made presentations on Hugo's novel on the aftermath of the French Revolution in Haiti, *Bug-Jargal*, and on Maryse Condé, about whom he also has published an article in the Italian journal, *Caribana*. He also has articles on Condé forthcoming for the Ist: Into Universitario Oriente in Naples and the African Literature Association.

ALESSANDRO PORTELLI teaches American literature at the University of Rome "La Sapienza" and is secretary of CAAR. Among his works are *The Death of Luigi Trastulli and Other Stories. Form and Meaning in Oral History* (Albany: SUNY Press, 1991); *The Text and the Voice. Speaking, Writing, and Democracy in American Literature* (New York: Columbia University Press, 1994); *The Practice of Oral History, The Battle of Valle Giulia and Other Stories* (Madison: University of Wisconsin Press, forthcoming). He has also written on African-American literature, Appalachian studies, popular music and culture, American and Italian folklore, and the American literary canon. He is the editor of *Acoma*, an Italian journal of American studies.

CLAUDINE RAYNAUD is a professor of English and American literature at the University François Rabelais, Tours (France). Educated in the United States (the University of Michigan, Ann Arbor) and in France, she has been working on autobiographical writings by African American writers and Black artists. (Brooks, Angelou, Lorde, Kennedy, Wideman, Isaac Julien/Hughes). Her essays have been anthologized in *Life/Lines* (1988) and *De-Colonizing the Subject* (1992) as well as in French publications. She has also headed the "Genesis and Autobiography" research group at ITEM-CNRS. Her recent work includes an extensive study of the manuscript of Hurston's *Dust Tracks on a Road* and a monograph on Toni Morrison. (*Toni Morison. L'Esthétique de la survie*, Belin, 1997). She has also published on Marvell, Herbert, Milton, Joyce, and Lowry.

DAVID RICHARDSON is currently a professor of economic and social history at the University of Hull, England. He has published a four-volume catalog of the slave trade from Bristol, an electronic data set of ships registered in the Liverpool Plantation Registers, as well as many articles on the transatlantic slave traffic, especially the African coastal origins of the trade. Some of these have appeared in the *Journal of African History, Research in Economic History, Journal of Economic History,* and *Economic History Review.* He is also editor and contributor to *Abolition and Its Aftermath* (1986).

MANISHA SINHA is an assistant professor of Afro-American studies and history at the University of Massachusetts, Amherst. She is the author of "Louisa Susanna McCord: Spokeswoman of the Master Class in Antebellum South Carolina" in Susan Ostrov Weisser and Jennifer Fleischner, eds., *Feminist Nightmares: Women at Odds* (New York: New York University Press, 1994) and is currently working on a manuscript on the politics of slavery and secession in antebellum South Carolina. Her dissertation, "The Counter-Revolution of Slavery: Class, Politics, and Ideology in Antebellum South Carolina," was nominated for the Bancroft Award at Columbia University in 1994.

MARIE TYLER-MCGRAW is currently a historian in the office of the Chief Historian, National Park Service, Washington, D.C. She is the author of *At the Falls: Richmond, Virginia and Its People* (Chapel Hill: University of North Carolina Press, 1994) and has published widely on contested issues in public history, African American history, and the antebellum South.

HANNA WALLINGER is a part-time assistant professor at the Institut für Anglistik und Amerikanistik of Salzburg University. Her main research interests are African American literature and women's literature. Her articles on Alice Walker, Paule Marshall, Zora Neale Hurston, Gloria Naylor and Dorothy Parker have appeared in European and American journals and essay collections.

Black
Imagination
and the
Middle Passage

Prologue

James A. Emanuel

The Middle Passage Blues

"Middle Passage:" the WORD means blues to me.
Look at it front or backside, it still means BLUES to me.
If I'da been a sailor on the Seven Seas
I'da sailed the seven ENDS and let the MIDDLES be. . . .
But if I'da been a sailor, I'da still been black.
THAT'S why the blues keeps sailin' back.
The blues keeps sailin' back.

I can HYP-NO-TIZE myself rememberin' Grandma's chair;
she had slave-girl mem'ries, and she rocked and hummed 'em there:
her daddy's neck and legs in chains, his own vomit in his hair—
stories Grandma told me—she rocked and hum-m-med 'em there:
Great-grandpa's neck and legs stretched out, with vomit in his hair;
and suddenly I'm runnin'-runnin'-runnin' through the town,
faces spinnin' round me while I'm runnin' through the town,
runnin' with my feelin's, tryin' to run my feelin's down,
Grandma hummin-n-n-n at my feelin's while I'm tryin' to run 'em down;
till suddenly . . . I see her chair, I feel she's got my han'
and she's sayin' "When you grow up you be a Middle Passage man."

Middle Passage mem'ries . . . they in a dungeon in my head.
Ain't no jailor, ain't no keys, ain't no judgment read;
but I hear clankin', I hear breathin' (all them dungeon folks ain't dead);

Great-grandpa's clankin' while he's breathin' (*chains* the only word he
    said).
He's breathin' and I'm listenin' and Grandma's got my han'
(Oh, if I'da been a sailor I'da sailed on past this lan'!).
I got the Middle Passage blues, and I can hardly stan',
but Great-grandpa's still there breathin' and Grandma's got my han'
(I ain't runnin', I'm just standin', but I had to have a plan,
somethin' to KEEP me on my feet, 'cause I'm in a dungeon lan').

I got the Middle Passage blues, but my folks gave me a plan
(Grandma said it, "When you grow up you be a Middle Passage man").
I'm a stand-up sailor.
I'm a Middle Passage man.

1

• • • •

The Middle Passage between History and Fiction

Introductory Remarks

Maria Diedrich
Henry Louis Gates, Jr.
Carl Pedersen

In the aftermath of the failed 1848 revolutions in Europe, one of the leading members of the Russian radical intelligentsia, Alexander Herzen, summed up the mood of disillusionment and distrust of the idea of progress among many of the Russian intelligentsia in a striking passage in his tract *From the Other Shore:* "If humanity went straight to some goal," he wrote, "there would be no history, only logic."[1] However, in the modern era, which arguably began with the encounter between Europe, Africa, and the Americas—and thus also with the beginning of the slave trade in the sixteenth century—the main trajectory of Western European thought seemed to aim straight toward "some goal" of human cultural progress, undergirded by the "logic" of unbridled economic development. Defenses of the slave system were based on discursive polarities that soothed the collective consciousness of Europeans. Eurocentric and hierarchical concepts of culture and, based on this Eurocentrism, the civilizing mission of Western European culture, relegated Africa to the subordinate position of the Dark Continent, which represented the fallen image of Europe's past, and the Americas to the Virgin Land, which contained the hope for Europe's future.

That future was predicated on the slave trade, its magnitude amply documented by historians using quantification methods. Indeed, much of the historiography of the slave trade has been a numbers game. The most comprehensive (and to date accurate) work has been carried out by

Philip Curtin, who estimated that a total of 10 to 11 million slaves were brought to the Americas from Africa. Of that number, more than 85 percent were brought to the Caribbean and Brazil. Owing to a variety of factors, from the modest number of about 600,000 Africans on the North American mainland grew the largest slave population in the Western hemisphere. The preliminary results of the Harvard Slave Trade Project, published for the first time in this volume, indicate that the "distribution of Africans in the New World was no more randomized than was its European counterpart."[2] It is important to remember that the conditions for population increase varied, depending on natural as well as man-made causes. The numbers of slaves who came to the Americas demonstrate the magnitude of the trade and point to the inhuman treatment and suffering endured by the captives.

One of the most striking images of the Middle Passage (the journey from Africa to the Americas) is the tight-packing of the slave ships, an illustration often used in history textbooks and anthologies on the African American experience. This image is no doubt familiar, even hackneyed. The injustice and brutality of tight-packing is unquestionable, the suffering and horror experienced by the slaves unimaginable. Add to that image the lack of proper diet, the unhygienic conditions that prevailed aboard the ships, affecting slave and crew alike, as well as the brutalities the Africans suffered at the hands of their white captors, and the inhumanity of the institution of slavery is laid bare. Apologists for the slave trade attempted to gloss over this inhumanity by claiming that Africans, at a lower stage of development than Europeans, were immune to this treatment. They believed that only by gradually learning civilized practices would Africans eventually escape from the cultural hold that strangled them. Opponents of slavery, on the other hand, pointed to the cruelty and violence of the trade as well as to the incongruity of supposedly civilized nations engaging in wanton inhumanity.

Generations of historians seeking justification for the trade transformed the physical contortions of the slaves into a cultural distortion of their experience in the Americas. Examining the work of British historians writing about the Caribbean, Eric Williams bluntly states that "[t]he dominant note in British historical writing between 1880 and 1914 is imperialism, the justification, encouragement, defence, and apology for colonies."[3] Williams's list of apologists for the imperial project includes James Anthony Froude, who visited the Caribbean in 1887 and wrote a book based on his observations, *The English in the West Indies, or the Bow of Ulysses* (1888). Froude defended the slave trade by casting the Africans in the role of children in need of imperial benevolence and guidance. Thus, slaves could be raised from their primitive state only with the aid of European civilization; without it, they would inevitably recede into darkness. This commonplace attitude is of course rooted in the Enlightenment's linear view of historical progress.

Ironically, opponents of slavery used images of physical contortion to condemn trade as inhuman and therefore incongruent with European notions of progress. According to the Guyanese writer Wilson Harris, these "ceaseless catalogues of injustice," promulgated by both nineteenth-century opponents of slavery and latter-day Caribbean intellectuals, had the unintended effect of confirming black inadequacy and cultural emasculation. Consequently, Harris would convert the image of the tightly packed ship into another, more potent image of the experience of the Middle Passage: the limbo dance of slaves brought up from the hold for a brief respite from their suffering. The beginning of African American culture is not to be sought in the image of tight-packing, he argued, but rather in the few moments and marginally expanded space on the deck (under the watchful eye of the crew), where the African captives replicated their physical contortions in dance. In this way, Harris seeks to formulate "a philosophy of history which is original to [the Caribbean] and yet capable of universal application."[4] This philosophy is thus defined by what Homi Bhabha calls the space in-between, rejecting the stringent opposition between above and below, between civilized and savage, that informs the discourses of slavery's defenders and its opponents.[5]

It is no accident that Harris focuses on the emergence of an African American folk culture as a way out of what he decries as the impasse of historical discourse. The study of folklife, which John Vlach has identified as "the total lifeway of a group of people including their verbal, material, and spiritual forms of expression," fuses culture and history, setting different cultural forms (like Harris's limbo dance) "against the backdrop of their pertinent cultural history."[6] In line with Harris's emphasis on the surfacing of an incipient African American culture from the holds of the slave ships, observers of twentieth-century African American folk practices claim the significance of these practices for a definition of African American culture that transcends the binary categories of oppressor and victim. Thus, Alan Lomax, in his recent book about blues cultures in the Mississippi Delta in the 1930s and 1940s, *The Land Where Blues Began*, claims that

> black African nonverbal performance traditions had survived virtually intact in African America, and had shaped all its distinctive rhythmic arts, during both the colonial and the postcolonial periods. It was this unwritten but rich African tradition that empowered the creativity we had encountered in the lower depths of the

Mississippi Delta. The error in African-American studies had been
to look to print and to language for evidence of African survivals.[7]

If we sidestep the potential dangers in this and similar statements
about the "authenticity" of African folk survivals, we can look for the
geographical dimensions of a Middle Passage sensibility in the Americas.[8] Constructing a cultural map of African America would arguably reveal varying degrees of cultural survival: in the United States, for example, in the Delta region and the Georgia and South Carolina Sea Islands;
in the Caribbean and Brazil, in mountain or jungle areas that had a high
incidence of maroonage. An African American concept of space had its
beginnings in the holds of the slave ships during the Middle Passage and
appears in different settings, such as the relationship between clandestine slave religious practices and the dominant center of the plantations
in the United States and Caribbean, or the idea of Anancy and the Great
House as a defining paradigm for the development of Caribbean literary
tradition. Other examples include the disquieting appearance of obeah
practices, upsetting the order of colonial domination in Caribbean fiction
from Claude McKay's *Banana Bottom* to Caryl Phillips's *Cambridge;* Paule
Marshall's first three novels charting the triangular slave trade in reverse;
the memory of the Middle Passage in Toni Morrison's *Beloved* (1987),
Fred d'Aguiar's *The Longest Memory* (1994), and Henry Dumas's "Arc of
Bones"; the return to Africa in Brathwaite's *The Arrivants* or Eddy Harris's
Native Stranger (1992); and exile in the imperial center in the work of
George Lamming or Sam Selvon.

The Middle Passage thus emerges not as a clean break between past
and present but as a spatial continuum between Africa and the Americas,
the ship's deck and the hold, the Great House and the slave quarters, the
town and the outlying regions. Undermining the imbalance of the power
of the surface and the weakness of the depths (deck/hold) is Edward
Brathwaite's notion of nation language. Submerged beneath the surface
of the dominant language, it constantly seeps through and inevitably affects it.

In arguing for a spatial and temporal continuum of a Middle Passage
sensibility, the editors and contributors in this volume define a topography that extends from the interior of Africa across the Atlantic and into
the interior of the Americas. For Harris, performance styles herald a new
configuration for African American expression, what Carl Pedersen has
called a transatlantic imagination.[9] Following Wilson Harris, we see the
need to construct such an imagination by reconceptualizing the meaning
of the Middle Passage for African American history and fiction. Several
intermeshing elements constitute this new conceptualization. Instead of

looking at the Middle Passage as a phenomenon of constricted space and limited time, the essays collected here extend its meaning in time and space from the particularities of internal African migration to current meditations on the relationship of African Americans to their past, from the hierarchical spatial relationships of above/below (the deck of the slave ship and its hold) and center/periphery (e.g., the Great House and the slave quarters; in a more abstract sense, the primarily European construction of an Africa as well as an African diaspora outside of history) to the syncretic notion of a space in-between that links geographical and cultural regions. The idea of a space in-between, voiced recently in Homi Bhabha's *The Location of Culture* and Paul Gilroy's *The Black Atlantic*, articulates this Middle Passage sensibility within and across the disciplines of history and literature, and within and across ethnic, racial, and national boundaries. In other words, the theory of the Middle Passage is necessarily interdisciplinary, comparative, and international.[10]

Essentialism—the Middle Passage as defined by British imperial historians and writers like Naipaul ("nothing was created in the West Indies"), digging a chasm between Africa and the Americas; the racial essentialism of negritudinists such as Aimé Césaire and Léopold Sédar Senghor; the construction of a monolithic Africa outside of history by Afrocentrists from Marcus Garvey to Kete Molefi Asante—must defer to hybrid theoretical perspectives. Edouard Glissant sets his dynamic notion of *antillanité*, a system of mutiple interrelated cultures, against the sterility of negritude; Paul Gilroy examines the discourse of the Atlantic world, touching the Americas, Great Britain, and Africa, thus challenging the one-sidedness of Afrocentric discourse. In Latin America, Gilberto Freyre's articulation of racial harmony rooted in biological and cultural miscegenation and Alejo Carpentier's idea of cultural *mestizaje* as the central metaphor in the aesthetics of *lo real maravilloso* offer an alternative mode of thinking to U.S. binary oppositions and the cultural exclusivity between black and white (Octavio Paz, of course, has developed a similar view of the difference between Mexican and American culture). In Joyce Jonas's metaphor for a new reading of Caribbean fiction, the presence of Anancy in the Great House produces webs of signification that undermine the Great House/ Slave Quarter topographical dichotomy.[11]

Heeding these models, the editors and contributors here argue that discourses of oppression (the deck of the slave ship over the hold, the Great House against the slave quarters, peripheral maronnage against imperial center) and resistance (rebellion and black nationalism, the biological determinism of negritude) perpetuate notions of exclusivity that obscure intricate networks of cross-cultural influence. In numerous examples of investigation, we demonstrate these oppositional discourses undermined by rituals of performance, by the construction and use of artifacts, and by linguistic practices.

The following essays stress the importance of these rituals and folk practices, as well as the significance attributed to them by Caribbean and Latin American intellectuals because they contribute to an interpretation of African American culture that is, in Stephen Greenblatt's formulation, at once "sensitive to the symbolic dimensions of social practice" and to "the historical dimensions of symbolic practice."[12] It is noteworthy that while slave historiography has traditionally fallaciously perpetuated an ultimately misleading dichotomy between Americanization and African survival, African American literary criticism in the twentieth century has vacillated between a sociohistorical and a "literary" approach. Franklin Frazier's claim that slaves had become fully Americanized was later countered by Melville Herskovits, who argued for a continuing African cultural legacy among black Americans.

The extended Middle Passage, with localized cultural webs of signification that form the generic metaphor of this volume, mediates within the disciplines of history and literature by arguing beyond essentialism to cross-cultural hybridization, attempting to blur the boundaries between history and fiction by using symbolic practices to undermine historical linearity. In George Lipsitz's words, "story-telling" (and for that matter performance art) combines "subjectivity and objectivity" and "employs the insights and passions of myth and folklore in the service of revising history."[13] Instead of an historical perspective that starts with totality and locates the particular within a given paradigm (Herzen's definition of logic as opposed to real history), the Middle Passage paradigm begins with local practices that intermesh and form a totality (Harris's limbo gateway to the transatlantic imagination). A quote from Harris's book of essays on literature, *The Womb of Space*, neatly sums up the concerns of the Middle Passage paradigm:

> It is necessary to make clear within the fabric of imaginative exploration we shall pursue that homogeneity is a biological hypothesis that relates all mankind to a basic or primordial ancestor, but as a cultural model, exercised by a ruling ethnic group, it tends to become an organ of conquest and division because of imposed unity that actually subsists on the suppression of others.
>
> The paradox of cultural heterogeneity, or cross-cultural capacity, lies in the evolutionary thrust it restores to orders of the imagination, the ceaseless dialogue it inserts between hardened conventions and eclipsed or half-eclipsed otherness, within an intuitive self that moves endlessly into flexible patterns, arcs or bridges of community.[14]

In February 1995 the Collegium for African American Research (CAAR), a Europe-based association of scholars working in the field of African American studies, hosted a conference in Puerto de la Cruz, Tenerife (Spain), inviting colleagues from Africa, the Americas, and Europe to discuss the history and the meaning of the transatlantic passage for African Americans. Tenerife, a beautiful island in the Atlantic Ocean, less than two hundred miles off the coast of Africa, seemed a most appropriate setting for the issues this international gathering was about to tackle: on their way to the Americas, the ships loaded with African slaves stopped at the Canary Islands for water, food, and other supplies. For a small number of Africans the islands became a new home; for most of the captives they were their last contact with Africa before they sailed off into the unfamiliar.

All contributions assembled in this volume are original, previously unpublished essays that were first presented at the CAAR conference in Tenerife. Though closely related to the theme of the conference, "Transatlantic Passages," the great variety of issues they study, as well as the wide range of approaches they take, not only represents the complexity and multifariousness of a process that became the definer of the African American experience as it changed the faces of Africa, the Americas, and Europe, of victims and victimizers alike, but also challenges us to recover the many voices silenced by the monologic master narrative and to embrace the polyphony of their re-memories. At the center of this collection we encounter departure, passage, and arrival; deprivation, transformation, and affirmation; loss, quest, and appropriation; the master narrative and subversive memory.

The essays were subdivided into three sections mirroring the three decisive stages of the transatlantic passage. Part I, "Voyage through Death . . . ," focuses on the trauma of dislocation that victims of the slave trade suffered as they were kidnapped from their communities, dragged across Africa in chains, and exposed to the horrors of the Middle Passage; part II, ". . . To Life upon These Shores," traces the process in which the involuntary black pioneers appropriated the unfamiliar—the master's "brave New World"—transforming the continent by their very presence and reinventing themselves as African Americans and as subjects of history; part III, "In Africa, There Are No Niggers," ventures to define the meaning which Africa acquired for the African American community and to understand that community's many attempts to rediscover and reimagine the African American Old World from a New World perspective.

"Transatlantic Passages," the title of our conference, pointed to the processual, continuous, international aspect of the experience, which again is mirrored by the international and interdisciplinary quality of the discipline we call African American studies. We editors paid tribute to this challenging heterogeneity and polyphony of the field by inviting scholars from the Old Worlds and the New, junior scholars and experienced colleagues, to join a process of intellectual quest and exchange that was bound to ask and face many questions, that will no doubt suggest a number of interpretations and perhaps even answers, and that we hope will stimulate new ventures of research and investigation, as well as new forms of international and interdisciplinary cooperation. We brought together people of very different backgrounds, whose motives for entering the field, whose approaches to and expectations of the discipline, differ dramatically. What we intended in assembling these individuals, interests, and readings was not a sentimental celebration of a "we" that could only parody community. To use Audre Lorde's words, "To acknowledge our dreams is to sometimes acknowledge the distance between those dreams and our present situation. Acknowledged, our dreams can shape the realities of our future, if we arm them with the hard work and scrutiny of now. We cannot settle for the pretenses of connections, or for the parodies of self-love." The volume thus embraces a collectivity defined by difference, by a multiplicity of visions; it is an endeavor to deal creatively with complexity and multiplicity, without succumbing to what Freud feared as the "narcissism of small differences." For, after all, there is a common denominator. As Gwendolyn Brooks reminds us,

> We are each other's business.
> We are each other's magnitude and bond.

Notes

1. Alexander Herzen, *From the Other Shore* [1850], quoted in Isaiah Berlin, *Russian Thinkers* (Harmondsworth: Penguin, 1979): p. 92.

2. See Philip Curtin, *The Atlantic Slave Trade: A Census* (Madison: University of Wisconsin Press, 1970). See also chapter 2 in this volume.

3. Eric Wiliams, *British Historians and the West Indies* (New York: Scribner's, 1965): p. 166.

4. Michael Gilkes, *Wilson Harris and the Caribbean Novel* (Trinidad: Longman Caribbean, 1975): p. 132.

5. Homi Bhabha, *The Location of Culture* (London: Routledge, 1994).

6. John Vlach, *By the Work of Their Hands: Studies in Afro-American Folklife* (Charlottesville: University Press of Virginia, 1991): p. xv.

7. Alan Lomax, *The Land Where Blues Began* (New York: Pantheon, 1993): p. xiii.

8. For a comprehensive study of early African American material culture, which is indebted to Edward Brathwaite's notion of creolization, see Leland Ferguson, *Uncommon Ground: Archaeology and Early African America* (Washington, D.C.: Smithsonian Institution, 1992).

9. Carl Pedersen, "Sea Change: The Middle Passage and the Transatlantic Imagination," in *The Black Columbiad: Defining Moments in African Ameerican Literare and Culture*, ed. Maria Diedrich and Werner Sollors (Cambridge, Mass.: Harvard University Press, 1994): pp. 42–52.

10. Paul Gilroy, *The Black Atlantic: Modernity and Double Consciousness* (London: Verso, 1993).

11. Joyce Jonas, *Anancy in the Great House: Ways of Reading West Indian Fiction* (Westport, Conn.: Greenwood Press, 1990).

12. Stephen Greenblatt, "Culture," in *Critical Terms for Literary Study*, ed. Frank Lentricchia and Thomas McLaughlin (Chicago: University of Chicago Press, 1992): p. 230.

13. George Lipsitz, *Time Passages: Collective Memory and American Popular Culture* (Minneapolis: University of Minnesota Press, 1990): p. 213.

14. Wilson Harris, *The Womb of Space: The Cross-Cultural Imagination* (Westport, Conn.: Greenwood Press, 1983): p. xviii.

Part I

• • • •

"Voyage through Death . . ."

(Robert Hayden)

· · · ·

> Our struggle is also a struggle of memory against forgetting.
>
> Freedom Charter
> (South Africa)

Olaudah Equiano—a name representing the African "I am," in which past, present, and future are one, the "I am" of an African self that could soar even though firmly rooted. They had always known who they were. They had always known their parents' names and their parents' parents'. They had always known where they came from and where they were heading within the circle that defined human existence. They had always known that they belonged. They had always known that to be human was to be black.

Gustavus Vassa—a name representing the Atlantic diaspora that threatened to wipe out the self, an unnaming and chaining down that signified the end of participation in history. For how do you spell "I am" when you are deprived of home, of place, of your sense of direction? How do you spell "I am" when the seamless web defining the self is torn? How do you spell "I am" when you are branded, when you are stacked away in the claustrophobic hell below the deck of a slave ship, when you are discarded because a commodity is damaged? How do you spell "I am" on water without boundaries? How do you spell "I am," how do you define "human," when the skinless (white Europeans) have acquired the right over definitions?

Centuries later historians would ridicule as a numbers game attempts to count the millions forced to suffer the trauma of the transatlantic passage. Yet for those who witnessed the murderous raids by Arabs, Europeans, or hostile black Africans upon their communities, for those who were discarded on their march to the African coast, for those who were banned to the hold of the ships, for those whose bodies were cast overboard, for those who made it to the unknown on the other side of the ocean, every single one mattered. For every single woman, every single man represented the difference between life and death, between the "I am" and chattel, between history and the void, between the voice and silence. For every single one defined the whole.

Thus, those who survived the passage not only commenced the struggle to defend the "I am" against the onslaught of definitions the "masters" imposed upon the "black other." They also memorialized the transatlantic passage in African American cultural memory, passed on and re-remembered from generation to generation. Denied a voice, exiled from human history by the master's monologic narrative, they remade, reimagined, and retold American history in the many voices of the black experience.

The six essays collected in part I deal with the complex meanings that this traumatic challenge of the African self acquired for African American and American cultures alike. At the center of each article therefore are black Americans as both victims and agents of history.

New data from the Du Bois transatlantic slave ship project allow a more detailed reconstruction of the direction and composition of the transatlantic slave trade than has been possible. These data, which David Eltis, David Richardson, and Stephen D. Behrendt present in "Patterns in the Transatlantic Slave Trade, 1662–1867: New Indications of African Origins of Slaves Arriving in the Americas," result from integrating, for the first time, data sets previously culled from the archives and in part from new archival research. Preliminary breakdowns of the origins, African region of embarkation, and the destination of slave ships in the Americas are presented. Broadly, the English slave trade is shown to be more important than previously thought, western central Africa supplied far more slaves than any region in West Africa, and there was a fairly marked geographic concentration in the departure of slaves from the African coast. On the American side, the British Caribbean was more important than previously realized. The supply of slaves to particular American regions was not a random process. Usually, and especially in Brazil, one or, at most, two regions of Africa supplied two-thirds of the slaves arriving at any given location in the Americas.

Geneviève Fabre's "The Slave Ship Dance" analyzes the first recorded dance during the Atlantic passage. Using descriptions found in a variety of sources—diaries, journals by witnesses or observers, legal papers, and testimonies—this essay documents the slave ship dance, underlines its fundamentally ambivalent character, and endeavors to grasp its scope and significance for the captains and their crews who ordered and partly controlled it, the travelers who saw it and were entertained, and mostly the performers themselves. More than a simple exercise meant to keep the human cargo alive and healthy, a break from work, or an amusement, the dance is seen here as a ceremonial performance, the symbolic enactment of a system of beliefs and a secret rite that seeks to give expression and meaning to the journey and to the suffering. The dance is also the prelude to action and insurgency, an experiment with all possible forms of escape, including freedom. Fabre also argues that the scene—with its careful orchestration of moods, emotions, ideas, skills, and devices—prefigures many other performances to come, some presenting complementary or

antithetical images to the slave ship journey. A response to the harsh realities, this "primal" dance brought into play many recreative capacities
and artistic strategies and blended many different legacies, thus creating
dramatic tensions between enslavement and freedom, memory and history, irretrievable past and uncertain future.

Jesús Benito and Ana Manzanas's "(De)Construction of the 'Other' in
The Interesting Narrative of Olaudah Equiano" initially dwells on the
process through which the image of the "other" as the ontologically different was generated in the reports of European travelers to remote regions of the world. Taking the "other" as a mobile category culturally
constructed, the essay focuses on how Equiano's autobiography con-
structs and deconstructs the image of the "other" in his dealings with
his white enslavers. A brief revision of Equiano's account of slavery in
eighteenth-century African societies, where slaves were not deprived of
their status as human beings, leads to an analysis of Equiano's strategy
to encode his Western enslavers as a homogeneous and indistinguishable
"other." In the creation of this "other," which takes place as he crosses
the Atlantic for the first time, Equiano consciously projects back onto the
Europeans most of the degrading misconceptions European travelers traditionally projected onto the Africans. Subsequently, as Equiano establishes closer connections with the English, his narrative presents a dynamic deconstruction of the "otherness" in the whites. His desire to erase
the barriers that separate him from the whites is met by the white man's
blind rejection of the slave's full humanity. This perception generates two
contrasting voices that will blend in the remainder of the autobiography.
Equiano's transatlantic passages parallel his personal experience: the
reader sees how the "other" crisscrosses the self and the self crisscrosses
the "other" to create an uneasy balance in the authorial voice. Equiano's
constant crisscrossing of the Atlantic is paralleled by his position as mediator between African and Western cultures, African natural religion
and Christianity, and, finally, between Africa's struggle for freedom and
Europe's imperialist economics.

The experience of the Middle Passage eluded those who lived it and
tried to write about it. It found early expression almost only in the de-
scriptions of those who shared in the responsibility of the slave trade,
Françoise Charras argues in "Landings: Robert Hayden's and Kamau
Brathwaite's Poetic Renderings of the Middle Passage in Comparative
Perspective." The difficulties in giving a narrative form to what seems to
resist language lasted until the late 1960s, when poetry broke the barrier.
Through a comparison of Robert Hayden's "Middle Passage" and the
Barbadian poet Kamau Brathwaite's *The Arrivants* (1973), this chapter
analyzes the poetic strategies that illuminated the experience of the

transatlantic passage in the English-speaking diaspora. By a reversal of meaning, Hayden's poem transforms this "voyage through death" to that of "life upon these shores." This paradoxical assertion of life in the destructive process of the Middle Passage becomes the central theme in Brathwaite's epic, in the context of a social and political debate on Caribbean culture. Most important in both poems is the defining of a voice to express the archetypal experience of the race, as well as the search for a language that would express the oral and visual qualities of this submerged voice that had already found expression in music and dance.

As Claudine Raynaud points out in "The Poetics of Abjection in Morrison's *Beloved,"* the evocation of horrors of the Middle Passage—a necessarily "borderline" text—is an attempt at representing abjection. The reconstructed voice of the slave daughter wrestles with meaning as it confronts the abject both outside (the "objective" experience of the Middle Passage) and inside (the "subjective" exploration of the pre-Oedipal). The poetics of the broken up, hollowed out prose of Beloved's monologue derive from the conception of the Middle Passage as a space of inbetweenness with its links to the origin, its reversibilities, its ambivalences. Wrested from Beloved's encounter with the unspeakable, her "unuttered thoughts" exemplify the struggle of perception (pictures) with speech (voice) and point to Morrison's definition of memory as "an act of willed creation." A close reading of the cameo passage where Sethe remembers the story of violation and infanticide told by Nan unveils the major metaphorical networks intertwined in the novel that relate to the body, language, memory, and creative imagination. The ultimate limit of the experience of the origin appears in the repeated notation of a sensation of burning ("a hot thing") while the difficult acknowledgement of the dead father's body as corpse (cadaver) spells another modality of the ab-ject. The poetic text of the Middle Passage is a revisiting of the beginnings (among others, a return to fusion and possession of the mother), which alone can bring about subjecthood in its coincidence with a genesis of utterance against/with abjection.

Finally, Claude Julien's "Surviving through a Pattern of Timeless Moments: A Reading of Caryl Phillips's *Crossing the River"* focuses on the three Phillips novels that hinge on the African diaspora. Reading *Crossing the River* as a fiction that perceives the diaspora as a global hurt, this chapter attempts to retrace the novelist's effort to match diegetic content and narrative structure through a fragmented narration that becomes a metaphor for fractured lives.

2

• • • •

Patterns in the Transatlantic
Slave Trade, 1662–1867

New Indications of African Origins
of Slaves Arriving in the Americas

David Eltis
David Richardson
Stephen D. Behrendt

The publication in 1969 of Philip Curtin's *The Atlantic Slave Trade: A Census* is generally noted as a landmark in the historiogaphy of transatlantic slavery.[1] Relying on published evidence, Curtin produced the first modern estimates of the volume of the transatlantic slave trade and of the regional distributions of slave departures from Africa and arrivals in the Americas. Since 1969, his work has been under close scrutiny, with various scholars producing new estimates of the British, French, Dutch, Portuguese, and other slave trades. Much of this new work, focused on the two centuries after 1660 when the transatlantic traffic in Africans peaked, has used archival shipping data unavailable to Curtin. Usually interpreted as more reliable than Curtin's, the new findings have nevertheless tended to corroborate rather than challenge Curtin's original estimates of the totals involved. The chief contributions of the new research have been in determinations of the temporal and geographic distribution of the trade, particularly in the patterns of slave departures from Africa.

In examining the geography of the trade, Curtin made perhaps the first overall systematic attempt to trace the African origins of slaves carried to the Americas. For instance, he used Rinchon's data culled from shipping records and Debien's plantation-based data to explore the African origins of slaves arriving in St. Domingue. He also used evidence from the British Parliamentary Papers to trace origins of those going to

Cuba and Brazil in the nineteenth century. More recently Geggus has extended Curtin's analysis of the origins of St. Domingue slaves, while other historians have sought to examine the origins of slaves arriving elsewhere in the Americas. Prerevolutionary South Carolina and Virginia, the early-nineteenth-century British Caribbean, and Bahia have received close attention, with the ethnicity of slaves as well as their geographic origins forming the subject of investigation. In this respect, important strides have been made in delineating connections between Africa and the Americas.[2]

Despite these advances, the precise origins of Africans arriving in the Americas still remain obscure. Further research on plantation records and other sources will doubtless clarify ethnic origins of Afro-Americans. Through shipping records one can trace the embarkation points in Africa of many, if not most, of the slaves shipped into various slave societies in the Americas between 1662 and 1867. Recent archival work has generated substantial data on the number, tonnage, and port of provenance of slave ships leaving European and American ports, on places of trade in Africa and the number of slaves taken on board, on mortality levels during the Atlantic crossing, and on the destinations of ships and numbers of slaves disembarked in the Americas. Many slaving voyages fitted out in Europe and America in the two centuries after 1662 have already been charted, and work tracing many others is well advanced. It is now possible to map fairly closely the transatlantic journeys of very large numbers of enslaved Africans. This chapter begins the process of establishing the connections between African and American regions involved in the slave trade after 1662.

The shipping, or more accurately, voyage, data used here derive from a data set of transatlantic slaving voyages created at the W.E.B. Du Bois Institute at Harvard and to be published by Cambridge University Press. The voyage records are drawn from several independently produced data sets of British, French, Portuguese, Dutch, and Brazilian slaving voyages. To date (at the end of 1995), the Du Bois data set contains records of almost 20,000 voyages. Of these, 1,700 failed to reach the Americas. Among the remainder, we have evidence on American destinations for about 15,200 voyages, on African departure points for 12,600, and on both African and American regions together for some 11,660 voyages. Where data on actual places of trade are not available, we have used intended ports of embarkation and disembarkation. Further, for about 15 percent of the voyages, we lack data on number of slaves carried; in these cases we have estimated the numbers of slaves on board from means computed from large sample sizes. We expect soon to have additional records available for about 6,000 voyages. Indeed, ultimately, we expect to have some information on about two-thirds of all the ships that made a transatlantic slave voyage.[3]

Our main findings are summarized in six tables. The first five provide information on the ports of provenance of ships, trading locations within Africa and America, and numbers of slaves shipped between 1662 and 1867. The final two tables present evidence of transatlantic connections from both American and African perspectives. Table 1 provides an indication of the organizational nexus of the trade. Three of the top four ports of departure were English, with the largest and most rapidly expanding urban center in the eighteenth- and nineteenth-century world—London—heading the list. However, while the English likely carried almost as many slaves across the oceans of the world as the Portuguese, Table 1 does overstate their dominance somewhat, for two reasons. First, the data sources for port of departure are better for England than for some other countries. Second, over 98 percent of slaving voyages from England left from London, Liverpool, and Bristol. This extreme geographic concentration was matched by no other slave trading power. In France, although Nantes was the clear leader, there were half a dozen ports from Honfleur to La Rochelle that were also of major significance. The key finding in Table 1, however, is the relative importance of ports of departure in the Americas. Bahia, Havana, Rio de Janeiro, and Bridge-

Table 1 Major Ports of Departure for Translantic Slave Ships, 1662–1867, in Descending Order of Importance

Port	Number of Voyages	Percent
London	2,654	13.3
Bahia	1,992	10.0
Liverpool	1,923	9.6
Bristol	1746	8.7
Nantes	1,510	7.6
Zeeland	693	3.5
Havana	686	3.4
La Rochelle	426	2.1
Le Havre	407	2.0
Bordeaux	396	2.0
Rio de Janeiro	382	1.9
Saint-Malo	217	1.1
Barbados	197	1.0
Amsterdam	175	.9
Lorient	154	.8
All Others		32.1
Total	14,886	100.0

Source: W.E.B. Du Bois Institute slave ship data set.

town, Barbados, are in the top thirteen on the list, and it seems fairly clear that a sizable proportion of the unknowns left from Brazilian ports in the nineteenth century when the trade was illegal. Indeed, there can be little doubt that Rio de Janeiro is seriously underrepresented on the list and really belongs in the top five or six. Eventually, it may be possible to show that two-fifths of the trade originated in the Americas, not Europe. At the very least, the traditional depiction of the trade as triangular in structure—Europe-Africa-Americas—needs qualifying.

Where in Africa did these ships go to obtain slaves? Tables 2 and 3 provide a broad answer to this question. The regions shown are defined as follows: Senegambia is the area north of Sierra Leone; Windward Coast ranges from Sierra Leone to the west of the Rio Assini and includes the Ivory Coast; the Gold Coast includes the Rio Assini to Cape St. Paul; the Bight of Benin runs from Cape St. Paul up to, but not including, the Rio Nun; the Rio Nun to Cape Lopez, inclusive, makes up the Bight of Biafra; and west-central Africa is the West African coast south of Cape Lopez; southeast Africa is any port north and east of the Cape of Good Hope. The sample size for ships is larger than the sample size for slaves; that is, a slave ship's point of embarkation is sometimes known but the number of people it took on board may be missing. Average numbers of slaves are thus calculated and used to fill in such blanks. Such averages are shown in column 2. The total number of slaves in Table 2—4.7 million—constitutes 40 percent of all slaves leaving Africa according to the last major synthesis of the trade.[4] This synthesis, however, covered the fifteenth to the nineteenth centuries and included slaves going to islands in the Atlantic and Indian Oceans, as well as those taken to Europe. If we focus on the transatlantic trade alone and the years 1662 to 1867, the limits of the present study, then 4.7 million probably represents a sample size of just over 50

Table 2 Estimated Slave Departures from Africa by Region of Embarkation, 1662–1867 (in thousands)

Region	Number of Slaves	Mean Slaves per ship	Number of Ships
Senegambia	146.5	213.6	686
Sierra Leone-Windward coast	251.3	276.1	910
Gold Coast	527.2	319.1	1,652
Bight of Benin	1,161.2	394.0	2,947
Bight of Biafra	507.5	323.9	1,567
West-central Africa	1,847.1	432.4	4,272
Southeast Africa	298.3	524.3	569
Total	4,739.0	376.0	12,603

Source: W.E.B. Du Bois Institute slave ship data set.

Table 3 African Ports of Embarkation in the Transatlantic Slave Trade, 1662–1867, in Descending Order of Importance

Port	Number of Slaves (thousands)	Mean Slaves per Ship	Number of Ships
Cabinda	272.0	443.7	613
Whydah	251.0	374.2	670
Benguela	204.1	470.4	434
Luanda	172.1	406.0	424
Mozambique	151.7	510.2	297
Malembo	112.9	404.6	279
Quilimane	98.5	597.2	165
Calabar	98.1	306.9	356
Senegal	76.4	245.8	311
Bonny	75.1	376.2	236
Ambriz	75.1	452.6	166
Congo River	71.1	483.5	147
Loango	68.0	395.5	172
Lagos	63.6	384.8	165
Gambia	41.7	201.5	223
Porto Novo	31.7	422.9	75
Ardra	31.0	360.3	86
Anomabu	24.9	304.0	88
Galinhas	24.3	292.5	83
New Calabar	23.6	251.3	94
All other known	264.0		902
Total	2,232.0	374.0	5,941

Source: W.E.B. Du Bois Institute slave ship data set.

percent. Even though this is a very large sample, bias is still possible. On balance, west-central Africa likely may be slightly underrepresented.

Table 2 shows immediately that more than 85 percent of Africans coming to the New World left from four of the six regions listed, all adjacent to each other. Collectively, they encompass one relatively short stretch of the African coast—from the Rio Assini in West Africa to just south of Benguela in Angola. Indeed, almost two-thirds of all Africans— 63.4 percent—left from just two regions: the appropriately named "Slave Coast" of the Bight of Benin, from Grand Popo to just west of Lagos, and west-central Africa from Mayoumba, north of the Zaire River to Cap de Sta Marta west of Benguela. These two regions cover about six hundred of the many thousands of miles of African coastline. And geographic concentration of departures was even more pronounced. While many departure points were recorded by region rather than a specific point of embarkation, table 3 shows that nearly 90 percent of those leaving from known points—as opposed to broad regions of embarkation—left from just twenty African ports. Likely a similar pattern pertains for European migrants to the Americas, but in the African case, the points of embarkation were not major urban centers in which the slave trade was just one of many other types of economic activity.

The sample of those arriving in identifiable American regions is slightly larger than for those departing from African regions (see Table 4). A sample size of 4.7 million Africans constitutes a larger share of arrivals in the Americas—after allowing for shipboard mortality—than it does of African departures. Perhaps the sample incorporates almost 55 percent of these arrivals in the 1662–1867 period. But we need to note bias here. Arrivals in the United States are underrepresented, as are arrivals in mainland Spanish territories. Furthermore, eighteenth-century south-central Brazil is probably not well covered.

It is clear that the geographic concentration of arrivals in the Americas is much more dispersed than that of African departures. Cuba in the north to Rio de Janeiro in the south—which absorbed 90 percent of the Africans coming to the Americas—is a much wider geographic range than the coastline of west and west-central Africa. Major ports of entry, as table 5 shows, were scattered within this range. More important, how

Table 4 Estimated Slave Arrivals in the Americas by Region of Disembarkation, 1662–1867 (in thousands)

Region	Number of Slaves	Mean Slaves per ship	Number of Ships
South America			
Guyana (French-British-Dutch)	268.4	284.6	943
Brazil Northeast	79.5	292.2	272
Bahia	706.1	321.2	2,198
Brazil South	1,069.0	415.9	2,570
Rio de la Plata	18.9	270.2	70
Caribbean			
Cuba, Puerto Rico	558.4	380.6	1,467
St. Domingue	674.1	302.0	2,232
Martinique, Guadalupe	141.4	241.0	587
Jamaica	553.7	280.2	1,976
British Caribbean (other) [a]	271.0	227.0	1,194
Barbados	190.7	214.3	890
Danish Americas	31.7	253.9	125
North America (mainland)			
Spanish Central America [b]	34.0	329.9	103
United States	120.4	217.7	553
Total	4,717.3	310.8	15,180

[a] Includesd all British Windward and Leeward Islands.

[b] Slaves landed in Dutch Caribbean and carried to Spanish America.

Source: W.E.B. Du Bois Institute slave ship data set.

Table 5 American Ports of Disembarkation in the Transatlantic Slave Trade, 1662–1867, in Descending Order of Importance

Port	Number of Slaves (thousands)	Mean Number of Slaves	Number of Ships
Rio de Janeiro	799.7	402.5	1,987
Bahia	705.0	321.1	2,194
Kingston (Jamaica)	512.6	284.2	1,542
Cap Français	353.8	310.3	1,140
Bridgetown (Barbados)	190.7	214.3	890
Martinique	122.9	247.2	497
Havana	119.6	326.1	367
Port-au-Prince	105.5	307.6	343
Leogane	74.7	303.8	246
Chesapeake	60.6	210.4	288
Les Cayes	56.0	268.0	209
St. Kitts	54.2	225.9	240
Pernambuco	53.4	296.5	180
St. George's (Grenada)	51.1	240.9	212
Saint Marc	47.5	295.2	161
Campos (Brazil)	46.9	446.9	105
St. John (Antigua)	41.4	208.1	199

Source: W.E.B. Du Bois Institute slave ship data set.

ever, is the broad distribution among American regions. South America accounted for just under half of African arrivals, with Brazil alone taking just under 40 percent of the slaves in the sample. The Caribbean absorbed a larger proportion—just over 50 percent of all slaves arriving in the Americas. The North American mainland, assuming that half the small number going to the Spanish mainland went to Central America and half to South America, took less than 3 percent of African arrivals (we expect to add additional data for this area when the data set is complete). Nevertheless, it is unlikely that arrivals in what became the United States amounted to as much as 7 percent of the whole. Eventually, we will augment our data for the mainland Spanish Americas, but the broad patterns depicted here are unlikely to change.

The key findings in this preliminary analysis, however, relate to neither Africa nor the Americas treated separately, but rather to the links between the continents. The great advantage of building a consolidated data set of this type is that it can focus on these links. The preliminary results displayed in Table 6 show the relative distribution among African regions of embarkation of an estimated 3.7 million slaves who landed in the fourteen American regions over two centuries. Breakdowns by 5-year periods will eventually be possible. Three preliminary points are of note. First, there is known bias in the table. Between 1811 and 1830, slaver cap-

Table 6 Slaves Arriving in the Americas: American Region of Disembarkation by Percent of African Region Embarkation, 1662–1867

	Senegambia	SL-Wind	Gold Coast	B. of Benin	B. of Biafra	W.C. Africa	S.E. Africa	Sample
French-British-Dutch South America	1.2	5.2	46.0	14.4	5.5	27.6	0	(235.0)
Northeast Brazil	5.0	1.7	0.9	0.9	1.4	86.0	4.1	(71.2)
Bahia	0.1	0.2	2.7	86.0	1.3	8.5	1.2	(642.4)
Brazil South	0	0	0.5	1.3	0.8	80.9	16.5	(969.8)
Rio de la Plata	0	8.2	4.7	1.2	31.1	54.8	0	(16.4)
Cuba/Puerto Rico	1.0	11.8	3.6	24.0	21.3	30.9	7.4	(205.7)
St. Domingue	7.2	9.9	5.9	22.3	4.0	47.6	3.1	(606.2)
Martinique-Guadalupe	6.2	8.2	9.9	32.5	11.5	31.2	0.5	(116.7)
Barbados	4.6	5.1	35.1	20.1	16.5	15.6	3.0	(113.2)
Jamaica	2.1	6.1	27.7	9.3	36.1	18.6	0	(360.8)
British Leeward	3.9	18.6	15.8	5.2	42.3	14.2	0	(205.0)
Danish Americas	0.4	7.1	47.4	3.2	13.2	28.6	0	(23.8)
United States	14.2	6.7	9.4	3.1	31.1	34.4	1.1	(74.2)
Central America	1.1	0	41.3	8.4	0	49.2	0	(23.5)
Total								(3661.8)

Note: Rows sum to 100; total number of slaves in thousands in parentheses.

Source: W.E.B. Du Bois Institute slave ship data set

tains arriving at Bahia frequently declared their point of departure in Africa as Angola, south of the equator, whereas in most cases they had obtained their slaves in the Bight of Benin. They reasoned that such deception was necessary because of the 1810 Anglo-Portugese treaty, which the British interpreted as allowing their navy to capture any Portugese slave ship trading north of the equator. In fact, the share of slaves arriving at Bahia from the Bight of Benin was probably in excess of 90 percent rather than the 86 indicated in the table. Second, the size of the regions of embarkation and disembarkation is misleading. Before 1830, at least, when suppressive measures ensured dispersed boardings and landings, almost all the slaves left from, or arrived at, a dozen or so points in Africa and the Americas. The only exceptions to this pattern were the mainland of North America and the Windward Coast, both of which played a relatively small role in the overall transatlantic trade. Third, despite this relatively small number of coastal points involved in the trade, there were major shifts in African provenance zones located away from the coast. Thus, Yoruba peoples, who overwhelmingly dominated the flow of peoples leaving Bight of Benin ports in the nineteenth century, formed a small minority of those leaving the same ports before the collapse of the Oyo empire, beginning in the late eighteenth century.

The new data reveal some rather striking patterns. The distribution of Africans in the New World was no more randomized than was its European counterpart. Broadly, with the exception of the area surrounding Bahia and probably the province of Minas Gerais, for which Bahia was a conduit, the African part in the repeopling of South America was as dominated by west-central Africans, as Europe was by Iberians. Peoples from the Zaire basin and Angola formed by far the greater share of arrivals in south-central Brazil—the largest single slave reception areas in the Americas—as well as in northeastern Brazil, and to a lesser extent, Rio de la Plata. West-central Africa formed the second largest provenance zone for all other South American regions. Bahia—one of the two most important points of entrance into the New World for Africans—was a major exception. Here, the dominance of peoples from the hinterland of the Bight of Benin was almost complete, although, as we noted, the ethnicity of those leaving the Slave Coast shifted drastically over time. A large West African presence is also apparent in the less important region of Rio de la Plata, the only region on the continent of South America where Africans from the Bight of Biafra—overwhelmingly Igbo and Ibibio peoples—were to be found in large numbers. West Africa is also well represented in the Guyanas and Surinam, but the Gold Coast, rather than the Bight of Biafra and the Slave Coast, supplied almost half of those arriving. This is the only region in the whole of South America where peoples from the Gold Coast have a major presence.

In the Caribbean, West Africa was as dominant as West-Central Africa in South America, though generally the mix of African peoples was much greater here than further south. Only in St. Domingue did Africa south of the equator provide half of all arrivals. And only in the French Leewards and Cuba did that ratio approximate one-third. Generally, a single West African region was a clear leader in the distribution, though the location of the leader varied. Barbados, the Danish islands, and Spanish Central Americas—drawing mainly on the Dutch entrepot of Curaçao here—drew disproportionately on the Gold Coast. The Bight of Benin played a similar role in the French Leewards. In Jamaica and the British Leewards, the Bight of Biafra was easily the single most important provenance zone, though in none of these cases did a single region provide as many as half of all arrivals, like the case in all Brazilian regions. In the Caribbean, "West Africa" effectively meant the Gold Coast, the Slave Coast (Bight of Benin), and the Bight of Biafra. Senegambia was of some importance in the French Caribbean. Sierra Leone, easily the most important part of the Windward Coast, was responsible for almost a fifth of disembarkations in the British Leewards, but generally these regions played a minor role in the slave trade to the major American regions, striking when one considers that passages from Senegambia to the Caribbean are typically half as long as their more southerly transatlantic counterparts.

Of all the receiving areas in the Americas, Cuba received the greatest mix of African peoples. No single part of Africa supplied more than 31 percent of Cuban arrivals, and the only major region not well represented on the island was the Gold Coast. In addition, the region that supplied the greatest number—west-central Africa—covered by the nineteenth century a very wide range of coastline and drew on vast slaving hinterlands, suggesting a further mixing of peoples. Moreover, there was no regional segregation within Cuba. Almost all the arrivals moved through Havana and ports west and ended in the sugar heartland that formed the hinterland beyond these ports. Large numbers of Yao from the southeast, Yoruba from West Africa, and Lunda from the Kasai valley in the Angolan interior intermingled on the plantation labor forces. All slaves arrived within a relatively short space of time in the first half of the century. The only other American region with a remotely similar pattern was Barbados, though here two adjacent regions in West Africa did account for 55 percent of all arrivals. When Barbados was receiving the basis of its African population prior to 1714, the Gold Coast and Bight of Benin predominated. Thus, language groupings, for example, must have been considerably more homogeneous in Barbados than in Cuba.

Finally, we should note the region that became the United States. The significance of the North American mainland derives not, as we have seen, from its importance in the overall slave trade, but rather in the fact that, as in the province of Quebec, a relatively small number of original arrivals grew into one of the larger minority populations in the two continents. In America the peoples of Senegambia played a larger role than in any other major region, though that share was still fairly small. The table does not show that Senegambia was of greatest relative importance in the very early years (before 1710), when the Chesapeake dominated. As in most of the English Americas, however (except Barbados), the Bight of Biafra supplied a third or more of arrivals and, together with west-central Africa, accounts for two out of three of all African migrants forced into mainland North America.

In broad terms, the new data confirm many of Curtin's findings. The data set is still not complete enough to address what was perhaps Curtin's central concern—the tendency of earlier historians to inflate the scale of the trade. It does, however call for some modification of the distributional patterns of the transatlantic traffic. On the American side, the new data highlight the importance of the British Caribbean, as well as the relative importance of the British slave trade that supplied the region. On the African side, the new data boost the relative importance of west-central Africa as a region of origin. West-central Africa may well turn out to have supplied more people for the slave systems of the Americas than all the major regions of West Africa (the Gold Coast, the Slave Coast, and the Bight of Biafra) together. The new data also raise the importance of the Americas as a source of slave voyages.

These results are clearly very preliminary. Three major improvements are imminent. First, at least 25 percent more data will be forthcoming by the end of the project. Second, more refined analysis—specifically linking smaller regions on one side of the Atlantic to smaller regions on the other—will be forthcoming. Third, more complex analysis incorporating a range of other variables (e.g., shipboard mortality, port of departure for slave ships, shipboard revolts, age and sex characteristics of deportees, slave prices, and eventually material from outside the present data set), is on the current research agenda. This is merely the first of a series of reports that should greatly increase both our knowledge of where black people in the Amerias came from and our understanding of the slave trade responsible for their presence. Perhaps now African Americans will eventually know as much about their origins as do their white counterparts.

Acknowledgments   We would like to thank Stanley Engerman for comments on an earlier draft of this chapter. The research on which this essay is based was supported by grants from the National Endowment of the Humanities and the Mellon Foundation.

Notes

1. (Madison, Wis.: 1969).

2. May Kahasch, *Slave Life in Rio de Janeiro, 1808–50* (Princeton, 1987); Barry Higman, *Slave Populations of the British Caribbean, 1807–1834* (Baltimore, 1984); David Geggus, "Sex Ratio, Age and Ethnicity in the Atlantic Slave Trade: Data from French Shipping and Plantation Records," *Journal of African History*, 30 (1989); David Richardson, "The Eighteenth Century British Slave Trade: Estimates of its Volume and Coastal Distribution," *Research in Economic History*, 12 (1989): 151–96.

3. For descriptions of some of these data, see Stephen D. Behrendt, "The British Slave Trade, 1786–1807: Volume, Profitability and Mortality" (unpublished PhD thesis, University of Wisconsin, 1993); David Richardson, *Bristol, Africa and the Eighteenth Century Slave Trade to America*, 4 vols. (Bristol, 1986–96); David Eltis, *Economic Growth and the Ending of the Transatlantic Slave Trade* (New York, 1987); Jean Mettas and Serge Daget, *Répertoire des expéditions négrières françaises au XVIIe siècle*, 2 vols. (Paris, 1978–84); Sv. E. Green Pedersen, "The Scope and Structure of the Danish Negro Slave Trade," *Scandanavian Economic History Review*, 19 (1971): 192–95; Johannes Postma, *The Dutch and the Atlantic Slave Trade* (New York, 1990); Herbert S. Klein, *The Middle Passage: Comparative Studies in the Atlantic Slave Trade* (Princeton, 1978). The consolidated data set will be called *The Transatlantic Slave Trade: A Data base on CD-ROM*.

4. Paul Lovejoy, "The Impact of the Atlantic Slave Trade on Africa: A Review of the Literature," *Journal of African History*, 30 (1989): 367–73.

3

• • • •

The Slave Ship Dance

Geneviève Fabre

We are almost a nation of dancers,
musicians and poets.

Olaudah Equiano
(1789).

Dance is for the African "the fullest expression of art."

Lee Warren,
The Dance of Africa (1972)

The central importance of dance in West and Central Africa has been often emphasized by historians, anthropologists, and Africans themselves. A communal activity, dance was also a crucial element in ceremonial life and created special bondings among all celebrants, thus united by certain beliefs and practices. In the cults honoring the gods or the ancestors, dance was a way of mediating between the godly and the human, the living and the dead. Deities were praised, called upon through a dance designed to invoke special features, proprieties, or abilities. Dance was thus used to solicit intercession, to thwart wrath or punishment that human action might have incurred, to flatter, or to appease. Dancers not only communicated with the spirits but also impersonated them through specific body movements, rhythms, or masks and became possessed themselves.

From a more worldly perspective, festive dancing could represent a feat, a battle, a victory, a particular domestic event; dramatize a crisis or a confrontation; or become a vehicle for comment, satire, or parody.[1] As a much valued art form, it required skills one learned. Dancers were honored, and officials were supposed to be good dancers; any deficiencies could threaten their status, whereas competence enhanced their aura. The characteristics of the dances could vary greatly from one society to the other—each boasting the best dancers and unique styles,[2] yet dance received in each the same consideration and was used for similar functions. Ceremonial or celebratory, dramatic or theatrical, parodic or satiric, it was pervasive everywhere.

In this chapter, I examine the first recorded dance on the way to the New World, when African captives were encouraged or forced to dance and sometimes "whipped into cheerfulness." It is highly symbolic and ironic that these performances should occur under the eye and whip of the slavers and their crew and on the deck of the slave ship. I shall therefore examine these dances' dual relation to the realities of the Middle Passage and to an African heritage. I question whether the slave ship dance constituted a definite assault on the captives' cultures and a dramatic break with former beliefs and practices, or whether it was a step toward the creation of a new culture in which still vivid memories of African dance could help bring shape and meaning to the experience of enslavement.

The slave ship dance had a wide range of witnesses and was often briefly mentioned in accounts and reports published on the slave trade. One of the first mentions occurs in the log of the English slave ship *Hannibal* in 1664: "Africans linked together were made to jump and dance for an hour or two. If they go about it reluctantly or do not move with agility, they are flogged."[3] The practice seems to have been widespread and was kept long after the abolition of the trade. The last record dates from 1860 when a slave ship, *Wildfire*, with 150 Africans from the River Congo, was taken in tow by an American ship in sight of Cuba and brought to Key West, Florida.[4]

Documents on the dance come essentially from three sources: slavers and captains who allude to them in logs or journals; observers who traveled on the ships as surgeons, guests, or visitors; the captives themselves, who endured the Middle Passage and mentioned their experience in their memoirs or autobiographies. From all these fragmented and scattered descriptions, one may grasp the scope of these dances, their significance and functions for the parties involved, and their underlying meanings for the "performers" themselves. Accounts by the slavers and captains present the dances as necessary, healthy forms of exercise; they emphasize the lightheartedness of the dancers inclined to "amuse themselves with dancing" and proclaim the captain's intentions to take good care of the captives and promote their happiness. Thus, James Barbot, owner of the *Albion* that voyaged the coast of Guinea near the Calabar River in the late seventeenth century, insists in his account on the good care the slaves received during the passage and describes the dancing as a happy pastime "full of jollity and good humor that afforded an abundance of recreation."[5] Practiced as a regular activity necessary for the health of the cargoes (we are told slaves "jumped into their irons for exercise"), dancing had a healing effect on slaves' suicidal melancholy. There was a common belief that if "not kept amused" and in motion slaves would die: these pleasant exercises were keeping the slavers' stock "in good condition" and "enhancing [their] prospects of making a profitable journey." Keeping the slaves in good shape was a major concern in the general economy of the trade at a time when losses in human lives through disease, epidemics, or suicide were high and caused much alarm. Captains had to commit themselves to carry the captives safe, whole, and fit for sale. When in the 1780s the slave trade came under attack and closer scrutiny, captains were requested to answer inquiries concerning the load, space, and provisions allotted on their ships, and laws were passed in 1788 to enforce stricter regulations, stipulating the load of each cargo. When called before Parliament, captains protested against the bill, declared it superfluous, and often referred to the dances as evidence of their goodwill and of the pleasant atmosphere that reigned on their vessels.

Opponents to the trade sent petitions for its abolition and tried to gather evidence that would question the captains' proclamations of innocence. Thus, in a publication that became famous, Thomas Clarkson collected testimonies from less biased witnesses.[6] Their observations offer a very different picture of the dance scene. The captives are described as "compelled to dance by the cat" or jump to the lash—this "jumping" termed "dancing."[7] A surgeon, Thomas Trotter, who traveled on the *Brookes* in 1783, sees the dance as a joyless ceremony that he called "dancing the slave." "Crew members paraded on deck with whip and cat o' nine tails."[8] Captives danced in shackles (except women and children) and on crowded decks. Dancing by the cat was perceived as a violent and painful exercise: "the parts . . . on which their shackles are fastened are often excoriated."[9] Physically damaging, the dances were also often humiliating. Captives left the hold for another kind of confinement: hampered by their shackles, the once free and expert dancers of Africa became the butt of mockery. Observers thus often emphasized surveillance and coercion and noted that slavers, who rarely mentioned the use of whips, ignored the complaints of the dancers.

The strict control or even violence were exerted to prevent any carry-over of indigenous practices. Fear was great indeed that the enslaved would use these exercises to develop some kind of secret coding and prepare a mutiny: the ships' guns were sometimes aimed at the dancers to intimidate them, and constant watch was secured. Whip and gun were used to set the limits and avoid transgression. "Dancing the slave" was part of a deliberate scheme to ensure subordination by destroying former practices, to curb any attempt at recovering freedom of movement, action, or thought.

Slave ship dances were also used to entertain captains, their crews, and their guests. These amusements were slightly more formal; musicians were requested (and the great number of advertisements asking for musicians attest to the importance of such shows). If no professional musician were available, a sailor would play the fiddle or bagpipe, or a captive would be designated to play a European instrument or to improvise on a broken drum or banjo. He could also use whatever was available: utensils, ship equipment, or kettles. The captives often brought with them instruments that they were sometimes allowed to play.[10] Meant to enliven the journey, some dances could turn into "wild, lewd parties" in a parody of primitive naked rejoicing.[11] After the trade was abolished, illegal slavers were careful not to attract attention of patrol ships or pirates. Yet in spite of the high risk, they were unwilling to relinquish a practice that was a source of profit and amusement. Dances continued but were carefully planned, either at night—a device that slaves would later use once ashore to escape surveillance—or by summoning only a portion of the captives at a time.

Rewards or liquor were also offered to the best performers. This practice can be seen either as a way of acknowledging and encouraging skill or as a means of buying talent and disarming resistance. This system introduced a hierarchical order and encouraged competitiveness among dancers. The rewards the best dancers received designated them as an elite, leaders who could perhaps be used to control others, who could organize or curb revolt. One needs to determine whether the best performers selected by the "rulers" were the same the captives tacitly chose and managed to impose. Performing skills were quickly singled out and endowed some slaves with a form of power that had to be promptly rechanneled.

All these strategies devised by whites prefigure many of the methods used in the "management" of plantations—ranging from intimidation to reward and privileges. Dancing the slave may seem to have been confined to the slave ship journey, but it endured under many other forms. Slaves may not have had to dance under the lash, yet the whip was always present physically or symbolically, conceived as the best instrument to punish insubordination or to "fix and season" independent-minded

Africans. Significantly, lash and fiddle were used in coffles in the same manner as they had been on the ships, this time to urge chained "niggers" to march on and accept this other passage to another unknown destination, sale, and uncertain fate.[12]

On the other hand, slave ship "entertainments" prefigure these performances when slaves' musical and dancing skills would be appreciated, and used. Captains and plantation owners took the same pride in showing how talented the captives were, and these plantation dances did not escape the attention of those who organized the first traveling minstrel shows in the 1830s.

Thus, even before the ships' arrival into the New World, performance was an important stake, essential in many cultural events but also determinant in white and black relations, with its web of ambivalent feelings: hatred and attraction, contempt or praise, condescension or respect. It created secret bonds and interdependence. Performance was at the same time a well-planned necessary event, a duty and an artistic accomplishment that could be rewarded.

If dancing the slave involved many strategies and much scheming on the part of the slavers, one may surmise that the captives responded with equally elaborate devices to develop—secretly but purposefully—a form of dancing that could escape control and manipulation.

The slaves' point of view is rarely mentioned in the accounts and was no concern to slavers except when they suspected plotting and mutiny; the grief, indignation, or resignation, the aspirations or strivings the dance might have expressed, were ignored or denied. Only a few perceptive observers—mostly, as we saw, the surgeons—were attentive to the moods of the performers. Occasionally a document hints at this hidden dimension of experience, such as this short poem, "The Sorrow of Yomba" (1790):

> At the savage Captain's beck,
> Now like brutes they make us prance:
> Smack the Cat about the Deck,
> and in scorn they bid us dance.[13]

Fear seems to have prevailed. Testimonies of African slaves to the Select Committee of the House of Lords[14] or early narratives—like that of Olaudah Equiano, who, as an Ibo boy of eleven, boarded a slave ship in 1756—underscore the terror and horror. If slaves near the coast were familiar with the trade, those who came from the interior had no notion of their captors' intentions. After the trauma of capture, the long march on land or water to the sea, they boarded the ships in unspeakable terror.

Many preferred suicide to the brutalities they would endure at the hands of voracious traders. Their "imagination ran wild" as Equiano says; rumors, reinforced by sailors or interpreters who sought to exploit the captives' fear, spread from Senegambia to Angola that the slavers, whose appetite for human cargo had become prodigious, were insatiable cannibals (in a strange reversal of the stereotype ascribed to Africans). Equiano tells us that when he saw "a multitude of black people of every description chained together" near a "large furnace of copper boiling," "every one of their countenances expressing dejection and sorrow," he was convinced they were about to be eaten; and many Africans thought that the captives who never returned had been eaten or murdered.[15] Another slave, Augustino, recalls that when the younger ones were allowed to come on deck, several jumped overboard in fear they might be fattened to be eaten.[16] The white man's cannibalism explained his hunger for slaves and hence the trade. It was not uncommon among Africans to express such suspicions toward the neighboring peoples they distrusted. It is therefore not surprising that they ascribed the same features to white traders, who were stranger to them, and saw themselves as the new sacrificial victims. Furthermore, many slaves who were familiar with canoes on rivers, but had never seen a ship, imagined that it was some object of worship or magic brought to their shores by the white man for a general slaughter. The fear and horror persisted and led not only to acts of despair but also to murderous revolt. Fright remained, says Equiano, until they reached the West Indies and bitter cries could be heard through the nights. Historians tell us that the *Amistad* rebellion off the Cuban coast in 1839 occurred because the captain's slave informed the captives that they were about to be eaten. "Desperate, they rose in revolt, murdering most of the crew, saving only a few to navigate the ship back to Africa."[17]

Thus, one can understand how the idea and image of death informed the slave ship dance and brought with it a whole train of associations. For the captives who identified with the roaming and restless spirits of the dead, beliefs about death and the journey to the other world could help them negotiate this unfamiliar voyage to unknown shores. Death was less feared than enslavement. And if it meant the only possible reunion with those who had been left behind—ancestors, friends, and kin—and with the home country, this "journey back" could be ceremonially performed or physically accomplished. The dance was the symbolic enactment of a whole system of beliefs, reinforcing worship rites and calling forth the gods, or the dead, or supernatural forces that could perhaps counteract white schemes. Or it could be the prelude to action: the collective meeting with death or revolt against the slavers. Death should be self-willed and not inflicted by others. And it was not merely an escape, a relief from hardships; it was seen as the only path to resistance that could wreck the slavers' project and challenge their power.

Beliefs associated with death, and the attitudes they engendered, accompanied the slaves through their journey and their New World odyssey—just as they later shaped their burial and death rituals. The African heritage was thus very much present on the slave ship—a heritage consisting of a set of beliefs and practices but also of a body of knowledge that could serve as tools to help them out of their present predicament.

Significantly, the dance was informed by certain frames of mind and occasionally signaled appropriate moments for action. The torpor of some of its movements featured death itself; the twists and contortions of body and limb figured the anxiety and the pain; the sudden clapping of hands and stomping of feet, the jumping and leaping, contrasting with the swaying of bodies and slow shuffle, evoked the possibility of escape or of greater freedom. The dance thus stages the various moods and moments of the slave ship experience—the temptation to surrender and despair, the suffering and humiliations, the awakening of energies, the call for daring or insurgent acts. Improvised, and yet purposeful, the dance is both an experiment with, and a rehearsal of, all possible forms of "escapes." All moods, emotions, and ideas are made physically present through the body in carefully orchestrated gestures that, as they express and try to make sense of the plight, suggest certain basic African rhythms; the body, that was so central to the lived and felt Middle Passage experience, is entrusted with the task of representation and figuration, just as it also must perform the actual acts the dance may induce.

Also important were the sound and vocal structure of the dance—the humming and whispering that burst into outcries of pain or jubilant shouting, the way emotions broke into moaning and singing, the language of voice and song and the tunes brought from Africa, the use of African tongues often mentioned by witnesses and of "talking drums" whenever they were allowed as well as all the substitutes found to replace them, and the devices sought to deaden the sound and disguise its meaning. The possibility of recreating familiar tunes with whatever was available enabled the captives to keep their musical tradition alive, its beats and rhythms, the subtle combination of vocal and instrumental effects.

Codes of silence were also developed. Silence was another answer to the humiliations suffered, alternating with moments of extreme vocal expression and shrieks of grief. The silence of "sealed lips" (that is evoked in a Yoruba sculpture) accompanied the silence of the drum—often described as "an instrument of significant silence" all the more powerful when it was suppressed[18]—and it became a critique of the cruelty and violence inflicted. Silence was also a bond cementing solidarity between captives who would not betray one another. This tacit pact agreed upon on the slave ship endured; it became a crucial code of behavior, severely punished when it was broken.

In the slave ship dance, the basic principles of many performances to come were set: the blending and interplay of dance, song, and music; the call-and-response pattern between dance and music, between voice and instrument, body and song, and mostly between leader-caller and the assembly of dancers (later called celebrants or worshippers when the "performance" would be conceived more as a ceremony); the gift for improvisation; the combination of spiritual and practical purposes; the implicit reference to the spirit world; the emphasis on communication, on the sharing of information and meaning as well as on the necessity to disguise any signal or message; the techniques of deceit to avoid surveillance, to conceal one's mood or designs. These skills and devices, found among all generations of captives, were passed on and improved upon by slaves through several decades.

Codes of kinship and loyalties were also asserted in which slaves acknowledged their common origin, thus reacting against the brutal exigencies of the trade, the cruel separations already experienced on the coast and in the pens, the deliberate destruction of their culture. African identity had to be proclaimed when it was most threatened. It became a mooring that could ensure survival, a thing to remember, a structure around which to create strong bonds in anticipation of other partings and bereavements.

Shipmates and countrymen took silent vows either to find a way back home—a constant preoccupation for early Africans—or to cultivate ties to sustain new communities. Later, after their arrival in the New World, these shipmates' groupings would assume a more official existence, be organized into "societies" that held multiple functions; inaugurated by a formal ceremony, they invented their own rituals, among which oaths of allegiance and mutual assistance figured prominently, and had their feasts, pageants, and marches.[19] In these ceremonial events celebrating the endurance and survival from the soul-destroying slave ship experience, the Middle Passage was symbolically evoked in its three moments: violent displacement, rebirth, and reunion, the memory kept and reactivated in order to cement the new communities.

In a sort of antithesis of the passage, some ceremonies, oriented in time and space toward Africa, symbolically staged the reunion with countrymen, the travel back to the motherland and home of the ancestors. This return is accomplished even more powerfully by spiritually potent Africans who could fly back to Africa, whose feats are reported or sung in that other ceremonial space, the storytelling session.

It is interesting to note that in the New World, many images antithetic to the slave ship journey were to emerge. Some were generated by the exegesis and reinterpretation of the biblical text inspired by the Evangelical movement. The cruel Middle Passage was opposed by the triumphant return similar to the crossing of the Red Sea by the children of Israel. The experience of conversion was pictured as a rebirth after a long journey through hell; the black church itself was conceived as a ship where "storm-tossed" people can assemble, worship, and "labor the spirit."[20] Ironically, the dreaded ship becomes the instrument of salvation in a religious and a practical sense. In a totally different mood, insurrectionary New World slaves saw slave ships as potential instruments of their liberation: they would use whatever ship they could capture to prepare a revolt. The mere sight of a ship inspired them to action. Thus, at the time of the Montserrat insurrection of 1768 in the Leeward Islands, slaves took advantage of the presence of three Dutch vessels offshore to prepare a mass escape by seizing the ships and sailing off perhaps to Puerto Rico, and they improvised a "Fire on the Mountain" song for the occasion.[21] In another inversion, slaves mastered their former fear of white cannibalism by inventing drinking toasts in calypso fashion at elaborate dancing feasts in Port-of-Spain and, playing on elements of the Catholic communion, made a song (often sung by market women): "The flesh of white people is our bread, their blood our wine."[22] One could find many other instances of inversion; one of the most intriguing is perhaps the famous Jonkonnu carnival in Jamaica and North Carolina that stilled the fright inspired by white traders by celebrating, in song, mask, and dance, a powerful African middleman and a major slaving place on the Guinea Coast.[23]

The slave ship experience itself, encapsulated in the dance, became a site of memory that informed many performatory or ceremonial events. I would like to dwell on one such event that probably has the strongest connection with the Middle Passage dance. It offers in a different setting a reinterpretation of that scene and introduces a new dynamic of time and space that highlights its symbolic significance.

In Caribbean cultures the slave ship dance received a name that is both specific and generic, "limbo," and became the prototype for other dances still practiced today. The limbo dance begins precisely on the slave ship, on the cramped deck where slaves were summoned, and is informed with this primal scene. Suddenly emerging from the ship's bowels, the figures of the shackled dancers of the limbo dance suggest a play with contrasts. The posture of the slaves in "limbo," hampered by their chains, trying to set their bodies in motion first, evokes what Wilson Harris has called in an insightful essay, "the eclipse of the resources of sensibility."[24]

But the dance also asserts the possibility of movement: it sets body and limb in motion and arouses the senses. The disabled bodies are able to perform a dance that is potentially the dance of life, a dance that can imaginatively break the chains and defy traders or captains and their crew. Thus, dancers translated the blunt order to instill life in their numbed and prostrated bodies into a secret call to be born again; they assembled all their energies to transcend the agony and pain. The healthy exercise that the chains turn into a grotesque pantomime that reinforces images of inferiority becomes a ritual of rebirth. The dance to ensure that the cargo of living flesh will arrive safe on the other shore is channeled to other ends. Neither mind nor limb will be so easily manipulated and conquered, and the survival will serve other purposes.

In the limbo dance, the possibility of renascence is evoked through metamorphosis: the dancer moves under a bar that is gradually lowered "until a mere slit of space remains through which with spreadeagled wings he passes like a spider."[25] In this symbolic reenactment of the slave ship dance, the leap to freedom is dramatized, visualized, and narrated. The spider image connects this choreography with another form of performance, storytelling, and with the animal trickster tales of West Indian and African folklore. Inadvertently and ironically, the rulers who order the dance provide an occasion for escape; the performer finds a way out of a desperate situation. This trickster's device announces and prefigures many other tricks and strategies, such as "stealing away," that slaves would later use to find a more appropriate space for their gatherings, dances, frolics, or worship. Onlookers on the ship would pay no more attention to a spider sneaking out through a slit of space than they did to the slaves' real "performance"; the meaning of the dance eluded them.

Invisible or perceived only as bodies and commodities that were shipped away, the enslaved would turn this liability—their invisibility as human beings and as magnificent and crafted performers—into an asset and proclaim with vehemence of limb and voice their humanity and vitality, as well as their capacity to outwit and "put on massa." They developed performatory skills to communicate in explicit or secret codes their grievances and strivings.

The slave ship dance was therefore not simply an atavistic spectacle or a meaningless, grotesque dance "under the whip" but a creative phenomenon of importance for the newly enslaved. Haunted by memories of Africa, beset by the slave trade whose laws and economic proscriptions violate their inner beings, the dancers perform an epic drama that announces the emergence of the New World Negro. Many elements in the slave ship setting supply figurative meaning. On one level, the dance expresses the predicament of the captives, caught in the prison of history, the vessel or the trade born of the inordinate ambition of the slavers. In an age of violence and despair, Africans experience the soul-destroying effect of the Middle Passage: their country irretrievably lost, the New World still unknown and forbidding. On another level, a craving for meaning enables them to deal with their dilemma symbolically; the "limbo imagination," as Wilson Harris calls it, "points to new horizons"[26] and announces the necessity of a new drama. As the dance reenacts the tragedy of dismemberment and dislocation, it stages the possibility of transformation through recollection, reassembly and movement. This inarticulate, obscure desire to be born again infuses the performance with mental design, with a sense of time and space.

This dance born on the slave ship found its way into many other performances: in feasts where the limbo is performed, in carnivals where its ironic replica appears: the dancing on high stilts evoking elongated limbs and the ability to confer with superior creatures or the gods. Slaves were thus encouraged to deliberately seek occasions to assemble; devise counterperformances that would magnify all the movements, gestures, and voices confined or repressed on the ship; and express more freely their feelings and emotions. In the words lent to a slave, if "slaves' bodies were owned by the masters in their dances, slaves skip about as if their heels were their own."[27]

The slave ship scene also prefigures a form of gathering essential to all performances, creating new bonds and solidarity to be translated in the image of a circle or ring: the chaotic heaping of bodies would be reordered into a different pattern or architecture.

Exploring other essential forms of performance in worship, or what Raboteau has called "danced and sung religion,"[28] would be interesting. In praise and hymn singing, the worshippers performed songs that seem resonate within the slave ship experience, with frequent references to the belly of the whale or "the fiery furnace" from which singers ask to be delivered, as in the song "O Lord give me the Eagle's Wing."[29] Significantly, the ring shout appears as an ironic duplication of the steps of the slave ship dance, a further stylization of which the worshippers have reached fuller command: the slow movement of heel and toe, the double shuffle, the low sound, the sudden bursting of voice and motion.

Performance brought into play many recreative capacities, as a response to harsh realities—dislocations, dismemberment, violations. Born of many interactions, it also created new bridges connecting continents and expanding boundaries. On the slave ship the enslaved were exposed to discrete African cultures whose singularity was assessed, as well as to the culture of the traders. The captain forcing them to dance to the music of some European instrument became the unexpected agent of a form of acculturation. In this "gateway to the New World," the process from destruction to creation, begun through a complex blending of legacies, transformed into new configurations.

In new settings after the Middle Passage, African Americans actively sought places and moments that would offer occasions to perform their new culture. Many artistic strategies of concealment were devised to avoid interference, censorship, or punishment and to resist "seasoning" and manipulation. They reaffirmed that, even if control were exerted, the imagination is free. Performance became a site for acts of resistance and liberation. The rehearsal of freedom took place at different levels: as a quest for space and movement, as freedom to summon gatherings, as freedom from bondage in fixed roles and representations, freedom to play with and transgress imposed forms and conventions. It spelled out a new grammar of social behavior. Thus imaginatively enacted, the idea of freedom was made visible; its advent became more urgent.

As the first New World performance, the slave ship dance established an interesting relation and dramatic tension between history and memory, between past and future. It asserted at the same time the will to remember and to reconstruct, however painfully, a chain of memories and simultaneously forget in order to invent a future, later acted out on casual and improvised stages. Most important, it created a fleeting relationship between gesture and vision, whether, as Herbert Blau writes, "you make the gesture to have the vision or you have the vision so that the gesture can be made."[30] The slave ship performance was a creative and daring act that proclaimed, with the sovereignty of the body, the vibrant intensity of one's imagining power.

Notes

1. On African dance: Michel Huet, *The Dance, Art and Ritual of Africa* (New York: Pantheon Books, 1978); John Miller Chernoff, *African Rhythm and African Sensibility* (Chicago: University Press of Chicago, 1979); Sterling Stuckey, *Slave Culture* (New York: Oxford University Press, 1987); Dena Epstein, *Sinful Tunes and Spirituals* (Urbana: University of Illinois Press, 1977); Robert Farris Thompson, *African Art in Motion* (Los Angeles: University of California Press, 1974); Katrina Hazzard-Gordon, *Jookin': The Rise of Social Dance Formation in African American Culture* (Philadelphia: Temple University Press, 1990); *The Interesting Narrative of the Life of Olaudah Equiano, or Gustavus Vassa, the African* [London: 1789], in Ama Bontemps, ed., *Great Slave Narratives* (Boston: Beacon Press, 1969), 1–192.

2. Thus, Equiano claims that the dances in the kingdom of Benin had "a spirit and variety which [he] had scarcely seen elsewhere." Bontemps, 7.

3. Quoted in *The Art of Exclusion*, the account was published in England in 1788.

4. The dance was meant "to keep the cargo alive long enough to reach the market." Epstein, 14.

5. George Francis Dow, *Slave Ships and Slaving* (Westport, Conn.: Grayson & Grayson, 1933), 84–85.

6. *An Abstract of the Evidence Delivered Before a Selected Committee of The House of Commons in the years 1790 and 1791 on the Part of the Petitioners for the Abolition of the Slave Trade* (London: James Phillips & George Yard, 1791), 37. Clarkson also wrote a *History of the Rise, Progress and Accomplishment of the African Slave Trade by the Parliament* (London: John W. Parker, 1839). On the trade, see Philip D. Curtin, *The Atlantic Slave Trade: A Census* (Madison: University of Wisconsin Press, 1969); W.E.B. Du Bois, *The Suppression of the Slave Trade to the United States of America* (reprint: New York: Dover, 1971); Daniel P. Mannix and Malcolm Cowley, *Black Cargoes* (New York: Viking, 1962); Edmund B. D'Auvergne, *Human Livestock* (London: Grayson & Grayson, 1933); E. Donnan, ed., *Documents Illustrative of the Slave Trade to America*, 4 vols. (Washington, D.C.: 1930–1935).

7. Clarkson, *History*, 304–305.

8. See George Howe, "The Last Slave Ship," *Scribner's Magazine*, July 1890, 114, 123–24.

9. Ecroide Claxton, surgeon, who sailed on the slave ship, *Young Hero*, in 1788. In Clarkson, *History*, 304–305.

10. Some Africans were enticed on board the slave ships and offered rewards to perform tribal dances. When the dancing was over, they were taken below, and given intoxicating drinks. When they awoke, they were far out at sea. See Edward Thorpe, *Black Dance* (Woodstock, N.Y.: Overlook Press, 1990), 10.

11. A surgeon on a Brazilian ship Georgia witnessed such a scene around 1827: members of the crew "stripped themselves and danced with black wenches . . . rum and lewdness reigned supreme," in Dowe, 241.

12. When slaves were transported from Virginia to the better markets of the cotton territories, they marched, "their feet heavily loaded with irons," to the sound of a fiddler who was supposed to enliven their spirit. Among the songs they sung was the famous "song of the coffle gang": "We came to be stolen and sold to Georgia" (quoted in George W. Clark, *Liberty Minstrel*, 5th ed. [New York: published by author, 1846]).

13. Rare Book Collection, Cornell University, Ithaca, N.Y.

14. "Report of the Select Committee of the House Of Lords, Appointed to Consider the Best Means Which Great Britain Can Adopt for the Final Extinction of the African Slave Trade: Session 1849," London, 1849.

15. In Bontemps, 47.

16. "Report of the Select Committee," 1849, 163. For more detailed analysis of the belief in white cannibalism: W. D. Piersen, *Black Legacy: America's Hidden Heritage* (Amherst: University of Massachusetts Press, 1993), chap. 1, 1–34; Michael Mullin, *Africa in America. Slave Resistance in the American South and the British Caribbean 1736–1831* (Urbana: Illinois University Press, 1992), 35.

17. Edwin P. Hoyt, *The Amistad Affair* (New York: 1970), 37.

18. Robert Farris Thompson, *Flash of the Spirit* (New York: Random House, 1983), 327.

19. Mullin, 15, 32, 35.

20. Joseph M. Murphy, *Working the Spirit. Ceremonies of the African Diaspora* (Boston: Beacon Press, 1994), 172.

21. Mullin, 219.

22. Mullin, 223.

23. See Geneviève Fabre, "Festive Moments in Antebellum African American Culture," in Werner Sollors and Maria Diedrich, eds., *The Black Columbiad* (Cambridge, Mass.: Harvard University Press, 1994), 42–53.

24. "History, Fable and Myth in the Caribbean and Guianas" (first published in Georgetown: National History and Arts Council, 1970), revised in *Explorations* (Mundelstrup: Dangaroo Press, 1981), 20–42. Reprinted in: *Selected Essays of Wilson Harris*, ed. Andrew Bundy (New York: Routledge, 1999), 152–166

25. Harris, 159.

26. Harris, 159.

27. In an imaginary dialogue between a slave and his master, in *Friendly Advice to the Gentlemen Planters of the East and West Indies by Philotheos Physiologus* (London: A. Sowle, 1634), 146–148.

28. Albert J. Raboteau, *Slave Religion* (New York: Oxford University Press, 1978).

29. These songs found echoes in the jubilant or mournful hollers and tunes of firemen and regiment marchers observed in 1862 by Thomas Wentworth Higginson in his *Army Life in a Black Regiment* (Boston: Fields, Osgood, 1870), 23–24.

30. *The Eye of Prey* (Bloomington: Indiana University Press, 1987), 178.

4

• • • •

The (De-)Construction of the "Other" in *The Interesting Narrative of the Life of Olaudah Equiano*

Jesús Benito
Ana Manzanas

Throughout the seventeenth and eighteenth centuries, European travelers in remote regions of the world easily found new subjects for the position of "the other," that elusive and mobile entity that constitutes the opposite of self. "The other" becomes a discursive concept upon which the so-called "civilized" imagination projects its fantasies and anxieties. Nowhere did travelers blend fact and fiction in their accounts as much as in their description of Africa. The tradition went back to classical historians such as Herodotus and Pliny, who had already peopled Africa with monstrous wonders such as beings without heads and with mouth and eyes in their breasts.[1] These monstrous "others," along with Acridophagi (insect eaters), Ichthyophagi (fish eaters), Ilophagi (wood eaters), Spermatophagi (seed eaters), and the common Anthropophagi as described by classical writers, were to fertilize the Elizabethan imagination, thirsty as it was for the details of savage life, which the Elizabethans located in the newly opened world overseas.[2]

Travel literature in the eighteenth century confirms and refutes the previous accounts with facts and supposed eyewitness reports. Discussions about the monstrous "other" who inhabited Africa heightened in the debate about the legitimacy of slavery. New explorations reached the most unknown parts of Africa in search for the "Noble Negro" and therefore offered new material for antislavery writings like John Atkins's *Voyage to Guinea* (1735). Other accounts, such as William Snelgrave's *New Ac-*

count of Guinea (1734), provided the familiar description of the Africans
as lascivious, anthropophagous pagans given to the worship of snakes.

Deeply influenced by the works of antislavery writers such as Benezet
and his *Some Historical Account of Guinea* (1770), which Equiano credits
in two footnotes,[3] Equiano creates in his *Narrative* an account that contrasts African primitivism with the barbarity of Western civilization. His
autobiography can be considered a peculiar kind of travel literature that
works as an ironic counterpoint as it subverts the categories the Europeans established in their encounters with the unenlightened or uncivilized. For Equiano, as an accidental tourist or traveler taken into a world
of wonders, the white man is "the other."

Slavery, as we read in the *Narrative*, was already known and practiced
in Africa. There were "orthodox" ways of obtaining slaves, who were
"prisoners of wars,"[4] and "unorthodox" ways through abduction. But
these slaves within Africa do not seem to fit the category of "the other," of
the opposite of the self, which Equiano presents in his descriptions of the
whites. The line that separated a slave from a free man was indeed very
tenuous, and any African could become a slave to the rest of the community if he committed a serious crime. In Africa, slavery would imply moral
corruption and a state of degeneracy. The slaves caught in wars would
approximate the concept of "otherness" since, as Jordan explains, "war-
fare was usually waged against another people"[5] and captives were usually foreigners or strangers to the community. But in any case, a slave's
situation in Africa was radically different from his condition in the West
Indies. Equiano explains that "they do no more work than other members of the community" and that "some of these slaves have even slaves
under them, as their own property, and for their own use" (19). As described by Equiano, slavery in Africa seems to represent a relationship of
service rather than one based on power. Slavery refers to a social status
but does not deprive the slave of his status as a human being. Loss of freedom was not viewed as loss of humanity. The term "slave" was therefore
rather circumstantial and did not seem to qualify the bearer as "the
other" in African society.

Equiano's first intuition of whiteness (as associated with otherness) is
a brief reference in chapter 1 mentioning light-colored children within
his community who were seen as deformed.[6] Equiano's view of white
complexions as a sign of deformity confirms the impressions of an English traveler, Sir John Mandeville, who in the fourteenth century already
noted that the people of Egypt "are black in color, and they consider that
a great beauty, and the blacker they are the fairer they seem to each
other. And they say that if they were to paint an angel and a devil, they
would paint the angel black and the devil white."[7] The category of "the

other" as the ontologically different appears when Equiano first encounters the white crew of a slave ship in chapter 2. When Equiano sees the white crew, he does not think of the Europeans as "deformed men"; they are not only not human but spirits with evil tendencies. Tossed and handled by the crew, Equiano is persuaded he had "got into a world of bad spirits" (33). The features Equiano emphasizes render the Europeans as a homogeneous, indistinguishable "other," deprived of individual qualities. Interestingly enough, like the Europeans when they came into contact with Africans, Equiano uses color, together with the whites' long hair, to categorize them. Subtly, Equiano reminds the reader that, for the African, the white man is "the other." The white man automatically embodies in Equiano's imagination savage tendencies, as he confirms when he "saw a large furnace or copper boiling and a multitude of black people" (33), a clear indication for Equiano that he was going to be eaten by these white spirits.

Clearly, Equiano demonstrates his limited comprehension of his new situation as a slave. The narrator can give a subjective account of his perceptions but knows nothing of causality.[8] Equiano's naïveté and his lack of knowledge of the workings of the slave trade are, at the same time, a subtle deconstruction of one of the key tenets of proslavery theoreticians such as William Snelgrave: that Africans had degenerated into cannibalism. In fact, the image of Africans as anthropophagi occurred frequently in the accounts of classical historians such as Pliny. The association of slaves and the anthropophagi is clear in the revealing title of G. Fitzhugh's *Cannibals All! or Slaves without Masters.* Fitzhugh's book reminds the reader of the Africans' natural tendencies and the necessity to keep them under slavery. Perhaps aware of numerous eyewitness reports and proslavery literature, which maintained that Africans eat each other, either alive or dead, with the same casualness with which Europeans eat beef or mutton,[9] Equiano subverts one of the practices that in the Europeans' eyes made Africans Wild Men. In Equiano's eyes, "those white men with horrible looks, red faces, and long hair" (33) are the degenerate and wild "other," the feared anthropophagi.[10]

Gradually, Equiano forges the image of the white man as "the other," the obverse of the travel books' idea of the Negro as "the other." Like an accidental and involuntary traveler, Equiano notes the "irrationality" that rules the world of the white "spirits." Equiano observes how "the white men had some spell or magic they put in the water, when they liked, in order to stop the vessel" (35). Astonished at the vision of whites on horseback, Equiano claims "these people [were] full of nothing but magical arts" (37). The naive and uninitiated voice of the young slave wonders at the so-called "civilized" ways of the whites but also subtly reminds the reader that only the eye of the beholder determines what is magic or irrational and what is perfectly logical and rational. Equiano subverts the common belief that Africans were all inveterate conjurers given to the study of black magic, as they appear in Herodotus's account,[11] and projects it onto "the other," thus implying that the European travelers who emphasized the irrationality of the Africans revealed only their own misconceptions and their own ignorance about the ways of "the other." In Equiano's *Narrative*, the accounts that presented the ultimate "otherness" of the Africans undergo Bakhtinian "dialogization" as they are relativized and parodied. As Equiano writes his own travel book, the subjectivity and the relativism implicit in the authoritative discourse peculiar to proslavery travel tales are laid bare.[12]

Yet Equiano starts to deconstruct his initial image of the whites on his way to England and after he is purchased by a new master, Henry Pascal. If the people to be "othered" are always homogenized, the individuation of one of them paves the way for the dissolution of the category of "the other." In the *Narrative* an individual, Richard Baker, appears in whom, we read, Equiano finds a faithful companion and friend. Moreover, Equiano seems to forget that whiteness for the African equates "otherness" and harbors, at least unconsciously, the desire to become white: "I therefore tried oftentimes myself if I could not by washing make my face of the same colour as my little play-mate, Mary, but it was all in vain; and I then began to be mortified at the difference in our complexions" (44). This anecdote, situated in the *Narrative* at a moment when Equiano is about to convert to cultural whiteness, appears quite symbolic. Convinced of the impossibility of "washing an Ethiop white," Equiano seems to realize that his Africanness and blackness are there to stay. Three years after he was taken to England, Equiano completed the deconstruction of his previous vision of whites as spirits. Whites are not strangers anymore, as Equiano explains: "I no longer looked upon them as spirits, but as men superior to us; and therefore I had the strongest desire to resemble them" (51–52). Equiano can turn into the perfect mimic man[13] as he imitates the English customs and mores. However, as he is unable to erase his blackness, his identification with the English, with the colonizer and slave holder, will never be complete.

White spirits turn into men, thus erasing the insurmountable difference—of kind—between white (spirits) and black (men). The only difference Equiano now perceives is a difference of degree, a quantitative differentiation because white men are superior. This new perception of what used to be "the other" as superior involves a new perception of the self as inferior or incomplete. Disturbing as this new category— superior/inferior—may sound, it reveals how Equiano, perhaps conditioned by the fluid barriers in African slavery, views the border between free men and slaves as tenuous, permeable enough to disappear in three years or, more astonishing, in a few pages. It seems on the one hand that Equiano feels the need to soften his ways and his perceptions of Englishmen once he is living among them. On the other hand, Equiano's fascination with European culture and morality reveals more than blind imitation. His admiration for English culture works as a critique of the uses and abuses it was put to by a majority of Europeans who, as we see throughout the *Narrative*, failed to live up to their own standards. Further, Equiano's understanding and admiration for the ways of the Europeans only confirm his qualities as a perceptive traveler on a foreign ground who is well trained in cultural relativism. Unlike some of the travelers who ventured into Africa and looked at Africans from a "literary" distance—as established by their predecessors' accounts—Equiano illustrates the notion that once one immerses oneself in the ways of "the other," barriers are removed. That might be one reason why Equiano finds that whites, contrary to his first intuition, were not spirits; neither did they live in a world of magic. Away from the horrific scenes he witnessed in the slave ship during the Middle Passage, Equiano seems to "convert" to whiteness. The barrier between the self and "the other" is therefore "blurred." Equiano has absorbed the principles and the language of "the other" and describes himself in the terms set by the English. In just two chapters Equiano has constructed and deconstructed a myth of whiteness, thus creating two contrasting voices that will blend in the remainder of the *Narrative*.

But this deconstruction of "the other" is far from definite in Equiano's *Narrative*. The alleged superiority of the whites is compromised when, against Equiano's expectations, his "benign" master, Henry Farmer, sells him to Captain Doran. At that moment and during his crossing of the Atlantic on his way to the West Indies, Equiano finds out that even though he had been baptized and "by the laws of the land" no man had a right to sell him, he was still will-less merchandise in the eyes of the whites. Even though Equiano considers himself an Englishman, Englishmen "proper" do not consider him an Englishman. If heathenism were a fundamental "defect" that set Africans—and Equiano—apart from Englishmen, the conversion of Africans to Christianity did not imply they had become civilized and were the same kind of men. Being a Christian, as Jordan explains, "was not merely a matter of subscribing to certain doctrines; it was a quality inherent in oneself and in one's society" (24), a quality intimately related to racial issues. Although a Christian, Equiano finds out that he does not participate in the "unity of man" and the continuity of mankind the Christian faith postulated. Despite being a Christian, he was still "the other" in white society. Equiano's conversion does not eradicate the difference that separated him from the whites. Equiano realizes that, even though he has traveled "transatlantic distances" to convert to the Christian faith, he is not fully accepted as a Christian. Further, as he states in the *Narrative*, he finds that "otherness" is a mobile category that encompasses other peoples like the Indians and changes according to the interests of the white majority, always including Negroes. What remains stable and fixed is that insuperable barrier or difference that separated slaves and masters and gives, in Equiano's words, "one man a dominion over his fellows which God could never intend" (80).[14] Instead of erasing differences, slave masters intensify and perpetuate them by denying the slave access to education, thus fixing him as irreversibly other, as Equiano denounces. Equiano's *Narrative* advocates the removal of racial and religious barriers in the inscription on the title page of the abolitionist slogan: "Am I not a Man and a brother."

Sailing back to the West Indies with his new master implies his return to the "land of bondage" and, accordingly, his reconstruction of whites as the deceitful, uncivilized "other." Even though Equiano is bought by another benign master, Mr King, who does not treat him "as a common slave" (71), Equiano always maintains a detached and ambivalent position toward whites, as Paul Edwards has demonstrated.[15] As the *Narrative* progresses, Equiano still fixes whites in the category of "the other," but as he learns their ways and their language, his discourse becomes visibly influenced by the white perspective. This double position is illustrated in Equiano's indirect participation in the economics of slavery, as an overseer on Dr. Irving's estate who managed to keep Negroes cheerful and healthy (76) and as an assistant on slave ships in numerous Middle Passages: "After we had discharged our cargo there, we took in a live cargo, as we call a cargo of slaves" (98). Perhaps one of the most disturbing aspects of this kind of statement (which appears repeatedly, pp. 90, 107) is the inclusion of Equiano within the "we." Striking as well is Equiano's detachment when he refers to "a cargo of slaves" as "live cargo" without further comment. Equiano is clarifying his position, which is closer to the whites—to whom he is linked through the inclusive "we"—and remains more distant from his fellow slaves, who are referred to in the third person. In addition, the references to slaves (not to "Africans") are followed by completely different subjects, as if Equiano intended to delete from his narration further engagement with other slaves and at the same time emphasize his perfect knowledge of the workings of slavery. It seems that when Equiano accepts the language and roles of the more "civilized" culture, he frequently runs the risk of adopting the distorting stereotypes inherent in that language.

The *Narrative* keeps an uneasy balance between Equiano's desire for personal freedom and his forced passivity when he witnesses the abuses committed against other Negroes during many Middle Passages. On such occasions Equiano carries out a superb exercise in negotiation between his silence and his role as critical witness to the sexual abuses perpetrated against female slaves. His silence and passivity are compensated for years later by his exposure of the atrocities of slavery in his *Narrative*. Equiano's African name—meaning "one favoured, and having a loud voice and well spoken" (20)—endows him with a natural gift for eloquence. His mastery of words proves decisive in negotiating between his "two souls" as a European and as an African and between his indirect acquiescence to a dominant ideology—as exemplified in the economic and religious voice that predominates in the *Narrative*—and his larger commitment to the abolition of slavery and his race. It seems that Equiano has to incorporate "the other" as part of the self if he wants to preserve that very self. This double perspective is noticeable from the opening of the autobiography in Equiano's dedication, when he first ponders his predicament since his abduction from Africa and finally justifies the horrors of slavery by his initiation into the Christian doctrine. In a way, both Equiano and Wheatley (among other writers such as Jupiter Hammon) echo the alleged positive effects of slavery vaunted by slavery supporters such as William Grayson, John C. Calhoun, or Howell Cobb, among many others. Although Africa remains in Equiano's mind and he is linked to it through "tender connections," Equiano distances himself from the characters in African American folktales for whom Africa is the paradise away from the white man.

As a slave planning to escape from the West Indies, Equiano never thinks of Africa as his final destination but chooses to return to England. Although his decision sounds paradoxical, it may imply that for Equiano, as for Martin Luther King many years later, a man's return to Africa would imply avoiding a problem. For King, as for Equiano, the fight against slavery first, and segregation later, demanded a courageous decision to claim full American or—in Equiano's case—English citizenship. When Equiano intends to return to Africa, he does so in the capacity of a missionary of the Church of England and later as a commissary on the Sierra Leone expedition. In both attempts he tried not to recover his Africanness or the simplicity of his old African religion but to convert his countrymen to the Gospel faith. When he decides to return to Africa, he is not planning to return merely as an African but as an African European committed both to the Negro cause and to the spreading of the culture of the West. Equiano clearly measures the power of such disruptive forces as Christianity and imperialist economics and sees no radical escape to a primitive and undisrupted African past. He is conscious that this "past" (the Africa he evoked in the first two chapters of his *Narrative*) is no longer there after the African encounter with the white man. Consequently, he adopts the role of a knowledgeable mediator. He seems aware that the clash between African and European value systems and religious beliefs is more dramatic when it emanates from different ethnic and racial groups, but rather less significant when it comes from individuals within the same ethnic group, as he acknowledges in his letter to the Lord Bishop of London.

Equiano's dual identity as an African and a European is clear as well in his encounters with the Musquito Indians. Although there are common ties between Equiano and the Indians (both were part of the category of "the other" in the Caribbean colonies), Equiano adopts the position of the mediator who introduces the Indians to the Holy Word. Unlike the figure of the colonizer, who would impose the new religion on the savage, Equiano is willing to acknowledge the moral superiority and religious fervor of the Indians. Equiano finds in the natural religion of the Musquito Indians echoes of his own African religion (neither has places for worship or is acquainted with swearing), and he considers these unenlightened Indians more enlightened than many Christians. However, in his fluid role as intermediary, he crisscrosses the line between both religious practices as he personally transcended the barriers separating the white man and the black other. He tries to bring the Indians to the Holy Word, but his attitude is not that of imposition as much as of persuasion. Even if Equiano is instrumental in the conversion of the pagan and unenlightened to the Christian faith, his suspicions about the so-called Christians are present throughout the *Narrative*. Very characteristic of his style is the ironic usage of "christian" when he wants to emphasize a master's special cruelty. He finds as well that there are Christians, like the Assembly of Barbadoes, who rather deserve the appellation of "savages and brutes." Also ironic, Equiano—a convert—takes the liberty of teaching or reminding old Christians of some excerpts from the Bible they frequently forget: "I told him [Mr. D—] that the Christian doctrine taught us 'to do unto others as we would that others should do unto us'" (74–75).[16]

Equiano's commitment and questioning—"dialogization"— of white ideology and culture "from within" is present as well in the economic voice with which he closes the *Narrative*. As Houston Baker has demonstrated in his analysis of Equiano's *Narrative* in *Blues, Ideology, and Afro-American Literature*, Equiano appropriates the mercantile and calculating voice of the white man, the same voice that quantified and translated the African's life into economic terms. Although Equiano denounces a system that establishes the value of the African in purely economic terms, as stated by the Assembly of Barbadoes, he is fully aware that he needs to master the economic mechanisms of slavery in order to ameliorate and alter his status as property.[17] When he records his initial commercial transactions with the diligence of a trader's secular diary in chapter 7, Equiano is not passively mirroring or imitating white mercantilism but subverting the economics of slavery to effect the "ironic transformation of property by property into humanity."[18] Equiano's economic voice disrupts the economic mechanisms and the language of slavery from within, through the knowledge he has acquired as marketable property. Once Equiano manages to buy his freedom from Dr. King, his mastery of mercantilism is finally stated in the theory of trade that would replace the slave trade with "a commercial intercourse with Africa." Fully aware of British economic interests and at the same time devoted to the abolitionist cause, Equiano transforms African slaves into African customers, who would "insensibly adopt the British fashions, manners, customs, &c." (176) and therefore perpetuate their condition as dependents or colonial subjects. Equiano's margin of negotiation when he makes this abolitionist appeal is indeed very narrow. He seems aware of the impossibility that Africans aspire to absolute freedom and, very cautiously, suggests a compromise for both Europeans and Africans.

Equiano's crisscrossing of the Atlantic takes him to a crisscrossing of identities. Equiano oscillates between his Africanness, with his vision of whites as "the other," and his desire to become part of that other and convert his countrymen to the superior white culture and religion. This crisscrossing of identities constitutes Equiano's "double consciousness," to use Du Bois's words. Equiano manifests his peculiar "twoness," "two souls, two thoughts,"[19] but his strivings are intricately interwoven and reconciled in his *Narrative*. "The other" crisscrosses the self and the self crisscrosses "the other" to create a difficult and uneasy balance in the authorial voice. Equiano's ultimate exercise of negotiation, the utopian commercial imperialism, which runs parallel to his Christian utopia that he advocates in the conclusion of the *Narrative*, stands as his ultimate compromise. This utopian commercialism would indeed end slavery— and therefore show the fruitful results of Equiano's infiltration in the world of "the other"—but would perpetuate the infiltration of "the other" in Africa, for it would also make the African settle for a new kind of servitude, and thus satisfy "the other" in him.

Notes

1. Pliny, quoted in Eldred D. Jones, *The Elizabethan Image of Africa* (Amherst: Folger Books, 1971), p. 5.

2. See Winthrop Jordan, *White over Black: American Attitudes toward the Negro, 1550–1812* (New York: Norton, 1977), p. 25.

3. For a detailed comparative analysis of Benezet's *Some Historical Account of Guinea* and Equiano's *Narrative*, see Angelo Costanzo, *Surprizing Narrative: Olaudah Equiano and the Beginnings of Black Autobiography* (New York: Greenwood Press, 1987).

4. Olaudah Equiano, *The Interesting Narrative of the Life of Olaudah Equiano, or Gustavus Vassa, the African*, in Henry Louis Gates, ed., *The Classic Slave Narratives* (New York: New American Library, 1987), p. 17. All subsequent references to this edition appear parenthesized in the text.

5. See Jordan, *White over Black*, p. 55.

6. Deformity as a quality associated with whiteness appears clearly in Chinua Achebe, *Things Fall Apart* (New York: Fawcett Crest, 1959).

7. Sir John Mandeville, *The Travels of Sir John Mandeville* (Harmondsworth, England: Penguin, 1983), p. 64.

8. Susan Willis, "Crushed Geraniums: Juan Francisco Manzano and the Language of Slavery," in Charles T. Davis and Henry Louis Gates, Jr., eds., *The Slave's Narrative* (New York: Oxford University Press, 1985), p. 202.

9. See Jordan, *White over Black*, p. 25.

10. For the captive Allmuseri in Johnson's *Middle Passage* (New York: Plume Book, 1991), white men were "barbarians shipping them to America to be eaten." The Allmuseri, like Equiano, saw the white men as "savages," p. 65.

11. See Jones, *Elizabethan Image*, p. 4. In Shakespeare's *Othello*, Brabantio accuses Othello of having corrupted his daughter "By spells and medicines bought of mountebanks," I.iii.v, 61.

12. See M. M. Bakhtin, *The Dialogic Imagination* (Austin: University of Texas Press, 1981), pp. 342–343, 412–414.

13. See Homi K. Bhabha, *The Location of Culture* (London: Routledge, 1994), pp. 85–92, for the importance of "mimicry" in colonial discourse.

14. Perpetuity is indeed a very characteristic aspect of slavery in America. See Jordan, *White over Black*, pp. 52–53.

15. Paul Edwards, "The West African Writers of the 1780s," in Davis and Gates, eds., *Slave's Narrative*, pp. 187–195.

16. See Katalin Orban, "Dominant and Submerged Discourses in *The Life of Olaudah Equiano* (or Gustavus Vassa?)," *African-American Review* 27 (1993): 655–664.

17. Houston A. Baker, Jr., *Blues, Ideology, and Afro-American Literature: A Vernacular Theory* (Chicago: University of Chicago Press, 1984), pp. 34–35.

18. Baker, *Blues*, p. 36.

19. W.E.B. Du Bois, *The Souls of Black Folk* (New York: Bantam Books, 1989), p. 3.

5

• • • •

Landings

Robert Hayden's and Kamau Brathwaite's
Poetic Renderings of the Middle Passage
in Comparative Perspective

Françoise Charras

The ideas developed in this essay proceed from a series of reflections evoked by Toni Morrison's comments on her treatment of the slaves' narratives in her novel *Beloved*, where she assumed that she was giving a voice to the former slaves' "interior life" that had remained, up to then, veiled. In this experience, which had found almost no expression in the various slaves' narratives, the collective and individual ordeal of the Middle Passage, also situated at the core of *Beloved*, was central.

Looking into the past, to verify Toni Morrison's claims, I tried to find literary attempts by previous African Americans to lift up the veil that had hidden the Middle Passage so deeply in the memories and consciousness of their past. The most obvious texts in the English-speaking world were Equiano's *Narrative* (1792) but also the work of Cuguano who, in a very brief part of his antislavery tract published in 1787, had already evoked the horrors of the transatlantic passage. Except for these two historical testimonies, the theme seemed to have remained latent until Robert Hayden's very popular treatment in a poem, "Middle Passage," first published in *Phylon* in 1944, then in a revised form in *Cross Section* (1946), to be finally included in *Ballad of Remembrance* in 1962—a long gestation, which I will trace further.

There was apparently very little more on the Middle Passage, except in the Caribbean, where this theme had already become the object of a debate. Indeed, in 1955, the Barbadian writer, George Lamming, published his first novel, *In the Castle of My Skin*. At the core of this semi-autobiographical novel, as in Toni Morrison's *Beloved*, the theme of the Middle Passage is developed in a lyrical stream-of-consciouness central chapter, which claims a reversed if not paradoxical approach to this historical ordeal. With the publication of *The Pleasures of Exile* in 1960, Lamming developed at length a new interpretation of what was to become the Caribbean Caliban myth and began a long debate on Caribbean culture with V. S. Naipaul. This was to continue with the latter's journal, or report, on a voyage back to the Caribbean, provocatively entitled *The Middle Passage: The Caribbean Revisited* (1962). In 1973, Kamau Brathwaite's published *The Arrivants: A New World Trilogy*. As indicated in its title, it consists of a poetic triptych (the first of a series of such related poetic compositions that seem recurrent in Brathwaite's work)—namely, *Rights of Passage* (1967), *Masks* (1968), and *Islands* (1969).

In these authors' work, I anchor my present study of the theme of the Middle Passage, which, even though resisting literary expression, has first and only recently emerged in poetic form. This essay studies two somewhat antithetic poetic renderings: Hayden's and Brathwaite's.

Most significantly, the traumatic experience of the Middle Passage seems to have made way only into the "literature" of those who participated in the trade. It appears in the form of logbooks, or testimonies and reports, to be produced before the tribunals or committees that were constituted in eighteenth-century England, under the pressure of the anti-slavery and abolitionist campaigns that led to the suppression of the slave trade. Hayden's poem, by its central use of such documents, highlights this absence of a voice that would inform the African American experience of the Middle Passage.

Rachel Ertel's most poignant essay, *Dans la langue de personne: Poésie Yiddish de l'anéantissement*, may offer a clue to analyze the aporia confronting the Negro writer and to explain why the poetic form might have seemed the only vehicle to convey what, to its victims, appeared to be the inexpressible. Rachel Ertel quotes from George Steiner's essay "La longue vie de la métaphore" (1987) his assertion that the only language in which the horrors of the Shoah might be expressed was German, "du dedans, de la langue-de-mort elle-même" [from inside in the language of death/the Dead] (9). And yet, she notes that the Yiddish poetry of annihilation—the poems of the victims as well as the survivors—is an attempt to utter the inexpressible:

> Il incombe au poète la tâche insoutenable de trouver une expression symbolique pour un référent qui récuse tous les signes. . . .
> Devant la folie de l'histoire, devant l'anéantissement, devant

l'opacité de cet événement, la raison se trouve désarmée, impuissante. . . . La parole étant impuissante à dire la *réalité* de cet événement, est amenée, pour atteindre la *vérité* à taire ce qui n'est pas dicible, tout en le signifiant. (12)

[It is the poet's task to give a symbolic expression to a referent that evades and challenges all signs. Reason confronted by the insanity of history is powerless, and, speech being incapable of enunciating the reality of the event, is led, in order to attain truth, to keep silent what is unutterable, while signifying it.]

The parallel with the Holocaust must have appeared relevant to Hayden when he began writing or, at least, revising "Middle Passage" for publication. The shock of these two appalling genocides seems to have struck him to the point that, in *Ballad of Remembrance*, he resorts to the form of the collage that he had already used from the very first in the composition of "Middle Passage." He accordingly juxtaposed poems dealing with the horrors of the Shoah with those that delved into the African American memory of the Enslavement.

The ellipses, the condensation of suffering involved in the silences to be filled by the audience's own knowledge or imagination, are reflected in Hayden's comments on his Middle Passage poem, "The Poet and His Art," and in "Reflections," where he defines poetry as "the illumination of experience *through language*" (*Collected Prose*, "Reflections," 11, my emphasis). The form of the collage—the spacing, the interruptions, silences, and pauses—as Hayden generally indicates, is essential to poetic language: "The poem is built on silences as well as on sounds. And it imposes a silence audible as a laugh, a sigh, a groan" (*Collected Prose*, "Reflections," 13).

Voyage through death,
        voyage whose chartings are unlove.

A charnel stench, effluvium of living death
spreads outward from the hold,
where the living and the dead, the horrible dying,
lie interlocked, lie foul with blood and excrement (*Collected Poems*, 51).

These lines sound as an echo to Equiano's personal relation of the same experience and to Cuguano's preterition:

It would be needless to give a description of all the horrible scenes which we saw and the base treatment which we met with in this dreadful captive situation, as the similar cases of thousands, which suffer by this infernal traffic are well-known. (11)

Yet in Cuguano's narrative the most eloquent exposure of the horrors of the inhuman condition appears only in the apocalyptic catastrophe: "And when we found ourselves at last taken away, death was more preferable than life and a plan was concerted amongst us that we might burn and blow the ship and so perish altogether in the flames" (Cuguano, 10). Just as Frederick Douglass's novel *The Heroic Slave* had been the necessary complement to his *Narrative*, the account of the Amistad revolt also arises from the horrors Hayden elliptically suggested, when completing the poem's purpose—an ending that was part of his attempts to revise for stronger emphasis. "I would like to change it somewhat, make it stronger. I have the feeling now there's something more I should say in order to round the poem off" (*Collected Prose*, "Art," 171).

Speaking of the circumstances that led him to write his "Middle Passage" Hayden later explained:

> That grew out of my interest in African-American History in the forties. It was part of a long work, a series of poems dealing with slavery and the Civil War. I had read Stephen Benet's poem *John Brown's Body* and was struck by the passage in which he cannot sing of "the black spear," and that a poet will appear some day and will do so. I hoped to be that poet and I also hoped to correct the false impression of our past, to reveal something of its heroic and human aspects (*Collected Prose*, "The Poet and his Art" 122).

A Ballad for Remembrance was finally published in England, thanks to Rosey Pool, Anne Frank's teacher. (Hayden was later to write an introduction to her own diary.) In this collection, as emphasized above, the African American history theme is introduced by the two poems on the Shoah: "Perseus" and "From the Corpse Woodpiles, from the Ashes." Evoking the genocide of World War II and other episodes of human racism and destruction, they are followed by a poem that brings forth the solace that may be found by the poet in the Baha'i faith. Foremost in these two poems is the author's use of the poetic "I" when confronted with a vision of horror, as compared with the "impersonality" conveyed by the use of voices and collage in "Middle Passage":

> Yet even as *I* lifted up the head
> and started from that place
> of gazing silences and terrored stone,
> *I* thirsted to destroy (*Collected Poems*, 44),

and again,

> Through target streets *I* run,
> in light part nightmare
> and part vision fleeing
> What *I* cannot flee (*Collected Poems*, 46, my emphasis).

Yet if parallels may be drawn between these two moments, brought thus together for Hayden by the circumstances of personal life and history, there remains an obvious difference, which was already underlined in Cuguano's denunciation of the slave trade. For the latter, as for the antislavery activists, at stake was the responsibility for the "Evil and Wicked Traffic of the Slavery and Commerce of the Human Species. This same traffic Hayden also emphasizes: "Standing to America, bringing home / black gold, black ivory, black seed" ("Middle Passage," I, 48, as again further on in the poem). Not only was survival possible, but, for obvious economic reasons, it had to be the outcome of the transatlantic slave trade.

Although the aim of slavery then was not annihilation, as in the Shoah, Hayden's reflections echo the words of the surviving Jewish poet, who, haunted by the image of the necrophore, feels his work feeds on the destruction of his people: "Maudit soit le poème qui chante aujourd'hui le martyr et maudites soient mes mains de n'être pas devenues cendres avec lui" (Ertel, 15) [Cursed be the poem that today sings of the martyr and cursed be my hands not to have been turned to ashes with him]. In "Reflections on Poetry," Hayden, commenting on "Elegies for Paradise Valley," reverts once more to the Perseus metaphor:

> Poems for him were often a means of catharsis, a way, he often thought, of gazing upon the Medusa without being turned into stone, the poem being his mirror shield. Anyway he was a survivor. *He had broken through* somehow. (*Collected Prose*, 13, my emphasis)

According to Hayden, the form of "Middle Passage" gradually suggested itself to him in its different elements, written here in a kind of paraphrase of his essay, "The Poet and His Art" (129–203):

> Different voices inform the design and dramatic progression of the poem. The poet comments on the action and the moral implications, "and at times, his voice seems to merge with voices from the past, voices not intended to be clearly identified. . . . The voices of the traders, the hymn singer's and perhaps the dead." These voices combine the irony and parody of intertextuality evolving from the collage of the (pseudo?)-historical documents with echoes of Coleridge, Shakespeare (*The Tempest*), as well as Melville, and lines from hymns or spirituals.

The use of the iambic verse with variations, irregularities "to avoid woodenness," suggests a "cinematic style or method" eluding transitions between scenes.

The structure is composed of three sections: (1) the dreadful conditions (ships' logs, eye witnesses' testimonies and depositions by the traders), announcing the motifs and themes: man's cruelty to man, the Negro's heroic struggle to get free, and the irony involved in the reference to Christianity; (2) the reminiscence of the old trader, a composite of various stories, meant to suggest the ballad (guilt and complicity—the African kings' part in that triangular trade); (3) finally, climactic, the Amistad mutiny, recapitulating all the themes and focusing on the heroic resistance to slavery.

By thus paraphrasing at length Hayden's later analysis of his poem, I wish to emphasize the poetic components also found in Brathwaite's epic poem, although put to different uses and purposes, most particularly the emphasis on language. I will not focus here on the obvious contradictions between the two poets—their antithetic stances concerning black aesthetics (Hayden being in a similar position in this debate to Derek Walcott regarding Brathwaite)—or on the different cultural and historical contexts that inform their respective poems. I wish to emphasize the affinities that, more deeply, conjoin these two renderings of the Middle Passage.

In Hayden's elaborate construction, the Middle Passage culminates on an assertion of, and claim to, life: "Voyage through death / *to life upon these shores*" (my emphasis). This line is repeated twice in the poem, once at the beginning, as a definition of the Middle Passage and, at the very end, as a conclusion, echoing the "voyage through death / voyage whose chartings are unlove" in the middle of the poem. Thus, by a striking reversal, the sense/direction of the voyage is transformed into the exaltation of "the black spear," as the first sign of the African American "breakthrough."

In the Caribbean, memories of the horrors of the transportation seem to have given way to a vision of rebirth, as the Middle Passage came to signify the arrival of a new people on the scene of the New World—a metamorphosis Brathwaite presents in his *Arrivants*, transmuting the very movement and signification of the transatlantic voyage. Yet, if for Hayden the recovering of one's past, rememoration, is commemoration, for Brathwaite it is incorporation and foundation, dispossession and possession, and evolves from the larger, longer cycle of an exodus begun long ago in Egypt.

As a transition, and before I address the interpretative and formal treatment of this theme by Brathwaite, I want to point to the transformation of the meaning of the Middle Passage into a mythical genesis pattern, in the debate that pitted G. Lamming and V. S. Naipaul, foreground for my comparative approach to Brathwaite's poem.

In chapter 10 of *In the Castle of My Skin*, through a mythopoietic process, the past is seen as informing and modeling the future of the race, of the people of the diaspora. As in Hayden's "impersonal" poem, the text, through the punctuation and the verbal expression, is denoted as "another language," a "strange voice" emerging from elsewhere, almost foreign. Rhetorically, almost visually, by the length and the rhythm of the balanced sentences and repetitions, it imposes its control and structuring on the experience of severing and dispossession. By an act of the will, expressed in a single sentence repeated twice in the chapter as a leitmotif, the Caribbean metamorphosis of the Middle Passage is thus enacted: "*I make my peace with the Middle Passage* to settle on that side of the sea the white man call a world that was west of another world" (210–211, my emphasis).

In the context of the struggle for independence and the failure of the Federation of the West Indies, Lamming resumes the same recurrent images in *The Pleasures of Exile*, particularly focusing on the deconstruction of the Shakespearian archetypal theme of Caliban and meanwhile opening a long debate with Naipaul on the subject of West Indian culture. "Few words are used more frequently in Trinidad than 'culture.' . . . It is like a special native dish, something like a callaloo. Culture is a dance. . . . Culture is, in short, a night club turn" (Naipaul, 70). To Naipaul, no West Indian culture derived from Africa. There is no West Indian culture:

> For nothing was created in the British West Indies, no civilization as in Spanish America, no great revolution as in Haiti or the American colonies. There were only plantations, prosperity, decline, neglect: the size of the islands called for nothing else. (27)

In the late 1960s in England, Brathwaite published his poetic trilogy. He was an historian, an exile, who had completed in reverse the triangular. The first of his three-volume epic poem was composed after a seven-year stay in Ghana. There the poem was partly conceived, to be continued and completed on his return to the Caribbean. Of that period of gestation he later said, in 1970 :

> [M]y verse until 1965 had no real centre. The "centre" is connected with my return to the West Indies in 1962, after 12 years absence. . . . I had at that moment of return, completed the triangular trade of my historical origins. West Africa had given me a sense of place, of belonging; and that place and belonging, I knew, was the West

Indies. My absence and travels, at the same time, had given me a
sense of movement and restlessness—rootlessness. It was, I recognized, particularly the condition of the Negro in the West Indies
and the New World. (quoted in Rohler, 12–13)

Whatever the differences that led Brathwaite later on to modify his ap-
praisal of Lamming's work, his epic can be read as evolving from the dispossession and betrayal themes introduced by the ancestor's voice in
Lamming's novel, as well as from the transformation of the Middle Passage into a ritual of cultural and historical repossession:

In 1953, George Lamming's *In the Castle of My Skin* appeared and
everything was transformed. Here breathing to me from every pore
of line and page, was the Barbados I had lived. The words, the
rhythms, the cadences, the scenes, the people, their predicament.
They all came back. They were possible. (quoted in Rohler, 3)

This actual living presence will substantiate the repeatedly resound-
ing void of "nothing" that, in Brathwaite's trilogy, echoes Naipaul's
assessment:

> and now nothing
>
> nothing
> nothing
>
> so let me sing
> nothing
> nothing : now . . .
>
> And so without my cloth,
> shoulders uncovered
> to this new doub
>
> and desert I return
> expecting nothing . . . (*The Arrivants*, 13, 177)

I cannot complete here a thorough analysis of Brathwaite's 270-page
epic. I refer the reader to Gordon Rohler's *The Pathfinder*, a most complete
exegis of the trilogy established in the context of the critical elaboration
the poet was conducting at the time, as well as against the historical and
political background of events in the Caribbean—in which Rohler himself was strongly involved.

In 1980, in "Articulating a Caribbean Aesthetic," Rohler describes *The
Arrivants* as moving "with the faith of spiritual dialectics towards an
equilibrium of negation and affirmation, void and structured form, si-

lence and widening circle of sound" (14). Building on the mythical importance of the Middle Passage, Brathwaite's triptych reintegrates the diaspora theme into a larger pattern of exile in the epigraph from Exodus that introduces *Rights of Passage* ("And they took their journey from Elim . . . after their departing out of the land of Egypt" [16.1]). However, the long, restless migration that opens the triptych does not found itself on the fatality of the biblical text but enlarges it by building up upon an archetypal cyclic pattern of rootless ordeal and suffering. The concentric circles of migration, exile, journey, and quest gradually evolve into rebirth and opening. "Beginning," the final chapter of the last part of the triptych, "will be an ingathering of themes and images, which is part of the process of closing of the circle as well as an attempt to make projections in the future" (Rohler, *Pathfinder*, 302).

Similarly, the various personae of the protagonist, by means of the various masks, develop from the enslaved, alienated, exiled individual to the impersonal/personal "I" of the reconstructed self, once he has accomplished the return to Africa and, as the African "omowale," has reclaimed African myths and gods. The "I" will fuse into the collective "choric voice" with the reenactment of the Caribbean dances and rituals.

The last part of the trilogy, "Islands," develops this process of re-memorying and "possession" through vondun, Kumina, and other Caribbean rituals. Calling forth the submerged voice of "the-self-in maronage" (*Caribe*, 8), "Rebellion" here is not the ultimate act or the final word in this process of nomination and possession. It most significantly leads to the ritual of "Jou'vert," the opening announcement of the carnival that symbolically forecloses the anachronistic historical quest that underlies the epic.

"Limbo" ("Islands," II) marks the possession process taking place through the rites of passage that develop from poem to poem, from "The Cracked Mother":

> I cried. But on the seas
> three nuns appeared
> black specks stalked the horizon of my fear
> Santa Marias with black silk sails (180),

through the drumming rhythms of "Shepherd":

> Drum
> dumb
> dumb there is no face
> no lip
> no moon,

to "Caliban":

> And limbo stick is the silence in front of me
> *limbo*
>
> .   .   .   .
>
> *limbo*
> *limbo like me*
>
> stick is the whip
> and the dark deck is slavery (194).

The reference to "Limbo"—the title of the poem that initiates the posses-sion—is explicated by Brathwaite in the glossary, again as in an echo to Naipaul's previous indictment.

> A dance, . . . which is said to have originated—a necessary therapy—after the experience of the cramped conditions between the slave-ship decks of the Middle Passage. Now very popular as a performing act in the Caribbean night clubs. (*The Arrivants*, 274)

Yet the very use of the limbo in the lines of Brathwaite's epic poem dis-claims Naipaul's pronouncements. The symbolic impact of that ritual dance had been explored by Lamming in *Season of Adventure* (1960), and its historical and mythic importance as a reenactment of the Middle Pas-sage will be made even more explicit by Wilson Harris in an often-quoted essay. (See also chapter 3, this volume.) Referring to "Masks," Harris says:

> *Sound* becomes *sight* because of the discontinuous line of the drum, of the mask that allows for the breath and life of the icon. . . .
> He [Brathwaite] has been affected by African images but in an evolutionary way as I understand it. Evolutionary in that, it seems to me, a discontinuous line makes for areas of overlap or gateway drama between Africa and the West Indies—*between sound and sight* (Harris, 40).

As recorded by Anna Walmsley, Brathwaite's own voice in his first public reading of *Rights of Passage* was the breakthrough that inaugu-rated the advent of the new Caribbean Artists' Movement in 1966 by demonstrating the *orality* of the new Caribbean poetry (59–62). The im-portance of the aural effect in Brathwaite's poem has been very bril-liantly described by Rohler and also by Brathwaite himself in the *The Love Axe* and *Jah Music*. Thus, one sees the intrinsic relation of Brathwaite's poetry to the rhythms of jazz and Caribbean music that give their form and structure to the work itself. The evolutive quality of his poetry emerges through variations in different interpretative modes—musical, dramatic, and choreographic. Intertextuality, music, and dance structure the reading of the poem, since "echoes in Brathwaite are generally deliberate, and are part of an architecture built on the power of allusion, improvisation and tonal variation" (Rohler, 265).

Brathwaite continues the theme of the cyclical passage through discovery/recovery, enslavement/delivery, dispossession/possession, in his second trilogy, *Mother Poem, Sun Poem, X/Self,* and then in "Third World History," with his *Middle Passages* (1992), published after the poet's emigration from the island (Jamaica) to New York, to the "other continent." This new volume seems to mark another passage (to me, less powerful) in Brathwaite's work, from *oral/aural* poetry to *visual* tactics with the blatant use of computer effects (already begun in *X/Self*).

This new mode of oral intertextuality, rhythmical and musical, is central to both Hayden's and Brathwaite's poems, whether in their reference to African American jazz music or, for the latter, the evocation of the Caribbean calypso. For Hayden, it is the pattern of poetic language itself, the iambic meter, that has to be broken, "submerged," while Brathwaite at times breaks the verse into fragments that are reconstructed into the metallic rhythms of the trumpet, the steel band, or the drum. The two poets seem here to be drifting apart, as Wilson Harris's comments on Brathwaite's public readings of *Rights of Passage* in contrast to his own use of the novel may explain:

> The difficulty of using a voice or music with words was that, 'one may be adding to that burden of persuasion.' And part of the crisis in the novel is in fact to implode, or explode internally, that kind of encrustation, that kind of accretion that has grown upon words. (quoted in Walmsley, 65)

The structuring of Hayden's poem, by its typographical effects, its reference to silences, is not the mere expression, or representation, of the variations and improvisations of the "oral" voice and its rhythms, as in some of Brathwaite's poems. It is the use of the most *visual* art form of the "collage" that causes the "exploding" of those accretions burdening the words, these other voices, whether those of the slave traders, or Shakespeare's and Coleridge's. Yet, in his criticism of Brathwaite's emphasis on dialect and popular music, Harris adds:

> There is no persuasion, there is no voice, there is no drum. The whole historical accretion which has grown on that word and which has become part of one's prison—begins to break up in this implosion. . . . And therefore part of the task of the creative

writer is to implode these words that you take for granted. (quoted in Walmsley, 65)

Yet in Brathwaite's poems this implosion of words is made *visual*, not by the use of dialect, but by the morphological and synctatical splitting up of the English language—a reconstructing of the fragmenting experience begun with the Middle Passage (Brathwaite in Martini, 18–19). What is at work is the process of repossession of the power of language through poetic creation, repeating thus the genesis of the "nation language," as described by Brathwaite:

And we had the arrival in our area of a new language structure. It consisted of many languages but basically they had a common semantic and stylistic form. What these languages had to do was to submerge themselves. . . . So there was a very complex process taking place, which is now beginning to surface in our literature. (*History of the Voice*, 7–8)

These linguistic strategies, which are best implemented in the poetic use of language, whether in Brathwaite's or Hayden's poetry, or in the form of the experimental novel as written by Wilson Harris, are evidence enough that what is at stake in this process of "re-memory" is the retrieving of the power of language, of naming. Whatever the differences that may separate the African American and the Barbadian poets, Hayden's endeavor to reclaim history runs parallel to Brathwaite's recovering of space. Language thus makes possible the reconquering of a territory, the landscape, "the manscape."

From Hayden's "Middle Passage" to Brathwaite's *The Arrivants*, drifting on the currents that relate the Caribbean to the North American continent, I have tried to explore some of the submerged meanings of the Middle Passage in poetic expressions that emphasize the centrality of language in the reconstruction of the shared ordeal of the black diaspora in the New World.

References

Brathwaite, Kamau, *The Arrivants: A New World Trilogy* (London: Oxford University Press, 1973).
Brathwaite, Kamau, "Caribbean Culture. Two Paradigms," in *Missile and Capsule*, Jürgen Martini, ed. (Bremen: 1983, pp. 9–54).
Brathwaite, Kamau, *History of the Voice: The Development of Nation Language in Anglophone Caribbean Poetry* (London: New Beacon Books, 1984).
Brathwaite, Kamau, *Jah Music* (Mona, Jamaica: Savacou Cooperative, 1986).
Brathwaite, Kamau, *Middle Passages* (Newcastle Upon Tyne, England: Bloodaxe Books, 1992).

Cuguano, Ottobah, *Thoughts and Sentiments on the Wicked Traffic of Slavery and Commerce of the Human Species, Humbly Submitted to the Inhabitants of Great Britain by Ottobah Cuguano, A Native of Africa* (London: 1787).

Equiano, Olaudah, *The Interesting Narrative of the Life of Olaudah Equiano, or Gustavus Vassa, the African* [1789]. In *The Classic Slave Narratives*, Henry Lous Gates, Jr., ed. (New York: Signet, 1987).

Ertel, Rachel, *Dans la Langue de Personne: Poésie Yiddish de l'Anéantissement* (Paris: Seuil, 1993).

Harris, Wilson, *History, Fable and Myth in the Caribbean and Guianas.* Selwyn Cudjoe ed. (Wellesley, Mass.: Calaloo Publications [1970], 1995, pp. 13–29).

Hayden, Robert, *Collected Poems*, Frederick Glaysher, ed. (New York: Liveright, 1985).

Hayden, Robert, *Collected Prose*, Frederick Glaysher, ed. (Ann Arbor: University of Michigan Press, 1984).

Lamming, George, *In the Castle of My Skin* (Ann Arbor: University of Michigan Press, 1994).

Lamming, George, *The Pleasures of Exile*, 2nd edition (London: Allison and Busby, 1984).

Morrison, Toni, "The Site of Memory," in *Inventing the Truth: The Art and Craft of Memoir*, William Zinsser, ed. (Boston: Houghton Mifflin, 1987), pp. 103–124.

Naipaul, V. S., *The Middle Passage: The Caribbean Revisited. Impressions of Five Societies—British, French and Dutch—in the West Indies and South America.* 5th edition. (London: Andre Deutsch, 1978).

Rohler, Gordon, "Articulating a Caribbean Aesthetic: The Revolution of Self-Perception," *Caribe* (Trinidad: 1980, pp. 7–14).

Rohler, Gordon, *The Pathfinder* (St. Joseph, Trinidad: College Press, 1981).

Walmsley, Anne, *The Caribbean Artists Movement, 1966–1972: A Literary and Cultural History* (London: New Beacon Books, 1992).

6

• • • •

The Poetics of Abjection
in *Beloved*

Claudine Raynaud

Nous, vomissures de négriers
Césaire, *Cahier du retour
au pays natal*

Kunta wondered if he had gone mad.
Naked, chained, shackled, he awoke
on his back between two other men in
a pitch darkness full of steamy heat
and sickening stink and a nightmarish
bedlam of shrieking, weeping, praying
and vomiting.

Alex Haley,
Roots

In Morrison's *Beloved*, the evocation of the Middle Passage is no sea yarn.[1] A layering of different moments painstakingly brought to the slave daughter's consciousness, the passage takes the shape of a strangely circular text composed of fragments of "images" that hardly add up to a narrative.[2] In between the laconic notations, the textual blanks bear witness to the effort to find words that would translate the visions into language. All the while, for the reader, the text itself represents a thwarted attempt at articulation, the gaps not pauses for breath but "real" blanks, suffocating loci of barred meaning, silences that spell the insistent closeness of chaos.

The reconstructed "voice" of the monologue, which the reader identifies as that of the slave daughter, wrestles with meaning as it confronts abjection both outside (the "objective" experience of the Middle Passage) and inside (the "subjective" exploration of the pre-Oedipal). Kristeva writes:

> There is in abjection one of these violent and obscure rebellions of being against what threatens it and seems to emerge from either an outside or an inside which are exorbitant, thrown besides what is possible, tolerable, thinkable.[3]

She goes on to define abjection as "a state in between subject and object." The abject is "a fallen object, etymologically a castaway, [which] pulls one to the place where meaning collapses." Beloved, thrown beside her self, ab-jected, cast off, consciousness struggling with the senseless, encounters the unassimilable (like the body unable to keep down food). Morrison renders that encounter in four pages of a broken poetic borderline text, Beloved's "unuttered thoughts."[4]

The Middle Passage confronts the real, the horror, and the ensuing necessity of escaping that deadly encounter to conjure up abomination— "ab-homen," that which is not human—and thus to achieve "humanity." In *Beloved*, it is intricately linked to the individual psychic experience of the daughter's relationship to the mother. The difficulty of reading lies in the complex convergence of the psychoanalytical and the insistence of the referent: the unspeakable experience of the slave trade, the collective trauma, the re-presentation of the black genocide. In a narrative of repetitions, echoes, mirrorings, and correspondences, the monologue tells yet another version of the struggle of the daughter to free herself from the murderous mother while the mother, by dying, by disappearing, has abandoned her. Going as far back to the origins as possible, this version is the most archaic, the most primal. The passage constantly loops back, resists linearity. The tension rests between the necessary chronological layering on the page of the signifying chain and the traumatic assault of split images wrested from a memory that had been engaged in an ambivalent life-saving process of repression. Like Sethe, the slave daughter is "remembering something she had forgotten she knew."[5]

The Middle Passage, this inevitable progress—drifting?—from a lost origin to a forced destination, is a space of in-betweenness, the place of the motion from home to hell, from a lost homeland to (in)hospitable lands that must become home, "Sweet Home," and finally "spiteful," "loud," and "quiet" 124. Morrison can thus be said to poetically explore the fluidity of the in-between, its links to the beginning:

> In-betweenness is a form of break-link between two terms, yet the space of the break and that of the link are greater than one thinks and each of the two terms is always already part of the other. There is no no man's land in between the two; no single edge sets them apart; there are two edges but they touch or are such that fluxes circulate between them.[6]

The "maternal narrative" is told by a daughter—the slave daughter—who emerges from her close contact with abjection bereft by her successive losses: she loses the mother three times and also loses the man who was close to her. Motherless, fatherless, the black daughter is an orphan of history. Forced to discard the mother's tongue and to utter the language of exile, the language of the white fathers, she gradually manages to articulate her losses, to make them "governable."[7]

Using initially a broken syntax and later an increasingly more complex grammar, the daughter attempts to translate the experience of abomination. This necessary progression goes from flesh to body to voice, from matter to language, from abjection to subjecthood. The title of Hortense Spillers's essay "Mama's Baby, Papa's Maybe: An American Grammar Book," which attempts an opposition between "flesh" and "body," fits Morrison's word "images" and the deliberate casting of the experience from a female point of view:

> I would like to make a distinction in that case between "body" and "flesh," and impose that distinction on the central one between captive and liberated subject positions. In that sense, before the "body" there is the "flesh." . . . If we think of the flesh as a primary narrative, them we mean its seared, divided ripped-apartness, riveted to the ship's hull, fallen or "escaped" overboard.[8]

Yet the text reconstructs that progress backwards in different moments whose chronological dis-order corresponds to the struggle of perception with utterance. The surface of the text—the text as surface—is worked through by what Sibony calls the "surface effect" inherent in images: "The image is cut out from our psychic space: this chaos of memories and perceptions is too rich for it; it salvages from it what it can, it's a cut-out, with the 'superficial' meaning that it entails."[9] Distinctions are gradually made among the confusion of sensory perception; images are detached, separated from their origins: "How can [Beloved] say things that are pictures" (210).

Together from the Sea

Before the core of the novel, where the reader is kidnapped on board the slave ship, the Middle Passage is first alluded to by Nan, the one-armed slave woman, Sethe's wet nurse, her "nanny," the woman who took care of her and other white and slave children while her mother was working in the fields (203). Written following the conventions of the realistic novel and framed as a memory, this passage functions as a cameo. Representative of Morrison's writing, it foreshadows both Sethe's telling of the murder and Beloved's monologue. It foregrounds the act of reporting and its embeddedness in the process of memory.[10] It anchors the narrative in history so that the text may later be free to break away from verisimilitude.

Prompted by Beloved, Sethe is forced to recall memories of her own mother. At night Nan told Sethe the story of violation and child murder—her mother's story, a story that reiterates the story told by the novel, Sethe's murder of her baby daughter to save her from being returned to slavery. The "horrors" of slavery displace the horrors of the Middle Passage, whose atrocity is told by women whose voices must be invented:

> She told Sethe that her mother and Nan were together from the sea. Both were taken up many times by the crew. She threw them all away but you. The one from the crew she threw away on the island. The others from more whites she also threw away. Without names, she threw them. You she gave the name of the black man. She put her arms around him. The others she did not put her arms around. Never. Never." (62)

These words, remembered by the "grown-up woman Sethe," constitute what can be narrated of the experience of the Middle Passage and, as such, are emblematic of the creative process, which leads to re-membering the crossing of the ocean. They are the slave's rendering of the fear of "swift unnavigable waters," which, in Stamp Paid's reflections, is one of the metaphors the whites have for the black man, who is also the savage, the cannibal.[11] This information about her origins came to Sethe in a language that she no longer understands as an adult but she understood as a child—her mother's tongue, the African language lost to her memory, a language whose meaning she might recall, but whose words she cannot repeat. Sethe believes that "that must be why she remembered so little before Sweet Home except singing, dancing, and how crowded it was" (62). As Sibony reminds us, this being in-between two or more languages is also specific to the poet's expression. The repressed mother tongue returns in the language of exile, which is the poet's language: "Poetic impulse springs off from the sharing of the word (*parole*), . . . it enacts the sharing of the origin, stages the fact that intimate words have their places of nakedness where they are exposed to the most vivid and multiple otherness."[12]

The narrative—what can be told—is doubled up by the unsaid in a forgotten language. Beyond this laconic text, looming much larger, wrestle images that cannot be put into words, but that will nonetheless have to be "imaged."[13] That might be why Sethe's and Beloved's eyes are expressionless, open wells and why the mother-figure on the slave ship "empties out her eyes"(211).

The use of indirect discourse ("She told her that her mother and Nan . . ."), together with the gradual passage from free indirect discourse into direct discourse, seems to belie the fact that the words are lost to Sethe's memory. The play between first and third person places the narrator in the ambiguous position of mastery (he or she is reporting) and submission (words have been said by another person and are remembered by yet another person). Free indirect speech in this case represents the impossibility of narration.[14] On the one hand, the narrator prompts the words without which meaning collapses. On the other, the simplicity of the sentences, the unadorned syntax and plain words, mimetically betray the link to the other language filtered through memory, the language of the (m)other, the language of the origin, the language of love. Direct discourse, for its part, also shows the difficulty of moving out of a child's representation of the world. A childhood memory is arrested in childish language. In Nan's narrative, complements are repeatedly anteposted, creating a rhythm: "The one from the crew," "the others from more whites," "you," "the others." This list amounts to counting the dead *and* to accounting for the survivor, the loved one, the beloved. Those rejected are part of the "sixty million and more" of the epigraph, to this day "unaccounted for" (274, 275).

The first distinction effected in the text lies between the nameless (and beyond, the unnameable) and the named (Beloved-Sethe). It opposes the one who will eventually be given a chance to achieve "identity" because she had a name (her father's, the black man's name, Sethe) to those offsprings of racial rape who are lost to the Middle Passage. Their fate is either death by drowning or the hope of survival on an unnamed yet specific island, "the island" (Caliban? Friday?). Repetitions abound, language stutters, meaning hides, appears, against a tragic compulsive gesture of rejection: "threw away" is repeated three times. The mother throws away, casts away, expels, ab-jects.

To "re-present" this impossibility of bringing back Nan's words to memory, the passage is outlined by the same sentences in direct speech: "Telling you. I am telling you, small girl Sethe." The Middle Passage must be told at the cost of confronting repressed memory, the "origin" (the cloaca, rape, and child-murder) and this shape of hope, the chosen child from the beloved black man. Expulsion is framed by the appeal to retain, to salvage, to keep, and to pass on. Memory's ambivalent working of casting off and (s)electing is spelled out at this moment in the novel, for memory is repeatedly defined as an act of resistance. Figuratively, then, memory is a mother who kills and saves her children. As the passage also makes clear, the four (or more) networks constantly intertwined in the novel in a ceaseless motion of metaphorical crisscrossing, are always already present: the body (life-giving/death-giving), language (naming/refusing to name), memory (retaining/getting rid of), and creative imagination (generating a text with and against the constitutive inadequacy of language). They lie at the core of Morrison's conception of her art as a black novelist. "Memory is an act of willed creation," she writes.[15]

An (Unmanageable) Emergency

The limited allusion to the Middle Passage is expanded in Beloved's monologue at the center of the novel. Having undertaken the task of telling Margaret Garner's story, Morrison had to go back to the experience of the Middle Passage despite her unwillingness. She says:

> Beloved was also—and it got to be very exciting for me then—those black slaves whom we don't know, who did not survive that passage, who amounted to a nation, who simply left one place, disappeared and didn't show up on the other shores. I had to be dragged, I suppose by them, kicking and screaming, into this book, because it is just too much.[16]

Beloved is both the baby girl killed by her mother who returns as a ghost to haunt her *and* the slave daughter on the ship who sees her mother disappear and who surfaces again. The three interior monologues—respectively, the voices of Sethe, Denver, and Beloved—then blend in a threnody whose meaning cannot be constructed from the outside (214–217). The three women have found their ideal other.[17] The loss is over and fusion total. As Stamp Paid remarks, "[W]hat he heard he could not understand" (172). His second attempt leads him to decipher, if not the words, at least who is uttering them; the confused voices are the spirits of those who have died in horrible circumstances: "The people of the broken necks, of fire-cooked blood and black girls who had lost their ribbons. What a roaring" (181). Thus, the broken linear sequence is a privileged glimpse into the undecipherable, into the unspoken:

When Sethe locked the door the women inside were free at last to
be what they liked, see whatever they saw and say whatever was on
their minds. Almost. Mixed in with the voices surrounding the
house, recognizable but undecipherable to Stamp Paid, were the
thoughts of the women of 124, unspeakable thoughts, unspoken.[18]

Thoughts, not necessarily words, are "reproduced" on the page: paradoxically, these voices are both silent and terribly loud. The monologues
resound with silence. The conflicting convergence of thoughts with the
graphic arrangement of the words on the page force writing into voice, a
voice which appears in inner, rather than outer discourse. The "negative"
(the unsaid) speaks louder than words. The black genocide, unspoken,
covered up, and repressed, must return with the ripping violence of a primal scream to America's historical memory.[19]

After Sethe (200–204) and Denver (205–209), at last Beloved speaks in
a attempt at describing the other side, the world she comes from, the
realm of the dead. She describes what it was like being dead. Morrison
says:

[Beloved] tells them what it was like being where she was on the
ship as a child. Both things are possible, and there is evidence in the
text that both things could be approached, because the language of
both experiences, death and the Middle Passage—is the same.[20]

Yet the monologue also hints at a desire for fusion, for a world where
mother and daughter can be together, reunited in an embrace that repro-
duces the oneness of pregnancy. It attempts to line up the shattered and
dislocated moments of a narrative. However, it is a collection of verbal
fragments that fails to amount to a re-collection. As such, these scraps
stigmatize memory's ultimate failure, its borders: what it comes up
against when it collapses.[21] The chaos of experience and the preverbal
(the inarticulate) must and will be left behind but nonetheless constitute
the daughter's memory, its material.

The process of differentiation, at work in the break-link between
mother and child, is the dominant metaphor of the experience of the
Middle Passage in Morrison's text. This process goes through three stages.

(1) The act of sorting out and separating in order to collect: "[filling]
the baskets," "[opening] the grass."[22] This first evocation of the mother
in Africa is barred, inaccessible. The "clouds" are in the way.

(2) The fusion. The primary narcissism of the baby daughter totally
engulfed in the mother translates into the disappearance of distinct
boundaries: "I am not separate from her   there is no place where I stop"

(210). The daughter is the mother and she is limitless. This stage of one-ness with the mother echoes Nan's phrase, taken literally: "we were to-gether from the sea." In a movement of inversion, typical of the ambiva-lence of in-betweenness, Sethe, the surviving daughter from the Middle Passage, becomes Beloved, the murdered child, one generation later. And Beloved is also the surviving slave daughter on the ship who loses her mother to the sea. Thanks to the fluidity of "displacement" as well as to the conflation at work in "condensation" (two of the primary workings of the unconscious), the one will be the other and the other the one.[23]

(3) The space of desire. The mother-daughter relationship first re-mains at the stage of demand: "I have to have it" . . . "I want to be the two of us I want the join" (213). Later, however, desire becomes an inven-tion of the ghost-daughter: "Beloved invented desire" (240).

As the most repressed voice of all, that of the slave daughter on the ship, attempts to speak, she comes to language both like and unlike a child uttering her first words. The baby girl's narrative of beginnings refers to the moment before being taken on board the slave ship. The "pri-mal" vision stages the mother in Africa separating flowers from leaves, a symbolic task of sorting out, a gesture of parting, which recalls the vision Sethe, as a child, had of her own mother, working away in the rice pad-dies: "I didn't see her but a few times in the fields and once when she was working indigo" (60). It also later finds another modulation in Sethe's poignant attempt at making Sweet Home her own by displaying salsify, yellow flowers, or myrtle at Mrs. Gardner's (22). It becomes the compul-sive repetition of Sethe's actions by the haint Beloved : "She filled basket after basket with the first things warmer weather let loose in the ground—dandelions, violets, forsythia—presenting them to Sethe, who arranged them, stuck them, wound them all over the house" (241). Thus, this element, which highlights the compulsion for repetition and its link to both collective and individual memory, exemplifies the novel's intricate narrative patterns. On the limited scale of Beloved's monologue, the movements of the text are also circular and repetitive, like loops that con-stantly double up on themselves to get closer to the truth of experience and constantly confront truth as the unsayable.

There Is No Place. . . . All of It Is Now.

Although space is denied by the roomlessness of the hull, several scenes are evoked in succession. The pastoral scene (Africa and, by extension, the slave mother in the rice fields) moves into the sea scene (the drowning of the mother and reunion with her daughter) and then on to a scene

situated before Beloved's apparition from the river, one of the novel's beginnings: "A fully dressed woman walked out of the water."[24] The last
moment is that of a resurrection, the emergence out of the water and the
promise of a home to come, the syncopated 124. Through a gradual
process of crystallization, more and more elements coalesce. It is not a
question of achieving accuracy in the description, which would appeal to
the referent, but rather of getting as close yet as far away as possible from
the "hot thing," where the depth of perception and memory precludes
evocation, yet leaves a residual sensation of burning, the ultimate limit of
the experience of the origin. In Sibony's words:

> The origin is a withdrawal which conditions the space in between
> two terms; it withdraws from that state of in-betweenness yet im-
> plies it and its withdrawal originates it. That is why states of in-
> betweenness are figures of the origin, dissipation of the origin, the
> origin being *too hot* and too traumatic to be experienced as such.[25]

This repeated notation—a "hot thing"—signals the moment of the encounter with abjection, what lies beyond the re-presentable: the hot iron,
the branding, the "fire-cooked blood," rape, the moment of birth, the saw
on Beloved's throat.[26] Abjection resurfaces in the very ambivalence, in
the impossiblity of a definite referent, of that recalled burning (searing?)
which points to consummation, to death by fire, or to sexuality. It also
represents the effort of the future subject to separate itself from the pre-
Oedipal mother. Abjection helps the subject to create a sense of "I," for it
is in the process of ab-jection that "I" comes into being.[27]

If one attempts to restore a chronology to these four pages, which precisely defy it, the first tableau is that of an arrested present: "all of it is
now   There will never be a time when I am not crouching" (210). Repetitions ("always," "now," "crouching") insist on the difficulty of telling,
the paucity of language, the fixity of experience, the violence of the
situation. The speaking voice is intent on going beyond the element that
surfaces in order to "string" together a narrative, an enterprise doomed to
failure because of the everlasting present. The eternity of the present coincides with lack of space, with the undifferentiated mass of the bodies
from which the daughter's voice emerges. In its turn, the physical impossibility of displacement, roomlessness echoes an impossible self-
contained biological cycle of bodily fluids: drinking, urinating, crying,
sweating, drinking ("if we had more drink we could make tears   we cannot make sweat or morning water" [210]). In this timeless present where
drink cannot become tears and sweat, relayed by the abject body of the
other, urine is drink: "the men without skin bring us their morning water to drink" (210, twice). Paradoxically, abjection cannot exist: "in the

beginning we could vomit   now we do not   now we cannot" (210).
Kristeva notes that vomiting is the zero degree of abjection, "the most el-
ementary and the most archaic of its forms."[28]

The Man on My Face Is Dead

In the stasis of that first scene, there is a question of both dying and surviving, of fusion and separation, of identity (selfhood) and distance together with loss (otherness). Boundaries are porous. The living are one
with the dead; dying requires an effort and lasts forever ("it is hard to
make yourself die forever" [210]). Such a confrontation with death is
summed up by the piled bodies in the hull and produces strange graphic
statements: "the man on my face is dead." In the workings of the narrative, this moment recurs, and the image is taken up again by Beloved later
in the novel: "She said when she cried there was no one. That dead men
lay on top of her. That she had nothing to eat. Ghosts without skins stuck
their fingers in her and said beloved in the dark and bitch in the light"
(241). The reference is to rape, the transition aptly preceded by the semantic ambivalence of "lay on top of her." The rape in the monologue
("he puts his finger there" [212]) is also thematically linked to Sethe's exchange of sex for the name of her daughter on a tombstone.[29] The climax of the novel, the epiphanic moment of Beloved's disappearance, has
Sethe "run into the faces of" the assembled women. It coincides with the
vision of the man without skin looking at Beloved:

> Now [Sethe] is running into the faces of the people out there join-
> ing them and leaving Beloved behind. Alone. Again. Then Denver,
> running too. Away from her to the pile out there. They make a hill.
> A hill of people, falling. And above them all, rising from his place
> with a whip in his hand, the man without skin, looking. He is look-
> ing at her. (262)

The white man's "look" spells distance, domination, torture, while his
"skinlessness" paradoxically sends him back in the eyes of the slave
daughter to incompleteness, to "flesh," thus reversing her own predicament, since she was the one who had been flesh in the slave master's system. Symbolically rising on top of the pile of falling bodies, which recalls
"the little hill of dead people" of the monologue (211), the white man's
distancing gaze contrasts with the confusion of smiles present in the
monologue ("she is my face smiling at me" [213]) and of laughter ("she is
the laugh . . . I am the laugher"[212], later to become "she is the
laugh; I am the laugher" [216]). However, the desire to be the mother's

face, that smile, includes an equally poignant acknowledgment of the father's death.

In the daughter's narrative, the central foregrounded element of the passage is the corpse of the father, the father's death, his presence/absence, which obviously echoes Halle's death as well as the atrocious deaths of the other Sweet Home men. The ultimate abjection, the acknowledgment of the dead father's body as corpse, cannot happen. Quite logically, dying is also impossible because there is not enough room: the body cannot be left behind, cannot be detached or expelled: "there is no room to tremble so he is not able to die." Kristeva explains:

> The cadaver (from *cadere,* to fall), what has irremediably fallen, cloaca and death, upsets even more violently the identity of the one who confronts it like a fragile and fallacious coincidence. Refuse like the corpse *signal to me* at what I permanently discard in order to live. These humors, this dirt, this shit are what life barely, painfully, puts up with when it comes to death. . . . [I]f refuse means the other side of the limit where I am not and which allows me to be, the corpse, this most sickening of all refuse, is a limit which pervades everything.[30]

After the stifling motionlessness of the first tableau, the monologue tells of the dead bodies pushed into the sea once the slaves are on the deck. This removal results in more room for the slaves ("now there is room"), thus making abjection possible. The vision of the mother in Africa, obscured by the clouds of gunsmoke, is also barred by the promiscuity of bodies. Once the man on her face is dead, the daughter can see: "I do not see her until he locks his eyes and dies on my face . . . my dead man was in the way like noisy clouds when he dies on my face I can see hers" (212). The father's death/absence, resulting from his murder, calls for a return to the mother. Yet the vision of the mother was also illumined in the song sung by the man before he dies: "I love him because he has a song. . . . his singing is of the place where a woman takes flowers away from their leaves and puts them in a round basket" (211). After losing the man she was close to, the slave daughter loses to the sea the woman-mother with whom she identifies.

In the Beginning . . .

In a ceaseless return to beginnings, the different sections of the text attempt to start before the preceding one: "in the beginning we could vomit" (210), "in the beginning I could see her" (211, repeated twice), "in the beginning the women are away from the men" (211). Speaking means looking for the origins (of the narrative). It means writing a narrative of origin that denies that the Word was the beginning and coincides with a genesis of utterance against/with abjection: "In the beginning there were no words. In the beginning there was the sound, and they all no knew what that sound sounded like" (259). This comes down to rewriting Genesis, reminiscent of other famous formulae: "In the beginning was emotion" (Céline) or "In the beginning was action" (Goethe).

The aborted attempt to write the beginning—it will be only a series of renewed tentative beginnings—affirms the indeterminacy of language, which will be gradually lifted. Throughout these four pages, the words used are purposely monosyllable or disyllable words (the only trisyllable words are "Beloved," "swallowing," "beginning"). One-syllable words, such as "see," "the," "he," "she," create meaning out of a minimal number of letters, which, in a certain order, spell "Sethe," the mother's name that bears the trace of the father's name and a word close to the sound "sth," "the interior sound a woman makes when she believes she is alone and unobserved at her work."[31] The degree of indeterminacy is heightened by the constant use of pronouns and of the words "do," "thing," "have," "be," "it." The sequence is anything but chronological, and it works through accretion of fragments that build layers of incomplete images, all to be summed up later in a more compact and more articulate paragraph (see p. 214).

The eternal present has given way to the succession of days and nights, the presence of time ("there is night and there is day again again night day night day" [212]). After the father's death, the mother goes in, following the pile of bodies: "they push my own man through they do not push the woman with my face through she goes in" (212). As she is about to smile back at Beloved, she dives into the sea. The mother's ambivalence is explicitly stated toward the end of the text in the form of an opposition between light and darkness, day and night. While the mother's face can be made out in the water ("in the day diamonds are in the water where she is" [212]), the dark side of that enticing smile is cannibalism. The profound ambivalence toward the mother—who is also the devouring mother—becomes the central tension in the evocation of the Middle Passage: "in the night I hear chewing and swallowing and laughter" (212). Yet it is not the ghost daughter Beloved who will later swallow the mother Sethe, but rather the mother, as monster, who swallows her daughter.[32]

The last section of the monologue is a movement of resurrection: "I come out of the blue water. . . . I am not dead." Mother and daughter can finally join: "she is my face smiling at me doing it at last a hot thing now we can join a hot thing." After a thwarted search for the mother's smile, Beloved has found it. In such a positive moment, this ambiguous burning, which spells destruction by fire, also bears connotations of sexual consummation. It echoes another ambivalent and epiphanic moment of abjection and *jouissance*, Paul D's lovemaking to Beloved: "in the midst of repulsion and personal shame, he was thankful too for having been escorted to some ocean-deep place he belonged to."

In this poetic splintering, where literature approaches abjection (the "hot thing") and moves away from it in a motion of ebb and flow, fragments of the narrative remain as traces that will be inverted, inscribed in the history of slavery. For instance, the smiling Sethe as the slave mother echoes her own mother's smile brought out of her bit by bit. She wore it to such a degree that when "she was not smiling she smiled, and Sethe never saw her own smile" (203). The daughter's desire comes ironically and tragically true and is negated through one of the abominations of slavery. On the slave ship the refused smile of the mother stigmatizes the acknowledgment of abandonment. Pieces of the novel's narrative that include scraps of the story, such as the earrings ("she does not have sharp earrings in her ears or a round basket" [212], "we are in the diamonds which are her earrings now" [213]) or the turtles ("in the day diamonds are in the water where she is and turtles" [212]), prove that Beloved is truly the historical consciousness of the slave community emblematized by Sethe's story.[33] Like elements in a dream, they are overdetermined. At the same time, the process of signification fights the scattering of the images, the dis(re)memberment of the narrative, Beloved's explosion: "I am going to be in pieces" (212). Of Beloved, the reader was earlier told that "among the things she could not remember was when she first knew that she could wake up any day and find herself in pieces. She had two dreams: exploding, and being swallowed" (132).

In *Beloved* the Middle Passage is rewritten as a ritual, the enactment of Beloved's conjoining with the mother after the trauma of the father's death. Subjecthood (individual and collective) and "identity" become possible but only at the price of abjection. Sibony writes:

> In-betweenness is the identity drive in so far as it is alive. It is precisely that drive which prevents from complete identification with one or the other of the two terms; it renews the ordeal of the passage and of displacement without turning it into wondering.[34]

Genuine survival (as opposed to drifting, wondering) is achieved at the cost of revisiting the horror of the Middle Passage. In this stark poetic rendering, Morrison mimicks the gradual verbalization of meaning, the translation of experience in language in order for it to be transmitted. A female child's voice doubles back upon itself so as to conjure new pictures and to add new words to a sentence and make it more "complete." At the same time, the return to beginnings leads to a revisiting of the origin—that is, total fusion with and possession of the mother, a passage through the site where subject and object are undifferentiated in mutual narcissistic possession, a return to abjection.

Notes

1. The 1988 Picador edition of *Beloved* is used throughout this essay.

2. See pp. 210–213. As such, it differs from narrative renderings of the passage that rely on realistic conventions and traditional representation. See, for instance, Alex Haley's *Roots* (London: Picador, 1977), 144–182, or Charles Johnson's *Middle Passage* (New York: Plume, 1990). It would also be useful to contrast Morrison's poetic text with Robert Hayden's poem, "Middle Passage," in *Collected Poems*, Frederick Glasher, ed. (New York: Liveright, 1985), 48–54, or Clarence Major's "The Slave Trade: View from the Middle Passage," *African American Review* 26, 1 (1994), 11–22. See also Imamu Amiri Baraka's play, "Slave Ship: A Historical Pageant" (1964). For a review of the treatment of the Middle Passage in African American literature, see Wolfgang Binder, "Uses of Memory: The Middle Passage in African American Literature," in Wolfgang Binder, ed., *Slavery in the Americas* (Wurzburg: Konigshausen & Neumann, 1993), 539–564.

3. Julia Kristeva, *Pouvoirs de l'horreur: Essai sur l'abjection* (Paris: Seuil, 1980; tr. Léon S. Roudiez; New York: Columbia University Press, 1982), 9. The translations are mine.

4. The reviews of Stanley Crouch, "Aunt Medea," *New Republic* (19 October 1987), 38–43, and of Ann Snitow, *The Voice Literary Supplement* (September 1987), which have accused Morrison of writing holocaust literature in blackface, should then ironically be taken at face value: *Beloved* wrestles with a history of abjection.

5. P. 61. If Beloved speaks the traumatized language of the Middle Passage, Sethe must also bring herself to recall and to tell the murder of her own daughter in order to be at peace with herself. These two textual moments answer each other.

6. Daniel Sibony, *Entre-deux: L'origine en partage* (Paris: Seuil, 1991), 11.

7. P. 122. Cf. Marianne Hirsh's work on *Beloved* as a maternal narrative, *The Mother-Daughter Plot: Narrative Psychoanalysis, Feminism* (Bloomington: Indiana University Press, 1989). See inter alia, Elizabeth B. House, "Toni Morrison's Ghost: The Beloved Who is Not Beloved" *SAF* 18 (1990), 17–26; Mae Henderson, "Toni Morrison's *Beloved*: Re-membering the Body as Historical Text," in *Comparative American Identities*, ed. Hortense Spillers (London: Routledge, 1991), 62–86; Jennifer FitzGerald, "Selfhood and Community: Psychoanalysis and Discourse in *Beloved*," *MFS* 39, 3 and 4 (Fall–Winter 1993), 669–687; Jean Wyatt, "Giving Body to the Word: The Maternal Symbolic in Toni Morrison's *Beloved*," *PMLA* 108 (1993), 474–488; Helene Moglen, "Re-

deeming History: Toni Morrison's *Beloved,"* *Cultural Critique* 24 (Spring 1993), 17–40.

8. Hortense J. Spillers, "Mama's Baby, Papa's Maybe: An American Grammar Book," *Diacritics* 17 (Summer 1987), 67.

9. Sibony, *Entre-deux*, 267.

10. Cf. Nellie McKay, "An Interview with Toni Morrison," *Contemporary Literature* 14 (1983), 413–429.

11. P. 198. White cannibalism was feared by the Africans (cf. *The Interesting Narrative of the Life of Olaudah Equiano, or Gustavus Vassa, the African* [1789]). Episodes of cannibalism are frequent in sea voyages.

12. Sibony, *Entre-deux*, 42.

13. I am borrowing this term from Audre Lorde and Maya Angelou, who both use it to speak of an African American women's poetics that foregrounds images (metaphors or "thought-pictures" in Hurston's vocabulary). See my *Rites of Coherence: Autobiographical Writings by Hurston, Brooks, Angelou and Lorde* (Ph.D. diss., University of Michigan, Ann Harbor, 1991), chapter 1.

14. The use of the name (Nan) as opposed to the pronoun (she) could actually mean that, when addressing the little girl, Nan referred to herself as "Nan" (third person) and did not use the first person ("I"). The sentence would not be written in free indirect discourse but in indirect discourse. The hesitation between first and third person (singular and feminine) repeats the possible conflation between "I" and "she" present in "I am Beloved and she is mine," which constitutes the core of the novel (210, 214).

15. Toni Morrison, "Memory, Creation and Writing," *Thought* 59 (December 1984), 385–390.

16. Amanda Smith, "Toni Morrison," *Publishers Weekly* (21 August 1987), 51.

17. Morrison, Public reading of her work, University of Paris VII, Jussieu, 8 November 1993.

18. P. 199. Cf. Morrison's "Unspeakable Things Unspoken: The Afro-American Presence in American Literature," *Michigan Quarterly Review* 18, 1 (Winter 1989), 9–34.

19. Morrison wants silence to scream in her narratives. Cf. *The Bluest Eye*.

20. Morrison with Marsha Darling, "In the Realm of Responsibility," *Women's Review of Books*, 5, 6 (March 1988), 5.

21. Within the space of this essay only the broader interpretative lines of the monologue can be given.

22. Biblical connotations are always present: "The grass in the flesh."

23. This motion is reversed in the diegesis of the novel where the daughter feeds on the mother; eventually, Denver cannot make out the one from the other: "Beloved bending over Sethe looked the mother, Sethe the teething child" (250).

24. P. 50. The image of the bridge comes up twice to stigmatize that moment: "Sethe is the face I found and lost in the water under the bridge"; "I lost her three times . . . once under the bridge when I went in to join her" (214). The emergency of urinating coincides with Beloved's apparition (51). Beloved drinks impossible quantities of water and Sethe's bladder empties itself in a seemingly endless stream, which sends her back to animality: she is peeing

"like a horse." The bodily metaphor coincides with that of the breaking of the waters in childbirth. Quite fittingly, Beloved suffers from incontinence when Denver nurses her. The body's fluids circulate from daughter to mother, from mother to daughter(s). For instance, breast-feeding, a central metaphor for the production of the story and the act of telling it, has its converse in the three women's milk drinking after their ice-skating escapade.

25. Sibony, *Entre-deux*, (emphasis mine).

26. Death by burning is a recurrent motif in Morrison's work. In *Sula* Eva kills her son Plum by setting him on fire and is helpless in saving her daughter Hannah from the flames. Sixo is burnt and shot in *Beloved*. In *Jazz*, Dorcas is an orphan as a result of the fire that destroyed her house during the East St. Louis riots. For study of the ambivalence of death by burning and the sexualized metaphors linked to fire, see Gaston Bachelard, *La Psychanalyse du feu* (Paris: Gallimard, 1949) and Gilbert Durand, *Les Structures anthropologiques de l'imaginaire: Introduction à l'archéologie générale* (Paris: Bordas, 1984).

27. Concurrently, if one reads the pages following the three monologues as summing up the fragmented text (214–217), possession (en)closes the text, locks the protagonists in a circle of belonging: "You are mine / You are mine / You are mine" (217). The word *mine* will be the only one heard by Stamp Paid, a figure of the reader, as he approaches the house (172).

28. Kristeva, *Pouvoirs de l'horreur*, 10. See the metaphor of revulsion in francophone Caribbean literature in Mireille Rosello, *Littérature et identité créole aux Antilles* (Paris: Khartala, 1992), 126–134. Vomiting is linked to the metaphor of nursing (breast-feeding), which runs through the novel.

29. See my "Figures of Excess in Morrison's Beloved," in Geneviève Fabre and Raynaud, eds., *Beloved She Is Mine* (Paris: Presses Universitaires de le Sorbonne Nouvelle, 1993), 139–151.

30. Kristeva, *Pouvoirs de l'horreur*, 11.

31. P. 172. "These" is also an anagram of Sethe.

32. On the ambivalence of and toward the mother, see Barbara Johnson, "My Monster/My Self," *Diacritics* 12 (Summer 1982).

33. The turtles are associated with sexuality (105, 116). See Ousseynou B. Traoré, "Mythic Structures of Ethnic Memory in *Beloved:* The Mammy Watta and Middle Passage Paradigms," in Fabre and Raynaud, eds., *Beloved She Is Mine*, 77–89.

34. Sibony, *Entre-deux*, 341.

7

• • • •

Surviving through a Pattern
of Timeless Moments

A Reading of Caryl Phillips's
Crossing the River

Claude Julien

If we admit that identity is founded on memory, fictions about the Middle Passage have proved to be *the* medium where the hurt of being torn away and dispersed can well up from its watery tomb. For example, Alex Haley's *Roots* (cliché-ridden as it is with the guilt feelings of liberal America) stands out as a pioneering story, and the mysteries, wonders, mysticism, and nimble sarcasm of Charles Johnson's *Middle Passage* have given the full measure of poetic creation in this respect.[1]

Literary exploitation of this theme by black novelists is part of a broader exploration. The transatlantic passage is currently being quantified in the Du Bois Institute's slave ship database. Historical and archival probing confronts the African diaspora in the very countries that engaged in and prospered from the slave trade—a prominent example being the "Les anneaux de la Mémoire" exhibit in Nantes. Also in France, Bernard Giraudeau's ten-year long movie project "Les caprices d'un fleuve"[2] will delineate the character of a governor posted on Gorée Island, a cynic, a libertine, and an elitist contemptuous of inferior people, who gropingly engages on his own spiritual revolution in 1787.

Fiction has the capacity to unseal the silent lips of official history. Recent fictions, whether French or American, try to trace the hurt the African diaspora created and look beyond both bland silence and militant simplifications. Both Giraudeau's movie script and Caryl Phillips's *Crossing the River*[3] suggest the complex calamities the slave trade has imposed on our world even though Giraudeau's nonbelieving nobleman is anti-thetic to Phillips's captain Hamilton, a staunch middle-class Christian.

A Story That Resists Protest-Novel Clichés

Crossing the River consists of six parts. It opens with a brief unmarked Prologue in which an African father whose crops have failed laments his "desperate foolishness," the sale of his three children to the captain of a slave ship. It closes with an unmarked Epilogue spoken 250 years later by the same African father to the sound of the tom-tom and a "many-tongued" chorus swelling on the other bank (or is it *shore?*) echoing the love these forsaken children took with them from Africa. The years be-tween the opening and closing segments, dated 1752 and 2002, project the transsecular hurts of the African diaspora into our future.

The first narrative, "The Pagan Coast," is set in Liberia in the 1830s. Nash (one of the children sold to captain Hamilton, now a manumitted slave and his master's favorite "son" specially educated for the purpose of colonization) comes back a stranger to his fatherland. His sycophantic letters to his "dear father" in Virginia, all of which call for material assis-tance and spiritual guidance never reach their addressee. They simply chronicle the tragic inadequacy of America's best intentions to redress the wrongs of slavery. Nash, ostracized by colonial society for marrying an African woman, dies from an epidemic—his bones irrecoverable from the African soil.

The second narrative, "West," takes us to pre– and post–Civil War America. Martha, the daughter sold to the slave captain, and now a for-mer fugitive with a "westward soul" (94), seeks freedom and respect but meets a solitary and nameless death on her way to California in the Den-ver winter while she dreams of being reunited with the daughter sold away from her in slavery days.

The third part, "Crossing the River," sweeps back to 1752 on the slaver gathering its cargo off the African coast. This narrative is composed of Captain Hamilton's matter-of-fact logbook and passionate love letters to his bride at home in England. This is Hamilton's first command and the young man is haunted by his father's mysterious death on the African soil while trading for slaves.

The fourth narrative, "Somewhere in England," rushes forward to World War II Britain, where Joyce, a working-class Yorkshire woman, di-vorces her no-good shopkeeper husband who is serving a prison sentence for black-marketing farm produce. Joyce marries Travis, the third child sold back in 1752, who has developed into a black GI from Alabama. Re-

spectful and loving Travis loses his life at dawn on an Italian beach in
1944, and Joyce finally yields to the social worker—a threatening shadow
of a character in a dissonant blue coat and maroon scarf. When giving
baby Greer up for adoption, Joyce symbolically becomes the African father's own daughter and starts a new life.

Sketchy as it must be, this synopsis shows that *Crossing the River* neither romanticizes Africa nor demonizes American slavery and racism. Indeed, whereas the misguided unfortunate father of the Prologue sells his
children into slavery to assuage want in a desperate situation, Captain
Hamilton laconically mentions in his logbook an African king eager to
trade. Contrary to his probably racist and now dead father, young Hamilton himself is not a bad man. He is very business-like when purchasing,
but cost is not uppermost in his mind when slaves are lost to disease.
Though slaves go by numbers on the ship, "This morning buried a fine
woman-girl (n° 123) of a fever" (121), he harbors no hostility—which
does not mean he understands his captives' gloom and sullenness. In a
way, Hamilton, who pens such naive adoring letters to his young bride
back in Britain, is a lost child: the misguided heir of a tradition, who follows his father's trade to fulfill his dream of material success, happiness,
and a family at home. Although he confesses to his wife he feels deep revulsion toward the blacks, he as yet fails to understand how this occupation soured his father's mind and ultimately made him an orphan; a victim in turn offering his finer nature on the altar of greed.

Crossing the River is similarly devoid of blame or anger toward American whites. There is no questioning Edward Williams's bumbling sincere
wish to do "God's work" (10) on behalf of his "black charges" (12) and of
the ignorant pagan Africans. The Denver woman who takes pity on the
dying Martha and offers her shelter is also a good soul, though she can
see no farther than her limited charitable urge. Even the Hoffmans who
purchase Martha are good persons who do their best to help their
bondswoman. But their best stops with taking nonbeliever Martha to a
revival. When their Missouri prospects turn sour, they decide to seek better opportunities in California and perfunctorily inform her she will be
sold back across the river to finance their trip. Such people are clearly
trapped by the social conventions they live by, a point readers must infer.
Limited as it is, the Denver woman's benevolence does not elicit the word
charity in the text. Martha's lifelong hurt is beyond mitigation. A drink of
water and a failed attempt at lighting a stove in a freezing shed are too little and too late.

Fair as the novel is to its white characters, the hurt of the diaspora is
ever-present. There is the "shameful intercourse" (1) of the Prologue.
There is Martha's and Lucas's helpless distress before and during the sale

that disperses their couple and family: the shrill song of the crickets out-side sounds "like twigs being broken from a tree"(76), an analogy that makes their affliction universal. There is the American Colonization Society whose early Pilgrim-father overtones quickly turn dissonant as these *letters from an African farmer* speak of black settlers exploiting the natives, of some of "the less respectable emigrants" (31) stealing two young boys to carry them to a slave factory, and of Nash's being ostra-cized from the American circle for marrying into the African community. There is the hurt of Uncle Sam's racist army. Above all, there is the quiet but insistent plea for the right to belong. History being a "pattern of time-less moments,"[4] the chains of the middle passage are roots of a sort to be planted in the soil you are treading because that is where your *final passage* brought you. Home is not where you come from, but where you are.

The Textual Strategy of a Fragmented Continuo

The coherence of *Crossing the River* arises paradoxically from fragmenta-tion. Here is indeed a novel from which stylistic unity is deliberately ban-ished. The voices are heard from their times in carefully crafted pastiches. The author acknowledges his debt to John Newton's *Journal of a Slave Trader* for the contriving of Captain Hamilton's account, but Nash's letters also ring superbly authentic with their nineteenth-century florid clichés and archaic words. Joyce's distinctive Yorkshire English and the village pump spirit in which she characterizes Chamberlain as "[t]hat silly brummie bugger" (76) help conjure up the specter of social disunion.

Fragmentation also emerges from the voices telling the stories as, apart from Joyce's first person narrative, several voices tell each strand. "The Pagan Coast" is perhaps the most complex in this respect. First, there is a heterodiegetic narrator describing Edward Williams in Virginia and on his later voyage to Liberia, a voice that mixes compassion and scathing mockery. Then, there are Nash's letters that become a pathetic monologue twisting the "Why have you forsaken me?" (42) motif the Prologue strikes in one of its variegated echoes. Finally comes Edward's own unsent letter. A similar voice meshing occurs in "West" when Martha's stream of consciousness on the threshold of death gives way to a heterodiegetic narrator that fully blends into the old woman's words and thoughts. Only a full stop signals the coming of another voice; not even a period breaks the continuum. All of "Crossing the River" flows from the same pen, but Hamilton the captain and Hamilton the lover are different persons. Last but not least, Joyce's narration looks like a diary whose sheets have been scrambled. But this is deceptive as the text is woven with hindsight, as shown in such comments as "I should have known then" (131) and "he's decent and honest. Or so I thought" (141). Except in the first two parts, reported dialogues are routinely deprived of quotation marks, so that people seem to be walled apart or to withdraw into themselves, even when Joyce has a cup of tea with Sandra, her only friend in the village, or speaks with her lost son after eighteen years. The earliest occurrence of this blurring of people confuses the reader in the Prologue, where the African father's and Captain Hamilton's thoughts form a lexical chain and can be differentiated only graphically with the help of italics: "We watched a while. And then approached. *Approached by a quiet fellow*" (1). Thus will people derive different sorrows from the same source. This one's loss is the other's theft, and both breed despair. In turn, despair breeds diasporan hope: naive, curtailed, threatened, and killed—in this order.

The almost uniform landscape, or rather the erasing of the topological individualities, supports the theme of unity through multiplicity. Topicality is kept minimal, as in a nightmare. There is hardly any description of Africa, of American plantations, or of Joyce's Yorkshire village, yet the text insists on elements that sever places, such as the coastal bar, the downs up from Leeds, the climb to Denver and the Rocky mountains, the Mississippi River Martha does not want to cross back to slavery, or Saint Paul's River, whose steep and slippery banks shelter Liberia's wilderness from American intrusion.

Coherence through fragmentation is projected through the manipulation of time. *Crossing the River* plays with time like a ship breaking erratic cross currents, tossing the reader here and there, lurching backward and forward. The overall course reaches from 1752 to the present, but individual segments pursue their own time schemes. "The Pagan Coast" begins in 1841, sweeps back to 1834, and then inches on to the painful truth in 1842 that *civilization* kills. "West" is not really dated, covering twenty-five years on either side of the Civil War, shuttling back and forth from the dying woman to her still smarting life's wounds and the disappointed hope of a haven in California until the past merges with the present into death. Whereas Hamilton's 1752 logbook is naturally chronological, the captain's love letters are not inserted according to their writing dates, suggesting that business matters supersede personal matters, which are sidetracked as the world sweeps towards modernity. Chronological disjointedness constantly affects the reading process. The Prologue mixes the African father's 1752 thoughts with Captain Hamilton's logbook, thus projecting a consubstantial flow of ideas into the fictional future. "The Pagan Coast" moves from innocence to despair in a circular way for Edward Williams and in a linear way for Nash. "West" follows a backward and forward trek through evil. "Crossing the River" follows the linearly bland course of evil unaware of itself. "Somewhere in England" begins with the awareness of inescapable evil and is the most chronologically disjointed of all, a constructed disorder hemmed in between 1936 and 1963, dates whose final digits read like an inversion. The Epilogue juxtaposes the year 2002 with quotations from earlier periods, thus duplicating the pattern of the concluding part of "Somewhere in England," in which 1963 becomes 1944 and 1945, joys leading to foretold sorrow. Dechronologization culminates in the novel's last part, thanks to a controlled effect of systematic parceling out. For instance, out of a total of sixty-five segments (the shortest of which is a mere five lines), six segments are in a row dated December 1940, and the January and February 1941 segments that follow also really belong to the same sequence. Such chronological carving simply fragment the reader's time base. Manifesting Joyce's moral and social wounds, this erratic time scheme shatters one's sense of history and metaphorically translates the dismal unity of fractured lives. As the epilogue says, these people are survivors, all of them.

Survivors All

Perhaps the most arresting aspect of "Somewhere in England" is the way Joyce the rebel erases Travis's blackness early on in her diary, as if she were trying to hide it from herself. The first description that comes of Travis pictures him as a tall and gap-toothed man (162). Earlier cryptic statements such as "I suppose we were all shocked" or "I wanted to warn them" (129) are easy to overlook because they make sense only much later through allusions to Travis's hair "like thin black wool" (167), or when his nameless and faceless companion (fuzzily defined through size only, "the not so tall one, but he wasn't short either" [149]), alluding to the regiment's band, jokingly says, "you hear us play, you can't help but dance" (149), or again when the townspeople stare at Joyce for walking out with Travis (202), or again when Len calls her a "common slut" and a "traitor to [her] own kind" (217).

What matters is not the color of the "Yanks" but their looking "sad, like lost little boys" (129). They are like the evacuee children no one wants in the village. They are like Joyce herself: a stranger among the village people to whom her bridegroom does not even bother to introduce her, as if she were indeed at worst a slave, at best the helper he needed in the shop after Sandra left his employ. They are like pregnant Sandra whom

Joyce nastily hurts. They are like Edward Williams, the plutocratic planter who is denied admittance at the Monrovia club because his wife has committed suicide. They are like Greer, whom the widowed Joyce gives up for adoption so she can start life anew after the war. When Greer seeks his mother in 1963, he comes to find her in the afternoon while *the children* are at school. Joyce is obviously relieved (and proud) her son has been smart enough not to force himself into her new (white) household: thus will uncomfortable questions be avoided and her personal history once again hidden (132). This cruel reunion (probably a one-time occasion) shows how the diaspora can hurt right at home, even in the heart of a loving wife and mother. Perhaps the African father of the Epilogue calls Joyce his "daughter" not because she loved Travis but, rather, because she has been "sensible" (in the words of the social worker) and given up their son for the sake of convenience—or is it survival? For, at this point, Joyce has turned into a rebel without a cause. The closing sections of "Somewhere in England," just like "The Pagan Coast" and "West," begin at the end and end at the beginning. Indeed the second part of "Somewhere in England" elicits a *dejà-vu* feeling as the last 1963 segment reaches toward the past from different angles, even quotes extensively from the earlier supposedly happy armistice celebration. Joyce's telling Greer by way of apology that life was not easy for a racially mixed couple (223) is the last resonance suggesting that the diaspora is an inescapable circle for those who have, as Captain Hamilton writes laconically, "lost sight of Africa," or, in Joyce's particular case, lost sight of themselves. To the African father's economic distress the modern world has added the evil of racism.

The Path to a Diasporan Fictional Form

From Caryl Phillips's works to date—*Higher Ground* followed by *Cambridge*—*Crossing the River* is the capping stone of the representation of the global hurt slavery imposed on mankind. Not only black people are crossing the river of racism but all men are caught in the current. In a way, the novel takes its cue from James Baldwin's italicized statement in *The Fire Next Time* that *"whoever debases others is debasing himself."*[5]

From this vantage point, it can be argued that *Higher Ground* presents the African diaspora as the starting point of mankind's drift into racism. Beginning with the inequities of the slave trade ("Heartland"), moving on to the American prison system ("The Cargo Rap"), and closing with Nazi madness ("Higher Ground"—whose title uses a traditional spiritual where the character involved is a Polish Jew), *Higher Ground* focalizes on the hurt perpetretated upon the victims. The nameless narrator of "Heartland" suffers mentally and bodily; insanity lies in wait for Rudy, who likens time served in prison to the Middle Passage, as well as for Irene, who escapes the Warsaw ghetto to confront ordinary British racism just across her room's partition. *Cambridge* also touches on the ravages of the diaspora on its black victims. But Phillips's second novel of the African diaspora dwells on the deadening of white hearts and souls through Emily Cartwright whose abolitionist self-given mission goes awry when she visits her father's plantation, only to be stranded for life on a Caribbean island with the haunting memory of her illegitimate still-born baby. Like Emily, all men and women in *Crossing the River* lose their bearings. Joyce's case is the ultimate instance of this racist madness because she does the expedient thing, not the motherly one. The reader is left to fill the gash this unacknowledged wound has opened by providing a meaning. Joyce's diary does not even grope its way to an answer to Greer's (unasked) question ("why have you forsaken me?") beyond the lame excuse that life was not easy for an interracial couple then, let alone (but this is a mere repsychologization of the character) a war bride widowed with a colored baby. Even though Greer is her son, he is still different. It was easier for Joyce then to get back into line, and it is probably best for the typical English housewife she has become to keep her past buried.

Does the diaspora imprint a form upon the novel? However moot and subjective this point may be, the case deserves argument. Narratively speaking, *Crossing the River* is fluid. Thoroughly adidactic, it acts as a current that sweeps the reader along. Structurally and chronologically, its 250-year diegesis turns the reader into a swimmer lost at sea. As doxic memory struggles with and against text-induced memories that scatter the years and shatter time, mnemonic fragmentation becomes a metaphor for fractured communities, fractured families, and fractured hearts.

The African and Western voices (past and present and future) that blend in the Prologue introduce, yet leave pendant, quotations from passages to come later that really belong to the same narrative moment. Only the (visual) trick of italics sets them apart. Similarly, the Epilogue quotes from the past four narratives to point to the story's global future. Again, a theme seems to emerge from a comparison of Phillips's three African diaspora novels: *Higher Ground* disperses its three fragments to different locations and different periods. The three stories can be approached as self-contained novellas but build to maximum impact from association. *Cambridge* does not manipulate time or location to the same extent because it is the same story seen from different vantage points. *Crossing the River* is similar to *Higher Ground* in time and location manipulation but establishes a filiation in a global hurt when an African father and a British mother are seized by an unnatural dizziness. Each of the three diasporan novels illustrates the search for a synergy between idea (hurtful dispersion) and form, which *Crossing the River* achieves when, as a fragmented continuo, it masters time.

Crossing the River invites the reader to look at the African diaspora with sorrow rather than anger. It also invites the awareness that diasporan hurt reaches beyond color. The novel's hurt line stretches taut from Africa to the new world and back, on to the Yorshire downs, and finally a battlefield somewhere in Italy, at dawn, a dawn more like dusk because the hurt line extends from 1752 to the present and on to the future, like an all-encompassing discontinuity.

If identity is built from the story we tell ourselves of our past, then rootlessness in *Crossing the River* threatens and affects not only those who suffered from the Middle Passage but also those leading isolated lives, like defiant Joyce in the home of her intolerant mother. Joyce, who survived being jilted by her first lover. Who survived Len's blows and drunken selfishness. Who survived the sorrow of losing Travis to war, then baby Greer to the British welfare system. Partial self-delusion, as in "And so we were sensible, my son and I. My son who hadn't asked me to turn him over to the lady with the blue coat and maroon scarf" (228), reveals Joyce's twisted mind in a modern world whose societies are disjunctive rather than conjunctive. The "muddy boots" that have trampled African soil to procure manpower for the new world are everywhere. *Crossing the River*'s essential idea is that African slavery is a fence post planted in mankind's heart, that on our side of the fence people have been drifting into modernity—away from humanity. In this global wasteland, *Crossing the River*, with its fragile characters, shores up fragments against mankind's ruin. Meanwhile, a "many-tongued chorus continues to swell" from "the far bank of the river" where the drum beats, and the African father builds some solace from this communication with his sons and daughters across the river.

Notes

1. A fine study of Johnson's complex path across the ocean and back is Ashraf H. A. Rushdy's "The Phenomenology of the Allmuseri: Charles Johnson and the Subject of the Narrative of Slavery," *African American Review*, 26, 3 (1992).

2. Giraudeau's "The Whims of a River" and Phillips's *Crossing the River* are continents apart but communicate lexically and conceptually through their titles. Giraudeau was born in La Rochelle, a French harbor the slave trade made prosperous. He has drawn from Albert Jacquard's *L'éloge de la différence* for his film.

3. All parenthetical references in this essay are to the 1994 Picador edition of *Crossing the River.*

4. Caryl Phillips chose to head *The Final Passage,* his first novel, with the following lines from T. S. Eliot's "Little Gidding":

> A people without history
> Is not redeemed from time, for history is a pattern
> Of timeless moments. So, while the light fails
> On a witner's afternoon, in a secluded chapel
> History is now and England.

5. James Baldwin, *The Fire Next Time* (New York: Dell, 1962), 113.

Part II

• • • •

". . . To Life upon These Shores"

(Robert Hayden)

• • • •

Would America have been America
without her Negro people?

W.E.B. Du Bois

When Milkman Dead, Toni Morrison's protagonist in *Song of Solomon*, first enters the Southern black community of Shalimar on his search for gold, he watches children play a ring game of African origin and sing what he dismisses as "some meaningless rhyme."[1] This same song later becomes a revelation for the initiated Milkman who, having learned to listen, suddenly realizes that these children sing about his ancestors—his grandfather Jake and his great-grandfather Solomon, who possessed the skills of his African forefathers: he could fly. Like the griot's disciple, Milkman memorizes the words, triumphantly claiming kin with "That tribe. That flyin motherfucking tribe" (332) and their descendants, the people of Shalimar, as well as the members of his own family.

However, at the very point when Morrison's protagonist achieves a sense of wholeness by rediscovering his African past, she also documents that her approach to history is neither exotic nor nostalgic by insisting on the validity of her differentiation between "those things of the past that are useful and those that are not."[2] With Milkman, she rejoices at his glorious revelation of the flying ancestor, who "ran up some hill, spun around a couple of times, and was lifted up in the air. Went right on back to wherever it was he came from" (326). But the blunt question of one of those whom Solomon left behind to suffer and fend for themselves—a woman's challenging "Who'd he leave behind?" (332)—forces Milkman to realize that flying off by oneself cannot be the African American alternative to the Atlantic diaspora: "You just can't fly off and leave a body" (336). Thus, Morrison's message to her contemporaries derives not from this glorious and powerful flying African but from his wife and children who, proud of Solomon's skills, stayed behind to weave a new web that would empower them to cope creatively with their American reality.

The essays collected in the second part of our volume deal with the various ways in which the uprooted, disoriented, and apparently voiceless Africans who had been forced to cross the Atlantic appropriated the territory and learned to cope with the people they encountered in the New World, transforming the unknown into their home, and reinventing themselves as African Americans.

In "Dislocation, Violence, and the Language of Sentiment," Cynthia S.

Hamilton examines slave narratives, their presentation of violence and victimization, and their articulation of a dislocation that resulted from an experience traumatic enough to destabilize the individual's view of self and his or her position in society. The slave narrative is viewed not as a culturally isolated phenomenon but as a genre related to other literary traditions such as the Indian captivity narrative, the sentimental novel, and the Gothic. Consequently, its treatment of violence, victimization, and dislocation is discussed in relation to intergeneric borrowings from these different traditions. Hamilton argues that the importance of these intergeneric borrowings lies in their introduction of conventions that effectively place the subject of the narrative, the narrator, and the reader in predefined relationships, setting expectations that are implicitly or explicitly acknowledged, and foreclosing some possibilities yet enabling others. If one is to understand some of the tensions and contradictions exhibited by the evolving form of the slave narrative, she insists, one must look closely at these intergeneric borrowings.

After approaching the intersections of gender, money, and slavery on a theoretical level, Eva Boesenberg's "The Color of Money: Economic Structures of Race and Gender under Slavery" contrasts representations of this constellation in two classic slave narratives: Frederick Douglass's *Narrative of the Life of Frederick Douglass* (1845) and Harriet Jacobs's *Incidents in the Life of a Slave Girl* (1861). If wage labor and the assumption of the provider role signal the transition from slavery to freedom and the attainment of manhood in Douglass's case, Jacobs's story offers no solution to the complexities of freedom, money, and the female gender role but provides a detailed analysis of economic structures in her life. Boesenberg shows that Jacobs's description preprares the ground for the clear-eyed perspective on money and gender relations that characterizes later black female cultural productions such as the blues.

Manisha Sinha's "Judicial Nullification: The South Carolinian Movement to Reopen the African Slave Trade in the 1850s" argues that most historians have underestimated the significance of the Southern movement to reopen the African slave trade in the 1850s. While the slave trade agitation found a home in only the lower Southern states, it was an important expression of proslavery discourse, slavery expansionism, and Southern nationalism in general. Advocates of the slave trade used sophisticated proslavery and constitutional arguments to justify their movement. Their agitation was linked to the sectional conflict over slavery expansion: most slave traders wanted to expand slavery into nonslaveholding territories rather than turn nonslaveholders into slaveholders. Southern opposition to reopening the Atlantic traffic was compromised by the fact that Southern leaders refused to condemn the trade

morally; they sympathized with the slave traders' arguments and opposed federal suppression policies. Proslavery opponents of the slave
trade based their opposition on mere "policy" and conceded the principle
to the slave traders. The refusal of Southern juries and judges to implement the slave trade laws revealed the true nature of the slave traders' triumph. Even though slave traders failed to revive the African slave trade
both in and out of the Union, they had successfully initiated an ideological reevaluation of the African slave trade issue.

Grace Nichols's sequence of poems *I Is* originates in her dream of a
young African girl swimming from Africa to the Caribbean with a garland of flowers around her waist, possibly in an attempt to purge the
ocean of the misery her ancestors had experienced. Other contemporary
African American writers, such as Alice Walker, have explored both the
Middle Passage and its mirror image, the quest for Africa—often, as
Nichols's garland might suggest—from a feminine angle and aesthetics.
Generations of women of African descent before Nichols and Walker
dreamed up Africa as well, though their notions of the continent and its
people differed considerably from contemporary ones. Mamie Garvin
Fields's *Lemon Swamp and Other Places: A Carolina Memoir* (1983), which
Clara Juncker discusses in "Africa in South Carolina: Mamie Garvin
Fields's *Lemon Swamp and Other Places,"* articulates not only a Charleston
woman's desire to go to Africa as a missionary in 1909 but also her parents' refusal to grant her their permission. "When I found that nothing
would change their minds," Mamie writes, "I decided to be that missionary right in South Carolina." As a teacher in her home state, Mamie
transplanted, so to speak, the Africa of her dreams to the culturally and
socially isolated John's Island, thus living out her own quest for the ancestral home. However, as other explorers before and after her time,
Mamie molds "Africa" according to her own needs and visions. Her reminiscences of the landscapes and people of various South Carolina islands
communicate above all the dreams and realities of an educated African
American woman living—and surviving—in the Jim Crow South.

In "'The Persistence of Tradition': The Retelling of Sea Islands Culture
in Works by Julie Dash, Gloria Naylor, and Paule Marshall," Lene Brøndum addresses the manner in which the filmmaker Julie Dash and the
novelists Gloria Naylor and Paule Marshall employ Sea Islands culture in
Daughters of the Dust, Mama Day, and *Praisesong for the Widow,* respectively. As theoretical points of departure, Brøndum employs Mae Gwendolyn Henderson's essay, "Speaking in Tongues: Dialogics, Dialectics, and
the Black Woman Writer's Literary Tradition" and Trinh Minh-ha's
Woman, Native, Other. Her analysis reveals that Dash, Naylor, and Marshall seek to liberate the discussion of African American women artists'

relationship to power and discourse from overused, stereotypical settings by placing their works on the Sea Islands, which come to occupy a cultural and psychological space "in the middle" between Africa and America. The Sea Islands, in other words, become a new und unfamiliar trope for the syncretic nature of African American cultures and for the existence of mythic ties to Africa. Primarily through storytelling and mythic memory, these artists also disrupt and revise history and historiography, thereby replacing oppression with celebration as their primary concern.

Hélène Christol's essay "The African American Concept of the Fantastic as Middle Passage" depicts the fantastic mode with its dialogical, interrogative, and unfinished styles of discourse, on the one hand, and its strong political, social, and ethical thrust, on the other, as a dominant mode in recent literatures. African American texts are shown to be part of that transcultural movement, and their use of the fantastic can be viewed as a crucial way to explore and reveal forgotten middle passages between Africa and America, mimesis and figuration, possibility and impossibility. Founded itself on Morrison's novel *Beloved*, this essay first analyzes how the fantastic works as the favorite locus for intertextuality, inserting itself consciously in the Western tradition of the fantastic. Even when it signifies resistance, by bringing back to life a revenant as the figure of re-memory and subversion, it still inscribes itself in that Western conception of the fantastic as a figure of transgression, underlining ruptures and discontinuities. Yet in the African American text, the Middle Passage goes both ways: permitting cross connections of African mythical and historical structures, the ghost restores a lost code and works as the necessary instrument in the healing of personal and collective wounds, taking readers and characters back to Africa, to language, and to reality. Christol also suggests, though, that the more recent African American texts might be less interested in the fantastic as a Middle Passage between different cultures and traditions than in the exploration of the fantastic as an art of limits, a play on boundaries.

Notes

1. Toni Morrison, *Song of Solomon* (New York: Signet, 1983): p. 267. All quotations in this text are taken from this edition.
2. Thomas LeClair, "Interview with Toni Morrison," in *Anything Can Happen: Interviews with Contemporary American Novelists,* ed. Thomas LeCiair and Larry McCaffery (Chicago: University of Illinois Press, 1983): p. 253.

8

• • • •

Dislocation, Violence, and
the Language of Sentiment

Cynthia S. Hamilton

Dislocation and violence provided evocative material for the slave narratives published before the Civil War, but more interesting than the continuing presence of such material are the changing literary conventions used to handle it. By examining these conventions, one can begin to see the impact of other popular literary genres on the slave narrative. Through wide availability and popularity, the Indian captivity narrative and later the sentimental novel provided both authors and reading public with conventions and expectations on which the slave narratives could draw. The Indian captivity narrative, which anticipated the slave narrative by over half a century, provided its earliest formal template.

In the Indian captivity narrative, the experience of captivity and subsequent enslavement is represented as an apocalyptic experience. A violent clash of cultures is shown here in terms of its affects on the life and consciousness of a particular individual uprooted from a familiar culture, lifestyle, and world view and confronted with an alien landscape, an alien society, and an unknown language. The captive's powerlessness in this new world is marked by deprivation, abuse, and alienation as the individual is placed in an alien landscape, cut off— by death, distance or separation—from friends and relatives, forced to travel great distances in circumstances for which the captive is unprepared, and deprived of sufficient food, clothing, and shelter. In Puritan captivity narratives, the sense of dislocation is also marked by the sudden wrenching apart of the captive's sense of spiritual and physical well-being. Captivity becomes a test of faith as the captive experiences a sudden discontinuity between the worldly and spiritual levels of experience, which had, up to that time, run in parallel. The captive declares himself or herself beloved of God, but chastened, marked to show the power of God's saving grace and to bear witness to the dire consequences of a lapsed covenant. Violence is experienced and witnessed within this wider framework. The captors are not seen as all powerful or the victim as degraded. In the captivity narrative, the captive maintains a sense of superior status despite having an inferior position within the captor's society. For those who survive the experience of captivity, victimization is a temporary state. Violence is not seen in personal terms but as the result of larger forces and is often described in a surprisingly dispassionate manner. This is not to say that the brutality of the violence is minimized. The mode of representation makes violence appear starkly, even numbingly horrific. In his *Memoirs of Odd Adventures, Strange Deliverances, etc. in the Captivity of John Gyles* (1736), Gyles describes the tortures suffered by his fellow captives in these terms:

> Sometimes they will take a captive by the hair of the head and stoop him forward and strike him on the back and shoulder till the blood gush out of his mouth and nose. Sometimes an old shriveled squaw will take up a shovel of hot embers and throw them into a captive's bosom, and, if he cry out, the other Indians will laugh and shout and say "What a brave action our old grandmother has done!" Sometimes they torture them with whips, etc.[1]

The strategy used here has been called, by Philip Durham, the objective technique, which he defined as "a peculiar artistic technique—an exclusive concentration upon what Ernest Hemingway called the 'sequence of motion and fact,' which produces an emotion, rather than on the direct portrayal of emotion or thought or upon any obvious rhetorical effort—such as calling attention to a tear-jerking scream—to arouse or direct the responses of the reader." Durham adds, "By using this technique these authors appear to create an attitude of casualness and detachment which makes the emotional reaction all the more effective when it is subtly and indirectly received."[2]

The sentimental novel treats violence and victimization very differently. One can see the way violence is sensationalized in the sentimental novel by comparing the description of torture from Gyles's *Memoir* with a description of impending Indian violence from the sentimental tradition, in this case from James Paulding's *The Dutchman's Fireside* (1831):

"Let us drink his blood!"—"Let us tear out his heart!" echoed the rest, as they brandished their weapons and came furiously towards Sybrandt. At this moment the soul of the young man bowed to the supremacy of these accumulating horrors; but it sunk only for a moment, and then regained its level.[3]

In this passage, the threatened violence is represented schematically by stock gestures and postures that act as prompts and models for appropriate emotional responses. Such treatment is typical of the way violence and victimization are handled within the sentimental framework. The philosophy of moral sentiments that underpins the sentimental novel sees empathy as the bedrock of morality; the man or woman of sincerity and sentiment exhibits the stamp of moral rectitude and of fine feeling both in his or her own behavior toward others and in his or her reactions to the distress of others.

The sentimental novel is a test of sensibility. The hero or heroine who undergo afflictions without renouncing their fine feelings or rectitude prove the purity of their sensibility. Characters also demonstrate their sensibility through their reaction to the suffering of others by striking appropriate gestures and postures. The author demonstrates an acceptable level of sensibility through comments, often "Dear Reader" comments, on the sufferers. And a reader's sensibility is vindicated as he or she reaches for a handkerchief. The victim of violence in the sentimental novel, therefore, quickly becomes an object of ego gratification, a process that sits ironically at odds with the more egalitarian bent of the philosophy behind the sentimental novel. This treatment of violence and victimization invites an unpleasant voyeurism. Furthermore, the increasing codification of the language of gesture associated with sentimentality encouraged a commodification of suffering, evidenced both in the popular literature of the day and in the elaborate etiquette and custom surrounding death and mourning.

In the sentimental framework, suffering is the product of a fall into knowledge or from social grace, marking the danger areas within the society. A fall into knowledge—suffering that results in a fully developed sense of duty and an appreciation of the meaning of womanhood—may be treated as a fortunate fall, necessary preparation for matrimony. A fall from social grace may be used to point a moral lesson or to implicate larger forces within society, giving the sentimental novel the potential to act as a vehicle for social criticism. Social criticism in the sentimental novel is likely to be decidedly double-edged, however. The victims of social injustice become litmus tests of sensibility before they provide incentives for reform. In Ned Buntline's *The Mysteries and Miseries of New York*

(1848), for example, we are asked to remember a "poor little sewing girl" who "cannot possibly last long. One winter of destitution—one bitter season of toil amid starvation and wretchedness, must sicken her. If she sickens, she dies; for then she cannot labor." While she might support herself by casting herself "into the hot-house of vice," this is a possibility dismissed with horror: "let us rather hope to see her freeze, starve, die in misery, with purity still in her soul, than to yield to the fatal step which would engulf all that is precious and beautiful in her character."[4] The narrator's harshest strictures are reserved for the victim, placing the reader's voyeuristic gratification above the claims of social justice. Indeed, as David Reynolds has shown, the sentimental novel is a parasitic tradition, presenting social trauma as spectacle in the name of reform.[5]

In sharp contrast to the handling of dislocation in the captivity narrative, the sentimental novel provides no adequate mechanism for exploring dual consciousness. The problem of dislocation—of being confronted with an experience traumatic enough to destabilize the individual's view of himself and his position in society—cannot be adequately expressed or explored within the mannerisms of the sentimental novel, where characters are defined through gestures and postures that have a predetermined social currency.

It is to the captivity narrative, therefore, that one must look for depictions of a dual consciousness that maintains an internalized set of values and view of self in the teeth of an environment that would deny it, while recognizing the need to take cognizance of the alien perspective offered by the society in which the individual must survive. In the consequent struggle for self-definition, the Indian captivity narrative assumes the reader will identify with the captive's "home" society, though the captive's attitude toward his or her captors is not as straightforward as this might imply. John Marrant's *A Narrative of the Lord's Wonderful Dealings with John Marrant* (1785), which is often cited as both an Indian captivity narrative and, less accurately, as a slave narrative, provides an extreme example of ambivalence, for Marrant's experience of captivity is inextricably linked to his adolescent rebellion against his family.[6] Marrant runs away from home in a fit of indignation, and while he welcomes the opportunity offered by his captivity to forge an alternative identity with enhanced social status, he has not switched his allegiance completely to his captor's society, for the values and religion that give his new social status meaning are firmly rooted in the "home" society he has temporarily rejected.

More usually, captivity narratives exhibit a nuanced response to the captor's society by recording acts of kindness as well as acts of cruelty. In *The Redeemed Captive* (1707), John Williams recalls a visit to "a small company of Indians" during his captivity, and says "they were after their manner kind to me and gave me the best they had, which was moose flesh, groundnuts, and cranberries but not bread."[7] Admiration for the Native American's stamina and survival skills in a hostile environment is also evident, though credit is sometimes given to Providence rather than to the Native Americans. In *The Soveraignty and Goodness of God* (1682), Mary Rowlandson comments that she "can but stand in admiration to see the wonderful power of God in providing for such a vast number of our enemies in the wilderness where there was nothing to be seen from hand to mouth."[8] Whether the praise is oblique or straightforward, approval is significant, for it marks points of commonality and shared values, indicates an effort to understand the experience of captivity in a manner that extends beyond the moral oppositions which structure the narrative, and provides the reader with a more textured depiction of Native American lifestyles. The captive's celebration of his or her own feats of survival within the hostile environment also adds to this textured depiction. In *Narrative of the Capture and Subsequent Sufferings of Mrs. Rachel Plummer, Written by Herself* (1839), Plummer proudly recounts two fights in which she bested Indian women charged with her management, and in so doing earned more respect from her captors.[9] The richness of texture added by such details is often lost in narratives related by a third person, such as those in Cotton Mather's *Decennium Luctuosum* (1699) or in *The Manheim Anthology* (1794); both works concentrate on cataloguing incidents of barbarous cruelty.[10]

In the slave narratives that draw heavily on the Indian captivity narratives, in these European captivity narratives, the reader is more likely to be associated with the captor's society than that of the captive. The estrangement from the captive's home society is further intensified in narratives written by, with, or edited by individuals who lack knowledge of the captive's home society, individuals whose affiliation is to the captor's society rather than the captive's. The dislocation of captivity and enslavement in *Some Memoirs of the Life of Job* (1734) is viewed by Thomas Bluett, the European recorder and interpreter of Job's story, not as a test of faith in the wilderness but as a providential opportunity for education. Not surprisingly, the violence of captivity is minimized, for this is a captor's view of a benevolent captivity, anticipating the proslavery apologetics of the antebellum period. Even within this narrative framed by the consciousness of its European interpreter, there is an attempt to provide a picture of the captive's home society, particularly in sections one and three. In the *Memoirs of the Life of Job*, as in the Indian captivity narratives, there are points of commonality, of shared values and norms between the captive's home society and that of his captors, societies other-

wise placed in juxtaposition. In the *Memoirs,* such points are endowed
with increased significance, for they are used to justify Bluett's admiration for Job and to explain the influences that shaped Job's noble character. In the hands of a skilled interpreter of one's own culture, like
Equiano, such points of commonality can be used not only as a way of
validating the captive's pride in his home culture but as a means of social
criticism, as Klaus Ensslen has ably argued.[11]

The slave narrative also provides more subtle opportunities for critical
observations of the captor's society. Although European society and values are used as the basis for judgments and appeals to the reader, the captive's apparently naive perspective can provide a telling point of contrast
between sanctimonious pronouncements and social practice. In James
Albert Gronniosaw's *A Narrative of the Most Remarkable Particulars in the
Life of James Albert Ukawsaw, an African Prince, Related by Himself* (1770?)
we are shown the educative value of captivity and enslavement, but here
the benefits of enlightenment are noted more wryly than in the *Memoirs
of the Life of Job.* When Gronniosaw lands in Portsmouth, England, his
outsider's perspective exposes the social hypocrisy of his adopted countrymen. Gronniosaw's misplaced trust when it comes to matters of
money and his immunity from avarice contrast with the attitudes and
practices in English society at large and provide a significant leitmotif
within the narrative.

In its treatment of dual consciousness, the slave narrative exploits po-
tentialities that remain underdeveloped within the Indian captivity narrative. The morality play and clash of cultures played out in the wilderness of the Indian captivity narrative are more fully internalized in the
slave narrative. The most pithy example is to be found on the tombstone
of Venture Smith, "African": "Though the son of a King, he was kidnapped and sold as a slave, but by his industry he acquired money to purchase his freedom."[12] In Venture Smith, the African nobleman coexists
with Franklin's Yankee. The internalized clash of cultures summarized so
neatly on Venture Smith's tombstone is explored much more fully in *The
Interesting Narrative of the Life of Olaudah Equiano, or Gustavus Vassa, the
African* (1789).

Later variants of the captivity narrative such as Solomon Northup's
*Twelve Years a Slave. A Narrative of Solomon Northup, a Citizen of New York,
Kidnapped in Washington City in 1841, and Rescued in 1853, from a Cotton
Plantation Near the Red River, in Louisiana* (1853) contrast Northup's life in
his home state of New York with his experience of captivity and slavery
south of the Mason-Dixon line. Northup's dual consciousness sets him
apart from those on the plantations who have been slaves from birth, and
one feels this awareness of distance in his comments about his fellow

sufferers in slavery. Northup recalls that when he and two other free-born men planned a mutiny on board the ship carrying them into slavery, they dared not trust any of the other slaves. "Brought up in fear and ignorance as they are," he explains, "it can scarcely be conceived how servilely they will cringe before a white man's look. It was not safe to deposit so bold a secret with any of them, and finally we three resolved to take upon ourselves alone the fearful responsibility of the attempt."[13]

Whether the clash of societies represented is that of Native American and English, Canadian French Catholic and New England Puritan, English and African, or Slave and free, the captive has two different identities and two different definitions of himself and his experience on which to draw. This is both painful, in that it produces a sense of dislocation, and positive, in that it offers creative choices with redemptive potential. In *Twelve Years a Slave*, Northup attempts, by answering questions about his life in the North, to give two of those imprisoned with him in a Washington slave pen a life-enhancing alternative vision of identity, an act recognized as dangerously subversive, for it denies the captor's ability to control a fundamental aspect of the captive's existence while asserting the individual's disposition and ability to act independently.[14] The reviled captive refuses a degrading definition of himself offered in one world system and looks to a more positive definition of self offered in another.

The captive's sense of special status, of undergoing and overcoming the ordeal of captivity as a demonstration of divine guidance and protection, which we saw in the Indian captivity narrative, can be seen in some slave narratives as well. Gronniosaw's narrative is prefaced by a commentary that finds in "the experience of this remarkable person" evidence that God's saving grace can operate "in regions of the grossest darkness and ignorance" by influencing the mind of "those whom he hath foreknown" to bring them to an understanding of His truth.[15] The political implications of divine guidance here are admittedly rather different from those of the Indian captivity narrative, but the sense of the individual's chosen status is the same.

The redemptive potential of an alternative social identity can also be seen in the treatment of violence. In *A Narrative of the Life and Adventures of Venture* (1798), Venture Smith maintains, and assumes that we will share, a view of himself very different from that offered by his temporary social position as slave. In the passage I am about to quote, the injustice of the whipping is indicated but not dwelt on. The superior self-possession of the slave is apparent, and although he suffers his mistress's blows, his superior power is established. This is not the portrait of a victim; it is the portrait of a man whose sense of self-worth easily discounts his momentarily disadvantaged position. While the image of the hand raised to ward off the blows is a stock image of passivity and appeasement, it does not stand here as a gesture that derives its meaning from the sentimental framework of victimization. Smith transforms the "great black hand" into a symbol of restrained power:

> I earnestly requested my wife to beg pardon of her mistress for the sake of peace, even if she had given no just occasion for offence. But whilst I was thus saying, my mistress turned the blows which she was repeating on my wife to me. She took down her horse whip, and while she was glutting her fury with it, I reached out my great black hand, raised it up and received the blows of the whip on it which were designed for my head. Then I immediately committed the whip to the devouring fire.[16]

Here we are presented with "the sequence of motion and fact" that characterizes the objective technique. It is assumed that interpretation is unnecessary because the reader will identify with the narrator and be shocked and offended by the violence without being given prompts in the form of the coded gestures of sentimental posturing. Clearly, the way violence and victimization are presented in the slave narrative has important implications, placing the reader in a particular kind of relation to the victim and anticipating a particular kind of response. An example will place the differences between the objective and sentimental approaches in sharp contrast. The following passage from *Running a Thousand Miles for Freedom; or, The Escape of William and Ellen Craft from Slavery* (1860) shows the tendency of the sentimental mode to transform individuals into stereotypes and to insulate the reader from the true horror of events, transforming actions into gestures:

> On Hoskens entering the apartment, in a state of intoxication, a fearful struggle ensued. The brave Antoinette broke loose from him, pitched herself head foremost through the window, and fell upon the pavement below.
>
> Her bruised but unpolluted body was soon picked up—restoratives brought—doctor called in; but, alas! it was too late: her pure and noble spirit had fled away to be at rest in those realms of endless bliss, "where the wicked cease from troubling, and the weary are at rest."[17]

Antoinette is placed before the reader as a suitable stimulus for sensibility. She is objectified and displayed, victimized by both the slave trader and by the teller of her story. And the reader, handkerchief at the ready, knows when to weep.

There are, of course, ways of subverting the sentimental agenda, as happens in the *Narrative of Sojourner Truth* (1850). Olive Gilbert, whose sentimental inclinations gave form to Sojourner Truth's story, and censored it according to the dictates of propriety, allows her subject to interject a comment that disrupts the conventional presentation of violence:

> He whipped her till the flesh was deeply lacerated, and the blood streamed from her wounds—and the scars remain to the present day, to testify to the fact. "And now," she says, "when I hear 'em tell of whipping women on the bare flesh, it makes *my* flesh crawl, and my very hair rise on my head! Oh! my God!" she continues, "What a way is this of treating human beings?" In these hours of her extremity, she did not forget the instructions of her mother, to go to God in all her trials, and every affliction; and she not only remembered, but obeyed. . . .[18]

Sojourner Truth's words establish her as a woman of sensibility in her own right, removing her from the voiceless posture as victim, and declaring her equal status. Her comment also replaces the condescension of pity with a more egalitarian empathy.

Harriet Jacobs's *Incidents in the Life of a Slave Girl* (1861) poses interesting problems for standard tests of sensibility, for in Jacobs's narrative the older writer who relates the events of her past life exhibits the gestures and postures that mark her as a refined woman of sensibility, while the younger self she presents to the reader as the object of empathetic involvement has violated one of the most basic tenets of sexual propriety under the domestic ideology. The result faces the reader of sensibility with an interesting dilemma and poses a case that should, according to the logic of sensibility, not be possible: a "fallen woman" of "refined sensibilities":

> But, O, ye happy women, whose purity has been sheltered from childhood, who have been free to choose the objects of your affection, whose homes are protected by law, do not judge the poor desolate slave girl too severely! If slavery had been abolished, I, also, could have married the man of my choice; I could have had a home shielded by the laws; and I should have been spared the painful task of confessing what I am now about to relate; but all my prospects had been blighted by slavery.[19]

The exemption Jacobs claims for herself is not one the sentimental novel was quick to offer. Heroines of sensibility had regularly been killed off amidst weeping and eulogies to avoid just such a situation, as we have seen with Antoinette and the poor sewing girl.

Jacobs wreaks even more profound havoc with the sentimental framework by introducing strong elements of the Gothic tradition. Such a blending of the sentimental with the Gothic is possible because of the strong ties between the two. Both are concerned with the home and with woman's place within it, and both are grounded on the domestic ideology of separate spheres. However, the home of refuge featured in the sentimental novel is replaced in the Gothic novel by a house of horror, where corruption infects and violation threatens. As a result, the sentimental novel tends to uphold the basic assumptions of the domestic ideology, while the Gothic novel confronts contradictions and tensions in a more radically fundamental manner. As Kate Ferguson Ellis has pointed out in her discussion of eighteenth-century English Gothic novels, the Gothic is "a set of conventions to represent what is not supposed to exist"; its conventions, she says, "speak of what in the polite world of middle-class culture cannot be spoken." As she also notes, one such unspeakable subject is violence against women.[20]

This is precisely the ground covered by Jacobs, and as Lydia Maria Child, who introduced and edited *Incidents in the Life of a Slave Girl* fully realized, Jacobs's removal of the veil that cloaked the more "delicate" or "indelicate" aspects of slavery was very definitely in questionable "taste": it violated the polite separation of public and private space and placed unmentionable subjects before a mixed audience. And worst of all, it was done by women well aware of the dictates of polite society. To treat such unacceptable material on generic shared ground, where revelation could be combined with insistently demanding and compelling appeals to the reader's sensibility, was a masterstroke that helped to sanction the forbidden exercise, providing it with both literary precedents and useful structural and stylistic conventions. In Jacobs's *Incidents*, domestic moral platitudes and sentimental postures are undercut by revelations that expose their irrelevance or falsity. The Southern home "of a sunny clime, and of the flowering vines that all the year round shade a happy home" is the plantation where the husband "pays no regard to his marriage vows," fathering children "of every shade of complexion" (36). Through such generalizing comments, Jacobs presents the defiled home of Dr. Flint as representative of the deep and widespread wrongs attendant on "the peculiar institution."

Jacobs's depiction of Dr. Flint is central to the shift from sentimental to Gothic, undermining Southern ideology and apologetics. Jacobs transforms Dr. Flint from an artful seducer in the sentimental mold into a Gothic villain: powerful, scheming, manipulative, ruled by guilty passions, and intent on the violation of the innocent. She turns a Southern gentleman, whose privileged status and wise and benevolent paternalism could, in accordance with Southern ideology, expect due deference and respect, into a lecherous old man unable to control himself. When Jacobs tells her persecutor that she is expecting a second child, he becomes "a restless spirit from the pit" who subjects her to "such insults as no pen can describe." Jacobs refuses to describe them, adding that she "would not describe them if I could; they were too low, too revolting" (77). Her refined sensibility, self-possession, and dignity contrast sharply with the behavior of her persecutor.

Within the Gothic tradition, the violation of the innocent, and the impending threat of such violation, forms an important leitmotif, shaping reader expectations and providing suspense. "My master met me at every turn, reminding me that I belonged to him, and swearing by heaven and earth that he would compel me to submit to him" recalls Jacobs. "His footsteps dogged me. If I knelt by my mother's grave, his dark shadow fell on me even there" (28). Here, as elsewhere in the narrative, a few suggestive details are supplied as indicative, leaving the conventional expectations of the Gothic to supply the suspense while shielding Jacobs to a certain extent from the need for fuller revelations.

These evasions can be both compelling and protecting. But other types of evasion take us back to the posturing of the sentimental, as in the following passage. Here, in jealous rage, Dr. Flint confronts Jacobs with the accusation of having taken a new lover and hurls her young child, who has sought to intervene, across the room. The scene is related as a series of standard poses with reactions depicted in the unsubtle language of melodrama:

> "Not yet!" exclaimed the doctor. "Let him lie there till he comes to."
> "Let me go! Let me go!" I screamed, "or I will raise the whole house." I struggled and got away; but he clinched me again. Somebody opened the door, and he released me. I picked up my insensible child, and when I turned my tormentor was gone. Anxiously I bent over the little form, so pale and still; and when the brown eyes at last opened, I don't know whether I was very happy. (81)

Such mannered treatment shields Jacob's privacy and obviates the need for her to confront a disturbing incident more directly, but it also shields the reader, allowing a conventional response to a melodramatic scene. The final sentence forces a reevaluation, however. It contradicts the expected response; Jacobs expresses not joy and relief at the recovery of her son, but a more complex ambivalence.

It is not surprising that the authors of slave narratives resort to sentimental formulations when dealing with emotionally painful or disturbing incidents, using the sentimental posturing as a mask or cushion. It is telling that in the *Narrative of the Life and Adventures of Henry Bibb, an American Slave* (1849), Bibb employs the objective technique when relat-

ing his near fatal accident after being tied to a horse, while choosing the
sentimental mode when he tells of being caught with his family as they
attempt to escape from slavery.[21] Nor is it surprising that in the *Narrative
of William Wells Brown, a Fugitive Slave* (1847), Brown shrouds in sentimental posturing his parting from his mother when she is sold down the
river as a result of their unsuccessful attempt to run away. But whether
the sentimental treatment is used in an effort to protect the self-liberated
slave from a painful past or to pander to the sensibilities of middle-class
readership, the result is a facile and dangerous evasion that commodifies
suffering. Such sentimental posturing contrasts sharply with Charles
Johnson's simple statement in *A Narrative of the Incidents Attending the
Capture, Detention, and Ransom of Charles Johnson* (1827):

> The sight of these scalps, thus unfeelingly placed immediately in
> my view; the reflection that one of them had been torn from the
> head of a female by our ferocious captors; the other from a man
> who had engaged my esteem and friendship; with whom I had em-
> barked on a plan of business now utterly frustrated; and that
> a much more cruel destiny than his was probably reserved for
> me, operated with an effect which I should in vain attempt to
> describe.[22]

Here the unspoken emotions are hauntingly evoked, the circumstances
presented in a way that forces the reader toward empathic involvement.
This is in stark contrast to the heightened, but artificial emotionalism of
the sentimental appeal. When it comes to exploring the psychology of
dislocation and violence, the sentimental mode is equally superficial, especially when contrasted with the Gothic, or with the captivity narrative
with its exploration of dual consciousness. One can understand the appeal of the sentimental mode, however, for its evasions were more comfortable for all concerned.

Such evasions continue to offer critics a means of validating their sensibility while insulating themselves from the full horror of the experiences narrated. A fuller understanding of these narratives awaits a closer
examination of their contradictions, tensions, evasions, and silences. If
we are to appreciate the slave narratives as mediated accounts of experience, it is imperative that we look more closely at the consequences, for
both authors and readers, of borrowings from other generic traditions.

Acknowledgments   I am indebted to the Manchester Metropolitan University
and to the British Academy for funding the release from teaching and admin-
istrative duties that has enabled me research and write this essay.

Notes

1. John Gyles, *Memoirs of Odd Adventures, Strange Deliverances, etc. in the Captivity of John Gyles, Esq., Comander of the Garrison on St. George's River* (Boston, 1736), reprinted in Alden T. Vaughan and Edward W. Clark, eds., *Puritans among the Indians: Accounts of Captivity and Redemption, 1676–1724* (Cambridge, Mass.: Belknap Press of Harvard Univ. Press, 1981), 102.

2. Philip Calvin Durham, "The Objective Treatment of the 'Hard-boiled' Hero in American Fiction: A Study in the Frontier Background of Modern American Literature," Ph.D. diss., Northwestern University, Evanston, Ill., 1949, 3–4.

3. James K. Paulding, *The Dutchman's Fireside; A Tale*, ed. William I. Paulding (New York: Charles Scribner, 1868), 100. The first edition was published in 1831.

4. Ned Buntline (E Z C Judson), *The Mysteries and Miseries of New York* (London: Milner & Co., n.d.), 68. The first edition was published in 1848 in New York.

5. David S. Reynolds, "The Reform Impulse and the Paradox of Immoral Didacticism," in *Beneath the American Renaissance: The Subversive Imagination in the Age of Emerson and Melville* (Cambridge, Mass.: Harvard Univ. Press, 1989).

6. The text of the 1788 London edition is reprinted in Richard VanDerBeets, ed., *Held Captive by Indians: Selected Narratives, 1642–1836*, revised edition (Knoxville: Univ. of Tennessee, 1994).

7. Williams [1707] (Amherst: Univ. of Massachusetts Press, 1976), reprinted in Vaughan and Clark, 167.

8. Rowlandson, 1682 Boston edition, reprinted in Vaughan and Clark, 69.

9. Plummer, 1839 edition, reprinted in VanDerBeets, 353–355.

10. The first edition of the *Manheim Anthology* was, according to VanDerBeets, published in 1793. I have used Mathew Carey's edition of 1794, reprinted in VanDerBeets's collection. Mather's work is reprinted in Charles H. Lincoln's *Narratives of the Indian Wars, 1675–1699* (1913; reprint: New York: Barnes & Noble, 1959).

11. Klaus Ensslen, "Sea-Changes and Identities. Dislocation and the Narrative Formation of Cultural Self-Concepts, (Olaudah Equiano, James Baldwin, William Gardner Smith)," a paper delivered at the Collegium for African American Research, Tenerife, 18 February 1995.

12. Smith, 1897 edition, reprinted in Arna Bontemps, ed., *Five Black Lives* (Middletown, Conn.: Wesleyan Univ. Press, 1971), 31.

13. Solomon Northup, *Twelve Years a Slave*, ed. Sue Eakin and Joseph Logsdon (Baton Rouge: Louisiana State Univ. Press, 1968), 44–45.

14. Northup, 29.

15. James Albert Ukawsaw Gronniosaw, *A Narrative of the Most Remarkable Particulars in the Life of James Albert Ukawsaw, an African Prince, as Related by Himself* (Bath, England: S. Hazard, [1770?]).

16. Smith, 14–15.

17. Craft, reprinted in Arna Bontemps, ed., *Great Slave Narratives* (Boston: Beacon Press, 1969), 282.

18. Olive Gilbert, *Narrative of Sojourner Truth*, ed. Margaret Washington (New York: Vintage Books, 1993), 15.

19. Harriet A. Jacobs, *Incidents in the Life of a Slave Girl, Written by Herself*, ed. Jean Fagan Yellin (Cambridge, Mass.: Harvard Univ. Press, 1987), 54. Subsequent page references will be included parenthetically in the body of the text.

20. Kate Ferguson Ellis, *The Contested Castle: Gothic Novels and the Subversion of Domestic Ideology* (Urbana, Ill.: Univ. of Chicago Press, 1989), 7.

21. Both Bibb's *Narrative* and that of William Wells Brown are reprinted in Gilbert Osofsky, ed., *Puttin' On Ole Massa* (New York: Harper Torchbooks, 1969).

22. Johnson, reprinted text based on 1905 reprint of first edition (1827), in VanDerBeets, 255.

9

. . . .

The Color of Money

*Economic Structures of Race and
Gender under Slavery*

Eva Boesenberg

In this essay, I shall approach the complexities of "race," gender, and
money under slavery in the American South. Particularly, I want to explore the slaves' own representation of the nexus between money and
gender once they had escaped the masters' symbolic economy where
their place was predetermined, immutable, and ambiguous with regard
to gender.[1]

Black people deported to North America might have experienced slavery on the African continent, but their commodification in the New
World represented a new dimension of dehumanization. Quite literally,
freedom and personhood depended on money in a slaveholding economy.
The profit motive, which had occasioned the slaves' transatlantic passages in the first place, was inscribed in the social structures of the "peculiar institution" with startling consistency. Treated as chattel and assigned a cash equivalent, the slaves were depersonalized further by the
degree of abstraction inherent in monetary language, which screens
contextual relations and reduces vastly different activities, objects, and
relations to a common denominator.

As economist Mascha Madörin has pointed out, for our times, the language of money, spoken by those who actually determine its value—
bankers, brokers, international monetary fund officials, and so forth—
functions like a binary system of oppositions such as valuable versus
worthless, predictable versus unpredictable, and reasonable versus irra-

tional. This calculating language shows an all too familiar conflation of stability, rationality, and financial success, a combination so overdetermined that one need hardly observe that this pole is also tacitly marked as "white" and "male." The "unpredictable" factors, such as women, children, and nature, become invisible in its reckoning.[2] As Patricia Williams notes, "given the way we use money, we . . . dispense with the necessity of valuing or considering . . . whatever is outside the market."[3]

One should be careful when applying these analyses to the past, especially since the language of money had not yet achieved the independence from material analogues that characterizes its present circulation. Yet, although money did not function as a free-floating signifier to the extent it does today, when the global exchange of currency, bonds, stocks, obligations, shares, and so on is twenty times as high as the value of goods being traded around the world, African Americans noted just this erasure of "the human factor" as a characteristic feature of their reduction to property under slavery. The trope of invisibility, which achieved such prominence in African American letters, corresponds to this camouflage of social relations that characterizes the language of money. Visible only as pieces of property, slaves could not be *seen* as human beings.[4]

The denial of subject status was linked to the exclusion of slaves from participation in the gender system that structured the dominant society. As Thorstein Veblen, Marcel Mauss, Luce Irigaray, and others have shown, definitions of gender in white patriarchal societies cast the man as proprietor/provider and the adjunct woman as the embodiment of his success. It is *his* status mirrored in her precious outfit and attractive exterior. Irigaray describes this differentiation of the genders into producer-subjects and commodified "objects" as a foundational move of patriarchal societies.[5] She suggests that the transformation of females into objects of exchange establishes the symbolic order in such a manner that women, despite their value as producers, cannot be recompensed for their labor. For their remuneration would imply a dual system of exchange and legitimate them as trading partners and thus undermine the paternal monopoly on the proper name, together with its power of appropriation.[6] In a patriarchal economy, according to Irigaray, all commodities (*especially* women) serve to mirror the value *of* the male *for* the male. Yielding to him their bodies as the physical site of such reflection or "speculation," as Irigaray calls it, their properties become the space where he imprints and imagines his activity. The woman is thus split into two irreconcilable bodies, her "natural" body and the exchangeable, socially valuable body that is the mimetic expression of male value.[7]

Under an economy of slavery, both male and female slaves are feminized or "ungendered" in the manner outlined by Irigaray. Pawns in their owners' jostling for status and social preeminence, slaves served not only as producers of wealth but also as its tangible representation, through their overall physical appearance or in particular contests of wit and skills between slaves of rivaling slaveholders. They, too, could not be paid for their labor, for such an economic interchange would have validated their status as human beings. Rather, master-slave relations, as Williams points out, "pursued a vision of blacks as simple-minded, strong bodied economic 'actants.' Thus, while blacks had an indisputable generative force in the marketplace, their presence could not be called activity; they had no active role in the market."[8]

Hortense Spillers has further suggested that the extremity of slavery rendered gender questionable as a category altogether. As a slave, the African American man was legally barred from "the prevailing social fiction of the father's name, the Father's law."[9] Enslavement also deprived the black woman of the parental function.[10] Spillers thus argues that kinship—and established notions of gender with it—"loses meaning, *since it can be invaded at any given moment by the property relations.*"[11]

Yet economic considerations structured black people's lives under slavery in paradoxical ways. For although slaves could never be "male" or "female," properly speaking, gender translated directly into cash value and served as a stratifying force among slaves in other contexts. When slaves were sold, a male slave would be advertised for his capacity to work, either his sheer physical strength or a particular manual skill, while a woman's ability to bear children, "to reproduce the master's property without cost," functioned as a major economic asset in addition to her value as a worker. Slave prices suggest interesting differences in the valuation of gender between African and American slave markets. While female slaves brought consistently higher prices in Africa, they would usually be sold for less money than their male counterparts on the American continent. As Herbert S. Klein suggests, this imbalance may be due to the central role of women in African agricultural production and matrilineal kinship systems.[12]

Gender was also a consideration in the distribution of labor. Both the duties assigned the slaves by their masters and labor within the community of slaves followed gendered patterns. While black men might be trained as shoemakers, carpenters, or masons, African American women would be taught skills such as spinning, sewing, weaving, or tending the sick.[13] Although slave women performed strenuous physical labor such as fieldwork, which was considered a "male" occupation in the society at large, the reverse was extremely unusual. Male slaves did not, as a rule, practice "female" duties or share equally in a slave household's domestic tasks. Cleaning, washing, and spinning remained the responsibility of women.[14]

As Susan A. Mann says succinctly, "Although slave women experienced a masculinization of their roles, slave men did not experience a corresponding feminization of their roles."[15] Both in slave households and in those of sharecroppers after emancipation, Mann observes, women worked longer hours than men. Mann also notes how patriarchal property relations in sharecropping families led to relatively greater power for freed*men* after emancipation.[16] Deborah Gray White's thesis that the absence of property in slave families allowed for the equality of men and women thus appears to need modification.

If the traditional male gender role might thus very well appeal to a male slave who was barred from access to the provider role, the prerogatives of paternity, and so forth, the female gender role in a slaveholding system, where real women were generally imagined to be "white," might seem much less attractive for a slave woman. The primary task of white women in a patriarchal society such as the antebellum South was to guarantee the legitimacy of the paternal bond as a prerequisite for the uninterrupted transmission of economic and other power from one (male) generation to the next. Their second major function—what Irigaray termed "speculation"—was described with lucidity and precision by Thorstein Veblen in his 1894 article "The Economic Theory of Women's Dress":

> originally because she was herself a pecuniary possession . . . it has (ideally) become the great, peculiar, and almost the sole function of woman in the social system to put in evidence her social unit's ability to pay. That is to say, woman's place . . . has come to be that of a means of conspicuously unproductive expenditure.[17]

As Veblen noted, a man's success as a provider is immediately revealed in his wife's fashionable wardrobe, which renders her "manifestly incapable of doing anything that is of any use."[18] Women literally embody their husbands' monetary strength. Anthropologist Martin Page, who investigated tribal structures in companies such as IBM and Holiday Inns in the 1970s, observed that the effective display of a manager's economic power still involved his *wife's* clothing, jewelry, or car. Page adduced countless examples suggesting that the symbolic economy decribed by Veblen is alive and well today.

For female slaves, the attainment of femininity, defined in this way, was out of the question. Whereas the ostentatious display of leisure and physical frailty constituted key elements of white feminine self-representation, work was the very essence of black women's lives. Even after slavery, the dilemma set up by this opposition tended to plague many black women who, because of economic necessity, continued to perform hard physical labor and hired themselves out for wages. If the money obtained gained them a higher status, especially vis-à-vis black men, it also barred them from the desirable position of a respectable (house)wife.

In this patriarchal economy, true femininity was predicated not only on moral and physical restraint as well as physical beauty—a concept that by definition excluded black women—but further required the invisibility of economic relations between a woman and her husband. The injunction against speaking of money within the family, a taboo Susanne Kappeler has shown to be central to patriarchal power, functioned to keep women innocent of its workings and free of its taint.[19] The image of the prostitute, the woman whose profession makes *explicit* the cash nexus structuring male-female relations, thus becomes, for the respectable woman, the fiend against whom her own position must be secured and defended. If white Southern women's ostensible purity also masked anxieties about their own economic dependence, one might argue that the female slave, whose body was *already* sold, represented a similar "problem" for the wives of slaveholders. Thoroughly victimized in this socioeconomic and cultural construction, many black women later tried to reclaim virtue, so central to femininity, as a defining feature of their social group.

Considering this tangle of economic inscriptions during slavery, how did African Americans react once they were nominally free to play a different role in the monetary economy? Was limited economic power—or poverty, to put it more bluntly—the only factor that obstructed their eager appropriation of the dominant society's gender roles?

The texts that have become twin classics in African American literature courses, Frederick Douglass's *Narrative of the Life of Frederick Douglass* and Linda Brent's *Incidents in the Life of a Slave Girl,* together appear to me to offer the most illuminating commentary on the issue of money and gender relations during slavery and after. For Douglass, increasing control over money eases and accompanies the transition from slave to freedman. Specifically, the power to contract for and earn wages, that is, the role of a free agent in the marketplace, functions as a catalyst for his decision to attempt flight.[20] Physical power, literacy, and the capacity to earn money form the triad that results in Douglass's freedom. Economically speaking, the transformation from a slave into a man, for Douglass, amounts to the metamorphosis of a bondsman into a wage laborer:

I found employment, the third day after my arrival, in stowing a sloop with a load of oil. It was new, dirty, and hard work for me; but I went at it with a glad heart and a willing hand. I was now my own master. It was a happy moment, the rapture of which can be understood only by those who have been slaves. It was the first work, the reward of which was to be entirely my own. There was no master Hugh standing ready, the moment I earned the money, to rob me of it. I worked that day with a pleasure I had never before experienced. I was at work for myself and newly-married wife. It was to me the starting point of a new existence.[21]

So crucial is the motif of the just reward withheld that Douglass places it alongside the enforced prostitution of black women to exemplify the depravity of slavery in the final pages of his text.[22]

These feelings were shared by other ex-slaves. Jourdan Anderson, for instance, seized on the same issue to disclose the injustices of slavery and the hollowness of his ex-master's generosity:

We have concluded to test your sincerity by asking you to send us our wages for the time we served you. . . . I served you faithfully for thirty two years, and Mandy twenty years. At $20 a month for me, and $2 a week for Mandy, our earnings would amount to $11,680. Add to this the interest for the time our wages has been kept back, and deduct what you paid for our clothing and three doctor's visits to me, and pulling a tooth for Mandy, and the balance will show what we are in justice entitled to. . . . If you fail to pay us for our faithful labors in the past we can have little faith in your promises in the future.[23]

In Linda Brent's narrative, on the other hand, wage labor is not nearly as central; her story speaks of money in more complex ways. Her text confronts the issue of economics head on, detailing first her parents' fortunate financial situation, which sheltered Brent from much that slavery represented for other African Americans. The narrative then focuses extensivley on the effects of human beings being held as property, particularly the disruption of familial relations. Rather than the laborer who is defrauded of his just reward, it is the slave mother who serves as the emblem of the "peculiar institution" in Brent's text. The passage that contrasts the free woman's happy Christmas to the slave mother's dread of the separation possibly approaching with the new year, when some or all of her children may be sold, stands as one of the emotional centers of her story.[24]

But Brent also gives us a poignant representation of the manner in which the *slaveholders* are being dehumanized through money:

When this slaveholder died, his shrieks and groans were so frightful that they appaled his own friends. His last words were, "I am going to hell; bury my money with me."

After death his eyes remained open. To press the lids down, silver dollars were laid on them. These were buried with him. From this circumstance, a rumor went abroad that his coffin was filled with money. Three times his grave was opened, and his coffin taken out. The last time, his body was found on the ground, and a flock of buzzards were pecking at it. . . . The perpetrators were never discovered.[25]

In this uncanny passage, the man and the money have become identified so irreversibly that even the dead body will have no peace. If property relations are inscribed by means of the lash and the branding iron onto the slaves' bodies during their lifetime, they reinscribe themselves upon the master's body at a moment of the truth, the time of his death.

Close attention to money matters remains an underlying theme of the text. In narrating how her relatives were bought out of slavery, Brent gives us the exact cash value of their liberty. In her own case, a series of futile attempts to secure freedom by financial means is finally closed by a bargain that has in the meantime become odious to Brent. Having escaped from slavery, she rejects the notion of herself as property so vehemently that she refuses to be bought—even for the express purpose of liberation:

I received this letter from Mrs. Bruce: "I am rejoiced to tell you that the money for your freedom has been paid to Mr. Dodge. Come home to-morrow. I long to see you and my sweet babe."

. . . A gentleman near me said, "It's true; I have seen the bill of sale." "The bill of sale!" Those words struck me like a blow. So I was *sold* at last! . . . The bill of sale is on record, and future generations will learn from it that women were articles of traffic in New York, late in the nineteenth century of the Christian religion. . . .

I had objected to having my freedom bought, yet I must confess that when it was done I felt as if a heavy load had been lifted from my weary shoulders. When I rode home in the cars I was no longer afraid to unveil my face and look at people as they passed.[26]

In this comparatively happy ending, Brent begins to assume a "subject position" by making herself visible *and* actively looking at other people. Yet our sense of ambiguity deepens as Brent comes to the conclusion of her tale. Formally liberated, she continues to serve her former employer in much the same capacity as she did before:

Reader, my story ends with freedom; not in the usual way, with marriage. I and my children are now free! . . . The dream of my life is not yet realized. I do not sit with my children in a home of my own. . . . But God so orders circumstances as to keep me with my friend Mrs. Bruce. Love, duty, gratitude, also bind me to her side. It is a privilege to serve her who pities my oppressed people, and who has bestowed the inestimable boon of freedom on me and my children.[27]

While the threat of slavery has lifted, relations of dominance between Brent and Mrs. Bruce appear structurally unchanged. Brent remains bound by "love, duty, gratitude"—vestiges of the monetary transaction that secured her manumission. One might also argue that the restraints of a gendered and racially segregated labor market contribute toward keeping Brent "in her place." Compared to Douglass, Brent has very limited access to wage labor. Domestic service provided the single most important opportunity for gainful employment not just for Brent but for generations of black women after her. Needless to say, such labor in "the private sphere" was hardly ever conducive to financial, spatial, or temporal autonomy.

Brents's continuing obligation is made more odious still through a subtext of the narrative revealing that white women are in truth indebted to black women, rather than the other way around. The narrator herself, but even more expressly her grandmother, stands in the narrative as signal figures of a debt never properly repaid—whether it be her grandmother's loan of $300 to her mistress or promises of liberation routinely broken at the death of the former owner.[28]

At the end of her story, Brent has not yet achieved the financial security that would allow her to establish her own home and family. Interestingly, the family Brent imagines is not the one Spillers calls "the mythically revered privilege of a free and freed community": "the *vertical* transfer of a bloodline, of a patronymic, of titles and entitlements, of real estate and the prerogatives of "cold cash," from *fathers* to *sons* and the supposedly free exchange of affectional ties between a male and a female of *his* choice."[29] This portrayal would seem to answer to Douglass's ambition. Brent, however, envisions a mother/child constellation *minus* a father.

In imagining "a room of her own," Brent not only departs from black male fantasies of fulfillment but further sets herself against the ending decreed for heroines: "my story ends with freedom; not in the usual way, with marriage."[30] Closer scrutiny, however, reveals a more than superficial analogy between her condition and married life. In both cases, the woman's labor becomes "invisible" and is poorly recompensed, if at all. The centrality of the economic bond is obscured by noble and powerful emotions. Yet, if Brent's circumstances at the end of the tale result from multiple acts of dispossession, they prepare a ground for *different* inscriptions of "race" and, indeed, gender. Exposing the camouflage of social relations inherent in monetary language, Brent has effectively named the economic contours of her life. Her unladylike perspective on money matters helped pave the way for later generations of black women who, like the classic blues singers, addressed the issue of money in gender relations with a frankness hardly ever heard elsewhere. When Bessie Smith sings, "I've got what it takes" and "you can look at my bank book but I'll never let you feel my purse," her sexually charged, self-confident stance rests on a healthy understanding of economic matters. She certainly will not put romance before finance in a manner that leaves her "down and out" in the end. That downright sensible attitude of "safety first" clearly reflects, and responds to, Brent's earlier unblinking look at the power of money.

Notes

1. This inquiry is part of a more comprehensive investigation of money and gender relations in American literature.

2. Cf. Mascha Madörin, "Männliche Ökonomie—Ökonomie der Männlichkeit," *Manney Mythos, FORUM* Sonderheft, BUKO 1990, pp. 3–7. Karl Marx described similar effects in his discussion of commodity fetishism in *Das Kapital.* Cf. "Der Fetischcharacter der Ware und sein Geheimnis," *Das Kapital: Kritik der politischen Ökonomie* (Hamburg: 1890), pp. 85–98.

3. Patricia J. Williams, *The Alchemy of Race and Rights* (Cambridge, Mass.: Harvard University Press, 1991), p. 30. Cf. also p. 17.

4. Cf. also Williams, *Alchemy,* pp. 27, 40.

5. Cf. Luce Irigaray, "Noli me tangere—ou de la valeur des marchandises," *Waren, Körper, Sprache. Der ver-rückte Diskurs der Frauen* (Berlin: Merve Verlag, 1976), pp. 46–61.

6. Cf. Irigaray, "Noli me tangere," p. 47.

7. Cf. Irigaray, "Noli me tangere," p. 52.

8. Williams, *Alchemy,* p. 220.

9. Horense J. Spillers, "Mama's Baby, Papa's Maybe: An American Grammar Book," *Diacritics* (Summer 1987), pp. 65–81, p. 80.

10. Cf. Spillers, "Mama's Baby," p. 78.

11. Spillers, "Mama's Baby," p. 74.

12. Cf. Herbert S. Klein, *The Middle Passage: Comparative Studies in the Atlantic Slave Trade* (Princeton, N.J.: Princeton University Press, 1978), pp. 240–242. Klein further notes that the price differential in America may be attributed in large part to higher prices for skilled artisans, who tended to be male. Cf. p. 240.

13. Cf. Teresa L. Amott and Julie A. Matthaei, "We Specialize in the Wholly Impossible: African American Women," *Race, Gender and Work: A Multicultural Economic History of Women in the United States* (Boston, Mass.: South End Press, 1991), pp. 141–192.

14. While Angela Davis regards such domestic labor as a source of power

for the slave woman, Christie Farnham concludes that double duty did not ensure increased status for the female slave. Cf. Angela Davis, "Reflections of the Black Woman's Role in the Community of Slaves," *The Black Scholar* 3, 4 (1971), pp. 2–15, and Christie Farnham, "Sapphire? Dominance in the Slave Family," in *"To Toil the Livelong Day": America's Women at Work, 1780–1980*, ed. Carol Groneman and Mary Beth Norton (Ithaca, N.Y.: Cornell University Press, 1987), pp. 70–83.

15. Susan A. Mann, "Slavery, Sharecropping, and Sexual Inequality," *Signs*, 14 (1989), pp. 133–157, p. 154.

16. Cf. Mann, "Slavery," pp. 140, 142–143, and Deborah Gray White, *Ar'n't I a Woman? Female Slaves in the Plantation South* (New York: Norton, 1985), pp. 158–159.

17. Thorstein Veblen, "The Economic Theory of Women's Dress," (1894); reprinted in *Essays in Our Changing Order* (New York: Viking, 1954), pp. 65–77, pp. 68–69.

18. Veblen, "Women's Dress," p. 73.

19. Cf. Susanne Kappeler, *The Pornography of Representation* (1986; dt. *Pornographie. Die Macht der Darstellung*. München: Frauenoffensive, 1988)).

20. Cf. Frederick Douglass, *Narrative of the Life of Frederick Douglass*, in *The Classic Slave Narratives*, ed. Henry Louis Gates, Jr. (New York: Penguin, 1987), pp. 243–331, pp. 314–315.

21. Douglass, *Narrative*, pp. 324–325. We may also note that, in Douglass's case, freedom and the possession of money appear as prerequisites for love and sexuality. His future wife, Anna, appears in the text only after his successful escape.

22. Cf. Douglass, *Narrative*, p. 327: "The man who robs me of my earnings at the end of each week meets me as a class-leader on Sunday morning, to show me the way of life, and the path of salvation. He who sells my sister, for purposes of prostitution, stands forth as the pious advocate of purity."

23. Jourdan Anderson, quoted in *The Black Book*, ed. Middleton Harris et al. (New York: Random House, 1975), pp. 10–11. William L. Andrews notes that Elizabeth Keckley adopted an economic pattern much like Douglass's in her life history. Cf. William L. Andrews, "The Changing Rhetoric of the Nineteenth-Century Slave Narrative in the United States," in *Slavery in the Americas*, ed. Wolfgang Binder (Würzburg: Königshausen & Neumann, 1993), pp. 471–486, pp. 478–483.

24. Cf. Harriet Jacobs, *Incidents in the Life of a Slave Girl*, in Gates, *Classic Slave Narratives*, pp. 333–515, pp. 350–351.

25. Jacobs, *Incidents*, pp. 377–378. Douglass also notes how the humanity of both the slave and the slaveholder is damaged by the process of valuation. Cf. Douglass, *Narrative*, p. 282.

26. Jacobs, *Incidents*, pp. 511–512.

27. Jacobs, *Incidents*, p. 513.

28. Interestingly, the grandmother also serves to exemplify the forcible dispossession of black people in Douglass's text. Cf. Douglass, *Narrative*, pp. 283–284.

29. Spillers, "Mama's Baby," p. 74.

30. Jacobs, *Incidents*, p. 513.

10

· · · ·

Judicial Nullification

The South Carolinian Movement to Reopen the African Slave Trade in the 1850s

Manisha Sinha

With the exception of W.E.B. Du Bois's pioneering work and a 1971 monograph by Ronald Takaki,[1] most historians have viewed the southern movement to revive the African slave trade in the 1850s as an aberrant phenomenon, without much significance for U.S. or African American history. It has been ignored by historians of the slave South and the sectional conflict, who question slaveholders' support for the movement, and by scholars of the Atlantic slave trade, who in recent years have emphasized the relatively minor role of the British North American colonies in the trade. However, as I will argue, the African slave trade agitation was an integral part of the growth of proslavery ideology, political separatism, and slavery expansionism in the South during the years preceding the Civil War. And though the slave traders, as advocates of this measure were called, failed to gain their objective both in and out of the Union, they precipitated an unprecedented rethinking of the slave trade and effectively damaged the national consensus on its heinousness.

The effort to revive the African slave trade was the most audacious proposal for the justification and perpetuity of racial slavery in the United States. The movement made little headway in the slave-selling, noncotton upper south states, which were also less susceptible to the politics of slavery. The slave trade agitation and other contemporary manifestations of an aggressive political stance on slavery, which included the dream of a slaveholding empire in Central America and the Caribbean, found a more congenial home in the cotton states of the lower south. Furthermore, high slave and cotton prices during the 1850s, no doubt, bolstered the aggressive and expansive mentality of lower south slaveholders. Relatively immune to calls for a slaveholding empire emanating from the slave-buying Gulf states, South Carolina emerged as the "storm-center" of the African slave trade movement.

The agitation to revive the Atlantic traffic gained its largest following among rabid secessionists and slavery expansionists of the lower south. Isolated suggestions for the reopening of the African slave trade had been made earlier, but the rise of a concerted movement under the auspices of Leonidas William Spratt, editor of the Charleston *Southern Standard*, in 1853 marked the beginning of a new era. While it is not known whether Spratt was a slaveholder, he had close personal and political ties to South Carolina's planter oligarchy. Aptly dubbed the "philosopher of the new African slave trade" by Horace Greeley, he not only pursued his objective with a single-minded devotion but also produced several sophisticated proslavery tracts for the revival of the foreign trade.[2] Confronted by southern dominance of the national Democratic party and the federal government in the 1850s and the concomitant waning of immediate secession in the slave South, Carolinian secessionists, led by R. B. Rhett and Maxcy Gregg, found a new home in the slave trade agitation.[3] The movement soon spread to lower south states such as Mississippi and Louisiana and, to a lesser extent, Alabama, Texas, and Georgia and made individual converts of leading southern nationalists and proslavery ideologues such as William Lowndes Yancey, J. D. B. De Bow, John A. Quitman, Louis T. Wigfall, Henry Hughes, Edmund Ruffin, George Fitzhugh, and Edward Pollard.[4]

More significantly, slave traders managed to foster a questioning attitude toward the African slave trade restriction and an increasing reluctance to view the traffic as morally reprehensible in the slave South in general. The movement to reopen the African slave trade was, as Takaki has put it, a quintessential "pro-slavery crusade." But the slave traders' logic was hardly a result of an attempt to rest all moral doubts over slavery, as he further argues. In fact, it represented the triumph of proslavery discourse. Governor James Adams of South Carolina, in his famous 1856 message calling for the revival of the Atlantic commerce, argued that no consistent vindication of slavery could countenance the condemnation of the slave trade. In majority reports on the governor's address, state legislators Edward Bryan and Alexander Mazyck reiterated this point. Similarly, Fitzhugh demanded a "re-hearing" on the slave trade question in the name of the slave South.[5]

Proslavery ideology, which was based on a rigorous critique of democracy and natural rights theory, celebrated the principles of inequality in order to defend slavery. The rejection of revolutionary ideology was best embodied in the call to revoke the constitutional prohibition of the African slave trade. Bryan traced the efforts against the African slave trade to the influence of "French philosophy" and the founding fathers' "love of liberty," which had apparently carried them "beyond the limits of sound discretion." Spratt characterized the reopening of the African slave trade as the final justification of the values of slave society, which were a correction of the revolutionary dictum that "*equality is the right of man.*" Like Fitzhugh, he wanted to defend not just slavery but "the slavery principle."[6]

Spratt's has been strangely neglected by historians of proslavery thought. In his famous 1858 report on the African slave trade, he wrote that no society in history had progressed through "an unarticulated mass of pure democracy." It must be noted that Spratt's defense of racial slavery provided the basis for his celebration of hierarchy. The slave South, by basing its aristocracy on the so-called natural distinction of "race," he argued, provided the best hopes for the future of mankind.[7] Spratt's argument shows that scholars who posit a race versus class defense of slavery quite simply miss the point. The belief in racial inequality bolstered the belief in human inequality in general.

The slave traders' antidemocratic philosophy calls into serious question the view of some historians that the African slave trade movement was geared primarily to serve the interests of nonslaveholders in the South by making all white men slaveholders with an increased supply of slaves.[8] While Mazyck ignored this question, Spratt and Bryan devoted only a few lines to it. Adams, who emphasized most the idea of creating slaveholders out of nonslaveholders, was particularly suspicious of nonslaveholders' loyalty to the slave South, especially given the "outward pressure" of northern antislavery. With his well-known opposition to democratic reform, Adams was no advocate of liberalizing the southern slaveholding order.[9]

Debates over the slave trade in South Carolina reveal that, at least in this state, the notion is false that large slaveholders as a class opposed its reopening in order to safeguard the value of their human property. Voting records in the legislature show that the slave trade agitation derived greatest support from the plantation areas of the state. Prominent supporters of the movement were secessionist-minded low country aristocrats such as John Middleton, Gabriel Manigault, and John Townsend. On the other hand, the nonplantation areas of the state, dominated by the nonslaveholding yeomanry, were most opposed to the reopening. Sectional divisions complemented partisan divisions, with up country national Democrats pitted against low country secessionists. If Carolinian slave traders intended to make slaveholders of all white men, they were most unpopular among the class they were supposed to benefit.[10]

The slave traders' argument for the spread of slave ownership was part of a broader argument for the expansion of slavery and cannot be viewed in isolation. The reopening of the African slave trade was not supposed to revolutionize southern slave society but to fortify and expand its existing structure. The movement to legalize the African traffic paralleled the fight over whether Kansas would be a free or slave state. Right from the start, slave traders pointed out that Kansas could be made a slave state only with an increased supply of slaves and slaveholding immigrants to the state. The slave South would surely lose the battle for territories with the free North, which could rely on unrestricted immigration, while the South's "labor supply" was cut off. They also warned against the "drain" of slaves and the spread of free labor in the border and older slave states.[11]

By not paying sufficient attention to the slave traders' expansionist logic, historians have failed to fully appreciate the connection between the African slave trade movement and the sectional conflict over slavery expansion. *De Bow's Review,* a premier southern journal devoted to the cause of slavery expansion and southern nationhood, published an article that even visualized the spread of slavery to northern and northwestern territories with the revival of the Atlantic slave trade. Edward Delony, a state senator from Louisiana, also argued that the slave trade prohibition was designed to impede the growth of the slave states and announced his plans to "expand the area of slavery" by reclaiming Haiti and Central America for it. Most southern leaders seemed to have been influenced by the slave traders' expansionist logic, if not by the plea to reopen the slave trade. In a public speech, a relatively moderate southern rights man like Alexander Stephens would claim that the South could not create any new slave states unless it received a fresh supply of slaves from Africa.[12]

The dynamic of the discourse of slavery and separatism, infused as it was with the most "advanced" arguments for slavery and ideals of an independent slave nation, encouraged rather than discouraged the slave trade agitation. A majority of slave traders, starting with Spratt, were unreconstructed secessionists. Only a few, such as the Virginian ideologues Fitzhugh and Pollard, argued quixotically that the reopening of the slave trade would restore equality between northern and southern states and thereby strengthen the Union. Most slave traders realized that the northern states would never consent to overturn the constitutional ban on the slave trade and happily combined their devotion to the slave trade cause with that of an independent slave nation.[13]

With a few exceptions, slaveholders' adherence to the slave trade cause varied in direct proportion with their advocacy of slavery expansion and secession. Senator James Henry Hammond, a former secessionist who had earlier advocated the African slave trade, came out strongly against the reopening of the slave trade in 1858, after announcing his switch to a unionist and antiexpansionist position. Other southern and Carolinian leaders who condemned the movement, such as Benjamin F. Perry of South Carolina, H. W. Hilliard of Alabama, Sam Houston of Texas, Henry Foote of Mississippi, were known for their unionism, and James Orr, W. W. Boyce, and James Chesnut of South Carolina were moderate states' rights men who opposed aggressive schemes for the expansion of slavery.[14]

Like other southern nationalists, slave traders also made use of states' rights theory to question the authority of the federal government to abolish a trade that was vital to the interests of the southern states. Contrary to the aspersions of their opponents and historians, slave traders hardly ever appealed to a "higher law" than the Constitution. In fact, they indulged in detailed constitutional quibbling, which was a hallmark of southern political thought, to subvert the most obvious meaning and intent of the Constitution. In a debate over the slave trade in the southern commercial convention at Montgomery in 1858, Alabama secessionist Yancey fully explicated the "constitutional" argument for the revival of the Atlantic slave trade. He pronounced the slave trade laws "unconstitutional," as the exact wording of the constitutional clause on the African slave trade allowed only for its continuance until 1808 and did not call for its abolition. Significantly, the rather ingenious "constitutional" rationale for the reopening of the slave trade was not restricted only to those who openly identified with the slave trade movement. In a remarkable speech before Congress, Senator James Mason of Virginia, who apparently opposed the actual revival of the slave trade, declared unequivocally, "I am one of those who could never see any warrant in the Constitution by which the United States undertook to suppress the slave trade—never."[15]

The effectiveness of the slave traders' ideological appeal was best illustrated by the limitations of the proslavery critique of the African slave trade movement. Southern opponents of the African slave trade tried to distinguish between it and slavery. However, they shared the premises of proslavery discourse with the slave traders, which relegated their criticism of the African slave trade from one based on principle to expediency. In 1854 the South Carolina House of Representatives Committee on the Colored Population, chaired by J. Harleston Read, a national Democrat, issued the first antislave trade report, which conceded that the intercontinental slave traffic would increase the political strength of the slave South and that the trade was indeed a "blessing" for the Africans.[16] J. J. Pettigrew of South Carolina, in presenting the most well-known case against the reopening of the African slave trade, made too many ideological and practical concessions to the slave traders. He admitted that "the undersigned, as a friend of Africa, might well advocate the revival of the Slave Trade." He rested his argument on the narrowest grounds, that the slave trade was against the "best interests of South Carolina." It is noteworthy that Pettigrew added a postscript to his report stating that he favored rescinding the African Squadron clause of the Webster-Ashburton treaty of 1842, which provided for the joint naval patroling of the African coast by the British and the Americans, and that he was against the designation of the slave trade as piracy by a 1820 law.[17]

The compromised nature of proslavery opposition to the slave trade was also evident in the criticism that some clergymen leveled at the slave trade. In a pamphlet on the question, Reverend John B. Adger felt that slaveholders were "God's agents in partly reclaiming" Africans from their alleged savagery and felt that the plan to revive the foreign slave trade was "a signal failure, viewed simply as the discussion of a great question of state policy." Proslavery divines such as Adger, C. P. Gadsden, and J. H. Elliot took their biblical literalism seriously enough to condemn the slave trade as "man stealing." Reverends James Henley Thornwell and J. Leighton Wilson also opposed the slave trade. But not all southern clergymen did. Reverend Iveson Brooks, the vocal proslavery Baptist minister from South Carolina, argued that the "sin" of the slave South lay not in its participation in the inhuman traffic but in its acquiescence to its suppression. And while the Rocky Creek Baptist Church of Edgefield, South Carolina, issued a protest against the illegal importation of Africans, the Southern Methodist Episcopalian Church rescinded its rule against the enslaving of free persons in 1858, stating ambiguously at the same time that it did not wish to express an opinion on the African slave trade.[18]

The triumph of the slave traders lay more in the realm of ideology rather than in the enactment of measures. In South Carolina, reports and resolutions on the African traffic were tabled or "indefinitely postponed" rather than rejected. In 1858, the state senate passed a resolution for the rescinding of the eighth article of the Webster-Ashburton treaty by a nearly unanimous vote of 38 to 1 and the senate Committee of Federal Relations recommended the passage of a resolution declaring the 1820 piracy law "unconstitutional." In Mississippi, Henry Hughes tried to foster his African apprenticeship scheme by presenting a bill for the formation of an "African Labor Immigration Company," which was narrowly defeated in 1858, and an 1860 bill for the repeal of the state prohibition on the external slave trade failed in the assembly. Similarly, in

Louisiana, a bill to authorize the transportation of African indentured labor and resolutions demanding the repeal of the slave trade laws were tabled and indefinitely postponed. In Georgia, an effort to rescind the prohibition of the foreign slave trade in the state's constitution failed and resolutions for the reopening of the African slave trade in Alabama and Texas fell on deaf ears. However, Governor Hardin R. Runnels of Texas was a strong advocate of the slave trade and Governor A. B. Moore of Alabama called for the revision of the 1820 piracy law.[19]

Slave traders were more successful in pushing their agenda in the southern commercial conventions, which came to be increasingly dominated by "fire-eaters," men who may not have been representative of their region but who led the fight for an independent southern nation. From 1855 onward, slave traders regularly introduced resolutions calling for the reopening of the African slave trade in annual sessions of the convention. Debates over the resolutions were marked by an upper and lower South divide, with the former generally opposed to and the latter for the reopening of the Atlantic traffic. At the 1857 Knoxville gathering, the convention passed a resolution calling for the rescinding of the eighth article of the Webster-Ashburton treaty over the opposition of upper South delegates. The absence of upper South states and the predominance of lower South secessionists at the Vicksburg convention in 1859 ensured the passage of a resolution calling for the repeal of the slave trade laws. And Hughes formed the African Labor Supply Association to implement his favorite scheme of importing African "apprentices." Du Bois had argued that a substantial minority in the slave South and a majority in the Gulf states were for the reopening of the African slave trade. The slave traders' success in the southern conventions reveal that it would be fair to assert that a majority of lower South secessionists were advocates of the African slave trade in the late 1850s.[20]

Regardless of their position on the actual reopening of the Atlantic commerce, most southern leaders expressed growing opposition to the enforcement of federal laws and treaties against the slave trade. The ambiguity of mainstream planter-politicians on the slave trade issue is interesting, as it has been ignored by historians. In fact, there was an emerging consensus among antebellum southern leaders against the moral condemnation of the slave trade and federal suppression policies. William H. Trescot, scholar and diplomat, argued for the abrogation of the African Squadron clause but criticized Carolinian politicians' opposition to the piracy law. On the other hand, William Gilmore Simms, proslavery author, attacked the piracy law because it would make slavery into a crime. South Carolina congressmen Lawrence M. Keitt, William Porcher Miles, and Milledge Luke Bonham condemned all the slave trade laws but contended that they did not actually favor the revival of the traffic. Rhett announced his decision not to agitate the slave trade question in 1857, but the *Mercury* continued to condemn the slave trade laws and treaties. Governor R.F.W. Allston of South Carolina also questioned the federal government's authority to interfere in the international slave trade. Georgia politician Robert Toombs condemned both the 1842 treaty and the piracy law. Jefferson Davis, future president of the Confederacy, felt that the African slave trade should be reopened for the territories.[21]

Congressional debates over the African slave trade, which marked its emergence as an issue in the sectional conflict, further revealed the bankruptcy of southern leaders' anomalous position on the slave trade. In December 1856, Emerson Etheridge of Tennessee, a staunch unionist, introduced a resolution in the House of Representatives strongly condemning any proposal for the revival of the African slave trade as "shocking to the moral sentiment of the enlightened portion of mankind." Most southern representatives argued that while they did not advocate the reopening of the African traffic, they could not vote for a resolution that branded it as inhuman and immoral. Etheridge's resolution passed by a mainly sectional vote of 140 to 57, with 54 out of 71 southern representatives voting against it. A substitute resolution, proposed by James Orr of South Carolina, which merely declared that it was "inexpedient" to reopen the trade, passed by a vote of 183 to 8.[22] The passage of Orr's resolution did not indicate only that most southerners were opposed to the revival of the African slave trade but also that most were opposed to an explicit and moral condemnation of it.

Southern leaders' congressional pronouncements show that their opinions on the African slave trade were hedged with so many qualifications and contradictions as to make their position not only inconsistent but untenable. In 1859, some southern senators, under the leadership of Clement Clay of Alabama, opposed an appropriation for the suppression of the slave trade. Only a few upper South senators tried to defend the constitutionality of the slave trade laws and the appropriation. In the end, Clay's resolution failed by a vote of 40 to 12, the twelve dissenting votes coming from such prominent southern leaders as Davis, Toombs, Mason, Hammond, and Chesnut. In the House of Representatives, the appropriation passed by a narrow vote of 101 to 98, and Republican Representative Kilgore's resolution condemning the slave trade failed to pass by a two-thirds majority. In 1860 some southern leaders again voiced their opposition to appropriations for the repatriation of a thousand Africans, apprehended in an American slaver near Key West, Florida, to Africa. The appropriation merely implemented the 1819 slave trade law. Southern congressional opposition to the 1859 and 1860 slave trade appropriations was noteworthy as both measures were sponsored by the prosouthern, Democratic administration of James Buchanan.[23]

Slave traders' efforts also served to effectively nullify the slave trade laws in some lower South states. In two famous slave trade cases, southern juries refused to convict persons involved in the illegal transatlantic slave trade. The slaver *Wanderer*, owned by rice planter and Confederate hero C.A.L. Lamar, landed over four hundred young African boys between the ages of twelve and eighteen in Georgia in November 1858, in the only well-documented instance of the violation of the African slave trade ban in the United States. The Africans were quickly sold and dispersed among the plantations of Georgia and South Carolina. Any attempt by the federal government to recover them would result in bloodshed, warned ex-governor Adams.[24] Earlier that year, the United States cruiser *Dolphin* captured the American slaver *Echo* off the coast of Cuba and brought the crew to Charleston, South Carolina, for trial. The *Echo*'s human cargo, 318 young African boys and girls, had been packed nude in the notorious "spoon fashion." Nearly 170 had died during the Middle Passage. Even Carolinian newspapers contained reports of the appalling state the survivors were reduced to, referring to their skeleton-like appearance. But Carolinian slaveholders soon started demanding the enslavement of the hapless Africans, and the federal government was forced to hastily repatriate them to Africa, despite southern opposition in Congress. Thirty-five more Africans would die on the journey back to Africa.[25]

The significance of the *Echo* and *Wanderer* cases became evident when the crew and owners of the slavers were brought to trial for violating federal slave trade laws. They touched off a national debate over the slave trade and invigorated the slave traders' campaign.[26] Prominent leaders of the slave trade movement offered their legal services to the *Echo* crew gratis and regurgitated the arguments for the reopening of the African slave trade in the courts. The sixteen crew members of the *Echo* were tried in two separate cases in the South Carolina federal district court and declared not guilty in quick succession in 1859. The captain of the ship, one Edward Townsend, was repatriated to Florida, where a jury also set him free.[27] In the *Wanderer* trials in Georgia, the Savannah grand jury indicted Lamar and his associates but declared that the South was no longer willing to obey the slave trade laws "because they directly or indirectly, condemn this institution [slavery], and those who have inherited or maintain it." Predictably, the *Wanderer* crew were declared not guilty by a Georgia jury, and a year later the government dropped its charges against Lamar and his associates. As John Cunnigham, who opposed the slave trade, observed, no southerner would ever convict a slave trader.[28]

The judicial nullification of the slave trade prohibition reached a climax in the case against William Corrie, the Carolinian captain of the *Wanderer*, in 1860. In his momentous decision, Judge A. G. Magrath, future governor of Confederate South Carolina, contended that the 1820 piracy law did not apply to the African slave trade because the slave trade was not specifically mentioned in the title of the law. Further, he argued that the law's listing of the decoying and enslaving of a "free negro or mulatto" as piracy did not apply to the purchase of slaves on a "foreign coast." The African slave trade, in his opinion, could be regulated as a "trade" or "business" but not by the criminal law of piracy. To reconcile this construction with his and Wayne's joint decision upholding the constitutionality of the slave trade laws in the *Echo* case, Magrath concluded that, though he conceded to Congress the authority to declare the slave trade piracy, in his opinion, it had yet to exercise this power! A couple of months later, Magrath and Wayne discharged the grand jury and Corrie, like the rest of the *Wanderer* defendants, went free.[29]

Magrath's slave trade decision and the universal applause with which it was greeted in the state revealed the true nature of the slave traders' victory. A staunch southern nationalist who claimed to oppose the revival of the Atlantic slave trade, Magrath epitomized slaveholders' ambivalence toward the African traffic. His decision more than met the "moral" demands of the slave traders: the slave trade was not piracy and the slaves were certainly not plunder. By nullifying the application of the 1820 law to the slave trade, he had wiped out the "insult" to the slave South contained in the African slave trade laws of the country. And he had applied the kind of literal legal and "constitutional" reasoning that had been established as a respectable precedent in South Carolina since its first nullification and had been employed effectively by the slave traders. Not a single public criticism of the decision was made by men who opposed the reopening of the African slave trade. Hammond actually undertook to defend the judge in Congress. Only Trescot privately quibbled at the flagrant misinterpretation of the 1820 law. But most slaveholders were no longer willing to condemn the slave trade as a crime against humanity or to take part in its suppression. And if the reopening or closing of the African slave trade were merely a matter of "policy," who was to say what policy or interest would dictate in the future?[30]

The judicial nullification of the African slave trade laws in the Deep South has been ignored by historians, who have been more interested in detailing the onrush of secession. Moreover, secessionists' efforts to play down the slave trade issue in order to ensure southern unity[31] and the Confederacy's decision to prohibit the external slave trade, over the protests of Carolinian planter-politicians, have minimized its significance.

However, the Confederate government's refusal to reopen the African slave trade was based on some practical calculations: the need to incorporate the upper South states who were against the Atlantic slave trade and to avoid a confrontation with the British government, to whom the slave nation looked for diplomatic recognition. In fact, in 1863, the Confederate government emphatically refused to sign any treaty against the African slave trade, and it is difficult to predict the action of the Confederacy on the slave trade if it could have maintained its independence. It was also no coincidence that the only U.S. citizen hanged for participating in the Atlantic slave trade was prosecuted by the Lincoln administration.[32]

The Civil War and the demise of slavery ensured that the African slave trade issue would be consigned to the dust heap of history in the United States. But the slave traders had successfully initiated an ideological reevaluation of the African slave trade through much of the slave South. By arguing mainly on the grounds of "policy" and conceding the "principle" to the slave traders, Southern opponents of the slave trade movement unwittingly recognized that the rationale behind the argument for the African slave trade was based on the same proslavery discourse that they themselves held. Moreover, they sympathized with the slave traders' "moral" and "constitutional" arguments, which culminated in the judicial nullification of the slave trade laws in the lower South. And while it represented perhaps the most controversial side of slaveholders' commitment to slave society, the South Carolinian movement to revive the African slave trade remains one of the best vantage points from which to view the discourse of slavery and separatism in the 1850s. The agitation to reopen the African slave trade was not a mere extremist fantasy. It derived its relevance from forces that increasingly started to dominate the slave South on the eve of the Civil War. For no matter how hard some slaveholders would try, they could not completely disown this unwelcome offspring of proslavery thought, slavery expansionism, and southern nationalism.

Acknowledgments   This essay is based on a paper presented at the W.E.B. Du Bois Institute for Afro-American Studies, Harvard University, in April 1993 and at the CAAR conference at Tenerife in February 1995. I am grateful to members of the institute and the audience at Tenerife for their questions and suggestions. I would also like to thank Eric Foner, Barbara Fields, Mrinalini Sinha and Karsten Stueber for their comments on earlier versions of this essay.

Notes

1. W. E. Burghardt Du Bois, *The Suppression of the African Slave Trade to the United States of America, 1638–1870* (Reprint: New York: Rusell & Rusell,

1969); Ronald Takaki, *A Pro-Slavery Crusade: The Agitation to Reopen the African Slave Trade* (New York: Free Press, 1971).

2. Spratt's name does not appear in the federal census schedules as a slaveholder. Most historians have automatically assumed that he was, therefore, a nonslaveholder. See Takaki, *A Pro-Slavery Crusade*, pp. 13, 19. Greeley is quoted by Ronald Takaki on p. 1, "The Movement to Reopen the African Slave Trade in South Carolina," *South Carolina Historical Magazine* 66 (Jan. 1965), 38–54; *Southern Standard* (July 3, 10, Sept. 20, Nov. 9, 1854).

3. The early conversion of Carolinian secessionists to the slave trade cause was signaled in the secessionist newspapers of the state. See especially *Charleston Mercury* (June 20, 28, July 7, 17, 21, Sept. 13, Oct. 24, 27, 31, Nov. 4, 8, 1854); *The Camden Weekly Journal* (June 20, Oct. 10, 1854); *Abbeville Banner* (Oct. 12, 1854), quoted in the *Southern Standard* (Oct. 17, 1854); *An Appeal to the States Rights Party of South Carolina: In Several Letters on the Present Condition of Public Affairs* (Columbia, S.C.: 1858), pp. 3–7.

4. For a profile of slave trade advocates, see Takaki, *A Pro-Slavery Crusade*, chap. 3.

5. *Message No. 1 of His Excellency Jas. H. Adams, Governor of South Carolina, To the Senate and House of Representatives, At the Session of 1856, With Accompanying Documents* (Columbia, S.C.: 1856), pp. 10–11; [Edward B. Bryan], *Report of the Special Committee of the House of Representatives of South Carolina, on so much of the Message of His Excellency Hon. Jas. H. Adams, as Relates to the Slave Trade* (Charleston, S.C.: 1857), p. 36; [Alexander Mazyck], *Report of Special Committee on so much of Governor Adams' Message as Relates to the Slave Trade* (no Publisher, no Date), p. 5; George Fitzhugh, "The Conservative Principle; or, Social Evils and Their Remedies," *De Bow's Review* 22 (May 1857), 461.

6. Bryan, *Report of the Special Committee*, p. 5; Edward Bryan, *Letters to the Southern People Concerning the Acts of Congress and the Treaties with Great Britain in Relation to the African Slave Trade* (Charleston, S.C.: 1858), p. 7; "Southern Convention at Knoxville," *De Bow's Review* 23 (Sept. 1857), 317; *Speech Upon the Foreign Slave Trade, Before the Legislature of South Carolina by L. W. Spratt, Esq. of Charleston* (Columbia, S.C.: 1858), pp. 7–8.

7. Spratt, "Report on the Slave Trade," pp. 473–475; L. W. Spratt, *The Foreign Slave Trade The Source of Political Power, of Material Progress, of Social Integrity, and of Social Emancipation of the South* (Charleston, S.C.: 1858), pp. 18–21.

8. See, for example, Lacy K. Ford, Jr., "Republics and Democracy: The Parameters of Political Citizenship in Antebellum South Carolina," in David R. Chesnutt and Clyde N. Wilson eds., *The Meaning of South Carolina History: Essays in Honor of George C. Rogers, Jr.* (Columbia: University of South Carolina Press, 1991), pp. 130–131, 134–138.

9. *Message No. 1 of His Excellency Jas. H. Adams*, p. 9; also see Spratt, *The Foreign Slave Trade*, pp. 11–13; Spratt, "Report on the Slave Trade," p. 485; Bryan, *Letters to the Southern People*, pp. 31–37; *Charleston Mercury* (Nov. 4, 1854).

10. See the carefully tabulated numerical data on the slave trade votes in the South Carolina legislature in Harold S. Schultz, *Nationalism and Sectionalism in South Carolina 1852–1860: A Study of the Movement for Southern Independence* (Durham, N.C.: Duke University Press, 1950), pp. 143, 159–164, 184.

11. *The Camden Weekly Journal* Oct. 10, 1854; *Charleston Mercury* (Oct. 31, Nov. 8, 1854; July 24, 28, 31, 1858); Spratt, "Report on the Slave Trade," pp. 481–483, 487, 490; Spratt, *The Foreign Slave Trade*, pp. 4–5; "Southern Convention at Vicksburg," *De Bow's Review* 28 (Oct. 1859), 208–210; *Message No. 1 of Jas. H. Adams*, p. 10; Bryan, *Report of the Special Committee*, pp. 25–29; C. W. Miller, *Address on Reopening the Slave Trade by C. W. Miller, Esq. of South Carolina, to the Citizens of Barnwell at Wylde-Moore Aug. 29, 1857* (Columbia, S.C.: 1857), pp. 3, 7–9.

12. "African Slavery Adapted to the North and North West," *De Bow's Review* 25 (Oct. 1858), 379–395; Edward Delony, "The South Demands More Negro Labor," *De Bow's Review* 25 (Nov. 1858), 494, 503; George Fitzhugh, "Missionary Failures," *De Bow's Review* 27 (Oct. 1859), 385; Stephens is quoted by Harvey Wish, "The Revival of the African Slave Trade in the United States, 1856–1860," *Mississippi Valley Historical Review* 27 (March 1941), 581.

13. Spratt, *The Foreign Slave Trade*, pp. 29–31; "Southern Convention at Vicksburg," *De Bow's Review* 28 (Oct. 1859), 469; George Ftizhugh, "The Administration and the Slave Trade," *De Bow's Review* 26 (Feb. 1859), 145; Edward Pollard, *Black Diamonds Gathered in the Darkey Homes of the South* (Reprint: New York, 1968), pp. 65–69; also see Jack K. Williams, "The Southern Movement to Reopen the African Slave Trade, 1854–1860: A Factor in Secession," *Proceedings of the South Carolina Historical Association* (1960), 21–31,

14. On Hammond's switch to a unionist and antislave trade position, see *Charleston Mercury* (Aug. 2, Nov. 2, 10, 17, 18, 1858); *Charleston Daily Courier* (Aug. 5, 6, Nov. 3, 1858); *Speech of Honorable James H. Hammond Delivered at the Barnwell Court House Oct. 29, 1858* (Washington, D.C., 1858); and Frank G. Ruffin to Hammond (April 24, 1858), W. H. Trescot to Hammond (July 27, Dec. 5, 1858), R. B. Rhett, Jr., to Hammond (Aug. 2, 1858), John Cunnigham to Hammond (Aug. 2, Oct. 9, 1858), Hammond to W. G. Simms (Aug. 13, 1858), J. H. Adams to Hammond (Sept. 22, Oct. 8, 1858), Hammond to M. C. M. Hammond (Nov. 28, 1858), in the James Henry Hammond Papers, Library of Congress. On Perry's opposition to the slave trade, see *Southern Patriot* (Oct. 12, 26, Nov. 2, 1854); Lillian Adele Kibler, *Benjamin F. Perry: South Carolina Unionist* (Durham, N.C.: Duke University Press, 1946), p. 282; "Late Southern Convention at Montgomery," *De Bow's Review* 24 (June 1858), 591–592; Earl W. Fornell, "Agitation in Texas for Reopening the Slave Trade," *Southwestern Historical Quarterly* 60 (Oct. 1856), 249–259; "Southern Convention at Vicksburg," pp. 214–220, 470–471; James L. Orr to J. J. Pettigrew (April 20, Oct. 30, 1857; Jan. 18, 1858), W. W. Boyce to J. J. Pettigrew (May 18, 1858), in the Pettigrew Papers, North Carolina Department of Archives and History, Raleigh; and *Charleston Mercury* (Sept. 3, 6, 7, 8, 9, 29, Oct. 1, 1859).

15. *Charleston Mercury* (Dec. 7, 1854; Aug. 11, 1858); Mazyck, *Report of Special Committee*, pp. 10–15; "Late Southern Convention at Montgomery," *De Bow's Review* 24 (June 1858), 584–585, 598–599; also see D. S. Troy, "Is the Slave Trade Piracy?" *De Bow's Review* 26 (Jan. 1859), 24, 26–28; Thomas Walton, "Further Views of the Advocates of the Slave Trade," *De Bow's Review* 26 (Jan. 1859), 54–59, 64–66; *Congressional Globe*, 36th Congress, 1st session, p. 2306.

16. General Assembly Index, African Slave Trade, Document 0010 004

1854 00010 00, South Carolina Department of Archives and History, Columbia; also see *Charleston Mercury* (Dec. 7, 1854).

17. [J. Johnston Pettigrew], *Report of the Minority of the Special Committee of Seven, To Whom was Referred so much of Gov. Adams' Message, No. 1, As Relates to Slavery and the Slave Trade* (Charleston, S.C.: 1858), pp. 4, 6, 23–37, 40.

18. John B. Adger, *A Review of Reports to the Legislature of South Carolina, on the Revival of the Slave Trade* (Columbia, S.C.: 1858) pp. 5, 12, 15–17, 35–36; B. M. Palmer, *The Life and Letters of James Henley Thornwell* (Richmond, Va.: Whittett & Shepperson, 1875), pp. 422–423; in his pamphlets, Reverend J. Leighton Wilson, a former missionary in Africa who, unlike most of his compatriots, supported British suppression policies, issued more strongly worded denunciations of the slave trade. See his *The British Squadron on the Coast of Africa* (London, 1850) and *The Foreign Slave Trade Can It be Revived without Violating the most Sacred Principles of Honor, Humanity and Religion?* (no publisher, 1859); *The Southern Episcopalian* 5 (March 1859), 657–660; Iveson L. Brooks, *A Defence of the South Against the Reproaches and Inchroachments [sic] of the North: In which Slavery is Shown to be an Institution of God intended to form the Basis of the Best Social State and the Only Safeguard to the Permanence of a Republican Government* (Hamburg, S.C.: 1850), pp. 42–43; *Charleston Daily Courier* (Jan. 6, 1859); Takaki, *A Pro-Slavery Crusade*, chap. 6.

19. *Journal of the Senate of South Carolina: Being the Annual Session of 1857* (Columbia, S.C., 1857), pp. 37, 68, 89; *Journal of the House of Representatives of the State of South Carolina: Being the Session of 1858* (Columbia, S.C.: 1858), pp. 129, 204–205; *Journal of the Senate of South Carolina: Being the Annual Session of 1858* (Columbia, S.C.: 1858), pp. 32, 109–110, 119–120, 200; *Reports and Resolutions of the General Assembly of the State of South Carolina, Passed at the Annual Session of 1858* (Columbia, S.C.: 1858), p. 436; General Assembly Index—African Slave Trade Documents 0010 016 1858 00019 00, 0010 016 ND00 00745 00, South Carolina Department of Archives and History, Columbia; *Journal of the Senate of South Carolina: Being the Annual Session of 1859* (Columbia, S.C.: 1859), p. 5; *Journal of the House of Representatives of South Carolina: Being the Annual Session of 1859* (Columbia, S.C.: 1859), p. 32; Stanford M. Lyman, ed., *Selected Writings of Henry Hughes: Antebellum Southerner, Slavocrat, Sociologist* (Jackson: University of Mississippi Press, 1985), pp. 18–61, 73–143, 146–148, 167–182; Takaki, *A Pro-Slavery Crusade*, pp. 96–102; *Charleston Mercury* (Feb. 25, 1858); Stella Herron, "The African Apprentice Bill," *Proceedings of the Mississippi Valley Historical Association* 8 (1914–1915), 135–145; Bernstein, "Southern Politics and Attempts to Reopen the African Slave Trade," *Journal of Negro History* 51 (1966), pp. 32–34; James Paisley Hendrix, "The Efforts to Reopen the African Slave Trade in Louisiana," *Louisiana History* 10 (Spring 1969), 99–111; Fornell, "Agitation in Texas for Reopening the Slave Trade," pp. 249–258; W. J. Carnathan, "The Proposal to Reopen the African Slave Trade in the South, 1854–1860," *Southern Atlantic Quarterly* 25 (Oct. 1926), 424; Wish, "The Revival of the African Slave Trade," p. 588.

20. *Southern Standard* (Jan. 16, 1855). See also *De Bow's Review* 22 (Jan. 1857), 89–94, 102; (Feb. 1857), 216–224, 23; (Sept. 1857), 226–238, 303–319; (Oct. 1857), 440, 24; (June 1858), 574–605, 27; (July 1859), 96–100; (Aug. 1859), 205–220; (Sept. 1859), 360–365, 28; (Oct. 1859), 468–471.

21. W. H. Trescot to Miles (May 30, 1858; Feb. 8, 1859), in the William Porcher Miles Papers, Southern Historical Collection, University of North Carolina, Chapel Hill; Mary C. Simms Oliphant et al., eds., *The Letters of William Gilmore Simms, 1858–1866* vol. 4 (Columbia: University of South Carolina Press, 1955), pp. 64–65; *Charleston Mercury* (June 25, Sept. 29, 1857; May 20, 22, 24, 1858; June 14, 1859); J. Holt Merchant, Jr., "Lawrence M. Keitt: South Carolina Fire-Eater," (PhD diss., Univ. of Virginia, Charlottesville, 1976), pp. 246–252; Eric H. Walther, *The Fire-Eaters* (Baton Rouge: Louisiana State University Press, 1992), pp. 284–285; *Charleston Daily Courier* (Nov. 23, 1858); *Congressional Globe*, 36th Congress, 1st session, pp. 224–227, 2307; Harold Schultz, "Movement to Revive the Foreign Slave Trade," (MA thesis, Duke Univ., Durham, N.C., 1940), p. 58; Wish, "Movement to Revive the African Slave Trade," pp. 579–580.

22. *Congressional Globe*, 34th Congress, 3rd Session, pp. 123–126; *Charleston Weekly Standard* (Jan. 6, 1857).

23. *Congressional Globe*, 35th Congress, 2nd session, pp. 1053–1057; 36th Congress, 1st session, pp. 1137–1139; 36th Congress, 1st session, pp. 2303–2309, 2956–2957, 2638–2644; and the *Charleston Mercury* (Jan. 29, 1859).

24. On Lamar's attempts to reopen the African slave trade and his involvement with the illicit slave trade, see "A Slave Trader's Letterbook," *The North American Review* 143 (Nov. 1886), 447–456; *Charleston Daily Courier* (June 1, 7, 8, 1858); *The Reply of C. A. L. Lamar, of Savannah, Georgia, to the Letter of Howell Cobb, Secretary of Treasury of the United States, Refusing a Clearance to the Ship Richard Cobden* (Charleston, S.C.: 1858); *Charleston Mercury* (June 3, 9, 14, Aug. 2, Dec. 22, 1858; March 28, 1859); for details on the landing of the *Wanderer*, see Tom Henderson Wells, *The Slave Ship Wanderer* (Athens: University of Georgia Press, 1967), pp. 1–34; J. H. Adams to James Chesnut, Jr. (Jan. 14, 1859), in the Chesnut-Miller-Manning Papers, South Carolina Historical Society, Charleston.

25. *The Sumter Watchman* (Sept. 1, 1858); *Charleston Daily Courier* (Aug. 30, 31, Sept. 1, 4, 15, 16, 17, Nov. 24, 1858); *Charleston Mercury* (Sept. 1, 2, 4, 7, 8, 15, 18, 1858); Lieber to Wade Hampton (Sept. 15, 1858), in the Francis Lieber Papers, South Caroliniana Library, University of South Carolina, Columbia; Huger to ? (Sept. 1, 1858), in the Alfred Huger Letterbook, Perkins Library, Duke University, Durham, N.C.; D. H. Hamilton to Hammond (Sept. 10, 24, 1858), in the James Henry Hammond Papers, Library of Congress; George to Krilla (Aug. 30, 1858), in the George A. Gordon Papers, Perkins Library, Duke University, Durham, N.C.; James Buchanan to Rhett (Sept. 3, 1858), in the Robert Barnwell Rhett Papers, South Carolina Historical Society, Charleston.

26. On the renewed agitation for reopening the African slave trade, see *Charleston Mercury* (Sept. 7, 11, 10, 13, 14, 15, 18, 20, 21, 23, 25, 27, 18, 19, 30, Oct. 5, 7, 8, 9, 11, 12, 14, 15, 16, 17, 1858); Van Tromp, *The Pirates of the Echo* (Charleston, S.C.: 1859); the *Courier*, after publishing articles opposing the repatriation of the *Echo* Africans, came out against the reopening of the slave trade, as did some other national Democratic papers in the state. See *Charleston Daily Courier* (Sept. 4, Nov. 10, 1858); *The Charleston Courier and the Slave Trade by Las Casas* (no Publisher, no Date).

27. *Charleston Daily Courier* (Sept. 7, 9, 10, 11, Dec. 7, 11, 1858; April 14,

15, 18, 1859); *Charleston Mercury* (Sept. 15, 1858; Jan. 19, Feb. 16, 17, 18, 24, April 8, 13, 14, 15, 16, 18, 20, 1859); *Report of the Trials in the Echo Cases, in Federal Court, Charleston, South Carolina, April, 1859; Together With the Arguments of Counsel and Charge of the Court* (Columbia, S.C.: 1859); also see Takaki, *A Pro-Slavery Crusade*, pp. 215–218.

28. In another case, a Charleston ketch by the name of *Brothers* was apprehended in 1858 for being a slaver. Its crew was not indicted by a Charleston jury and in the admiralty case, Judge Magrath ruled that there was not sufficient evidence to libel it and returned it to its owners. See *Charleston Daily Courier* (Jan. 3, 4, 8, 18, 21, Feb. 14, March 25, May 14, 19, 26, June 23, Nov. 17, 1859; May 30, June 20, Oct. 22, 1860); *Charleston Mercury* (Jan. 1, 3, 5, 13, 17, 18, 21, Oct. 26, 1859); "Charge of Mr. Justice Wayne of the Supreme Court of the United States Given on the Fourteenth Day of November, 1859, to the Grand Jury of the Sixth Circuit Court of the United States, for the Southern District of Georgia," in Paul Finkelman, ed., *The African Slave Trade and American Courts: The Pamphlet Literature* vol. 2 (New York: Garland Publishing, Inc., 1988), pp. 1–29; Takaki, *A Pro-Slavery Crusade*, pp. 209–211; Wells, *The Slave Ship Wanderer*, pp. 24–59, 63–83; "A Slave Trader's Letterbook," pp. 456–457, 460; John Cunnigham to Hammond (Jan. 15, 1859), in the James Henry Hammond Papers, Library of Congress.

29. *The Slave Trade Not Declared Piracy By the Act of 1820: The United States versus William C. Corrie Presentment for Piracy Opinion of the Honorable A. G. Magrath, District Judge in the Circuit Court of the United States for the District of South Carolina, Upon a Motion to Enter a Nol. Pros. in the Case* (Columbia, S.C.: 1860), esp. pp. 14–26; *Charleston Daily Courier* (April 19, 1860); *Charleston Mercury* (April 19, 1860); Wells, *The Slave Ship Wanderer*, pp. 59–62.

30. For Magrath's self-righteous explanation of his course of actions, see A. G. Magrath to Hammond (Jan. 21, 1859; May 30, 1860), in the James Henry Hammond Papers, Library of Congress; *Congressional Globe*, 36th Congress, 1st session, pp. 2269–2270; W. H. Trescot to Miles (May 12, 1860), in the William Porcher Miles Papers, Southern Historical Collection, University of North Carolina, Chapel Hill.

31. *Charleston Mercury* (March 9, 10, 31, April 21, June 14, 1859); *Charleston Daily Courier* (Sept. 29, 1859); undated newspaper clipping from the *Yorkville Enquirer*, in the Milledge Luke Bonham Papers, South Caroliniana Library, University of South Carolina, Columbia; *Speech of Hon. W. L. Yancey, Delivered in the Democratic State Convention, of the State of Alabama, Held at Montgomery, on the 11th, 12, 13th and 14th Jan., 1860* (Montgomery, Ala.: 1860), pp. 17–18; Schultz, "Movement to Revive the Foreign Slave Trade," pp. 66–68.

32. For Upper South and British concerns over the slave trade, see Editorial Letter by G. W. B., *Southern Literary Messenger* (*SLM*) 32 (Jan. 1861), 71–76; "Slave Trade in Southern Congess," *SLM* 32 (June 1861), 409–420; "The African Slave Trade," *SLM* 33 (Aug. 1861), 105–113; "Despatch from the British Consul at Charleston to Lord John Russell, 1860," *American Historical Review* (July 1913), 783–787; on Carolinian protests against the Confederacy's decision, see *Charleston Mercury* (Feb. 13, March 15, 1861); "The Philosophy of Secession: A Protest from South Carolina Against a Decision of the Southern Congress," *Living Age* 3rd series (March 1861), 801–810; *Journal of the Conven-*

tion of the People of South Carolina, Held in 1860, 1861 and 1862, Together with the Ordinances, Reports, Resolutions, Etc. (Columbia, S.C., 1862), pp. 207, 214–215, 236–264; A. L. Hull, ed., "The Making of the Confederate Constitution," *Publications of the Southern Historical Association* 9 (Sept. 1905), 288; *The African Slave Trade and the Secret Purpose of the Insurgents to Revive It. No Treaty Stipulation Against the Slave Trade to be Entered into with the European Powers. Judah P. Benjamin's Intercepted Instructions to L. Q. C. Lamar, Styled Commissioner, Etc.* (Philadelphia: 1863); Warren S. Howard, *American Slavers and the Federal Law, 1837–1862* (Berkeley: University of California Press, 1963), pp. 201–202.

11

• • • •

Africa in South Carolina

Mamie Garvin Fields's Lemon Swamp
and Other Places

Clara Juncker

Grace Nichols's sequence of poems *I Is* originates in her dream of an African girl swimming from Africa to the Caribbean with a garland of flowers around her waist, possibly in an attempt to purge the ocean of its burden—the misery and suffering her ancestors had experienced (Wisker 26). Other contemporary African American writers, such as Alice Walker, have explored both the Middle Passage and its mirror image, the quest for Africa—often, as Nichols's garland might suggest, from a feminine angle and aesthetics. Women of African descent belonging to generations before Nichols's and Walker's dreamed of Africa as well, though their notions of the continent and its people differed considerably from contemporary ones. Mamie Garvin Fields's *Lemon Swamp and Other Places: A Carolina Memoir* (1983) articulates a Charleston woman's desire to go to Africa as a missionary in 1909, and her parents' refusal to grant their permission. "When I found that nothing would change their minds," Fields writes, "I decided to be that missionary right in South Carolina" (105).[1] As a teacher in her home state, Fields transplanted, so to speak, her dream of Africa to the culturally and socially isolated John's Island, thus living out her own quest for the ancestral home. However, as other explorers before and after her time, Fields molds "Africa" according to her own needs and visions. Above all, reminiscences of the landscapes and people of various South Carolina islands communicate the dreams

and realities of an educated African American woman living—and surviving—in the Jim Crow South.

Mamie Fields's autobiography, which her granddaughter Karen Fields
helped assemble, originates in her resolution to "seize the territory" to in-
sert her life into the fabric of American literature and history (Jones 12).
Her territorial interests appear more concretely in the title of her life
story, whose emphasis on place suggests the Fieldses' southern roots. In
"The Search for Southern Identity," (in *The Burden of Southern History*) C.
Vann Woodward explains the significance of locality by quoting Eudora
Welty:

> Like a good many [regional] writers . . . I am myself touched off
> by place. The place where I am and the place I know, and other
> places that familiarity with and love for my own make strange and
> lovely and enlightening to look into, are what set me to writing my
> stories. (30)

Fields grounds herself with a controlling metaphor of houses and decors
as well as with her chapter headings, which all focus on place: "The Par-
sonage, No. 5 Short Court"; "Forbidden Places"; "A Place Behind God's
Back"; "Moving North"; "A School at Society Corner, James Island"; and
more. Her choice to relocate the African continent just outside Charleston,
thus uniting the African with the Southern in her life (text), constitutes a
move characteristic of Fields and of many a South Carolinian inhabiting
Lemon Swamp and Other Places.

The South that Fields consistently foregrounds is, not surprisingly, historically dense. Karen Fields mentions in her introduction to *Lemon
Swamp* her grandmother's "appreciation of history." This mindset, Karen
notes, determined Fields's doings, as well as "the way she recounts
events" (xxii).[2] As a girl in the 1890s, she had been surrounded with ex-
slave relatives, as well as with the visitors they brought to her home in
No. 5 Short Court. Two ladies in particular, Fields recalls, had long talks
with her Uncle J. B. The older one, she writes without fanfare, "was Harriet Tubman" (15).

Slavery and its aftermath give Fields's South its texture and occasionally erase the distinction between the past and the present. Stating that
"Charlestonians like their rice," Fields shifts to a plantation setting, where
owners refuse their slaves rice, and then to a vignette of her Aunt Harriet
cooking rice while telling Fields what other ex-slaves had done to boil it
properly (59). The autobiography's time frame shifts back and forth between the author's present, her past, and slavery days, thus arriving at
the characteristically southern "past in the present." Literally, the past

continues to exist in the South Carolina of a younger Fields, present as her acquaintance Dr. Evans points out to her. He takes her to an isolated plantation surrounded by locked gates and asks for her assistance in helping the people kept there to escape their cruel mistress. "Dr. Evans and I were about to step out into a place where they still had *slavery*," Fields writes. "S-L-A-V-E-R-Y. . . . Anybody that left had to steal away. Steal away in 1920-some, just like in slavery time!" (200–201).

Not just those unfortunate enough to be on the wrong side of locked gates experienced the South as a contained and containing environment. In the introduction, Karen remembers her family's summer trips from Washington, D.C., where she grew up, to Charleston as ventures into "another country." Loading the car with "huge provisions," her parents tried to make their "capsule" self-sufficient, due to "a determination to avoid insult, or worse." As Karen concludes, "we made our voyage with the cramped venturesomeness of austronauts" (xiii–xiv).

For most of Fields's life, Charlestonians of African descent literally moved within a space bounded by segregation. As a little girl in the 1890s, Fields sees, through the window of a white family's house, a man putting on Ku Klux Klan sheets; she learns early to maneuver outside or around the "Forbidden Places" of her chapter title. Textually, Fields inscribes and subverts racist practices by contrasting the activities of John C. Calhoun and Frederick Douglass, yet places the two in a parallel sentence construction with Douglass first: "At the same time that Douglass was preaching against slavery, John C. Calhoun was preaching for it" (57). In the South, African Americans wanting to speak and to write had, in short, to invent their own space. As Fields writes about segregated parks, "telling us to stay in our place didn't mean that we were going to get a place to stay in" (57).

If the statue of Calhoun commands the Citadel Green and used to remind Fields and others of keeping off the grounds, the old Public Market reminds rich Charlestonians, then as now, "where their wealth came from" (xxi). The Charleston of *Lemon Swamp* thus houses its own racial ironies. The Public Market has become a Confederate museum; tourists of African descent admire the flowers at Cypress Gardens plantation while gliding, Karen writes, "in 'battoes' poled by black teenagers through canals originally built by slaves" (xx).

In Fields's days, Charleston constituted an especially complicated landscape. Due to various city requirements, the African American–owned Hametic hotel became too expensive for Charlestonians of color, while segregation practices prevented white guests from staying there. "What do you think of that—a hotel for Negroes that Negroes couldn't go to?" Fields asks (32). And within the African American community, insider/outsider status was fixed by birth and by skin color, because, Fields explains, "Charleston had two segregations." Entering the Avery Institute, a segregated high school for African Americans, Fields finds light-skinned people on one side of the aisle, dark-skinned on the other.

With its various ironies and complexities, Fields's depiction of the South nonetheless overlaps with her image of Africa. In both spaces, the conception of time is fluid, frequently nonlinear. As in Alice Walker's *The Temple of My Familiar*, ancestors continue to exist in the lives of their descendants; Fields's great-great-uncle Thomas thus inhabits the mental landscape of No. 5 Short Court, where he moves in textually before Fields herself has appeared in the *Lemon Swamp* pages. In the "Genealogical Guide" that concludes the autobiography, he figures prominently as "Thomas Middleton (Africa-born)," thus reminding Fields' readers of historical and cultural continuities.[3] Karen Fields explains the more subtle links between her southern grandparents and their African counterparts, who "do not think of place in a mere physical sense separate from its warming by generations of sons and daughters" (xviii). Because of this "warming" of the earth by time, by history, and by people, both Africa and the South constitute in Fields's representation land(scape)s of plenty. She fondly remembers a generous Liberian classmate at Claflin University, who gets money from home to invite his friends to the Claflin/State football game and other outings, just as she consistently emphasizes her own plentiful supplies of food and clothes.

Fields inscribes Africa in her South Carolina memoirs through a dialogic form. She converses, of course, with the granddaughter, who constitutes her immediate audience, as well as with a wider circle of readers. She adds, moreover, dialogic genres such as letters to her life text, which in itself enacts a dialogue between autobiographical selves of various ages and experiences.

Yet Africa is unreadable to Fields. In describing her generous Liberian classmate at Claflin, she stresses that "he had a large mark branded on his forehead, which we all thought was ugly at first, and that it must have hurt." Trying to decipher this writing, she communicates to her audience that "it was a sign of his rank over there" and that she and her classmates "got used to it." Nonetheless, her next remark reveals her inability to understand this African discourse: "[B]esides, he was a fine-looking fellow in every other way" (93).

Despite this aversion of the African American gaze from African sign systems, Africa as such constitutes a magnetic field for Fields and her peers. They invent "Africa," so to speak, as an Iserly playspace, situated concretely in the Friends of Africa organization. Here, Fields writes rather vaguely, "we studied about Africa." More concretely, she adds, members focused on "the work our [Methodist] church was doing there" (102). She prefers, in short, her own inscriptions on African soil to African signs on American. Indeed, she wishes herself to go to Africa as a missionary, so as to put her own mark on the continent and its people. A poem she wrote for a Friends of Africa hymn-writing competition communicates her translation of Africa to "Africa":

> There is an island across the sea
> Where bands of heathen dwell
> Who hunger for the Living Word
> That saves a soul from Hell. (103)

As Fields looks towards Africa, her gaze is indistinguishable from a colonial one, whether religious or mercenary. She shares with imperialists in the contact zone, to use Marie Louise Pratt's term, the panoramic view that sets the beholder off from and over those beheld. As the author, Fields groups herself with the "we" who vow to help the "bands of heathen." The Africans of her poem become, in other words, the savage other, reduced by the imperial "I" to a generic horde. Also her "island across the sea" phrase, promininently displayed in the first line, emphasizes difference. Indeed, like other "seeing men" (and women), she cannot see the Africans she describes. They become invisible in the crowds hiding their individual identities and in Fields's religious focus. As "souls" longing to find the path to heaven, her Africans lack what her (African) Americans have: bodies and Bibles. The religious imagery of Fields's poem reinforces continental and cultural differences. With "that Divine Abode" as the ultimate goal for spiritual and narrative measures, Africans remain on a lower rung of the ladder leading towards higher spheres, whether religious or cultural.

This notion of Africa as an uncivilized other returns in Fields's representation of the continent as an infective space. Gertrude Townsend and John Coleman, Claflin graduates who go to Africa as missionaries, die, Fields emphasizes, from the "African fever" a few years later. Though she mentions that yellow fever kills people in South Carolina as well, Fields devotes considerable narrative energy to her parents' fear of sickness and death in Africa, to the many missionaries who never return from there, and to the death in Africa of William Demosthenes Crump, the first African American Collector of Ports in Charleston and later Ambassador to Liberia. To stay within her parents' goodwill and outside the chaos she associates with Africa, she displaces the continent to South Carolinian shores. Like Mary McLeod Bethune of the National Council of Negro Women, a role model and mentor, Fields decides to combat disorder of various kinds closer to home: "If I cannot give my millions / And the heathen lands explore / I can find the heathen nearer. / I can find him at my door" (106). Lemon Swamp of Fields's title, as well as John's and James Islands, where Mamie teaches in remote country schools, thus represents a fusion of African and Southern territories that allows her to inhabit both.

Lemon Swamp constitutes in the autobiography a wild zone, a space of alterity outside order and control. It is mirrored in John's Island, where Fields gets a teaching assignment in 1909. To go there, she has to leave behind all emblems of civilization—her trunks—and enter a territory still more liminal, erotic, and dangerous (112). This journey into darkness represents a process of deculturalization, in which Fields will have to renegotiate traditional concepts of nature and culture, seeing and blindness. As Karla Holloway observes, "sight and voice—seeing through a glass, albeit darkly, seem to be the way to effacement and effacement seems to be the way to internalize . . . the Other" (47). John's Island, in short, immerses Fields in difference. In crossing a gully separating her from what she calls "her future home" on the island, Fields slips and literally descends into a different space: "I went screaming, for I knew I was visiting the realm of snakes, lizards, spiders, and what-have-you. Although I could see none of them, the pitch black made me 'see' all of them!" (112). This encounter with the other allows her to open her eyes to what she has so far succeeded in not seeing.

Well outside the reach of the Methodist church, islanders practice vodoo and witchcraft, right in the house Fields comes to inhabit. In another island community, Miller Hill, Fields encounters "hag," a witch who for weeks invades her sleep and disturbs her peace of mind. Her decision to confront the hag, however, leads to a physical and mental initiation. When the witch appears in Fields's room, and the "instant of crisis" Houston A. Baker (*Workings* 85, 89) identifies as a feature of African American women's writing occurs, she is ready:

> I pulled his hands apart. I knocked him down and off the bed. When she came and jumped on me in bed, as usual, I caught her hand and pulled her fingers apart with all my strength, beat him or her in the face. . . . She got out of bed and ran away. She ran away through the keyhole. . . . (119)

Though Fields finds her body and mind invaded by the hag, she manages to extort this indeterminately gendered presence and delegate the sexuality and irrationality it represents to absence. For now at least, she has rejected the connection to African magic and power of island conjurers, though their craft remains in her text as "poetic distillates" con-

stituting "improvisational cultural wisdom" (Baker, *Workings* 85, 89).
Fields has won a battle for rationality and can begin to teach the island's
children.

But other battles block her way. As an erotic zone challenging the Vic-
torian moral codes to which middle-class African Americans of Fields's
generation subscribed (Perkins), John's Island teems with untamed sexuality and violence. Robert shoots his girlfriend Kitty in her private parts,
because she has performed an erotic dance called "ball the jack" in his absence (139). Like the African heathen she had longed to convert, the island population exists in "A Place behind God's Back," the chapter title
through which Fields communicates darkness and invisibility. It's not
just Fields's representation of John's Island that merges this space with
the "Africa" she had previously ima(gin)ed. "Back then," she notes in
Lemon Swamp, "you could still see houses built very much like the houses
in Africa" (119). The islanders' Gullah language further testify to well-
documented historical connections. At the same time, it opens a door out
of the linguistic prison in which Baker locates many a turn-of-the-
century autobiographer of African descent (*Journey Back* 47).

The South Carolina coastal and island swamps accordingly function
as mediating spaces between African, African American, and southern
systems of belief. The presence of a middle-class Methodist teacher on
John's and James Islands testifies in itself to cultural negotiations, but
also Fields's terrestrial descriptions suggest the liminality of the contact
zone. James Island, she writes, "was near and far" from her home in
Charleston (205); Lemon Swamp constitutes a similar jumble of contradictions. Listing what she likes about Lemon Swamp, she mixes heat and
coolness, light and dark, land and water, movement and stillness, and
pleasant and unpleasant smells, thus establishing the swamp as difference (67). Fields's domestic(ating) metaphors weave themselves around
the untamed vegetation of Lemon Swamp, which sets the scene, in short,
for the cultural mediation under way.

With her commitment to education and progress, Fields changes the
islanders. She fights stereotypes of them as "ignorant" and "dumb" and
sees the islands as reservoirs of talent. Her civilizing efforts include teaching her classes to say the Pledge of Allegiance and sing the national
anthem, to straighten hair, to can tomatoes, and to gain access to information. In short, her trust in American systems of belief results in a
strategy for racial "uplift" aimed at allowing the schoolchildren to enter
the American mainstream.

But the islanders change Fields as well. Their untamed sexuality, violence, and superstition represent what Fields's bourgeois socialization
has rendered invisible, but their deference to whites clarifies her own

racial position. By watching her pupils shuffle and avert their eyes in the company of local authority figures, she comes to resent the segregation and racism defining her own existence. "White people had so many ways to degrade the Negro," she observes. She proceeds to teach an island boy that he is "*somebody*" and to go over with her class "all the beautiful things that are black, starting with black satin and black crepe" (214). She begins to manipulate school trustees by "dramatizing" (225), a subtle way of sassing them into compliance reminiscent of Hurston and spunky African American autobiographers like her (Braxton 165). And Fields finds a role model in Mrs. Mary McLeod Bethune of the National Council of Negro Women, herself an accomplished educator and activist. By adding resistance to her own list of accomplishments, she changes her own life script, and that of her region.

In looking for Africa in South Carolina, Fields finds, like many a traveler, herself. In the meeting with a racial self less contaminated by (African) American middle-class codes, she invents, so to speak, a self more intent on eliminating the iron gates hemming it in. Yet her destination is neither the Africa that she does not know nor the South Carolina she knows too well. Fields navigates, in fact, toward a contact zone where new constellations of self and other, black and white, African and American might grow. By recording her story, she embarks upon a project of "denigration," in Michael Awkward's revision of the term an appropriative inscription of African American culture and expression upon Western systems of signification (Awkward 9). Predictably, her passage is stormy. As Baker writes in *The Journey Back*, "to understand our origins, we must journey through difficult straits. And in the end we may find only confusion" (1). Fields finds "The We Land," the title of her last chapter and a site of racial potentiality. Confusion may, after all, blossom into change, in the South and elsewhere. "Much was coming," Fields concludes, "that we couldn't imagine then" (241).

Notes

1. Further references to *Lemon Swamp* will appear parenthetically in the text.
2. CF. Holloway 33.
3. CF. Holloway 134.

References

Awkward, Michael. *Inspiriting Influences: Tradition, Revision, and Afro-American Women's Novels.* New York: Columbia UP, 1989.
Baker, Houston A. *The Journey Back: Issues in Black Literature and Criticism.* Chicago: U of Chicago P, 1980.

Baker, Houston A. *Workings of the Spirit: The Poetics of Afro-American Women's Writing.* Chicago: U of Chicago P, 1991.

Braxton, Joanne M. *Black Women Writing Autobiography: A Tradition within a Tradition.* Philadelphia: Temple UP, 1989.

Fields, Mamie Garvin. *Lemon Swamp and Other Places: A Carolina Memoir.* New York Free P, 1983.

Holloway, Karla F. C. *Moorings and Metaphors: Figures of Culture and Gender in Black Women's Literature.* New Brunswick, N.J.: Rutgers UP, 1992.

Jones, Gayl. *Liberating Voices: Oral Tradition in African American Literature.* Cambridge, Mass.: Harvard UP, 1991.

Perkins, Linda. "The Impact of the 'Cult of True Womanhood' on the Education of Black Women." *Journal of Social Issues* 39.3 (1983): 17–28.

Pratt, Marie Louise. *Imperial Eyes: Travel Writing and Transculturation.* London: Routledge, 1992.

Wisker, Gina, ed. *Black Women's Writing.* New York: St. Martin's P, 1993.

Woodward, C. Vann. *The Burden of Southern History.* New York: Mentor, 1969.

12

• • • •

"The Persistence of Tradition"

The Retelling of Sea Islands Culture in Works by Julie Dash, Gloria Naylor, and Paule Marshall

Lene Brøndum

Before the Civil War, the Sea Islands off the coasts of Georgia and South Carolina were one of the last areas in the United States to see a continued arrival of Africans who had illegally been transported to the United States to be sold as slaves. The last ship on record to have "imported" African captives is the slave ship, the *Wanderer*, which brought a cargo of 400 Africans to Jekyll Island, Georgia, in 1858, fifty-one years after the importation of Africans as slaves had been banned in 1807.[1] Julie Dash refers to the Islands as a "reverse Ellis Island" for the African slaves.[2] Isolated from the mainland, the Sea Island Gullahs, descendants of African captives, here "created and maintained a distinct, imaginative, and original African American Culture" (*Making* 27). In other words, the Sea Islands, as a U.S. geographical area, retain strong rural African cultural traditions. The Sea Islands, according to Dash, represent a greater degree of genuine cultural syncretism of African and American culture than that found anywhere else in the United States. Once a "reverse Ellis Island" to the African slaves, the Islands today have been reversed again into a more positive cultural "bridge" to Africa by such African American artists as Gloria Naylor and Paule Marshall, who use the rich Sea Island heritage in *Mama Day* and *Praisesong for the Widow*, respectively, as well as by filmmaker Julie Dash, who has made the feature film, *Daughters of the Dust*.

Mae Gwendolyn Henderson presents a useful paradigm for the motivation for using Sea Island culture in African American women's texts in her essay, "Speaking in Tongues: Dialogics, Dialectics, and the Black Woman Writer's Literary Tradition."[3] Henderson says that "black women writers have encoded oppression as a discursive dilemma, that is, their works have consistently raised the problem of the black woman's relationship to power and discourse" (24). Henderson explains further that African American women negotiate this dilemma by entering into both "testimonial" and "competitive" discourses with their readers (20). In *Daughters of the Dust*, for instance, Julie Dash speaks to African American women in an intimate voice by focusing on the stories of the Peazant women and by mythologizing their past and their present. In contrast to this personal discussion, Dash also enters into a public and political dialogue with the hegemonic systems, when, as I will explain later, she subverts the traditional standards of historiography. Henderson asserts that in "negotiating [this] discursive dilemma" African American women writers "accomplish two objectives: the self-inscription of black womanhood and the establishment of a dialogue of discourses with the other(s)" (30). These two objectives require "disruption" and "revision" of the conventional and canonical stories, and Henderson suggests the modes of disruption and revision as a model for reading African American women's literary expression. Disruption, which she defines as "the initial response to hegemonic and ambiguously (non)hegemonic discourse," occurs, for instance, when Dash inserts herself into a predominantly white, male film tradition by creating a film entirely about African American women's lives (30). Henderson defines revision as the "rewriting or rereading" of the conventional and canonical stories (30). Canonical stories are representations of hegemonic discourse. Therefore, to enter into that discourse, African American women writers must challenge those stories by rewriting them and, in the process, write themselves into the canon.

Julie Dash's *Daughters of the Dust* offers an example. Her film takes place on the Sea Islands in 1902, on the eve of the Peazant family's migration to the North. In the making of *Daughters of the Dust*, Dash had no intentions of making an "ethnographic" or "historically accurate" film about a Sea Islands family. Rather, she has used her extensive research on Sea Islands culture and history to present to her audience a film that reflects the "essence" of Sea Islands culture in a way intended to give her audience "mythic memory" rather than "ethnographic memory."[4] She wanted to "take [an audience] back, take them inside their family memories, inside our collective memories" (*Making* 5).

To create this mythic memory, Dash disrupts and revises the traditional standards of historiography by consciously using what I will term a "composite history" of the Sea Islands. I define a composite history as a nonchronological representation of history in which historical "facts" are selected for representation according to whether they effectively reveal something about the "essence" of a culture or a historical period, rather than according to "objective," historical demands for chronological accuracy. As such, a composite history functions as a revision of the traditional Western definition of history.

Bilal Muhammed, the Muslim Sea Islander and member of the extended Peazant family, is one example of Dash's use of composite history; Bilal Muhammed, or Bilali Mohamet, probably his real name, was an actual person who lived on Sapelo Island, Georgia, in the early part of the nineteenth century (and thus could not have been a 55-year-old man in 1902). The historical Bilali Mohamet was an African-born Fula Muslim from Timbo in Futa Jallon of present-day Guinea-Conakry, who brought his religion with him to America and who wrote from memory his own version of a Muslim religious text, the *Risala*, which Dash in the film has transformed into a "homemade Koran."[5] In *Daughters of the Dust*, Bilal tells Mr. Snead, the photographer, that he was brought over on the *Wanderer* in 1858. With Bilal Muhammed's arrival on Dahtaw Island on the *Wanderer* in 1858, Dash incorporates combined pieces of historical information that are relevant for her project but would have been difficult to include, if she had not turned to the use of composite history. Dash herself explains that it was important for her to include Bilal's character in her film to show "the persistence of tradition" and to show that African Americans draw on numerous religious traditions. In other words, Dash seeks to present an historical explanation for the existence of Islam in African American culture (*Making* 36–37).

Another example of Dash's use of composite history deals with the representation of Sea Islands agricultural history. Nana, the great-grandmother, describes the hardships of slavery by describing the slaves' hard toil with the poisonous indigo dye, as well as with the production of rice and Sea Islands cotton (Screenplay 31–32). Nana disregards the fact that, historically, the three crops did not (to any large degree) coexist but followed one another as the main Sea Islands crop.[6] She makes no distinction, because it is irrelevant. What is relevant is the total suffering, the composite hardships, because those experiences were all the same. To emphasize this point, Dash gives some of the women indigo-stained hands, thus creating a new and unfamiliar symbol of slavery in the toxically blue hands. She consciously ignores the fact that the poisonous indigo stain would not have remained on hands and that indigo was not cultivated after the end of the eighteenth century, about fifty years before Nana's birth. By presenting a composite history of the Sea Islands, Dash presents the Peazant family's scraps of mythic memories. Extracting and emphasizing the "essence" of Sea Island culture rather than presenting an historically accurate picture of it, Dash establishes her sense of mythic memory as a means of maintaining a sense of self and community and connections to Africa.

Trinh Minh-ha characterizes storytelling as "the oldest form of building historical consciousness in community" in her book, *Woman, Native, Other.*[7] This can be seen as an important revision of the representation of history. Storytelling attests to Dash's notion of the persistence of tradition, because it becomes a significant link to the ancestors. For African American women writers, storytelling is often important as a method of revision. In Dash's, Naylor's, and Marshall's work, for instance, storytelling becomes a significant means of revising traditional historiography, because it gives authority to the spoken word as a historical record. In other words, storytelling disrupts the discursive history of hegemony.

In much the same way that storytelling serves to disrupt the representation of history by revising it, so mythmaking emphasizes a reworking of tradition. In this context, I define a myth as a story that seeks to explain or give meaning to aspects of human life or a culture's origins and identity. Contemporary African American women's writing of stories that function as myths of origin and identity differs from the traditional notion of the mythical as something that points back to a distant historical time. In actuality, African American women's use of myth is another disruption of dominant discourse: first, by valuing myth in contrast to "history" and, second, by the writer's sense of agency and subjectivity in the discussion of a communal historic past. Hortense J. Spillers explains in "Mama's Baby, Papa's Maybe: An American Grammar Book" that Africans enslaved, kidnapped, and carried to America were removed from the source of earlier communal myths and, as a result, created new myths to replace the lost ones in part to explain the dispersal of their people and to facilitate survival, both on arrival and two hundred years later.[8] This, I believe, is what bell hooks means when she argues that *Daughters of the Dust* is intended to give its audience "mythic memory" rather than "ethnographic memory" (*Making* 30). Myth as memory then functions as a complementary story to the mercantile, labor-seeking history of early New World capitalism by exposing the other side, the Middle Passage below deck and in the fields. Perhaps more significantly late in the twentieth century, myth as memory also functions as a revelation of a positive, beautiful mosaic of images of African American women—of their past, present, and potential futures.

Both *Daughters of the Dust* and Gloria Naylor's *Mama Day* have as their spiritual center a strong, matriarchal figure.[9] Dash's Nana and Naylor's

Miranda are the keepers of the family spirit and are both deeply rooted in the culture and the history of the Sea Islands. Possessing ancestral knowledge and power gives these women a spiritual strength that they will pass on to their children through storytelling, creating an interconnection of cultural spirit and integrity that binds generations. In *Daughters of the Dust*, Nana functions as an African griotte who tells her family stories to the younger family members to give them strength and pride in themselves and their family/community. At the graveyard, for instance, when Eli, Nana's grandson, is questioning the power of the ancestors to protect the living, Nana says to him, "'Do you believe that hundreds and hundreds of Africans brought here on this other side would forget everything they once knew? We don't know where the recollections come from. Sometimes we dream them. But we carry these memories inside of us'" (Screenplay 22). Although Nana is not always aware of the origin of her mythic memories, they nevertheless form the basis of her deeply felt historical consciousness.

Nana says to her extended family, "'Take my 'Hand,' I'm the one that can give you strength" (Screenplay 86). The "hand," a small leather pouch that Nana has sewn, contains the collective family memories: a lock of Nana's mother's hair (Nana's only physical memory of her African-born mother), a lock of Nana's own hair, and various "scraps of memories" from her tin can (Screenplay 78). As she is sewing the hand, she tells the women who are fussing over her that, "'There must be a bond . . . a connection, between those that go up North, and those who across the sea'" (Screenplay 77). This bond is further emphasized when Nana brings together Yellow Mary, the prostitute, and Viola, the Christian missionary. Around her neck, Yellow Mary carries a charm of St. Christopher, the patron saint of travel, which works as a symbol of the Middle Passage. Nana ties her own "hand" of African beliefs to Viola's Bible with Yellow Mary's St. Christopher's charm, while exclaiming that "we've taken old Gods and given them new names" (Screenplay 85). The two women, who are juxtaposed in the film, are thus brought together by Nana's composite hand of gods and stories, which becomes an emblem of spiritual and cultural syncretism and thereby also a promise of spiritual regeneration.

Despite this image, however, the promise of the future seems less assured in *Daughters of the Dust* than in *Mama Day*. Dash's Peazants, after all, are leaving their ancestral home, and none of them knows what awaits them in the North. Historically, much black Southern culture was dramatically altered as a consequence of the migration to the North. But at the end of the twentieth century, Gloria Naylor reconfirms the promise of spiritual continuity and survival. At the end of *Mama Day* when

George has died in body but not in spirit, Miranda says to him, "'I can't tell you her [Sapphira's] name, 'cause it was never opened to me. That's a door for the child of Grace to walk through. . . . And there'll be another time—that I won't be here for—when she'll learn about the beginning of the Days'" (308). Metaphorically, Miranda here expresses her belief in mythic memory. This mythic memory will sustain Naylor's Cocoa at the beginning of the twenty-first century as it sustained the Peazant family a hundred years before.

Mama Day's fictitious Sea Islands community of the 1990s, Willow Springs, and especially the Day family, attests to the persistence of tradition, as they can be viewed as the spiritual descendants of the Peazants of Dahtaw Island as we encounter them in 1902. In a sense, Naylor assures us that, regardless of whether African Americans who migrated North were able to retain their unique culture, the syncretic Sea Islands culture existing *in* the area and passed on by those who stay behind is alive even at the turn of the twenty-first century. In Willow Springs, Naylor implicitly creates an island community different from the real Sea Islands communities of the late twentieth century, many of which have been, or are being, partly destroyed by tourism and commercialization.[10] Consequently, Naylor's Willow Springs, which has refused to sell the land and the community's integrity, appears as a creatively constructed utopian community in which both the present and the future have been mythologized. In other words, Willow Springs survives, whereas many of the Sea Islands have not. Naylor presents an imaginative survival of traditional Sea Islands culture, even if this survival ultimately seems threatened in reality.

Naylor creates this imaginary survival by inventing Sea Islands traditions that emphasize the mythical origins of the island community's independence and integrity. These myths and invented traditions function as a radical revision of the most canonical of all texts, the Bible. Naylor emphasizes the persistence of tradition by accommodation to changing times. The celebration of Candle Walk, for instance, has changed for every generation since its start in 1823, but the spirit in which it is celebrated has remained the same, namely, a celebration of the islanders' independence and past. Candle Walk, observed on Willow Springs on December 22, is celebrated instead of Christmas.[11] December 22 is the day when, according to one story, the African-born slave woman, Sapphira, took her freedom and went east over the ocean. The day of her rebellion and flight thus replaces the Christian day of celebration. So not only does Naylor replace Jesus Christ, with a fierce African slave woman as the savior, she also changes the inflexible Christian ritual of celebration into a flexible, dynamic ritual due to its purely oral transmission in the form of stories from one generation to another. In short, Naylor disrupts one of the most central Christian events and, in revising it, writes her own canonical story.

Naylor's depiction of the "standing forth" ceremony at Little Caesar's funeral is another ritual that serves to disrupt the dominant Euro-American Christian tradition. In the Sea Islands studies that I have consulted, I have found no records of any standing forth ceremonies, but I know that particular funeral traditions are unique to the area and can be traced back to West African funeral traditions.[12] However, Naylor's fictitious ceremony invokes the old African/Sea Islands belief in the survival of the spirit, when the people of Willow Springs stand forth and, directly addressing themselves to Little Caesar, tell him what he will look like when they next see him (269). As in her creation of Candle Walk, Naylor revises a Christian ritual. Little Caesar's spirit has not passed away in a moment of finality; it has merely passed on into another sphere of existence. In short, by inventing Candle Walk and the standing forth ceremony, Naylor creates and mythologizes cultural traditions much for the same reason that Dash mythologizes history, both in order to represent the "essence" of Sea Islands culture.

In *Daughters of the Dust*, *Mama Day*, and Paule Marshall's *Praisesong for the Widow*, we encounter the parallel myths of the Ibo Landing and that of the flying Africans, powerful myths of resistance. In fact, the myth of the Ibo Landing is so powerful that, in the course of research for *Daughters of the Dust*, Dash found out that almost all the Sea Islands have an area claimed as the "real" Ibo Landing (*Making* 30). Consequently, this is an essential aspect of Sea Islands culture, and so Dash has used it at a central point in her film when she makes an intertextual reference by quoting Marshall's presentation of it in *Praisesong for the Widow* (Screenplay 67–68). All three authors imaginatively recreate the myths of the Ibos and the flying Africans, thus further attesting to their potential as metaphorical markers of an autonomous and assertive cultural sense of self. *Daughters of the Dust* takes place *at* Ibo Landing, indicating the close association between the myth and the Peazant family's reality. In *Mama Day*, Sapphira's flight back to Africa becomes the celebration of the island's cultural, political, and economic independence from white America. In *Praisesong for the Widow*, Avey Johnson's Sea Islands heritage triumphs over her adult struggle for materialistic wealth.[13]

Avey has been named after Aunt Cuney's grandmother, Avatara, who actually saw the Ibos get up and walk back to Africa.[14] This grandmother had chosen Avey to carry on the tradition and to take over her Aunt Cuney's role as a culture bearer. The middle-aged Avey finally answers to the call of the ancestors while participating in a ritual celebration of the

African ancestors on Carriacou, a small eastern Caribbean island, after a series of experiences that prepare her for her cultural and spiritual reawakening. The celebration is the "Beg Pardon" or the "Big Drum," when Lebert Joseph's people beg the ancestors for forgiveness for whatever wrongs they have committed in the course of the year. The arduous boat trip from Grenada to Carriacou serves both as a purge for Avey's White Plains materialism and as a reversal of the Middle Passage. This disruptive reversal makes Avey's arrival on Carriacou—the representation of Africa—a homecoming.[15] In the company of this group of African Caribbeans, who have all returned to their home island for the Beg Pardon, Avey becomes reconnected to her Sea Islands heritage. She reconnects when she is finally able to do the Ring Shout, which the old folks of Tatem used to dance, in the company of these islanders whose equivalent local dance or shuffle is called the "Carriacou Tramp." Avey realizes that "these strangers . . . had become one and the same with people in Tatem" (250).

By having Avey come to terms with her cultural heritage on a Caribbean island, Marshall not only bridges the gaps for Avey between the North of the United States and the Sea Islands and between the Sea Islands and Africa, she also adds another cultural bridge that connects the African diaspora of North America with that of the Caribbean. Using the Sea Islands as the link between them, Marshall emphasizes the common ancestry of reconstructed African communities in America and the Caribbean, rather than focusing on any specific cultural differences between these communities. The African diaspora becomes rejoined in this novel through the modes of storytelling, dance, and song, which are the only remembrances of Africa. Avey realizes this at the Beg Pardon:

> It was the *essence* of something rather than the thing itself she was witnessing. . . . All that was left were a few names of what they called nations which they could no longer even pronounce properly, the fragments of a dozen or so songs, the shadowy forms of long-ago dances and rum kegs for drums. . . . And they clung to them with a tenacity she suddenly loved in them and longed for in herself. *Thoughts—new thoughts—vague and half-formed slowly beginning to fill the emptiness.* (240, italics mine)

The thoughts that are beginning to fill the emptiness are the stories of Avey's childhood and the half-forgotten mythic memories of Africa and of a long-ago spiritual and cultural wholeness. What is left is the "essence" of these memories. Avey realizes this when listening to the drum:

> The theme of separation and loss the note [of the drum] embodied, the unacknowledged longing it conveyed summed up feelings that

were beyond words, feelings and a host of subliminal memories
that over the years had proven more durable and trustworthy than
the history with its trauma and pain out of which they had come.
. . . The note was a lamentation that could hardly have come
from the rum keg of a drum. Its source had to be the heart, the
bruised still-bleeding innermost chamber of the collective heart.
(244–245)

On Carriacou, the drum, combined with the music and dance, is the
mythic memory of Africa and of the loss of wholeness. The function of
storytelling therefore gains a slightly different function in *Praisesong* than
in the previously discussed works. In *Praisesong*, storytelling puts words
to the mythic memories expressed through music and dance. Ultimately,
Aunt Cuney's recollection of the Ibos tells the same story as the drum-
beat, and they both come from the innermost chamber of the collective,
mythic memories of the heart. Storytelling, song, and dance thus function as historical records by defining and keeping alive the essence of the
past. In other words, they connect the African diaspora to history, tradition, self, and community. After Avey—or Avatara—fully realizes this
during the Beg Pardon, she consequently reconfirms her maternal ancestor Avatara's spiritual connection to Africa when she vows to pass on her
story: "Her body she always usta say might be in Tatem but her mind, her
mind was long gone with the Ibos" (254–255).

Mae Henderson's statement that African American women writers
have encoded oppression as a discursive dilemma in their writing is an
apt characterization of Dash's, Naylor's, and Marshall's use of Sea Islands culture in their works. These artists have directly confronted what
Henderson terms the dilemma of the African American woman's relationship to power and discourse precisely through their representations
of the Sea Islands heritage. As a trope, the Sea Islands function at least at
two levels. First, the Sea Islands geographically and culturally are located
"in the middle" between Africa and America and therefore occupy a cultural and psychological space that helps these artists liberate the discussion of power and discourse from overused, stereotypical settings, configurations, and representations. In the same way that Dash uses the image
of the women's indigo-stained hands as a new and unfamiliar symbol of
slavery, so these artists use the Sea Islands as a new and unfamiliar trope
for the syncretic nature of African American cultures and for the existence of mythic ties to Africa. Second, the Sea Islands historically represent some of the most seriously oppressive locations of plantation slavery.
At the same time, they also represent some of the strongest retention of
direct African cultural influences. This simultaneity allows for a multiplicity of likewise unfamiliar disruptions and subsequent revisions of

hegemonic systems, especially in terms of revisions of history and histo-riography, particularly through the modes of storytelling and mythic memory. Storytelling and mythic memory are not only means of revision; they also function as means of celebration. In other words, Dash, Naylor, and Marshall are not primarily engaged in a discourse about op-pression; they are engaged in a pursuit of the survival of body and spirit and the triumph of their people's cultural heritage against all odds. In a way, they confront the dilemma that Henderson asserts by replacing op-pression with celebration as their primary concern. This celebration is highlighted by the Sea Islands's gruesome historical past and, signifi-cantly, by an imaginary landscape where the Sea Islands are *both* Africa *and* America.

In *Mama Day*, Miranda says of the double-ring wedding quilt she is sewing for Cocoa that "'when it's done right you can't tell where one ring ends and the other begins. It's like they ain't been sewn at all, they grew up out of nowhere'" (138). Miranda is making the quilt out of rags of old clothing that her ancestors have worn. The quilt thus becomes a record of her family history. Dash, Naylor, and Marshall are likewise creating rings on a quilt of Sea Islands history and culture. They are creating their own contemporary, artistic tradition based on retelling the traditions of the old Sea Islands culture and history. They are thus simultaneously creating and upholding tradition and speaking to their readers/viewers in intimate, "testimonial" discourse. At the same time, their retelling of Sea Islands culture is also a process through which they write their own canonical sto-ries, thereby engaging in a "competitive" discourse of hegemony. Dash's, Naylor's, and Marshall's visions of the significance of the Sea Islands are remarkably similar. As a reader, I find it difficult to tell where one ring ends on their quilt and the others begin. I cannot think of a more appropriate metaphor for Dash's notion of the persistence of tradition.

Notes

1. See W.E.B. Du Bois, *The Suppression of the African Slave Trade to the United States of America 1638–1870* (New York: Social Science Press, 1954), p. 297. See also Juanita Jackson, Sabra Slaughter, and J. Herman Blake, "The Sea Islands as a Research Area" [1974], in Mary A. Twining and Keith E. Baird (eds.), *The African Presence in the Carolinas and Georgia: Sea Island Roots* (Trenton, NJ: Africa World Press, 1991), p. 156.

2. Julie Dash, *Daughters of the Dust: The Making of an African American Woman's Film* (New York: New Press, 1992), p. 6. References to this book will be cited as *Making*. The screenplay for *Daughters of the Dust* is printed in *Making* but has its own pagination. References to the screenplay will use this pagination and will be cited as "Screenplay." References to the feature film it-self will be cited as *Daughters of the Dust*.

3. In Cheryl A. Wall (ed.), *Changing Our Own Words: Essays on Criticism, Theory, and Writing by Black Women* (New Brunswick, NJ: Rutgers University Press, 1989), pp. 16–37.

4. The phrase derive from bell hooks. See "Dialogue between bell hooks and Julie Dash, April 26, 1992," in *Making*, p. 30.

5. See Allan D. Austin, *African Muslims in Antebellum America: A Sourcebook* (New York: Garland Publishing, 1984), p. 268. Harold Courlander claims that Bilali came from the Sudan, so there are conflicting accounts of his land of origin. See Courlander's *A Treasury of Afro-American Folklore* (New York: Crown Publishers, 1976), pp. 289–290.

6. See Paul Sanford Salter, "Changing Agricultural Patterns on the South Carolina Sea Islands" [1968], in Twining and Baird, *Sea Island Roots*, p. 20, and Guion Griffis Johnson, "The Staple Crops," Chap. 2 in *A Social History of the Sea Islands, with Special Reference to St. Helena Island, South Carolina,* (Chapel Hill, NC: 1930).

7. Trinh Minh-ha, *Woman, Native, Other: Writing Postcoloniality and Feminism* (Bloomington: Indiana University Press, 1989), p. 148.

8. Hortense J. Spillers, "Mama's Baby, Papa's Maybe: An American Grammar Book," *Diacritics* (Summer 1987), p. 75.

9. Gloria Naylor, *Mama Day* [c. 1988] (London: Vintage, 1990). All references will be to this edition.

10. As an example, see Patricia Jones-Jackson, *When Roots Die: Endangered Traditions on the Sea Islands* (Athens: University of Georgia Press, 1987), pp. ix–xvii and 165–168.

11. Jackson, Slaughter, and Blake speak of "special Christmas festivals" that, in some areas, have survived since slavery. They do not offer any details or references, though. See Jackson et al., "The Sea Islands as a Research Area," in Twining and Baird (eds.), *Sea Islands Roots*, p. 157.

12. As an example, see the Georgia Coastal Writers' Project, Savannah Unit, *Drums and Shadows: Survival Studies among the Georgia Coastal Negroes* (Athens: University of Georgia Press, 1940), Appendixes 56, 58 and pp. 236–237.

13. Paule Marshall, *Praisesong for the Widow* [c. 1983] (London: Virago, 1989). All references will be to this edition.

14. Avatara means "the incarnation of a deity" and somebody who "crosses over." See *Merriam Webster's Collegiate Dictionary*, 10th edition (Springfield, Ma: Merriam-Webster, 1993).

15. See Abena P. A. Busia, "What Is Your Nation?: Reconnecting Africa and Her Diaspora through Paule Marshall's *Praisesong for the Widow*," in Cheryl A. Wall (ed.), *Changing Our Own Words*, pp. 206–207.

13

The African American Concept of the Fantastic as Middle Passage

Hélène Christol

The fantastic allows multiple cultural and literary intersections. With its multilayered functions and strategies, the African American fantastic text can be analyzed as the perfect illustration of what Gates defined in "Critics in the Jungle" as a multiterritorial text-milieu, occupying a "rhetorical space in at least two [and often more] canons.[1] If, in addition, we consider Todorov's now classical study of the fantastic and/or more recent transcultural and ethnological studies, we realize that the fantastic could be a crucial literary mode that reveals forgotten Middle Passages between Africa and America, mimesis and figuration, possibility and impossibility.

The particular status of the fantastic in African American literature was of course determined in part by the particular position of African Americans in American history as a colonized people of former slaves, whose familiar culture was devalued, even at times suppressed, by the white colonizer and thus "made strange" in their own eyes. Their original culture's modes of belief and expression, termed "primitive," were thus ascribed to some kind of subculture unworthy of attention.

Yet dismissing the fantastic as "primitive," a term that usually reflects Western white devaluation of older different rituals and beliefs, and as a secondary literary subgenre ignores its importance in contemporary literature. Modernist and postmodernist interest in "a zone of hesitation, a frontier between this world and the world next door,"[2] in the irruption of the absurd and the emergence of surrealist struggles "to destroy the barriers between the rational and the irrational in literature,"[3] marks the emergence of the fantastic as a dominant mode in recent literatures, developing dialogical, interrogative, and unfinished styles of discourse as well as a strong political, social, and ethical thrust.[4] African American texts are part of this transcultural movement, which affects European as well as African, Asian, or South American authors.

Founding my discussion of the African American fantastic on Morrison's novel *Beloved*, I will first analyze the fantastic as a favorite locus for intertextuality, an interplay with other Western texts, which was after all the basis of African American strategies of survival in a white-dominant society. Figuration, "signifying," was implicit and explicit in ritual rhetorical structures in which words had multiple meanings. *Beloved* reads as a conventional fantastic novel in which forms, situations, themes, and figures belong to the romantic and more contemporary fantastic of Todorov, Caillois, Castex, or Genette. Yet behind the surface text hides another text, signifying resistance, rediscovering what Morrison called a "black cosmology," in which the black person's absence, as a figure of negation, is brought back to life, a black revenant, which is the figure of re-memory and subversion. Such black cosmology rests on an African text, the echo of African cultures and rituals in which the fantastic recreates a lost order, works as a tool that enables author, characters, and readers to seek and find the primitive entity that might heal the community and restore life and self to the individual.

Western Modes and Patterns

Morrison, who studied Faulkner and has taught European and American literature, has enlisted the tradition of the fantastic in the text of *Beloved*. Various external trappings listed by Todorov or Caillois as typical of that mode can be identified in the plot and themes of the novel. For instance, Caillois's study, which uses as references the novels and short stories of Western writers of the nineteenth and twentieth centuries, defines as typically fantastic themes such as "pact with the devil," "harried souls in search of peace, asking for specific actions," "ghosts condemned to endless travels," "personified forms of death walking among the living," "vampires," "curses provoking the death of animals and of persons," "spectral women seducing and killing men," "inversions of dream and reality," "rooms or houses in bizarre locations," and "repetition of time sequences."[5] Morrison has obviously picked out most of these "images" and introduced in *Beloved* the paradigmatic elements of a good fantastic story:

an old isolated house, haunted by a restless spirit who impersonates a person killed violently in the past; 124 functions as a secluded place in which supernatural events constantly happen: turned down slop jars, smacks on the bottom, red lights. The first pages of the novel also introduce a baby ghost, followed later by the enigmatic resurrection of Beloved's ghost, the supposed impersonation of Sethe's murdered daughter.

Another key element of the conventional fantastic story is the presence of a hysterical girl who can conjure up the spirits.[6] Several characters in *Beloved* can play that role: Denver, a young adolescent girl, on the verge of breakdown when the book opens; Sethe, who cannot forget her act of pride and freedom and might have called the ghost to deal with her past act. The novel hypothesizes that Beloved might not exist at all, hallucinated into being by Sethe, Denver, or Paul D. She constantly changes forms, and no one agrees on her physical description, neither Stamp Paid, the women who first saw her "and then they didn't" (267), nor the little boy who saw a woman in a tree with fish in her hair. Such individual and collective hallucination characterizes the Gothic tradition, which represented the dark areas of the psyche in similar ways and explored the unconscious of the characters, their fears and desires. Psychoanalytical readings of *Beloved* show how to read the fantastic element in the novel in such terms, which would be consistent with Todorov's conclusion that the fantastic disappeared with the emergence of psychoanalysis.[7] The emergence of the ghost substitutes for the inadmissible answer to the questions of Sethe and Denver, the surfacing of their unconscious. The indefinability of Beloved's identity—real girl, imagined ghost, or real revenant—helps create uncanny effects akin to the fantastic. In a continual state of transition or metamorphosis, Beloved acts as a supernatural force, a "semiotic haint."

Finally, the accumulation of rhetorical figures such as comparisons and metaphors, the modalization terms, and the constant use of internal focalization in the text point to Morrison's perfect understanding of the particular idiom of the fantastic, as developed by classical Western authors of the nineteenth and twentieth centuries.

The fantastic, however, is not only a matter of themes, figures, or supernatural creatures. More basically, it reflects a fracture or a scandal that affects a system imprisoned in absolute rule. "The fantastic indicates a rupture in recognized order, the irruption of the inadmissible in the midst of the unalterable everyday legality,"[8] like a crack in the spatial time continuum that serves as a framework to ordinary experience. In an analysis of the theory of "catastrophes," which might be pertinent to a study of the very nature of the fantastic, René Thom developed a theory of the dynamics of forms, calling catastrophe "that brutal leap which allows a system to survive whereas it ought normally to have died."[9] Catastrophes are maneuvers of survival for a system—mathematical, cultural, social, or literary—when it must abandon its normal characteristics to escape destruction. Such leaps are reflected in the disconnected structure of the early parts of *Beloved* in which ruptures, blanks, ellipses, transform the text into a puzzle, a "crazy quilt" characterized by repetitions, a circling narrative that stops but picks up speed again without any authoritative voice to organize its chronology and its space. Such multiple temporal frames with back-and-forth movements that blur the normal linearity and hierarchy of time sequences allow the fantastic to slide into a world in which order and the norm have been disturbed. In fact, three essential sources of disorder are explored as the narration develops: the Middle Passage is the first and essential catastrophe, provoking loss of space, culture, language, the uprooting from familiar faces and lands, and the irruption of new demons, "the men without skins," as the whites are termed. Then slavery develops, a colonizing experience, meaning loss of self and loss of humanity. Finally, amnesia symbolizes the ultimate loss, that of the past and of language, the loss of the code without which normality cannot be restored. The African American experience as a series of catastrophes, in the Thom meaning of the term, is indeed privileged ground for the development of the fantastic: it seems to be the very condition of the survival of the text itself, the only mode capable of dealing with such discontinuities and ruptures.

Obviously the sophisticated narration, the play on the reader's doubts as to Beloved's identity, the presence of the uncanny in the Freudian sense of the term, the theme of the double, even the staging of fearful effects, place *Beloved* in the classical tradition of the fantastic in literature. Morrison thus demonstrates how useful such appropriation of literary fantastic elements from the Western tradition can be for the African American contemporary text. Yet the text "signifies" more immediately. *Beloved* can indeed be analyzed as a "ghost story," but its haunted space is defined in the very first pages of the novel as haunted by "Negro grief" (5).

A House Haunted by Negro Grief

Bringing to life a black revenant is a way of underlining the absence, of the unnamed crowds of slaves who died in the Middle Passage or in slavery, sixty million and more. The black slave, who was a figure of negation, is resurrected, claiming his or her name, signifying protest and resistance, asking to be remembered and vindicated. In many interviews,

Morrison contended that she wanted to use black folklore, superstition, and magic as an act of affirmation of black specificity and history. Consequently, her novels, and more specifically *Beloved*, challenged the mimetic realistic Western vision of reality by looking at the world differently, introducing magic as another way of knowing things that combined "the very practical, shrewd, day to day functioning that black people must do, while at the same time they encompass some great supernatural element."[10] There she found the vast imagination of black people, that black cosmology she wanted her books to reflect.

In doing so, she questioned and transcended Western conceptions of time and reality, presenting the question in both literary and political terms—literary, as she questioned realism and the Western expectation of a mimetic realistic literature; but also political, as her vision of reality struck at the very heart of Western civilization, questioning a post-Enlightenment reason that objectified the other and unnamed millions of black people. In a conversations with critics, Morrison said that "what distinguishes the colonized from the colonist was viewing what is rational and what is not,"[11] thus opening the debate over the legitimacy of the irrational/rational norm. If the fantastic is a deliberate departure from the real and normal, the question becomes what are the limits of that norm, which depends on cultural and social definitions based on race, place, class, gender, and history.[12] By highlighting the instability, inconsistency, or underlying preposterousness of the normal, the fantastic permits an exploration of the potential that history fails to achieve. As Fuentes once wrote,"Art gives life to what history killed. Art gives voice to what history denied, silenced or persecuted. Art brings truth to the lies of history."[13] In *Beloved*, the fantastic becomes the art of subversion, calling the voices of the ancestors, calling the ghosts who are finally exorcized when Sethe directs her violence no longer at her children but at the white man with the whip. The fantastic allows the author to recreate the mental dislocation of the inner world of the slaves, opposing another vision of nature, humanity, and the world to the pseudo-scientific, rationalistic view of Schoolteacher and his nephews. Defying white hegemony over history and over the text, the fantastic assumes a transgressive manifesting function by taking the text away from the white law, by rediscovering a code that will no longer destroy but create.

Indeed Morrison still works within the limits of the fantastic tradition, for, to quote Todorov again, "the function of the supernatural is certainly to take the text away from the action of the law and to transgress it."[14] Yet she goes further than simply recognizing the act of transgression. She ultimately asserts that what is described by critics as supernatural or fantastic is just "the way the world was for [her] and for the black [she] knew."[15] Refusing to identify with "magic realism," as evidenced in her interview with Christina Davis,[16] she remarked that her shrewd, efficient people nonetheless had "this other knowledge of perception, always discredited but nonetheless there, which informed their sensibilities and clarified their activities. . . . It seemed impossible . . . to write about black people and eliminate that simply because it was 'unbelievable.' . . . That *is* reality."[17] Of course, the power of the writer has always been to name, to define reality. Morrison, however, not only linked this power to the art of writing but emphasized the conscious and sometimes unconscious resurgence in her writing of an old African text.

The Old African Text

By linking the resurrection of Beloved to Africa, as a child from the Middle Passage, and to the murdered daughter, coming from the dead, Morrison uses the fantastic as therapy that bridges the gap artificially created by white colonization between Africa and America, the living and the dead, the past and the present. Death and the Middle Passage, as Deborah Horvitz wrote, evoke the same language: "[T]hey are the same existence: both were experimented by the multiple identified Beloved."[18] The "other side," Africa, death, is never far away: bridges and rivers establish connections between the two worlds. Drawing from what Levine called "the sacred world of the slaves,"[19] and the network of belief and practices that emphasized the normality of spirits, signs, and omens, Morrison's *Weltanschauung* is very close to that described by Mbiti in his analysis of African religions and myths.[20] The concept of humanity as one with all matter, animate or inanimate, all spirits, visible or not, hints at another type of universe in which "trees can be outraged and hurt, and the presence or absence of birds meaningful."[21] As Levine wrote, "To an African, everything is real, very real, horribly real."[22] The supernatural is used to control the supernatural itself.

Such echoes of the cultures and rituals from Africa point to the attempt to tame the "strangeness," the deregulation of the universe, thus incurring a subtle interplay between continuities and discontinuities, ruptures and fusions, the ontological objective being the restoration of order preceded by its disruption. The final avatar of Beloved might very well be the African figure of Mami Water, as explored in the very interesting article by Osseynou B. Traoré, which focuses on the Mammy Watta and Middle Passage paradigms. Associated with the mermaid fish imagery, Mammy Watta, "alluring and extremely beautiful," highly sexual, a river creature, has the dual power to bless her lover with artistic gifts and to destroy him. "Even though Beloved is exorcized back into the water," concludes Traoré, "she symbolically frees Paul D. and Sethe from the destructive burdens of their slave pasts and carries them safely above the drowning waters onto the shores where they can live and love."[23]

The intervention of the fantastic thus frees the community and the characters. Connecting mythical and historical structures, the ghost makes life possible, restores the lost code and text, and becomes a necessary instrument in the healing of personal and collective wounds. The writer functions as a witch doctor, an ethnopsychiatrist exercizing "the influence that heals," the title of a recent book by Tobie Nathan, Professor of Clinical Psychology and Pathology at the University of Paris VIII and Director of the Devereux Center of Ethnopsychiatry. By inventing and feeding ghosts, Morrison traces the unsaid and the unseen of a culture and thus cures the trauma created by what has been silenced, repressed, or destroyed. Such technique, which provokes strong emotions such as fear, pain, or surprise, and entails the risk of death, leaving traces on the body, is based on the cultural specificity of the "village" examined. Tobie Nathan concludes about his mostly African migrant patients: "I was led paradoxically to feel that I obeyed the rules of deontology when I conjured up with my patients the dead, the spirits, or traditional rituals, rather than when I asked myself about their so-called unconscious desires."[24] One essential basis to his therapy is fear, as evidenced in his chapter entitled "An Apology of Fear," an essential element in the expected reactions of the reader to the fantastic, and a positive therapeutic concept for Nathan, since it allows an interactive etiology and provokes interactive healing processes that force the patients to reclaim their cultural and social environments.

In various parts of *Beloved*, flashes of memory brought back by the ghost allow Sethe and other characters to remember the religions practiced in Africa and carried over to America, as in the Clearing ceremony, stripped of the trappings of Western Christian conventions, or in the pictures of the antelope dance in which men and women "shifted shapes and became something other" (31). A revisited African subtext matches the function of the fantastic, its paradoxical twoness symbolizing fractures, yet essential to restore continuities both in the text, recomposed structurally at the end of the book, and in the epiphanies of the different characters. If illness and death are believed to stem from the acts of an agent, feeding that agent until it is satisfied makes it leave the haunted body that is then restored to health. Nathan's description of the various cases and their therapy strikingly echoes the strategies used by Morrison to bring her book to its denouement, and to a more pacified, if not totally appeased, vision of the world. Such a conception of the fantastic, which requires from the reader both an intellectual response and a "visceral, physical response,"[25] creates another Middle Passage, this time in reverse: from America to Africa, from oblivion to memory, from silence to language.

Interestingly enough, the fantastic has recently been used extensively by black female writers, who seem to find it the best mode to express conflicts and the resolution of conflicts. Gloria Naylor in *Linden Hills* started using the familiar stereotyped paraphernalia of Gothic fiction and the psychological substructure of Gothic monomania and Faustian psychotic visions. Affirming the Gothic's thesis that the world of form and substance is both illusory and real, she used it as a way of demonstrating the exploitation and reduction to silence of black women in American society. The haunted house of Luther Nedeed reminds one of 124: both signify a criticism of patriarchy and link the fantastic to a gendered conflict. *Mama Day* is also a multivocal text in which magic, memory, and fiction determine a space and a code ruled by the fantastic. The most recent novel, however, *Bailey's Café*, seems to use the fantastic in a slightly different way: no ghosts there, no conjure women, but the creation of a specific space, halfway between the finite and the infinite, with a door opening for those who find it, as in Hesse's *Steppenwolf*, and a void at the back. The café is situated nowhere and everywhere, a territory of the soul. *Bailey's Café* deals with the fantastic less in terms of opposition between reality and fiction, or the different ways of apprehending reality, than in terms of borders and limits, interrogating boundaries rather than questioning the identity of a culture. The exploration of that interface that hangs somewhere on the edge of the world might open onto a dark ontological void, threatening chaos and dissolution. Yet Naylor finally rejects such fascination for chaos, which "gives no answer and gets no answer."[26] The fantastic as transgression in her novel is an essential experiment in reality, the testing of which enables the writer to rewrite her own genesis and like God, to create her own world. The book affirms that when the concept of reality becomes so terrifying or horrific, as in the death of a child or the violence exercised against blacks or women, the only natural element is, in fact, the supernatural. *Bailey's Café* ends on the symbolic birth of a new Jesus, both black and Jew, from the Virgin Mariam, a Falasha girl who found her way from Ethiopia to the Café. The birth is described as a true miracle, the real miracle being certainly the way in which this birth invents less aggressive multicultural relations between blacks and Jews. Yet the void is still there in the drowning of Mariam. This void outback as a place of horror and death maintains a fantastic edge to the narrative, which uses the mode in a more subdued, less culturally demonstrative manner than the preceding texts.

In the same way, Paule Marshall's last novel, *Daughters*,[27] keeps the fantastic on the edges of the text, after *Praisesong for the Widow*, whose structure was woven in ritual, magic, and the resurrection of the old African Barbadian rites. *Daughters* tones down the fantastic effects by displacing most of the narration in the United States, though the space of the book alternates between the mainland and the island. The spirits and ghosts have been internalized by Ursa Beatriz and the constellation of women who finally communicate telepathically to become the instruments of the spiritual salvation of the island. The only aural presence of the other world is the sound "Keram," which might be the voice of the past, the eternal sound of waves breaking on the original beach of the Middle Passage, from which everything started and where everything ends.

The fantastic is thus a crucial element in challenging existing notions of reality, subverting the visions channeled by dominant cultures and provoking action to change both that vision and reality. Departing from consensus reality, the supernatural can signify the differences among culturally imposed ways of seeing; it can become a trope on reality. *Beloved, Mama Day,* or *Praisesong,* all invoke the supernatural as both a figurative and actual means to achieve reunion with the past, and a way of coming to terms with a collective and personal history that might lead to a different tomorrow, as Paul D. tells Sethe. In more recent novels, as in *Jazz,* or *Bailey's Café,* or *Daughters,* it seems, however, that the authors are less interested in the fantastic working as a text-milieu, a Middle Passage between Western, African American, and African traditions, than in the exploration of the fantastic as an art of limits, a play on boundaries. In *Bailey's Café,* the author leaves the reader free to prescribe action. The act of imagining, of becoming, is as much the responsibility of the reader as that of the author. Rushdie once wrote, "What's a ghost? Unfinished business is what."[28] The new African American texts invite us, as readers, to invent our own ghosts and to "finish business."

Notes

Quotations from *Beloved* are taken from Toni Morrison, *Beloved* (New York: Knopf, 1987).

1. Henry Louis Gates, Jr., *Black Literature and Literary Theory* (New York: Routledge, 1984), p. 6.

2. Neil Cornwell, *The Literary Fantastic: From Gothic to Postmodernism* (New York: Harvester Weatsheaf, 1990), p. 151.

3. Cornwell, p. 154.

4. See Cornwell, p. 211

5. René Caillois, *Images, Images* (Paris: Corti, 1966), pp. 36–39.

6. Tzvetan Todorov, *Introduction à la littérature fantastique* (Paris: Seuil, 1970), p. 155.

7. See the famous study of Sigmund Freud, *L'inquiétante étrangeté et autres essais* (Paris: Gallimard, 1985; 1st ed. 1919).

8. René Caillois, *Au Coeur du Fantastique* (Paris: Gallimard, 1965), p. 161.

9. Claude Fierobe, "Le'point catastrophe': l'éclairage de la théorie des catastrophes," in Max Duperray, ed., *Du fantastique en Litérature: Figures et Figurations* (Aix-en-Provence: Publications de l'Université de Provence, 1990), p. 36. See also René Thom. *Paraboles et Catastrophes. Entretiens sur les Mathématiques, la science et la philosophie* (Paris: Flammarion, 1984).

10. Nellie McKay, "An Interview With Toni Morrison," 1983, in Denille Taylor-Guthrie, ed., *Conversations with Toni Morrison* (Jackson: University Press of Mississippi, 1994), p. 153.

11. Bessie W. Jones and Audrey Vinson, "An Interview With Toni Morrison" [1985], in *Conversations*, p. 181.

12. See the very perceptive study of Rosemary Jackson and the even more challenging article of Anne Könen. Rosemary Jackson, *Fantasy: The Literature of Subversion* (London: Methuen "New Accents," 1981). Anne Könen. "Toni Morrison's Beloved and the Ghost of Slavery," in Geneviève Fabre and Claudine Raynaud, eds., *Beloved, She's Mine* (Paris: CETLNA, 1993), pp. 53–67.

13. Cornwell, p. 217

14. Todorov, p. 167.

15. Christina Davis, "An Interview With Toni Morrison" [1986], in *Conversations*, p. 226.

16. Davis, p. 225–226.

17. Davis, p. 226.

18. Deborah Horvitz, "Nameless Ghosts: Possession and Dispossession in *Beloved*," *Studies in American Fiction*, 17:2 (Autumn 1989): 162

19. Lawrence Levine, *Black Culture and Black Consciousness* (New York: Oxford University Press, 1977), p. 3

20. See John S. Mbiti, *African Religions and Philosophy* (New York: Frederick A. Praeger, 1969).

21. Levine, p. 58.

22. Levine, p. 59.

23. Ousseynou B. Traoré, "Mythic Structures of Ethnic Memory in *Beloved*: The Mammy Watta and Middle Passage Paradigms," in Geneviève Fabre and Claudine Raynaud, eds., *Beloved, She Is Mine* (Paris: CETLNA, 1993), p. 88.

24. Tobie Nathan, *L'influence qui guérit* (Paris: Odile Jacob, 1994), p. 332.

25. Bill Moyers, "A Conversation With Toni Morrison" [1989], in *Conversations*, p. 274.

26. Gloria Naylor, *Bailey's Café* (London: Heineman, 1992), p. 223.

27. Paule Marshall. *Daughters.* (New York: Atheneum, 1991).

28. Cornwell, p. 198.

Part III

. . . .

"In Africa,
There Are
No Niggers"

(Vernon Reid)

• • • •

We see things not as they are,
but as we are. Our perception is
shaped by our previous experiences.
                              Dennis Kimbro

Frederick Douglass spent a lifetime struggling for the right of African Americans to define themselves as Americans. He vigorously protested any white attempt to impose the ascription "African" on blacks residing within the territory of the United States because he realized that this white naming spelled the perpetuation of blacks' exclusion as the eternal "other" from American history, culture, and society. Yet when the elder statesman Frederick Douglass first encountered Africa on an excursion to Egypt in his sixty-fifth year, he was almost overwhelmed by a sense of recognition. On African soil he discovered and embraced his twoness—his Africanness and his Americanness, the tragedy of being both and neither. It was an experience shared by thousands of African Americans who returned to their Old World: Maya Angelou, Langston Hughes, Claude McKay, Richard Wright, Alice Walker, to name only a few.

As Charles Johnson's African rebel protagonists in *Middle Passage* acknowledged after they overthrew their white captivators, Africa and Africans would never be the same after black communities had been raided by fellow African, Arabian, or European slave catchers. Africa was transformed as her children were dragged in chains across the continent and dumped into the depth of slave ships. For the victims of the trade, a return to their old identities was impossible. Africa was lost for those who crossed over into the unknown. Yet Africa remained with them in the New World: as reality and myth, as dream and nightmare, as image and memory, as potential home and exotic tourist stop. It was and is central to the multifaceted "I am" that the black survivors of the transatlantic passage, their children, and children's children created out of whatever fragments of self and memory they had defended against the onslaught of the chattel definition. The nine essays that form the final section of our volume, ask about the meaning of Africa for modern blacks.

In contemporary African American fiction, the Middle Passage has come to be treated as a boundary permeable in one direction only, as Fritz Gysin insists in "The Enigma of the Return." These fictional journeys back to the source either stop short of reaching the tautological center of origins (i.e., Ellison's "Blackness of Blackness"), or turn out to be so confusing as to call the whole enterprise into question. Consequently the expected transformation, catharsis, or healing process remains highly elusive. Attempts to represent a return to Africa in artistically convincing postmodern novels frequently undercut the concept altogether: Milkman Dead, in Toni Morrison's *Song of Solomon*, imitating a highly questionable act of one of his male ancestors, learns how to fly but does not even think about returning to Africa; Rutherford Calhoun, in Charles Johnson's *Middle Passage*, realizes his African hybridity when he confronts the Allmuseri god while drifting back to America; and Mason Ellis, in Clarence Major's *My Amputations*, at the end of his long trip home experiences an Africa that functions as a superior trickster calling his bluff. The imaginative passage to the past seems blocked by the reality of the present—African and African American alike. Gysin suggests that the inversion of the Middle Passage paradoxically inscribes its centrality; if anything is essentialized, it is the condition of the in-between, the condition of the boundary.

The American Colonization Society, founded in Washington in late 1816 by an alliance of politicians and evangelical ministers, proposed to sponsor free blacks willing to emigrate to a colony on the west coast of Africa. That colony became Liberia. Although later denounced by Northern abolitionists and viewed with suspicion by many African Americans, it early attracted some of the most ambitious African Americans and represented a form of black nationalism available to those who were willing to make the sea voyage. In "The Hues and Uses of Liberia," Marie Tyler-McGraw focuses on the origins and nature of Liberian nationalism by studying the lives of antebellum Virginia emigrants and their emancipators and supporters. The existence of Liberia was used to argue for African American ability, freedom, and citizenship in the United States as well as Liberia. The proclaimed success of African colonization reified the American origins myth, just in the process of elaboration in the 1820s and 1830s, but hindered the ability of Liberian colonists to make connections with the indigenous Africans. The early dominance of Virginia colonizationists and their deep investment in American political culture and evangelical religion helped to create and sustain an African version of the Upper South's early republic.

Pauline Hopkins is one of the recent rediscoveries of a tradition of African American women writers before the Harlem Renaissance. Her novel *Contending Forces* (1900), her three serial novels—*Hagar's Daughters* (1901–1902), *Winona* (1902), and *Of One Blood* (1902–1903)—as well as her short fiction have recently been republished in the Schomburg edition and have gained some critical acclaim. Hopkins's texts not only cover a large number of contemporary issues, such as racial politics, phrenology, occultism, and feminism but also turn toward Africa. When Reuel Briggs, the protagonist *Of One Blood*, discovers that "in the heart of Africa was a knowledge of science that all the wealth and learning of modern times could not emulate," a reader familiar with twentieth-century multicultural knowledge may hear a truism, but it surely stirred the interest of the late-nineteenth-century reader, who had been trained to consider Africa as uncivilized and savage. It also spoke of a racial pride that the average colored American was not then used to hearing. In "Voyage into the Heart of Africa: Pauline Hopkins and *Of One Blood*," Hanna Wallinger puts Hopkins's "In the Heart of Africa" into context and reads *Of One Blood* as a contribution to the concept of "Ethiopianism," in terms taken from the discussion of colonialist literature, and against the background of the dominant post-Reconstruction racial and scientific discourse. One of Wallinger's main arguments is that Hopkins fuses the Ethiopian and the romantically African. So while the novel offers a very positive rewriting of African American history, while it leads to a profound rewriting of the science of racial origins and even offers a revision of accepted biblical readings, it yet is still not immune from contemporary stereotypes. In its ambiguous message, this novel is an early fictional rendering of the continuous search of the African American writer for his or her African origins.

Katja Füllberg-Stolberg's "African Americans in Africa: Black Missionaries and the 'Congo Atrocities,' 1890–1910" focuses on one of the most brutal events in Africa's colonial history, discussing especially the role African Americans played in the discovery of these crimes against people in Central Africa. In the late nineteenth century, the "Congo Free State" was under direct control of Leopold II, who regarded the territory as his personal property. Leopold's rule turned into a nightmare for the indigenous population when they were forcefully recruited by the colonial authorities to collect and transport rubber, the region's most important cash crop. William Henry Sheppard, a black American missionary of the American Presbyterian Congo Mission, was among the first to speak out against the severe punishment of the African people who tried to resist their recruitment as forced laborers. Sheppard's reports on the social and economic conditions in the Congo became the basic material for the mission's agitation for reforms in Leopold's colonial empire. Füllberg-Stolberg shows that the events in the Congo marked a turning point in the African Americans' attitude toward Africa. A critical debate about European colonialism and imperialism began that not only brought the suppression of the African people to the public eye but also intensified the confrontation with white racist attitudes and "Jim Crow" law practices in the United States.

In her essay "Sexual Violence and the Black Atlantic: On Alice Walker's *Possessing the Secret of Joy*," Giulia M. Fabi contextualizes Alice Walker's outspoken participation in the international movement to abolish female genital mutilation within her long-standing and often controversial literary battle against sexual violence. Walker's works, including "The Child Who Favoured Daughter," a story that deals with female mutilation in the United States, consistently represent "contrary women" who fight back. In *Possessing the Secret of Joy* (1992), however, the female protagonist, Tashi, seems completely trapped by her (absent) flesh. This condition may heighten the effectiveness of Walker's indictment of genital mutilation, but at the same time it weakens her portrayal of Tashi's agency and attempts at resistance. The sharp contrast between Walker's victimized fictional protagonist, whose eventual death emerges as a veritable suicide, and the author's own call for social change in her nonfictional note of "Thanks" creates representational tensions that we, as readers, have to decodify to appreciate the complexity of a book like *Possessing the Secret of Joy*, whose potential weakness, Fabi suggests, may paradoxically reside in the very breadth and effectiveness of its appeal.

Like Fabi, Tobe Levin, in "Alice Walker, Activist: Matron of FORWARD," perceives Alice Walker's heroines as exemplifying the issue of passages through both space and time. In the early 1980s, *The Color Purple* mentioned obliquely "a bit of bloody cutting" around puberty as characteristic of the (composite) Olinka but skirted the complex issue of female genital mutilation in Africa and its exportation to Europe, America, and Australia. In a bold and controversial move, Walker has joined an international abolition movement called into existence in part by the African diaspora. With her narrative *Possessing the Secret of Joy* (1992), accompanied by the book and film, *Warrior Marks: Female Genital Mutilation and the Sexual Blinding of Women* (with Pratibha Parmar, 1993), Walker accepts the responsibility to close ranks with activists and artists on five continents. Her fifth novel flashes back to Africa where Tashi, in a patriotic gesture preceding her emigration to America, opts to undergo the operation Kenyatta claimed, in his first act of state, represented the sine qua non of tribal ethics. Walker dramatizes, through Tashi's physical and mental anguish, this misguided scapegoating of women by patriarchal nationalist ideology, justified in opposing colonial oppression but not in continued insistence on subordinating women. This essay looks at recent developments in the international movement against female genital mutilation, focusing on both Walker's critics and allies. Levin asks: Can a womanist aesthetics of caring win commitment to the struggle for women's human rights and assure the death of harmful traditional practices?

In "Passages to Identity: Re-Membering the Diaspora in Marshall, Phillips, and Cliff," Johanna X. K. Garvey looks at fictional works by Paule Marshall, Caryl Phillips, and Michelle Cliff that evoke the Middle Passage and the Atlantic slave trade, depicting a spectrum of experiences in the resulting African diaspora. Their texts underscore the necessity of memory, and what Toni Morrison has termed "re-memory," to the process of uncovering and voicing the history so long repressed and ignored by the monologic master narrative. The three authors under study are ideally situated to perform these acts of re-membering: Marshall, born in Brooklyn to immigrant parents, raised in a tightly knit Bajan community, making trips "home" to the West Indies; Phillips, born in St. Kitts, almost immediately relocated to Britain, educated there and in the United States, and now resident in a variety of cultural spaces; Cliff, a Jamaican of mixed heritage, light enough to "pass" but choosing to identify as black, transplanted to the United States and educated in Britain. To examine the African diaspora and the passages that created it may necessitate a fundamental experience of displacement, a questioning of the meaning of "home" and "family." Garvey discusses each text in turn, with particular attention to narrative strategies, to illustrate how contemporary writers have begun to grapple with the immensity of what one critic calls "one of the greatest thieveries-of-history"—and the concomitant difficulties of representing both the literal passages of the slave trade and the passage into new identities forced on millions. Thus, Marshall opts for a unity of site and time with a cast of characters drawn from both the West Indies and the United States, while Phillips sections his narrative into four related eras and locales, with interlocking characters. Cliff offers the most "free" fiction, one that crisscrosses between the Caribbean and the United States, makes gestures toward Africa, but most clearly resists any notion of a "homecoming" to that Motherland. Following Paul Gilroy, Garvey argues that these authors share a *diasporan* cultural identity, and the essay shows their mutual rejection of any myth of return. All three demonstrate that the Middle Passage, buried and pathless as it may seem in the Atlantic, must be remembered by all of us who are its "heirs and descendants"; perhaps in the retelling its pain may be brought to the surface and the nine million recognized.

The theme uniting *Segu* and *I, Tituba, Black Witch of Salem*, two novels of Maryse Condé, is pride, Robert H. McCormick, Jr., argues in "Return Passages: Maryse Condé Brings Tituba Back to Barbados." In the first case, the source is the precolonialist African Bambara civilization. In the second, it is the resurrection of a "nationless" black woman who, after being a scapegoat in Salem, returns "home" to Barbados. Maryse Condé is depicted as a writer whose own locus has shifted from Africa, site of the author's infelicitous sojourn in Guinea, to the United States and the Caribbean. In Condé's first commercial breakthrough, *Segu*, she represents the cultural clash between the proud, indigenous Bambara civilization and the Islamic civilization that eventually subdues it during the course of the nineteenth century. In spite of Condé's disclaimers that *I, Tituba, Black Witch of Salem* is not a feminist novel, McCormick sees Tituba as a protagonist resurrected from the abjection of her birth and her condition as a slave to the pride of a black woman in her benevolent witchery. Facilitated by frequent communion with her ancestors, Tituba's supernatural powers are used, even when she is a postmortal spirit, to help create and sustain the struggle of "her" people for independence. Conceived not in Africa but by rape on a slave ship in the no man's land of the Atlantic, and brought to Salem at the time of the Witch Trials, she returns, at the end of the novel, to Barbados where, even after being hanged for plotting a revolt with her lover, she helps to work for political independence.

Last but not least, Alessandro Portelli's "Mediterranean Passage: The Beginnings of African Italian Literature and the African American Example" demonstrates that recent immigration from Africa, Latin America, and Asia has resulted in the beginnings of a literature written in Italian by authors of foreign birth whose first language is not Italian. Under some respects, this writing retraces the steps of African American literature: the discovery of blackness and whiteness, the confrontation with "two-ness," the question of bilingualism, the experience of coauthorship with editors and amanuenses. The scene of writing is also often similar, including such spaces as prison, the street, the underground. On the other hand, the relationship with the culture, language, and community of origin is different from African American writing: there is a combination of a sense of exile and a horizon of return, which generates a different relationship between narratives of immersion and emersion. According to Portelli, these "narratives of disappointment" accompany the sense of exhilaration often inherent with travel, exploration, discovery, with the cold and narrowness of the actual European space available to the immigrants. The sense that emigration is intended to be a temporary experience, and that Italy is to a large extent a country of passage, also contributes to a diminished concern for the creation of a community of African-Italian readers.

14

· · · ·

The Enigma of the Return

Fritz Gysin

R ecent novelistic attempts to deal with a real or imaginative return to
Africa more often than not foreground the enigmatic quality of that
endeavor. Not only is the path of the return frequently frought with insurmountable obstacles but the ties of African American fictional characters
to their African origins are much more ambiguous, precarious, and tenuous than some advocates of Afrocentrism would like us to believe. The
problem of direction emerges as a major issue. In contemporary, and especially in postmodern African American fiction, most aesthetically successful "re-memories" are repetitions of the enforced process of emigration
from Africa to *America.* In more theoretical terms, in a majority of novels
we witness attempts to return on the level of discourse (*narration*), such as
an intention to go back to the roots, or on the level of text (*récit*), such as
the use of analepsis, while on the story (*histoire*) level, the spatial, and
sometimes even the temporal, direction is forward. When we witness an
actual return to the source on the levels of story or text, the attempt stops
short of reaching the tautological center of origins, Ellison's "Blackness of
Blackness,"[1] or, if that center is reached, the confusion there calls the
whole enterprise into question, and the expected transformation, catharsis, or healing process remains highly enigmatic.

In the postmodern African American fiction I have examined, the
topic of the return to Africa appears most frequently in connection either
with problematic escape, or with what I call the alterity of one's origins,

or with a specific liminal quality of the quest. The return in these cases is either impeded, or causes a confrontation with a distorted mirror image, or leads into a trap. Above all, in a curious imitation of the complex processes taking place during the Middle Passage from Africa to America, representations of the inversion of this Middle Passage, the return to Africa, frequently relate it with the phenomenon of death. I restrict my analysis to a brief outline of three enigmatic forms of return, representational paradigms of the return in much of African American postmodern fiction: the legendary flight, the "historical" voyage, and the "contemporary" professional visit.

Whereas the classical topic of the liberating flight found sporadic expression in black writing of the midcentury,[2] recent African American authors have been increasingly fascinated with the celebration, in black folk tales, of the "Flying Africans," slaves who take one long look at the new country, turn around, and fly back to Africa, or of selected shamanic slaves who teach other slaves the magic word that allows them to fly back. Since Toni Morrison made flight the central topic of her fourth novel, *Song of Solomon* (1977), the interest in it as an expression of escape or resistance has caught the attention of authors such as Paule Marshall (1983), Richard Perry (1984), and Gloria Naylor (1988).[3] Interestingly enough, Morrison's treatment of the myth is at the same time more complex and more differentiating than that of her followers; as Hovert and Lounsberry show in great detail, the reason may be her early fascination with the motif of flying and her extensive experimenting with it in her two earlier novels.[4] According to these critics, Morrison not only has a history of associating flight with death but she also provides in her novels an intricate classification of forms of flying, based on direction, intention, and motivation.[5] Especially in *Song of Solomon*, however, these different forms of flying combine and fuse in ways that obscure the clear distinctions proposed by such a classification, so that the success of the magic flight as the central determinant of the male monomyth is called into question.

Milkman's life begins with the suicidal crash of pseudo-Daedalus Robert Smith and ends with his own death leap into the arms of Guitar, his friend and enemy. Both incidents are presented in ambiguous terms; neither is directly related to black resistance.[6] Furthermore, the object of his quest, the legend of his flying great-great-grandfather, is full of paradoxes: the revealing song addressed to Sugarman/Solomon contains in its center his wife's wail *not* to leave her and her twenty-one children back in bondage, and there is a report of the mother going mad when Solomon does fly off, so that his children have to be brought up by neighbors. In addition, the slave's legendary flight to Africa involves a considerable degree of selfishness and indifference, quite the opposite of the communal spirit that Milkman allegedly found during his quest. Finally, Milkman's metaphorical transcendence emulates his illustrious ancestor only in his achievement of freedom by surrendering to the air; the return to Africa is no longer mentioned. In other words, the repetition of the return remains an imitation whose goal seems doubtful and leaves open the question whether the original legends, as some scholars have claimed, were not intended to cover up, or compensate for, cases of collective suicide anyway.[7] Thus, the intentionally paradoxical and open end of the novel not only reflects Morrison's ambivalent concern with the mythical male hero[8] but also manifests her highly complex treatment of the return to one's origins. The act remains one of magic and transcendence; it refuses to be measured in terms of ideological failure or empowerment. Above all, as the model of Pilate's form of flying suggests,[9] it remains rooted in American soil: "Now he knew why he loved her so. Without ever leaving the ground, she could fly."

Charles Johnson's *Middle Passage*, originally entitled "Rutherford's Travels," has become the best-known recent example of an account of the voyage back to Africa. In this "Journal of a Voyage intended / by God's permission / in the *Republic*, African / from New Orleans to the Windward / Coast of Africa," the name of the game is inversion. Rutherford Calhoun's escape from the threat of marriage to a pious black schoolteacher takes him to a decrepit old slave ship, a patched-up affair in considerably worse shape than Melville's *Pequod* and run by a character considerably more sinister than Ahab and Stevenson's Long John Silver put together. Participating in a predominantly white endeavor,[10] Calhoun does reach the west coast of Africa, but during his short stay at a Senegambian slave port he is advised to "lie low" to avoid being captured by African slave traders. As a result, his actual "setting foot" on African ground does not seem to leave any lasting impression. A much more significant encounter with the "essence" of Africa occurs on board the *Republic*, when he gets to know their cargo, thirty members of the fictional tribe of the Allmuseri and their god, who is carried along in a crate in the hold of the ship.

This confrontation proves extremely disconcerting to the protagonist as well as to the reader. The protagonist is confused by the paradoxical quality of the Allmuseri,[11] a mixed, ancient tribe, whose system of beliefs, however, embraces the unity of being, a multicultural people, who disapprove of division and singularity. As Ashraf Rushdy points out in great detail, "the phenomenology of the Allmuseri" combines a "plurality of meanings of intersubjectivity"[12] with a view of the Real as "a shared hallucination."[13] Moreover, their pacifist and universalist world view strongly contradicts their revolutionary tendencies and the Black Nationalist behavior of their leader.[14] The readers are confused because on the discourse level this transcendental tribe not only incorporates the Heraclitean concept of flux and process[15] but its philosophy is so anachronistically a combination of Edmund Husserl's phenomenology and poststructuralist theories of writing[16] that the "Africa" represented by this tribe seems to be miles apart from the concepts of racial purity underlying Afro-American nationalist and Afrocentric concerns. Needless to say, this contradictory state of affairs receives a further twist in Calhoun's confrontation with the protean Allmuseri god, who appears to him in the shape of his father, but whose cultural hybridity, as represented by the living tattoos on his body,[17] mirrors, and competes with, present conditions in the United States. Thus, it seems that even at the utmost point of spiritual return to the essence of Africa, the protagonist confronts an extreme form of interracial and intercultural blending as well as a distorted mirror image. No wonder he begins to doubt his identity as "a marginalized American colored man."[18]

Significantly, this essential confrontation in the hold takes place while the *Republic* is drifting "back" to the West Indies in spite of the efforts by the mutinous blacks to steer it "back" to *their* home. As a result of this zigzagging of the ship (and of the contradictory definitions of "home"), the concept of "return" becomes highly ambiguous. Furthermore, Rutherford's gratuitous salvation from a ship conveniently sinking, with the dangerous part of the mutinous blacks conveniently drowning, fits in with the postmodern parodistic form of the novel, but it also connects his liminal experience with the concept of the Middle Passage in a way that makes any lasting return to Africa impossible and irrelevant, while still emphasizing the significance of handing down the enigmatic wisdom of the Allmuseri to the surviving generations of African Americans.

My third example refers to a protagonist's actual return to Africa, although the real Africa depicted here is just as much an Africa of the mind. Clarence Major's *My Amputations*[19] tells the adventures of Irish-African-American author Mason Ellis, who may or may not be an impostor, a petty crook impersonating a famous black writer. He seems to have received a generous fellowship from the "Magnan-Rockford Foundation"[20] and spends his time giving lectures all over the United States and Europe and running away from his double, who is trying to kill him, and from members of various secret organizations, who are either after his money or attempting to manipulate him.

In the last part of the novel, the protagonist, deliberating whether after his eventful journey across Europe he should accept the offer of an

African lecture tour, comes to a decision by oddly imitating Huckleberry Finn's famous moral choice. "'All right, then, I'll go to hell,'" says Huck, tearing up his denunciation of Jim.[21] And of Mason Ellis's reaction to his invitation, we read: "So, what the hell, he'd go to Africa!" And the old dream of flying returns: "He'd be a gray-eyed crow in Africa: He'd keep his wings clean and he'd fly!"[22] But a strange kind of hell it turns out to be.

For his professional trip to Africa, Mason is given a sealed envelope addressed to Chief Q. Tee in Monrovia and warned not to let anybody know about the contents. Again, Africa proves to be anything else but the welcoming mother country. Ghana is disappointing and dangerous; he meets quite a number of important people but has difficulties communicating, not least because of the continual interruption by acts of open violence in the streets. Moreover, his audience is unaware of the black American authors he mentions. The inversion of his implied quest is accompanied by frequent cynical greetings ("Welcome home, Brother"[23]). During a stopover at Abidjan, he is arrested as an "enemy to Ivory Coast" and made the butt of a few nightmarish police jokes, such as being locked into a coffin and having to submit to a game of fake Russian roulette.[24]

"Liberia was hope" we read, but at the same time we learn that "although he was in dirty, poor Monrovia . . . the enemies had surely closed in."[25] Mason begins to receive mysterious messages, is visited by a devilish figure on stilts, and is thus prepared for his summons to appear, his face hidden by a mask, in the village of Tabli-Gablah in Bomi Territory, whose inhabitants, according to the taxi driver, have a pact with the devil. The message in the letter, Mason finally learns from Chief Q. Tee, reads: "*Keep* this nigger!"[26] An elliptic version of the well-known letters in Ellison's *Invisible Man*,[27] this order turns Mason's African experience into a blind alley.[28] The old man tells him: "'One can carry the disease one covers oneself against on the fingers one uses to secure the cover. You, my son, have come to the end of your running.'" If we consider that Mason has been trapped in Liberia, the one African nation founded by returning American slaves, the last sentence of the novel assumes additional ironic significance: "The hut smelled of, of, cow rocks, turtle piss and smoke."[29]

To conclude, in contemporary African American fiction the Middle Passage has come to be treated as a boundary permeable only in one direction.[30] Attempts to represent a return to Africa in artistically convincing postmodern novels frequently tend to undercut the concept of the return altogether. The reasons for this may have to do with a postmodern understanding or subconscious awareness of African American cultural difficulties in coming to terms with the almost chaotic multicultural complexity of postcolonial Africa and a concomitant critical, or even satirical, artistic reaction to this state of affairs, which then focuses on the American black protagonists' inability to connect with such enigmatic representations of their origins. Thus, instead of celebrating the return, postmodern African American fiction creatively engages the boundary: Milkman Dead learns how to fly but does not even think about moving to Africa; Rutherford Calhoun confronts his hybridity as an African trait while drifting "back" to America; and Mason Ellis experiences an Africa that calls his bluff. The imaginative passage to the past seems blocked by the reality of the present—African and African American alike. Therefore, I think that the inversion of the Middle Passage paradoxically inscribes its centrality. If anything is essentialized, it is the condition of the in-between, the condition of the boundary.

Notes

1. Ralph Ellison, *Invisible Man* (New York: Random House, 1952), p. 7

2. E.g., Richard Wright, *Native Son* (New York: Harper, 1940), pp. 14–15; Ralph Ellison, "That I Had the Wings," *Common Ground*, 3 (Summer 1943): 30–37, repr. as "Mr. Toussaint," in *Negro Story* (Oct.–Nov. 1944): 3–11; "Flying Home," in Edwin Seaver, ed., *Cross Section* (New York: L. B. Fischer, 1944), pp. 469–485.

3. Toni Morrison, *Song of Solomon* (New York: Knopf, 1977); Paule Marshall, *Praisesong for the Widow* (New York: Putnam, 1983); Richard Perry, *Montgomery's Children* (New York: Harcourt Brace Jovanovich, 1984); Gloria Naylor, *Mama Day* (New York: Ticknor & Fields, 1988).

4. Grace Ann Hovet and Barbara Lounsberry, "Flying as Symbol and Legend in Toni Morrison's *The Bluest Eye, Sula,* and *Song of Solomon,*" *CLA Journal*, 27.2 (December 1983): 119–140. Cf. also Philip M. Royster, "Milkman's Flying: The Scapegoat Transcended in Toni Morrison's *Song of Solomon,*" *CLA Journal*, 24.4 (June 1982): 419–440.

5. Hovet and Lounsberry, 121–135.

6. In fact, Robert Smith's death leap is an act of despair, carried out *against* a task of black resistance. A different reading may be found in Gay Wilentz, "If You Surrender to the Air: Folk Legends of Flight and Resistance in African American Literature," *Melus*, 16.1 (Spring 1989): 21–32. Cf. also her later version, "Civilizations Underneath: African Heritage as Cultural Discourse in Toni Morrison's *Song of Solomon,*" *African American Review*, 26.1 (Spring 1992): 61–76.

7. To my knowledge, Morrison's modification of the popular legend was first pointed out by Hovet and Lounsberry (p. 134), although they do not stress the implication this has on the treatment of the topical return to Africa. Wilentz follows suit but reads this as a gender-specific version, contrasting Solomon's dropping of his son with a folk tale in which a woman escaping to Africa carries her child along (p. 31). Neither of the articles pays attention to the fact that by "riding the air" Milkman remains above American soil.

8. On Morrison's ambivalence regarding the male monomyth, see Mi-

chael Awkward, "'Unruly and Let Loose': Myth, Ideology, and Gender in *Song of Solomon,*" *Callaloo,* 13.3 (Summer 1990): 482–498; Kimberly W. Benston, "Re-Weaving the 'Ulysses Scene': Enchantment, Post-Oedipal Identity, and the Buried Text of Blackness in Toni Morrison's *Song of Solomon,*" in Hortense J. Spillers, ed., *Comparative American Identities: Race, Sex, and Nationality in the Modern Text* (New York: Routledge, 1991), pp. 87–109; Cynthia Davis, "Self, Society, and Myth in Toni Morrison's Fiction," *Contemporary Literature,* 23 (1982): 323–342.

9. Morrison, *Song of Solomon,* p. 336.

10. "[F]or much of the voyage Calhoun is a black man playing a white man's colonial game." S. X. Goudie, "'Leavin' a Mark on the Wor(l)d': Marksmen and Marked Men in *Middle Passage,*" *African American Review,* 29.1 (Spring 1995): 112.

11. The name is fictional; it may suggest "all misery," Cf. Fritz Gysin, "Predicaments of Skin: Boundaries in Recent African American Fiction," in Werner Sollors and Maria Diedrich, eds., *The Black Columbiad: Defining Moments in African American Literature and Culture* (Cambridge, MA: Harvard University Press, 1994), p. 291. It may also, as S. X. Goudie has proposed, be in part an anagram: "All-museri/*erimus,* meaning 'We shall be All'" (p. 119, note 8).

12. Ashraf Rushdy, "The Phenomenology of the Allmuseri: Charles Johnson and the Subject of the Narrative of Slavery," *African American Review,* 26.3 (Fall 1992): 376.

13. The term is from Charles Johnson's earlier novel, *Oxherding Tale* (Bloomington: Indiana University Press, 1982), p. 49. Cf. Rushdy, p. 391.

14. Goudie's suggestion that it is "ripped asunder" by enslavement (114) does not quite convince me; it happens too fast, and Goudie himself has to admit that Calhoun may have misread the Allmuseri.

15. Johnson, *Middle Passage* (New York: Atheneum, 1990), p. 124. Cf. Rushdy, 377.

16. Rushdy, pp. 376, 377.

17. For an earlier version of this phenomenon in Johnson's writing, see Gysin, pp. 288–291.

18. Johnson, p. 169.

19. Clarence Major, *My Amputations* (New York: Fiction Collective, 1986).

20. Major, p. 22.

21. Mark Twain, *Adventures of Huckleberry Finn,* ed. Walter Blair and Victor Fischer (Berkeley: University of California Press, 1986), p. 271.

22. Major, p. 180.

23. Major, p. 182.

24. Major, p. 192.

25. Major, p. 195.

26. Major, p. 204.

27. Ellison, p. 26.

28. Jerome Klinkowitz's suggestion that the protagonist at the end of the novel finds "a tribal sense of unity in Africa—precolonial and hence prepolitical where the separations so vexing to [him] do not exist" ("Clarence Major's Innovative Fiction," *African American Review,* 28.1 [Spring 1994]: 57) provides a strange contrast to an earlier review of the novel by James Robert

Saunders (*Obsidian ll*, 3.1 [Spring 1988]: 102), who writes that the novel "ends in despair as Mason is led off to what seems to be death."

29. Major, p. 205. For a brief mention of Mason's African experience as a failure to provide satisfactory answers to his questions about identity, cf. Lisa C. Roney, "The Double Vision of Clarence Major, Painter and Writer," *African American Review*, 28.1 (Spring 1994): 65–75; cf. also Stuart Klawans, "'I was a weird example of Art': *My Amputations* as Cubist Confession," *African American Review*, 28.1 (Spring 1994): 77–87.

30. For my classification of boundaries, see Fritz Gysin, "Centralizing the Marginal: Boundaries in Recent African American Fiction," in *Modernism, Modernity, and Ethnicity*, ed. Jeffery Melnick and Josef Jarab (forthcoming).

15

• • • •

The Hues and Uses of Liberia

Marie Tyler-McGraw

On December 28, 1816, the American Society for Colonizing the Free People of Colour, soon to become the American Colonization Society, was organized in the hall of the House of Representatives in Washington, D.C. Its goal was to send free persons of color, with their consent, from the United States to a colony to be acquired on the west coast of Africa. The recent and surprisingly successful conclusion to the War of 1812 encouraged a heady sense of national destiny and the moment seemed auspicious for grand schemes. One of those schemes was an effort to move beyond the cautious founding fathers and address the manifest contradictions between republican liberty and chattel slavery in the United States. The society was primarily the product of steady but separate agitation and organization by a Virginia congressman and a New Jersey minister and, in addressing the condition and prospects of the free black, focused on race more than slavery.[1]

A self-appointed committee recruited by those two gentlemen began writing a constitution in the Morris Hotel in Washington, D.C., but soon moved their labors to the House of Representatives. There the draft constitution was adopted at a general meeting of interested parties. A handwritten and much-amended memorial to the Senate and the House of Representatives accompanied the approved constitution. In it, the Society's reasoning was made clear: "This intermediate species of population cannot be incorporated so as to render the Body Politic homogeneous and consistent in all its [members] which must be [the] essential consideration of every form of government." The memorial added, "If they be permitted to remain among us, under this state of imperfect connection, just raised from the abyss of slavery, but not to the level of freedom, suspended between degradation and honor, this unfortunate race will [perish]."[2]

This small group of prominent men had named the central issue that persisted in any consideration of American republican destiny. Their concern for the "imperfect connection" of free blacks with a body politic sharing a common European culture reflected the reasoning of the Federalist papers rather than the realities of American society. The improbable scheme proposed for free-black removal simply raised again the question of the nature of African "degradation" in America, and on that issue colonizationists were deeply divided. "Degraded" was perhaps the most-used adjective in Colonization Society rhetoric because it could be used both by those who argued for an innate African inferiority and those who believed colonization necessary because of insurmountable prejudice against African Americans.

Free blacks shared the assessment that they were suspended between degradation and honor, yet most did not concur in the solution proferred. The American Colonization Society, roundly condemned by abolitionists and free blacks after its first fifteen years of existence, provided an important focus of debate for the black convention movement of the 1830s. Until the Civil War, African American leaders developed their critique of race and citizenship in the United States substantially in response to the rhetoric of African colonization. The critique that emanated from the North is well documented, but its availability has encouraged among historians an easy dismissal of the ambiguities in the colonization movement.[3]

Garrisonians and other abolitionist factions, as well as the black convention movements of the 1830s, understood that among their central tasks were energetic discrediting of the American Colonization Society and distancing themselves from the earlier and more moderate emancipationist tradition. They sought to portray colonization as a plan by slaveholders and their dupes to eliminate free blacks and make slavery more secure. For this task, the Colonization Society's national publications and national orators often gave them rich resources, as when such spokesmen described free blacks as the antithesis of the republican citizen—idle, thieving, deceitful, and morally debased. The fact that these traits might exist as a result of America's racial culture, not as the innate nature of African Americans, was not an ambiguity that abolitionists wished to explore, although it existed throughout the literature of the Colonization Society.

That central ambivalence in colonization made the American Colonization Society a truly contested site, so contested as to implode and shatter into diverse independent state societies within two decades while continuing to maintain a national office in Washington. Most twentieth-century historians have dismissed the American Colonization Society as part of the political history of the Jacksonian era and as a premier example of conservative social control, conceived by slaveholders and a declining Federalist elite and imposed on helpless, unwilling African Americans in bondage.[4] The reality is much more complex, rich, and diverse. A political interpretation of the Colonization Society inadequately describes its quixotic appeal, its rhetoric, or its local level persistence. The Colonization Society has been underutilized as a site for examining the antebellum cultural construction of race.[5]

Naming African Americans as saved or redeemed, as republican citizens, and as nation builders in Liberia made their inherent qualities and legal status in the United States open to question. The rhetoric of "liberty" and "republicanism" embedded in the colonization argument and the early republic permitted African American colonizationists to play ironic tropes on the themes of liberty and slavery in America. Another central theme of colonization, the conversion of the Africans by Christian African Americans, also represented an opening for commentary on the role of the Christian black in America.

Decades before the founding of the Colonization Society, African Americans in the North had shown interest in colonizing in the West Indies, on the African coast, or in the western part of the North American continent. Exploring the possibility of leaving the United States made apparent the two opposing yet intertwined strands in African American thought: a radical and complete African separatism, which was yet thoroughly American in its vision of the new society. The benefits to Africa of Christianity, civilization, and commerce were the frequently cited themes, but they were a superficial and decorous layer that covered the central questions of national identity and equality. In the period from the American Revolution to the War of 1812, as African Americans found themselves increasingly restricted politically and socially in the new nation, a note of African unity began to sound more frequently in their writings and oratory. But it was a unity of the African diaspora in America, not yet a unity with the people of the African continent. The African nation to be achieved was conceived as not only a geographic place, but a political construction with a constitution and trade policies. The first expressions of African nationalism were braided together with the political theory and practice of the era of the American Revolution.[6]

At the same time, the white founders of the American Colonization

Society were eager to do more than send free blacks to an African colony. They hoped to create another republic to show that the American experience was exportable and thus natural and sustainable. A developing sense of national identity, informed by the creation of an American origins myth, needed reification. This was, indeed, as important as the removal of free blacks and manumitted slaves, an activity that different members variously described as leading to emancipation or securing slavery more firmly. Weak and diffused at the national level, the society soon lost its political battle for federal support for Liberia and for a national fleet of ships for trade and transportation. Sectional suspicions then caused some states to sever their direct connections with the national society and to administer a state-based program. African colonization and its financing took diverse forms within the states and even between certain auxiliary societies, but regional differences were particularly important in Maryland, Pennsylvania, New York, and Virginia.[7]

An examination of the colonization movement in one state provides an opportunity to explore its complex meanings and its uses on a regional level. Despite the vigilance of southern slaveholders, the American Colonization Society offered space for a black and dissenting white commentary on slavery and freedom, liberty and human property, spiritual redemption and bodily restraint. The Chesapeake states of Maryland and Virginia provided at least half of the antebellum colonists to Liberia, and Virginia provided almost a third of them before 1860. Virginia also had more auxiliary societies than any other state. The politics of Virginia, not the demographics of black removal, made colonization appear possible in that state. The symbolic function of emigration to Africa was more important than its permanently low numbers.[8]

There had been, in Virginia, a certain confident slackness about slavery. As the colony that had codified slavery and experienced it the longest, Virginia did not usually trouble itself with enforcing every slave statute. The nation's largest and most populous state knew the contribution it had made to the republic with a dynasty of Virginia presidents, a preponderance of congressmen, and a vast expanse of diverse land reaching the Ohio River. Virginia's vulnerabilities became apparent after the War of 1812 as Tidewater plantations lost their greatest productivity and other states began to draw more population. The state stood to lose its primacy in Congress after the 1820 election, and the confidence with which the state had produced theories of liberty and the model slave-based economy faltered. The American Colonization Society, founded by a Virginia congressman, soon drew the suspicions of such conservative Virginia congressmen as John Tyler, who succeeded, within a decade, in taking the Virginia auxiliary branches out of the national society based in Washington and placing authority in a state society, based in Richmond.[9]

This act made the public face of colonization in Virginia exactly what northern blacks and abolitionists described—a slaveholder's organization to more firmly secure slave property by eliminating the presence of free blacks. To a noticeable extent, the creation of a Virginia Colonization Society with prominent slaveholding officers cooled the interest in African colonization of Virginia free blacks and emancipation-minded whites. But the concept was too important for too many reasons to be abandoned. A national society that addressed slavery, however indirectly, was important to nationally minded Virginia colonizationists, who continued to correspond directly with the American Colonization Society secretary in Washington. In addition, while the presidency and vice presidency of the Virginia Colonization Society were held by such planter elites as James Madison and John Marshall, the working offices of secretary and treasurer were filled by long-term antislavery evangelical small businessmen, such as Benjamin Brand and William Crane of Richmond.

Free blacks in Virginia found themselves further from true citizenship in the 1820s and 1830s than they had been at the beginning of the century when the Revolutionary glow was still reflected in the state's statute permitting emancipation and the lack of restriction on education. The initial response to African colonization by free blacks, especially those in the towns of the Tidewater, was receptive. A study of emigration registers and ship's lists (complete until 1844 and partial from 1845 to 1860) makes it possible to divide Virginia immigrants into three general categories: urban free blacks and manumitted slaves; rural manumitted slaves (and a few free blacks); and free mulatto families, some triracial in origins and never enslaved. In Virginia, free black families with high levels of literacy and skills emigrated in the first decade. Even before the abolitionist attacks of the 1830s on the American Colonization Society, many of them based their expectations on the support of black religious societies and on the reports of African Americans who returned from Africa. Their reliance on other African Americans for financial support and information indicated a growing sense of an African American nation within the American nation even below the Mason-Dixon line. Their written references to religion, republicanism, and race never argued that the black man in America lacked capabilities, but only that he would not be permitted to use them.[10]

In keeping with the construction of race taking place in the 1820s and 1830s, the exercise of citizenship was equated with manhood. Women, or soft feminine characteristics in men, could not survive the demands of a frontier to be forged into a republic. Black men must overcome tenderness, excessive affection, interest in pleasure, even the humility and concern for others evidenced in Christian ministers. Yet religious societies sponsored colonization in Africa, and the society sent many young and sensitive white seminarians to Liberia as colonial agents. One black Baptist minister from Richmond, Lott Cary, confronted with these conflicting paradigms, exhibited enough manly citizenship to become the evangelical as trickster.[11]

Cary, born a slave in New Kent County, was hired out to the Richmond tobacco factories in the early years of the nineteenth century. Through "overwork" (the custom of paying slaves for factory work beyond the standard day) and his position as foreman, Cary acquired the cash to buy his freedom. Taught to read and converted by an evangelical Baptist shoemaker from New Jersey, Cary and his colleague, Colin Teage, constituted themselves as a church and, with their families, left for Liberia in early 1821. Their venture was financed by Richmond's all-black African Baptist Missionary Society, so Cary felt little obliged to the Colonization Society. It was Cary's view that free blacks in America could not acquire either political or social freedom and that true liberty depended on removal to another place. Cary often evinced polite contempt for the Colonization Society and its earnest, inexperienced young agents.

Once in Liberia, Cary challenged the authority of the American Colonization Society and reported only to the Baptist Board of Missions. Shortly thereafter, he led a revolt of settlers who rejected the society's total control of the distribution of food and land. Cary claimed that authority rested in the immigrant community as a political body. This, he affirmed was the first step to becoming a republic. The society's agent in Liberia was confused at this assertiveness. Cary was seen as uncooperative at best and deranged at worst in letters by the agent to the Colonization Society. Cary's theory was always consistent, but it was not until he began to implement it that its implications became clear. If Africa were the black man's continent, then the black man was in charge. Although the Colonization Society office in Washington wanted him arrested, the agent in the field realized that this would invite insurrection. As the health of the agent, Jehudi Ashmun, faded, Cary became the acting agent for the Colonization Society. Cary successfully turned the values of republicanism and evangelicalism inside out in order to reverse the structure of power and prestige in Liberia. When Cary was killed in a gunpowder explosion, both the Baptist Board of Missions and the American Colonization Society hastened to turn him (in print) back into the pious and humble black Baptist minister that they thought they had in the first place.[12]

Among a group of rural emancipated slaves emigrating to Liberia, the

Lucas brothers received similar admonitions to manhood. In rural Loudoun County, Virginia, in 1829, Albert and Townsend Heaton emancipated Mars and Jesse Lucas and seven other members of the extensive Lucas family of slaves and free blacks. In January 1830, they left Norfolk for Liberia and, over the next six years, the two sets of brothers exchanged letters.[13] Loudoun County, at the edge of the northern Virginia Piedmont, was an area of mixed farming similar to those of Maryland and southern Pennsylvania. The county had two colonization auxiliaries, one formed by local Quakers. Letters from the Lucas brothers to Exedra, the Heaton farm, reveal a tension in the motives of the immigrants to Liberia. They have been at least nominally convinced by their masters that they can only be "true men" in Liberia. While immigration was apparently a condition of emancipation, the Lucas brothers assert their eagerness to work hard in Liberia and to become landholders and local officeholders on the models they have seen in Loudoun County. They see themselves as pioneers on a new frontier, clearing the land and facing hostile natives.

A letter from their former master, Albert Heaton, recites with amazing explicitness what they must do to become both manly and free:

> [F]ew indeed of the free blacks have done well here & Never Can—But you have gone to a Country where the No'blest feelings of Liberty will spring up . . . Liberty [is] the dearest right of man, the strongest passion of the soul, you have shewed the true dignity of man by imigrating to Liberia. . . . It is well to show feeling and mourn the loss of friends, but to distress yourselves about them over-much is unmanly and you ought not to do so. . . . You are now your own Masters and it depends greatly on your own conduct whether you will do well and prosper. . . . No Man can expect to do much for himself or others unless he is industrious, saving and correct and fair in his conduct.

In America, then, Africans can never know true freedom and thus can never be true men. The prize of liberty must be won; it cannot be bestowed. Heaton addressed his letter to the Lucas brothers, not to the entire family group.

Mars and Jesse Lucas viewed the Africans as lacking the qualities that would entitle them to respect. Mars wrote: "[T]he natives, here is not. very. much given to Industry. or the[y] would have had more land. Cleared, the most the[y] care about is Hunting and fishing, but that is only when the[y] have no Tobacco. nor Rum. that is the Cheaf Articles the[y] Care about, the[y] are about the Closest people I have ever seen, the[y] would not give one mouthful if we was diing for it." Mars has given the indigenous natives the characteristics frequently ascribed to American Indians, with one exception. Many immigrants to Liberia were surprised at the shrewd bargaining capabilities of the Africans whom they encountered and were even more suprised to find themselves traded out of their money and goods in a short time.

The Lucases also had a brief captivity narrative:

> [M]e and Brothr went down to Bassa to make money and while we was down there we had to saw out in the Bush & there were some insinuations past on the short & the heathens came in one night & destroyed 20 more or less of our American people & then came into our saw pit & took us away from our work & carried us to a native town, kept us some space of time & used us very cruel but throw the mercy of God we were delivered from the[m], & afterwards Mars went back & fought in the war but I did not.

Within four years, the brothers viewed the colony more pessimistically and criticized their fellow immigrants. Mars wrote: "But, the people. get, above their trades after the[y]. come. here, the[y] won't work but live from hand to mouth—but that would not. suit me." Jesse wrote: "plese to send none of my relation here until you see me. I am glad to here old perry [farm dog in Loudoun County] is alive wheath[er] he can tree oppossums or not but if he was her[e] the Leperds wold Ceatch him quicker than he Catch possums." At the end of the correspondence, they are hoping to sell their improved land and return to Loudoun County.

Internal evidence is strong for concluding that the letters from the Loudoun County Lucas brothers were indeed written by them and for people they believed they knew intimately. Over the years, Mars continued to make all pronouns "the" and to sprinkle periods for emphasis. Jesse, the family man, was the better and more fluid writer. Their descriptive passages, inquiries about local events, and requests for trade goods were direct and unaffected. Those who had official duties, such as Lott Cary, tended to write public letters. Didactic and persuasive, they were intended for publication or to transact business. They informed in a very different way. Lott Cary turned the language of colonization against itself to revolt against the established authority and thus begin a manly republic, while the Lucas brothers' discourse was more informal, perhaps less ambitious, yet based on the same values of enterprise, citizenship, and masculinity.

The epitome of early-nineteenth-century American values appears among the triracial and free black families who left Virginia for Liberia. Virginia has a long history of mulatto and triracial families, beginning no later than the mid-1600s, and both whites and Native Americans have, at various times, made vigorous efforts to stamp out all knowledge of it. Among the first (white) families of Virginia, it became convenient to trace all their Chesapeake Indian ancestry to Pocahontas.[14] When, in the early nineteenth century, the Virginia legislature began to assert that all the remaining consolidated tribal groupings on reservations had either died out or were hopelessly admixed with blacks, those who claimed tribal lands fought to keep them by denying African intermixture. Then and later, Indians claimed not to be connected with blacks. The political and economic price to be paid was too high.

In reality, many of the state's triracial and mulatto families were unofficially well known. Until the 1820s, their status was uncertain and they had no set racial identity. These families occupied an ambiguous place in Virginia society, but further restrictions on free-black mobility and the Virginia Assembly's efforts to revoke reservation rights for Native Americans made the situation nearly unendurable for many. Intensely aware of their genealogy and family connections, some of these families moved to Ohio, Canada, or Liberia because their prospects were hopelessly diminished as racial controls followed a reordering of racial meaning in the 1820s and 1830s. One large and extended triracial Pamunkey family, driven off their ancestral land in New Kent County, moved to Richmond, then to Ohio, and then on to Canada. In writing back to her grown children in Virginia from Canada, Lucy Scott still clung to her belief that "the good people in Virginia was sorry for us," and for the "poor mixed blood children," but "for the sake of you children you all mus part from you good friends also an come to a land whar you children can be men and women—butiful schools hear—you can school you child for 25 cent per mont an mak him a man up to business."[15]

Among apparently triracial families who migrated, in whole or in part, to Liberia were the Payne, Page, and Roberts families of Virginia and their kin in the James, Spriggs, and Yates families. One branch of the Roberts family was self-identified as Lumbee Indians who moved from the James River of Virginia to Robeson County, North Carolina. A triracial Payne or Paine family existed on the Accomack County Eastern Shore of Virginia in the 1660s, and Paines were emancipated by the Quaker parents of Dolley Madison in Hanover County, Virginia, before the Revolution.[16]

On the ship *Harriett*, arriving at Monrovia in March 1829, were nineteen members of the David and Eleanor Sprigg Payne family from Richmond, including Nancy Sprigg, the 80-year-old mother of Eleanor Sprigg Payne, and a cousin, Beverly Page Yates. On the same ship were nine members of the Roberts family from Norfolk, which was to provide Liberia's first president. As a member of those interconnected families and a vice president of the republic of Liberia, Beverly Page Yates explained, "Liberia is an offshoot from the United States, primarily from the *Southern states* and three-fourths of the people who laid the foundation of the Republic were from Virginia" (emphasis in original).[17]

Reversing the transatlantic voyage did not restore these African Americans to their native land because their native land was the United States first and the American South second. Edward Said has described nationalist movements as possessing the "desire to reclaim preempted culture and to search for and restore a concrete geographic identity."[18] The Virginia colonizationists expected to lay claim to an American identity in Africa, and the predominance of Chesapeake blacks, especially Virginians, particularly shaped the well-named Americo-Liberian, a new cultural persona.

When Joseph J. Roberts, formerly of Norfolk, Virginia, became Liberia's first president in 1847, he spoke in his inaugural address of the first African American colonists in Liberia, "a mere handful of isolated Christian pilgrims, in pursuit of civil and religious liberty, surrounded by savage and warlike tribes bent on their ruin and total annihilation."[19] This complete embrace of the emerging American origins myth may have been a transitional national identity under some historic circumstances, but, cut off from the main currents of African American postemancipation thought and dependent on Protestant missions, American corporations, and paternalistic American politics, Americo-Liberians made only modest adjustments to their surroundings and continued to interpret their history though the prism of antebellum American "whiteness."

Notes

1. Douglas Egerton, *Charles Fenton Mercer and the Trial of National Conservatism* (Oxford: University of Mississippi Press, 1989).

2. Container 4, Reel 304, Subject File VI 1792–1964, Papers of the American Colonization Society, Manuscript Division, Library of Congress, Washington, D.C. The important word *perish* is almost illegible.

3. William Lloyd Garrison, *Thoughts on African Colonization* (Boston: Garrison and Knapp, 1832). Historians of the last generation, attracted to the radical abolitionists and their critique of American society, have been too willing to accept Garrison's account of the black response without noting dates for anticolonization meetings.

4. See, for example, Egerton; Lawrence Friedman, "Purifying the White Man's Country," *Societies* (Winter 1976), pp. 1–24; Leonard Sweet, *Black Images of America 1784–1870* (New York: Norton, 1976); and David Rothman's *The Discovery of the Asylum: Social Order and Disorder in the New Republic* (Boston: Little, Brown, 1971).

5. Floyd Miller, *The Search for a Black Nationality: Black Colonization and Emigration, 1787–1863* (Urbana: University of Illinois Press, 1975); Howard H.

Bell, *A Survey of the Negro Convention Movement, 1830–1861* (New York: Arno Press, 1969); Winthrop Jordan, *White over Black: American Attitudes toward the Negro, 1550–1812* (Chapel Hill: University of North Carolina Press, 1968); David Brion Davis, *The Problem of Slavery in the Age of Revolution, 1770–1823* (Ithaca, N.Y.: Syracuse University Press, 1975); George M. Fredrickson, *The Black Image in the White Mind: The Debate on Afro-American Character and Destiny, 1817–1914* (New York: 1971); Marcus Cunliffe, *Chattel Slavery and Wage Slavery: The Anglo-American Context, 1830–1860* (Athens: University of Georgia Press, 1979). More recently, David Roediger, *The Wages of Whiteness: Race and the Making of the American Working Class* (London: Verso, 1991) and Alexander Saxton, *The Rise and Fall of the White Republic* (New York: Routledge, Chapman, Hall, 1992).

6. Dickson Bruce, "National Identity and Afroamerican Colonization, 1773–1817," *The Historian* 58 (Autumn 1995): 15–28.

7. For an institutional study of the forces that pulled power from the Washington center, see Philip J. Staudenraus, *The African Colonization Movement, 1816–1861* (New York: Columbia University Press, 1961).

8. Svend E. Holsoe, Liberian Research Institute, Department of Anthropology, University of Delaware, Newark, Delaware, summarized in *Liberia: A Land and Life Remembered* (Athens: University of Georgia Press, 1988), pp. 3–5.

9. Virginia Colonization Society Papers, Virginia Historical Society, Richmond, Benjamin Brand Papers, Virginia Historical Society, Richmond.

10. Many of these references are found in manuscript letters to the American Colonization Society and in the society's publication, *African Repository and Colonial Journal*, Manuscripts Division, Library of Congress; in the records of the Richmond Auxiliary of the American Colonization Society, Virginia Historical Society, Richmond; in the papers of Benjamin Brand, Virginia Historical Society, Richmond; and in the predominantly Baptist missionary publications of the day, including *The Latter-Day Luminary*.

11. Lawrence Levine, *Black Culture and Black Consciousness* (New York: Oxford University Press, 1979), pp. 106–108, 368, 400; Henry Louis Gates, Jr., *Figures in Black: Words, Signs, and the "Racial Self"* (New York: Oxford University Press, 1987), p. 237. See also Marie Tyler-McGraw, "Richmond Free Blacks and African Colonization, 1816–1832," *Journal of American Studies* 21/2 (1987): 207–224.

12. For a remarkable account of Cary as an angry and abrasive man, see the account written by the Colonization Society agent, Jehudi Ashum, and published by Miles Mark Fisher, "Documents: Letters, Addresses, and the Like Throwing Light on the Career of Lott Cary," *Journal of Negro History* 7/4 (Oct. 1922): 431–433.

13. The entire Lucas-Heaton correspondence has been published in Marie Tyler-McGraw, ed., "'The Prize I Mean is the Prize of Liberty': A Loudoun County Family in Liberia," *The Virginia Magazine of History and Biography* 97/3 (July 1989): 355–374.

14. Robert S. Tilton, in *Pocahontas: The Evolution of an American Narrative* (Cambridge: Cambridge University Press, 1994). Antebellum writing about Pocahontas was primarily in the form of poems and plays, and authors included Robert Dale Owen, Lydia Sigourney, Seba Smith, and William Thackeray. The Virginia colonizationist, George Washington Parke Custis, con-

tributed *Pocahontas, or the Settlers of Virginia, a National Drama in Three Acts* (Philadelphia: 1830) to the white appropriation of Pocahontas.

15. Lucy P. Scott, Columbus, Ohio (Sept. 5, 1854), and Brantford, Ontario (Oct. 29, 1854), to "my dear children," Richmond, Virginia, in the Norvell Wilson Papers, Southern History Collection, Manuscript Department, Wilson Library, University of North Carolina, Chapel Hill.

16. Jay Worrall, "The Friendly Virginians: A History of America's First Quakers" (unpublished manuscript in author's possession, 1992), 340, 377, 344; Virginia Easley DeMarce, "'Very Slitly Mixt': Tri-racial Isolate Families of the Upper South—A Genealogical Study," *NGS Quarterly* 80/1 (March 1992): 5–36, and "Looking at Legends—Lumbee and Melungeon: Applied Genealogy and the Origins of Tri-racial Isolate Settlements," *NGS Quarterly* 81/1 (March 1993): 24–45. See Helen Rountree, *Pocahontas's People* (Norman: University of Oklahoma Press, 1990), for a cautious evaluation of the Virginia Indian/European/African relationship over four centuries.

17. Beverly Page Yates, *African Respository*, 49 (1873), pp. 94–95; "Roll of Emigrants that have been sent to the Colony of Liberia, Western Africa, by the American Colonization Society and its Auxiliaries, to September 1843, and etc.," *Senate Documents*, 28th Congress, 2nd session, 1844, ix, 152–389.

18. Edward Said, "Yeats and Decolonization," in Terry Eagleton, Fredric Jameson, Edward Said, eds., *Nationalism, Colonialism, and Literature* (St. Paul: University of Minnesota Press, 1990), p. 77.

19. C. Abayomi Cassell, *Liberia: History of the First African Republic* (New York: Fountainhead Publishers, 1970), p. 143, quoted in Howard Temperley, "Black Separatism, American Values, and the Colonization of Liberia" [unpublished paper in possession of author], p. 28.

16

• • • •

Voyage into the Heart of Africa

Pauline Hopkins and
Of One Blood

Hanna Wallinger

R euel Briggs, the protagonist of Pauline Hopkins's *Of One Blood*, a
serial novel published between 1902 and 1903, discovers that "[i]n
the heart of Africa was a knowledge of science that all the wealth and
learning of modern times could not emulate."[1] This statement surely
stirred the interest of the late-nineteenth-century reader, who was
trained to regard Africa as uncivilized and savage. It was startling because it spoke of a racial pride that the average colored American was not
then used to hearing. In this essay I will put Reuel Briggs's and Hopkins's
"heart of Africa" into context and read *Of One Blood* as a contribution to
the concept of "Ethiopianism," in terms taken from the discussion of
colonialist literature, and against the background of the dominant post-
Reconstruction racial and scientific discourse.

Pauline Elizabeth Hopkins is one of the most interesting rediscoveries
of recent African American literary history, a rediscovery prompted in
part by the republication of her novel *Contending Forces* (1900), and by
her three magazine novels-*Hagar's Daughter, A Story of Southern Caste
Prejudice* (1901–1902), *Winona, A Tale of Negro Life in the South and South-
west* (1902), and *Of One Blood, Or, the Hidden Self* (1902–1903). With only
her nonfiction still remaining largely unavailable to the interested
scholar, it may be said that Hopkins has been lifted out of obscurity, an
obscurity that Ann Allen Shockley lamented in 1972 when she subtitled
her article on Hopkins "A Biographical Excursion into Obscurity."[2]

As editor of the *Colored American Magazine* from 1901 to 1904, as writer of many articles about current issues of her time, Pauline Hopkins was certainly aware of the dominant scientific discourse about race, race differences, and the origin of the races.[3] No doubt she was well acquainted with the ideas and writings of the two foremost race leaders Booker T. Washington and W.E.B. Du Bois.

Hopkins was also aware of the fact that one topic that made readers turn the pages, engaging the interest of a late-nineteenth-century reader, was Africa. Although Africa was unknown in terms of personal experience, Africa as a literary trope, however, was well known to most black Americans and was much discussed and debated. British colonialists, who, as Dorothy Hammond and Alta Jablow argue in *The Africa That Never Was*, brought forth a "tidal wave of literary production,"[4] including voluminous descriptions of flora, fauna, and scenic wonders, numerous travelogues, and innumerable scientific and literary tales, provided ready and available information to a reading public who were interested in exotic surroundings and certainly not restricted to the European continent.

Africa, the "Dark Continent," was usually associated with the negative side of what Abdul R. JanMohamed calls the central trope of colonialist discourse, namely, the "Manichean allegory," which is "a field of diverse yet interchangeable oppositions between white and black, good and evil, superiority and inferiority, civilization and savagery, intelligence and emotion, rationality and sensuality, self and Other, subject and object."[5] As a minority group, colored Americans were not at all exempt from sharing the belief in this oppositional discourse. Quoting the Italian Marxist Antonio Gramsci, Jackson Lears calls this period of American culture one of cultural hegemony in which "dominant social groups maintain power not through force alone but through sustaining their cultural hegemony—that is, winning the 'spontaneous' loyalty of subordinate groups to a common set of values and attitudes."[6] Nancy Leys Stepan and Sander L. Gilman speak of "internalization" as a strategy employed by minority groups to respond to racist ideology and refer to "the very profound psychological and social introjection of negative images and meanings contained in the stereotypes, in the construction and understanding of one's self-identity."[7]

As a minority writer, Hopkins was concerned with establishing her "Americanness," her right to live in America; as a colored writer, Hopkins was concerned with her tradition, her heritage, her connection with Africa; and as a woman writer, Hopkins was concerned with refuting the prevalent stereotypes of the black woman as mule, mammy, or whore. With *Of One Blood*, Hopkins moves—at least spatially—outside the confining racial prejudices of American society. African American writers at the turn of the century and even earlier usually dealt with Africa under the heading of Ethiopianism, which is a glorification and dramatization of the African past. In principle a biblical view of Africa, Ethiopianism takes its name from the verse "Princes shall come out of Egypt; Ethiopia shall soon stretch out her hands unto God" (Psalms 68:31). Wilson Moses identifies as the two components of Ethiopianism the themes of "Rising Africa" and of the "Decline of the West," which he summarizes as follows:

> Ethiopianism may be defined as the effort of the English-speaking Black or African person to view his past enslavement and present cultural dependency in terms of the broader history of civilization. It serves to remind him that this present scientific technological civilization, dominated by Western Europe for a scant four hundred years, will go under certainly—like all the empires of the past. It expresses the belief that the tragic racial experience has profound historical value, that it has endowed the African with moral superiority and made him a seer.[8]

Eric J. Sundquist suggests that this reading of Psalms 68:31 "portrayed colonized African or enslaved Africans in the diaspora as prepared for providential delivery from bondage." It could be seen "to prophesy a black millennium, a violent seizure of freedom through acts of revolt sanctioned by God and led, literally or figuratively, by a black redeemer from within Africa or, in some interpretations, from America."[9] In "Ancient Africa and the Early Black Historians," Dickson Bruce sees the origin of this movement in the discrepancy between the black Americans' segregationist reality and their integrationist goals. Bruce argues that, on the one hand, "their sense of the need for separate development required them to develop a rhetoric of racial pride and solidarity, a rhetoric that asserted the distinctive character of black people and their potential for independent achievement." As a consequence, however, "their integrationist goals required that any rhetoric of separate development or distinctiveness not compromise the basic case against segregation, namely that blacks had a right to full equality in American life and wanted to claim that right without limitations or qualifications."[10]

On the one hand, Ethiopianism was a much-needed movement that inspired racial pride; as such, it has to be discussed as a reaction to the dominant view of Africa being populated by people of an inferior race. Yet, on the other hand, one has to agree with Dickson Bruce, who interprets the emphasis on a glorious past at the expense of contemporary African reality as an example of "complex assimilationist underpinnings": "[Black thinkers] saw the African heritage as something to take pride in, but they ignored or even condemned modern Africa when they talked about that heritage. They preferred to focus instead on ancient Egypt and Ethiopia, and they took pride in that heritage precisely because of its direct connection with modern Western civilization."[11]

This dual view of Africa—the glorious past versus the insignificant present—will be the focus of the following analysis of Hopkins's novel *Of One Blood*. Is the main character's journey into the heart of Africa really a manifestation of an assimilationist spirit? Is it an addition to JanMohamed's "Manichean allegory"? How does *Of One Blood* relate to Hopkins's position as a minority woman writer?

Structurally, *Of One Blood* is divided into an American part and an African part. Its central theme is the struggle and suffering of Dr. Reuel Briggs, a talented physician who passes as white, and whose outstanding characteristic is the power of second sight. At the beginning of the novel the vision of a beautiful woman draws him away from suicidal thoughts. Some time later, he encounters the same woman in Dianthe Lusk, whose superior voice in a Fisk jubilee choir captures the audience's attention and his own. After a railroad accident, she then happens to be brought into the hospital where she is resuscitated by Reuel Briggs but suffers from complete amnesia. Her real name and her race are unknown to anyone but Reuel and his friend Aubrey Livingston. Livingston's fiancee Molly Vance invites her into her rich father's home; Reuel and Felice Adams, as she is now called, fall in love and marry. Immediately upon his marriage, due to straitened financial circumstances, Reuel Briggs sets out on an expedition into Africa organized by a group of British scientists. While he is away, Aubrey Livingston reveals himself as the villain of the novel; he lets his fiancée drown and then forces Dianthe to marry him after he has convinced her that Reuel is dead.

Even from this cursory glance at the novel's plot, it is clear that *Of One Blood* fits easily into the Hopkins canon as well as into the tradition of the nineteenth-century sentimental novel. As critic Claudia Tate puts it, the novel "relies on both the passing strategies and masked character identities of *Hagar's Daughter*, the mystery plot of a ghost story, Ethiopian legend, the familiar triangular love story, and enough intrigue to keep even a late-twentieth-century reader engaged."[12] Susan Gillman discusses the novel as an American race melodrama under which she groups a genre that "focuses broadly on the situation of the black family—almost always of an interracial genealogy—specifically on the issue of 'race mixture,' as a means of negotiating the social tensions surrounding the formation of racial, national, and sexual identity in the post-Reconstruction years." Its basic plot, as she sees it, is "the reconstitution of the black family separated under slavery, culminating in the revelation of secret identities, of hidden race mixture, and finally of separated and reunited parents and children."[13] As such, they combine the melodramatic and didactic.

Reuel Briggs travels to Africa with the group of scientists and archaeologists, accompanied by Molly Vance's brother Charlie and Aubrey Livingston's servant Jim Titus. When he is led to believe that Dianthe is dead, Reuel falls into despair. One night as he roams around the ruins of the ancient city of Meroe, he is captured by the survivors of this ancient Cushite civilization. It is discovered that because of a birth mark on his breast, he is a true descendant of their royal line, and he is, therefore, crowned King Ergamenes. Since he believes that his American wife is dead, marriage ceremonies between him and Queen Candace are prepared. By way of the Cushite's highly developed knowledge of supernatural forces, Reuel finds out about the misdeeds of Aubrey Livingston and his servant Jim Titus. In a quick wrapping-up of all loose plot lines, he travels home once more, finds Dianthe dying from poison, and confronts Aubrey with the knowledge, which he and Dianthe had acquired earlier, that the three of them are siblings, all "of one blood." Livingston dies by his own hand and Reuel goes back to Africa.

In its more interesting African section, *Of One Blood* moves outside the narrow American setting and offers a partly escapist, partly utopian view of an ancient black civilization. In *The Africa That Never Was*, Hammond and Jablow claim that the colonists were attracted to life in Africa because it "held out the possibilities of freedom of movement and a general independence from the constraints of life in Great Britain."[14] In Hopkins's case, it has to be added that it offered her narrator the freedom to think a thought barely possible in the American context: that all races are equal and that race distinctions are arbitrary and not traceable to behavior or innate values and virtues. Africa as the archetypal "other" of the European and also American imperialist mind becomes in *Of One Blood* the place of encounter in a positive sense with one's past. The Africa of the British explorers—it is no coincidence that the archaeological expedition is led by Professor Stone, a British scientist—the country of cannibals and savages, becomes the cradle of civilization in which this early African American hero finds his roots. Hopkins enwraps her central Christian argument "Of one blood have I made all races of men" (590) in the formulaic garb of the adventure story and the psychological ghost story. This message is conveyed in a very conclusive, convincing way to late-nineteenth-century readers used to plot intricacies; supernatural occurrences; tales of adventure, love, and sentiment; and tales about Africa, the "dark continent."

The novel's hero, Reuel Briggs, is acknowledged by his friends as "a genius in his scientific studies" (444); his origin is thought to be either Italian or Japanese. Making Briggs nearly white and endowing him with superior physical nobility allows Hopkins to have her hero move freely in his social surroundings, become a famed doctor of medicine and an authority on brain diseases, and join the British expedition as one of its leaders without being hindered by the problems a black man faced at the time.

In outward appearance, Briggs is blessed with "superior physical endowments," which include "the vast breadth of shoulder, the strong throat that upheld a plain face, the long limbs, the sinewy hands," an athlete's head "covered with an abundance of black hair, straight and closely cut, thick and smooth," and an aristocratic nose "although nearly spoiled by broad nostrils" (443). And possibly to alert the reader to his racial background, his skin is described as white "but of a tint suggesting olive, an almost sallow color which is a mark of strong, melancholic temperaments" (444). Reuel Briggs is clearly meant to engage the reader's sympathy. The intention of this early description is to establish him as a strong personality, a natural leader of men. In most respects, Reuel Briggs moves around with the freedom of the average white man; he has been trained in a scientific world dominated by white men; therefore, he has appropriated the bearing and worldview of a white man. At the same time it is also obvious that his double heritage will provide the novel with its basis for conflict and dramatic action.

The tenth chapter (out of a total of twenty-four)—or the fourth installment in the original serial novel—brings the transition of the archaeological expedition from America to Africa. Upon their approaching Tripoli, Reuel views "a landscape strange in form," a portion of Africa "whose nudity is only covered by the fallow mantle of the desert," a view that leads him to the conclusion "that the race who dwelt here must be different from those of the rest of the world" (509). Seen through Reuel's eyes (his attitude is assumed to be identical to that of the rest of the party), the expedition's first view of Africa combines the average Anglo Saxon–American fascination with exotic surroundings and an awareness of difference in the form of an immediate remark pertaining to its "uncivilized" status:

> At a few cable lengths away the city smiles at them with all the fascination of a modern Cleopatra, circled with an oasis of palms studded with hundreds of domes and minarets. Against a sky of amethyst the city stands forth with a penetrating charm. It is the eternal enchantment of the cities of the Orient seen at a distance; but, alas! set foot within them, the illusion vanishes and disgust seizes you. Like beautiful bodies they have the appearance of life, but within the worm of decay and death eats ceaselessly. (509)

Their first encounter with Africa's people is with "a horde of dirty rascals" who "waylaid" them (511). This description conforms to JanMohamed's definition of colonialist literature as "an exploration and a representation of a world at the boundaries of 'civilization', a world that has not (yet) been domesticated by European signification or codified in detail by its ideology."[15] So, while the group of explorers recoil at the jostling, noise, and general uproar, they are simultaneously drawn to its exotic scenario: "Under the Sultan's rule Tripoli has remained the capital of a truly barbaric state, virgin of improvements, with just enough dilapidated abandon, dirt and picturesqueness to make the delight of the artists. Arabs were everywhere; veiled women looked at the Christians with melting eyes above their wrappings" (512).

When the expedition finally reaches its destination, the island of Meroe, Reuel sees a "dirty Arab town" (526). He suffers from despair and a loss of heart when he is confronted with "a pile of old ruins that promised nothing of interest to him after all" (526). This is what the "real" Africa is like: "the desolation of an African desert, and the companionship of human fossils and savage beasts of prey" (526). Reuel clearly professes a view of Africa here that offers nothing for the future, no sign of a bustling, developing, or even progressive life:

> It was a desolation that doubled desolation, because his healthy American organization missed the march of progress attested by the sound of hammers on unfinished buildings that told of a busy future and cosy modern homeliness. Here there was no future. No railroads, no churches, no saloons, no schoolhouses to echo the voices of merry children, no promise of the life that produces within the range of his vision. Nothing but the monotony of past centuries dead and forgotten save by a few learned savans. (526)

No other quotation reflects in such a succinct way the novel's ambiguity. Reuel—in his role as colonizer and explorer—ponders about the common dichotomies: America represents progress, the future, modern life, industry, religion/Christianity, companionship, and education, while Africa lacks all these qualities. Some time later, roaming around the ruins of the once beautiful Meroe, an ancient center of learning and the arts, Reuel muses: "Now, however, her schools are closed forever; not a vestige remaining. Of the houses of her philosophers, not a stone rests upon another; and where civilization and learning once reigned, ignorance and barbarism have reassumed their sway" (538).

As an American, Reuel has been imbued with this view of Africa. To a certain extent, he has internalized the negative terms and norms of the dominant scientific and ideological discourse. A radical process of learning, which forms the core of the novel's message, will alert him to an awareness of "another" Africa of past glory and rich heritage. While the fictitious Reuel Briggs reflects upon the black man's divided nature in terms of his American identity and his African past, it must be pointed out that Hopkins employs the familiar Ethiopian and romantically African argument as a rhetorical strategy to counterpose this negative view of modern Africa.

So it is no wonder that soon after this description, the reader's attention is focused again on the ancient treasures of the country: Professor Stone produces a mysterious chart that "held the key to immense wealth" (528) and the promise of finding a hidden treasure. The history of ancient Ethiopia that Professor Stone elaborates upon now becomes the center of the novel's focus and replaces any concern for the present state of Africa.

As most literary historians point out, the vogue of Ethiopianism took its origin from the Bible, but even from bare historical facts, the past of Meroe and of the Cushite Empire can be regarded as a fit metaphor for the embryonic black nationalist movement. The splendor of ancient Meroe and the Cushite Empire, as well as historical evidence of a powerful Queen Candace, who was of Nubian—that is, African—origin substantiates the view that ancient Egypt was a black culture and ancient Ethiopia a predominantly black civilization. Although by no means unchallenged, this view continued to serve its purpose for black historians, scientists, and writers because it "contradicted racist assertions of black inferiority and dependence."[16]

The account of the Cushite-Ethiopian past that Hopkins's British scientist Dr. Stone gives is mainly biblical: he names as the progenitor of the Ethiopian race "Cush, the grandson of Noah, an Ethiopian" (531) and sees Chaldea between the Euphrates and Tigris rivers as their first home. Ham's grandson Nimrod then founded Babylon, the world's first great civilization. Professor Stone's expedition, as he says, will prove his theory that the Ethiopian civilization by far antecedes the Egyptian. His "greatest authority" is the Bible, as he explains to the members of the expedition, because it asserts that the world's race—the Egyptians, Ethiopians, Libyans, and Canaanites—"were ethnically connected, being all descended from Ham" (533).

His view is remarkable above all for the fact that in it the descendants of Ham are "blessed" by becoming the builders of the most ancient civilization, while in the popular mind they are usually "cursed" by being black. Certainly this effective undermining of the most common metonym for the Negro as the cursed son of Ham conveys an outspoken, radical message for Hopkins's contemporary reader who was well versed in the Bible. As such it is a contribution to the theme of Ethiopianism, which Hopkins here uses as a strategy of transvaluation of the dominant discourse based on biblical interpretation.[17] This strategy centers around the reversal of a negative into a positive image: the "cursed" sons of Ham are "blessed" as the founders of an ancient empire. And to give its voice more legitimacy, Hopkins lets a white British scientist utter this statement, which is later supported by the linguistic research he cites. But while Stepan and Gilman argue that this strategy of transvaluation suffers from the fact "that the terms of the dominant discourse were very far from being transcended,"[18] in *Of One Blood* it leads to a profound criticism of the science of race in general. As a consequence, the mere existence of racial distinctions is put into question, and the potential of the African heritage for an improvement in the status of the American Negro is emphasized.

This movement into the heart of Africa entails for Reuel a movement into his own self, a movement intricately linked to his own racial awakening. Thomas J. Otten calls his article about *Of One Blood* "Pauline Hopkins and the Hidden Self of Race" because he argues that race and mind have to be seen as "each other's doubles."[19] Otten connects the novel's subtitle with William James's article "The Hidden Self," a work with which Pauline Hopkins was most certainly familiar. Otten comes to the conclusion that "[r]ace is here construed as an interior element, as a secret buried within the personality, as a 'submerged' side of the self: in James's terms, an aspect of the self that is 'fully conscious' yet sealed off from normal consciousness, that preserves and represses memories of guilt and trauma."[20] Reuel's memories bring him a feeling of shame about his passing into the white world. But he soon realizes that the point of contact between him and his racial heritage is his power of second sight. In his Cushite mentor Ai he finds this power developed to the utmost precision. So it comes as no surprise that the one achievement that Reuel admires most in this African civilization is the science of occultism. When he says that "[i]n the heart of Africa was a knowledge of science that all the wealth and learning of modern times could not emulate" (576), "science" here means occultism, mesmerism, and supernatural powers. Although the nineteenth century developed a concept of science as "the dominant mode of cognition of industrial society," as "apolitical, nontheological, universal, empirical, and uniquely objective,"[21] Hopkins's identification of supernaturalism with science was not at all extraordinary at the turn of the century when "notions about clairvoyance, curative elixirs and mesmerism" circulated.[22] Without a doubt, the supernatural becomes the African heritage per se. It is the connecting link between the American present and the African past. As such, it serves Hopkins as a positive reminder of the richness of African culture—a richness that when appropriated by an American colored man can imbue with racial pride and lead to personal fulfillment.

In this sense, the hidden city of Telassar, in which Reuel Briggs confronts his family past and racial heritage, becomes the one side of the American Negro hidden from public view. The voyage into the heart of Africa is used to reveal a splendid richness and superior intellect that make the Negro people the equals of white people.

In the novel's predominantly Christian argument, however, it is the African civilization that supposedly will benefit from the contact with America. "'O Ergamenes, your belief shall be ours; we have no will but yours. Deign to teach your subjects'" (563). This plea by Ai comes after he has explained to Reuel the governing principles of their state. In rudimentary form, Ai here presents an alternative ideology based upon strict social rules, an elaborate hierarchical social and political structure, and a belief in an Old Testament "Supreme Being" (562). All of this has to be contrasted with the common view of Africans as childlike and primitive. Reuel is fascinated by Ai's explanations but immediately laments the lack of fundamental New Testament belief: "'What of the Son of Man? Do you not know the necessity of belief in the Holy Trinity? Have not your Sages brought the need of belief in God's Son?'" (562f). In this sense, Reuel is very much the colonizer/missionary who brings religion to the heathen race.

Despite all this, the dominant impression with which the reader is left is of Hopkins's fundamental rewriting of African American history. In chapter 15 Reuel-Ergamenes is solemnly crowned, the magnificent crown being "set with gems priceless in value" (553). Through this strange, solemn ceremony, he is acquainted with his real past as the descendant of an African king. To Reuel the surroundings appear as if out of the Arabian Nights, yet they seem vaguely "familiar" (551). To him, who had always carefully hidden his "Ethiopian extraction" (557), this ceremony seems a great privilege. The historical explanation for the downfall of the Cushite Empire from past glory is given in the form of a recitative in the language of the Old Testament.

In correspondence with the dream-like and visionary nature of Reuel's adventure, the emphasis of the Telassar parts is on atmosphere and on the depiction of a lush, luxurious, Oriental civilization. It is here that Reuel finds elements of a flourishing life: fertile fields, vineyards, moving crowds, and great buildings, all of which stand in vivid contrast to the Africa he knew before.

Hopkins may be making an ironic comment about the common fiction about Africa and India, in which the hero is usually found to have European aristocratic forefathers,when here a black American is found to have a royal African heritage—a heritage that accounts in large measure for his inherent nobility and qualities of leadership. But, still, it remains an ambiguous and ironic comment because the said black American may "pass" and, in effect, has been passing as a white man.

His female counterpart is a noble African version of the beautiful Dianthe Lusk. Queen Candace is described as a classical beauty, so beautiful that she can appear only in an unrealistic setting. She is described as a "Venus, a superb statue of bronze" with "long, jet-black hair" and "a warm bronze complexion" (568). Although it is true, as Hazel Carby maintains, that "[t]he idealization of black beauty within the text was classic in its pretensions rather than African,"[23] the salient characteristics of Queen Candace are her strength and power and exquisite femininity. In accordance with the novel's concept of male-centered civilization and the male-female power situation, Queen Candace appropriately lowers herself to Reuel-Ergamenes: "Grave, tranquil and majestic, surrounded by her virgin guard, she advanced gracefully, bending her haughty head; then, gradually her sinuous body bent and swayed down, down, until she, too, had prostrated herself, and half-knelt, half-lay, upon the marble floor at Reuel's feet"(567f).

The power situation is instantly made clear: the beautiful, civilized African woman lowering herself to the powerful, nearly white African American man and explorer. But Hopkins is not content to rest with this obvious, too simplistic dichotomy. It will be a reciprocal relationship: Reuel will learn from this ancient civilization and eventually find his ideal companion and "give to the world a dynasty of dark-skinned rulers" (570). In turn, he will teach the Cushite people about modern culture. Hopkins thus envisions a cross-cultural, pan-African, and cross-continental fertilization.

Although Hopkins does not quite succeed in transcending the central dichotomy between a mythic black past and a realistic African present, *Of One Blood* is nonetheless dominated by the vision of a blooming, well-ordered, civilized African culture and society. Her central argument about the common and unifying bond between all races of mankind allows Hopkins to criticize American racist tendencies, to express racial pride, and to call for a revision of history. By giving her African heroine the name of the historical Queen Candace, while her American, light-colored heroine has to die, the novel hints at the life-giving force and future potential that Hopkins envisions in the heart of Africa.

Notes

1. Pauline Hopkins, *Of One Blood, Or, the Hidden Self,* in *The Magazine Novels of Pauline Hopkins,* introduction by Hazel V. Carby (New York: Oxford UP, 1988), p. 576. All further references will be cited by page in the text.

2. Ann Allen Shockley, "Pauline Elizabeth Hopkins: A Biographical Excursion into Obscurity," *Phylon* 33 (Spring 1972), pp. 22–26. For a recent bibliography of Hopkins, see *The Unruly Voice: Rediscovering Pauline Elizabeth Hopkins,* ed. John Cullen Gruesser (Urbana: U of Illinois P, 1996).

3. See Carby's chapter "Of What Use Is Fiction?" in her *Reconstructing Womanhood: The Emergence of the Afro-American Woman Novelist* (New York: Oxford UP, 1987), for a discussion of Hopkin's role as founding member/editor/contributor of the *Colored American Magazine.*

4. Dorothy Hammond and Alta Jablow, *The Africa That Never Was: Four Centuries of British Writings about Africa* (New York: Twayne, 1970), p. 76.

5. Abdul R. JanMohamed, "The Economy of Manichean Allegory: The Function of Racial Difference in Colonialist Literature, *"Race," Writing, and Difference,* ed. Henry Louis Gates, Jr. (Chicago: U of Chicago P, 1986), p. 82.

6. Jackson Lears, *No Place of Grace: Antimodernism and the Transformation of American Culture 1880–1920* (New York: Pantheon, 1981), xvii.

7. Nancy Leys Stepan and Sander L. Gilman, "Appropriating the Idioms of Science: The Rejection of Scientific Racism," in *The Bounds of Race: Perspectives on Hegemony and Resistance,* ed. Dominick La Capra (Ithaca, N.Y.: Cornell UP, 1991), p. 89.

8. Wilson J. Moses, "The Poetics of Ethiopianism: W.E.B. Du Bois and Literary Black Nationalism," *American Literature* 47.3 (1975), p. 416.

9. Eric J. Sundquist, *To Wake the Nations: Race in the Making of American Literature* (Cambridge, Mass.: Belknap Press of Harvard UP, 1993), p. 553.

10. Dickson D. Bruce, "Ancient Africa and the Early American Historians, 1883–1915," *American Quarterly* 36.5 (1984), p. 685.

11. Dickison D. Bruce, *Black American Writing from the Nadir: The Evolution of a Literary Tradition, 1877–1915* (Baton Rouge: Louisiana State UP, 1989), p. 39.

12. Claudia Tate, *Domestic Allegorie of Political Desire: The Black Heroine's Text at the Turn of the Century* (New York: Oxford UP, 1992), p. 204.

13. Susan Gillman, "The Mulatto, Tragic or Triumphant? The Nineteenth-Century American Race Melodrama," in *The Culture of Sentiment: Race, Gender and Sentimentality in Nineteenth-Century America,* ed. Shirley Samuels (New York: Oxford UP, 1992), p. 222.

14. Hammond and Jablow, p. 78.

15. JanMohamed, p. 83.

16. Bruce, "Ancient Africa," p. 696.

17. See Stepan and Gilman, pp. 91–94.

18. Stepan and Gilman, p. 92.

19. Thomas J. Otten, "Pauline Elizabeth Hopkins and the Hidden Self of Race," *Journal of English Literary History* 59 (1992), p. 229.

20. Otten, p. 229.

21. Stepan and Gilman, p. 77.

22. Otten, p. 237.

23. Carby, p. 159.

17

• • • •

African Americans in Africa

Black Missionaries and the
"Congo Atrocities," 1890–1910

Katja Füllberg-Stolberg

The "Congo atrocities" were one of the most brutal events in Africa's colonial history. William Henry Sheppard, an African American missionary of the American Presbyterian Congo Mission (APCM) was among the first to speak out against these atrocities, thus playing a major role in the African American confrontation with European colonialism in Africa. The *Congo Mission* was founded in 1890 in the Democratic Republic of Congo which, from 1885 until its independence in 1960, was part of the European colonial empires, first as the Congo Free State, and, since 1908, as Congo Belge. The history of the APCM exemplifies the role African Americans played in the United States's involvement in Africa at the turn of the century and sheds light on the American economic and social interests in Central Africa at this time.

As a result of the colonial conquest of Africa, the late nineteenth century experienced a boom in Christian foreign missionary activities, and European as well as American churches extended their mission work into the African continent. The first African American missionaries came to the Congo territory in 1886 with the American Baptist Missionary Society. But black Americans working for the Baptists confronted strong disapproval and brought racial tension to the surface. Their presence in Africa was regarded by their white colleagues as an "intolerable interference in the God-given mission of the Anglo-Saxon race."[1]

Five years later, the foundation of the APCM jointly by the black missionary William Henry Sheppard from Virginia and the white missionary Samuel Norman Lapsley from Alabama, however, does not fit the picture of white missionaries' dominance. Were there special reasons for this decision of the Foreign Missionary Board of the Southern Presbyterian Church? The APCM became their first mission station on the African continent. Arguably, the Southern Presbyterians' engagement in Central Africa should be connected with American foreign policy in Africa at this time.

The U. S. Interest in Central Africa

Only at the peak of the so-called scramble for Africa were the European nations especially attracted to the Congo Basin. The vast resources of this region—ivory, palm oil, and (above all) rubber—were important to European industrial development. The Berlin Africa Conference of 1884–1885, initiated by the German chancellor Otto von Bismarck, was designed to end colonial rivalry through the official European annexation of most parts of the African territory. With participation in the conference, the United States, though not a colonial power in Africa, legitimized the conquest and the colonization of this continent.

While the European powers and the United States were still arguing over free navigation on the Congo River and free trade, King Leopold II of Belgium created the Congo Free State. Leopold's surprise tactics were rewarded when the European nations and the United States acknowledged the King's action as a *humanitarian* venture to enforce the abolition of slavery and the slave trade as well as to encourage free trade in Central Africa.

The Association Internationale du Congo (AIC) was founded by the Belgian King's initiative in 1882 as an international philanthropic organization to explore Central Africa. But in 1884, when the AIC merged into the Congo Free State, neither Europeans nor Americans realized that Leopold II used the association as an important political instrument to create his own colonial empire. Due primarily to the efforts of Henry Shelton Sanford,[2] a former American envoy in Brussels with good relations to the Belgian king, the U.S. government was the first power to recognize the AIC diplomatically—when other powers followed suit during the Berlin Africa Conference, the Congo Free State emerged.

The Congo Free State was an exception within the European colonial empires. The region was under direct control of Leopold, who regarded it as his personal property. His policy of economic exploitation turned into a nightmare for the indigenous population, who were forcefully recruited by agents of the foreign rubber companies, together with government officials, to collect and transport rubber, the region's most important cash crop, for the world market. Everybody who refused or tried to evade this arduous forced labor was draconically punished. Pictures of men, women, and even children with chopped-off hands shocked the world during the first years of the twentieth century.

The American interests in the Congo Basin seemed to have been determined by economic considerations. Due to Sanford, American businessmen became aware of the economic potentials in the region, which already had been anticipated by the explorer Henry Morton Stanley. Sanford created the ideological background for the activities of an American pressure group that tried to publicize the aims of "development" of this part of Africa.

In addition, the "race question" became an important impetus for America's involvement in Central Africa. John Tyler Morgan, senator from Alabama and member of the Foreign Relations Committee, supported the American engagement in Africa for what he called "humanitarian reasons." In the following years he strongly advocated African American migration to the Congo territory, which he considered the best solution for the "Negro question in the South." According to Morgan, black Americans' migration to Africa would rid the South of the more ambitious and "troublesome coloreds" and extend American influence and Christian civilization to a continent "badly in need of both."[3]

John Tyler Morgan knew the Lapsley family and owned for some years a joint law firm with the missionary's father. From the beginning, Morgan was interested in the establishment of the APCM at Luebo and exchanged letters with Samuel Lapsley about the social and economic conditions in Central Africa.[4]

The Foundation of the APCM

When Sheppard and Lapsley arrived in Central Africa in 1890, knowledge about this part of Africa was rather scanty and mainly derived from books such as Henry Morton Stanley's *Through the Dark Continent*. Stanley's rather grim picture of "uncivilized African heathens and cannibals" was shared by the majority of his readers and influenced black Americans' ambivalent image of the African continent.

The two young missionaries (Lapsley was 25, Sheppard 26 years old) began work enthusiastically. After a year-long intensive search, they finally chose the small trading center Luebo in the Kasai district in today's southern Democratic Republic of the Congo as a suitable site for their mission. Luebo, on the fringes of the Kuba Kingdom's 900 miles of the coast, was considered most remote and backward in European eyes. The Kuba Kingdom was actually a confederation consisting of several language groups, sharing a common culture.[5] The Kuba were surrounded by other groups, such as the Songye. Some of them—under the name of "Zappo-Zap" soon acquired a bad reputation as mercenaries of the "Free State."

The two Americans divided their work. Lapsley was in charge of the mission, responsible for organization, finance, and keeping contacts with the Belgian adminstration and the church at home. Sheppard, on the other hand, engaged in building relations with the Africans. He soon became known as a successful hippo hunter and supplied the surrounding villages with meat for the exchange of other foodstuffs. After a short while he could communicate on a basic level and familiarized himself with the ways of his African neighbors. But the successful cooperation between the two missionaries came to a sudden end when Lapsley died in March 1892 on a journey to the coast.

From then on, Sheppard was mostly on his own. He was temporarily supported by some white missionaries, but they all had to leave Luebo soon for reasons of health. When the Southern Presbyterian Church considered closing the station, Sheppard returned home for a lecture tour, pleading for financial and personal support of the APCM. Sheppard's gripping reports of his experiences in the "heart of Africa" sparked enthusiasm among the African American community. In May 1894, he returned to Luebo with four new missionaries, among them his wife Lucy Gantt Sheppard.

The activities of the African Americans in Luebo were regarded by the Executive Committee of Foreign Missions of the Southern Presbyterian Church with great suspicion. Sheppard, though de facto in charge of the station, was denied its official leadership.

Racial discrimination had always accompanied William Sheppard's career within this segregated Presbyterian congregation. It had taken him several years to convince the committee to send him to Africa, at least as an escort of a white missionary, Samuel Lapsley. The Executive Committee disputed Sheppard's ability to work independently in a foreign environment and to learn African languages, writing that "the sight of half-naked African women would subject Sheppard to irresistable attacks of lust" and finally agreeing that "only under supervision of a white man could a black missionary go to Africa."[6]

Sheppard was born in 1865 in Waynesboro, Virginia, to relatively affluent parents who belonged to the small group of black members of the Southern Presbyterian Church after the Civil War. He studied at the Hampton Normal and Agricultural School, and its founder, General

Samuel C. Armstrong,[7] became Sheppard's role model and considerably influenced his relationship to white people. Armstrong's idea of black education implied that "Negroes and Indians could learn their lessons of humility, cleanliness, thrift, and above all, the love of the white race."[8] During his studies at Hampton, Sheppard decided to dedicate his life to Africa. White teachers and reports of former pupils who worked as missionaries in Africa aroused Sheppard's interest in the continent. He decided to join Stillman College, the Southern Presbyterian Theological Seminary for Colored Men, at Tuscaloosa, Alabama. Here he learned about an African American's responsibility for the so-called "civilizing mission of the dark continent."

The theory of "providential design" served as a theological justification of colonialism and became fundamental to the American missionary movement in Africa. Providential design implied that God permitted enslavement of a part of the African population to enable them to enjoy Christianization and "civilization" in America. When this was achieved, slavery was abolished in the United States with God's will, so that African Americans could return to Africa to free their brothers and sisters from the yoke of "ignorance", "paganism," and "barbarity." In the 1880s, providential design was a major component of many Protestant movements and gained currency even among black church members. When Sheppard left Stillman, he was determined to have his part in the "redemption" of the "land of his forefathers."

Africa fulfilled Sheppard's expectations. For the first time he worked independently. In some way Africa became a second homeland for him. Here he gained all the authority and respect denied him in the United States. During his first years in Central Africa, Sheppard became known for his sympathetic and vivid reports about the Kuba. Sheppard was the first outsider to enter the ruling center of the Kuba Kingdom, and, following an invitation by the king, the Lukenga, spent several months there. "I had seen nothing like it in Africa. . . . [They] make one feel that he has entered a land of civilization."[9] "I grew very fond of the Bakuba and it was reciprocated. They were the finest looking race I had seen in Africa, dignified, graceful, courageous, honest, with an open, smiling countenance and really hospitable."[10]

Although the Kuba showed little interest in Christian religion, Sheppard was not disheartened. Again and again, he sought their contact. His voluminous notes illustrate that Sheppard, unlike the majority of missionaries in Africa, revised his original picture of the "backward, uncivilized" African and at least showed respect for "strange customs." Nevertheless, even in Sheppard's detailed reports of African life are notions like "spiritual darkness" and "moral gloom." But Sheppard, in contrast to his colleagues, always resisted the "chance to see himself as a black elect coming to save a continent."[11] He actively participated in the Kuba's everyday life and helped to build houses.

Sheppard's reports written between 1892 and 1896 are full of ethnographic descriptions and reflect peaceful living. But his "harmonious little world" was soon spoilt when the colonial reality reached the remote Kasai district and when finally a new head of the mission was appointed. William McCutchan Morrison, a white missionary with experiences in China, took charge in early 1897. He immediately began to reorganize the mission and risked an open clash with Leopold's government over the labor recruiting and concession policy.

The APCM's Fight against the Atrocities

The APCM, like other missions, was instructed to stay away from politics as much as possible to avoid confrontation with the colonial power. Cooperation with the authorities was important, especially in connection with the application for land to set up mission stations. In the Congo Free State the Protestant missionaries competed over the land question with the Catholics, who were strongly supported by the Belgian king.

With the founding of the Free State, Leopold II declared all the land not permanently used by Africans his personal property. Since 1890, he had personally held the monopoly on the extraction of rubber, ivory, and wood. Foreign companies could acquire concessions, but Africans were denied the right to partake in the economic exploitation of their own country's raw materials. From the middle of the 1890s onward, the number of reports about the brutal methods used by concession companies and administration officers in the recruitment of labor, mainly for the extraction and transport of rubber, proliferated. Apparently the Force Publique, an armed troop of Africans under the charge of European officers, forcefully recruited the people in the villages for labor services.[12] Those who refused suffered severe punishment. Pressure on the African population grew in 1898 when the colonial administration introduced a tax on foodstuffs. The missionaries of the APCM witnessed the flight of large groups of the indigenous population into the bush. At the beginning they gave little credit to the villagers' reports or thought them exaggerated, until the Pyaang, who lived next to the mission and had shown considerable interest in the conversion to Christianity, were invaded by Songye people. These "Zappo Zaps" provided the greatest number of soldiers for the Force Publique in the district of Kasai, were reputed to be very belligerent, and thus were feared in the whole region.

After Morrison's takeover, Sheppard stepped into the background. Morrison was accompanied by several white missionaries who soon tried to dominate the work at the station. In the United States opposition to the employment of African Americans as missionaries in Africa grew. Distrust and animosity toward black missionaries spread, and many were called back from their posts in the first decades of the twentieth century. The attitude of the American churches corresponded with the political and social climate in the United States, which was increasingly dominated by hatred and violence against black people. With the beginning of the World War I African Americans were no longer sent to the APCM. This policy supported the colonial government's argument that black Americans would stir up the Congo people's growing resistance to colonial rule.

During the following years, tensions between black and white mission personnel at the APCM intensified. The younger generation of African American missionaries especially did not easily accept the subordinated role assigned to them. Even Sheppard, who officially never uttered any critique of the Executive Committee's decisions, tried to evade Morrison's direct control when he took charge of the newly founded station at Ibanji, far from Luebo.

Yet Sheppard, with his long-established contacts to the Kuba and several other groups in the area and his position of trust within the African population, proved indispensable for the APCM. Sheppard provided the mission with the insider material about the social and economic situation of the Free State that became fundamental for the mission's active role in the Congo Reform Movement.

When there were rumors about plans of the "Zappo Zaps" to attack Ibanji, which had turned into a safe haven for many fugitives, Morrison ordered Sheppard on a dangerous surveillance tour to the Songye. All hopes to end the conflict obviously lay with Sheppard, as a letter by Morrison and two other missionaries confirmed: "Dear Brother Sheppard, we hear of atrocities being committed in the Pianga country by the Zappo-Zaps. We commission you immediately on receipt of this letter to go over and stop the raid."[13]

Sheppard's journey confirmed his worst fears and he found proof that the Songye were mutilating the population under the eyes of the state officials. Sheppard wrote a detailed report about his meeting with the Songye leader M'lumba N'kusa:

We saw the chief [M'lumba N'kusa, K.F.-S.] coming out. He reached us, greeted us and said: "Come, come to the camp." We started on. I said: "I see some dead bodies on the plain. I notice men with their heads off." "Some has taken a fancy to them", he said.

"They have taken their skulls to rub their tobacco with." . . . On we walked and saw flesh on pieces of bamboo around the fire to dry for future use. We spent two days inside the camp and we counted the frames of people as well as we could and there were three hundred they had murdered and eaten."[14]

Sheppard and his escort were allowed to return to Luebo. They informed the authorities and subsequently M'lumba N'kusa and 700 of his followers were arrested in the presence of Sheppard. The *Missionary*, the official monthly magazine of the Presbyterian Foreign Mission Board, published parts of Sheppard's drastic report in 1900. Then at least the American church communities received firsthand information about the gruesome deeds harming the population of the Congo Free State. But another four years passed before European governments and the American president, Theodore Roosevelt, addressed the matter, as a result of the formation of the Congo Reform Association (CRA) in England and the American Congo Reform Association (ACRA) in Boston. Meanwhile, the crimes against the population of the Free State increased in scope and cruelty.

William Sheppard had pointed out atrocities in 1899 in a report to Leopold. He had received no response. It was 1905 when Leopold established a commission of inquiry, which advocated reforms but blamed the unpredictable African soldiers solely for the atrocities.

In the meantime William Morrison was named official representative of the APCM by the church council. While most members of the Executive Committee of Foreign Missions of the Presbyterian Church were rather reluctant to get involved in an internal affair of the Congo's administration, the Committee's chairman, Rev. Samuel H. Chester, a friend of Morrison, called for Presbyterians to take an active role in the campaign for reform.

The missionaries of the APCM were supported by the American Baptist Missionary Union (ABMU). Together, their mission boards sent several delegations to the secretary of state for foreign affairs and President Roosevelt. Yet the United States was not a signatory power of the Berlin Act, and therefore any direct interference in Congo affairs seemed very unlikely. Thus, the church representatives decided to approach Congress. A *Memorial Concerning Conditions in the Independent State of the Kongo* was referred to the Senate Foreign Relations Committee, of which John Tyler Morgan was the ranking minority member.[15]

Finally, the campaign for Congo reform, initiated by protestant church members as well as the CRA and the ACRA, was successful. Under the pressure of the American and European governments, the Belgian state agreed to the annexing of the Congo Free State in 1908.

"Christian Fighter for African Rights"

William Morrison's contribution to the movement against the Congo atrocities is unquestionable. His correspondence with diplomatic circles and with officials of the State Department prove his dedicated work.[16] But most of his reports were based on information collected by William Sheppard, who, unlike Morrison, received little attention in the international media.

In the African American community, Sheppard, however, was well known and celebrated as a "Christian fighter for African rights" and "black hero of the Congo."[17] He even found some late acknowledgment when W.E.B. Du Bois declared him "Man of the Month" in *The Crisis* of May 10, 1915.

Morrison's dominent role explains only part of Sheppard's reluctance to take an active part in the reform movement. When the ACRA asked him to speak in Boston, he claimed that he wished to speak only of the Gospel work and that he, as a colored man, would not be understood if he criticized a white government before white people.[18] In Sheppard's cautious attitude, the profound impact of General Armstrong's educational doctrine lingers on. Yet, despite his reluctance to openly confront the white authorities, Sheppard described in detail the economic and social decline of the Kuba as a consequence of colonial misrule.

Sheppard reported the mistreatment of the Kuba by the agents of the Compagnie du Kasai, an amalgamation of different foreign companies, who acted as tax collectors for the colonial authorities. Their demand for forty hours of hard work per month as a payment of the so-called "labor tax" had not been met by the Kuba, who refused to obey. So in 1907, Sheppard journyed to the affected villages he had already visited three years before, when the prosperity of the area had made a great impression on him. His second visit, however, was characterized by a note of deep shock at the fate of the villagers:

> But within the last three years how changed they [the Kuba, K.F.-S] are! Their farms are growing up in weeds and jungle, their king is practically a slave. . . . Even their children cry for bread. Why this change? You have it in a few words. There are armed sentries of chartered trade companies, who force the men and women to spend most of their days and nights in the forest making rubber, and the price they receive is so meager that they cannot live upon it.[19]

Sheppard published an article in the mission's own circular, the *Kasai Herald.* Although Sheppard did not mention the Compagnie du Kasai, the company was outraged and in September 1909 brought a case against Sheppard and Morrison as the editor. The trial gained great publicity in the United States. But with exception of the African American media, the whole affair was referred to as the "Morrison case." Sheppard was only mentioned as "one Negro missionary." After several delays, the hearing finally took place in Kinshasa (former Leopoldville) in September 1909. The case against Morrison was withdrawn and Sheppard was acquitted. The court decided that, in his article, Sheppard had intended neither to maliciously offend the Compagnie du Kasai nor to make it responsible for the conditions and had in fact not mentioned its name.

For Sheppard the closure of the case also meant his departure from Central Africa. In 1910, together with his wife, he returned to the United States for good and took over a parish in Louisville, Kentucky, where he died in 1927. The reasons for Sheppard's departure are not fully clear. In his letter of resignation he stated that he was "fearful of being obliged to return from his work in Africa on account of broken health."[20] But the internal development of the APCM and the increasingly difficult relationship with his colleagues surely influenced his decision.

Obviously, Sheppard was deeply hurt at the reaction of some of his colleagues, who blamed him for not having talked explicitly in public about the Congo State's misgovernment and the atrocious treatment of the African population.[21] As a consequence of Sheppard's sometimes cautious behavior, part of Leopold's lobby, especially the Belgian legation in Washington, D.C., tried to use his reports and speeches for their own ends. For example, they asserted that Sheppard had not seen any atrocities with his own eyes, and the missionary seemed unable to confront these charges in a more aggressive manner.

Moreover, Sheppard's relationship with the Kuba had deteriorated in his last years in Africa. He tried, together with two other African American missionaries, to interfere in a dispute about the succession to the throne of the Kuba Kingdom. The missionaries hid the potential successor to the throne, whom they favored, in order to protect him from his opponent. This direct intervention strongly shook the long-established relationship of confidence and respect between Sheppard and the Kuba. He lost his position of trust within the Kuba society.[22]

In spite of critical statements by some of his contemporaries, William H. Sheppard was surely one of the most important and influential black American missionaries at the turn of the twentieth century. He was not the only one who wrote about life in the Congo, but his strong dedication and commitment to the fate of the African people made him an outstanding personality. His detailed and vivid descriptions of Kuba everyday life are of high ethnological value. Although Sheppard made an important contribution to the discovery of and fight against the Congo atrocities, as well as to the debate about European colonialism and imperialism in Africa in general, his work has so far been acknowledged only by some scholars within black American studies.[23] In the standard European literature on colonialism in Central Africa, William Sheppard is not mentioned.[24]

Before 1900, African American missionaries, like the majority of the black leaders in the United States, were seldom sharp critics of colonialism in Africa. They adhered to the "civilizing and Christianizing" theory and saw European imperialism as a justifiable method to accomplish that end. Yet the coverage of the atrocities in the black media caused widespread condemnation in the African American community and contributed to an intensive debate over European colonialism in Africa. Moreover, it appears that the brutal events in the Congo Free State vividly brought the suppression of African people to the public eye and necessarily intensified the confrontation with white racist attitudes and "lynchjustice" practices in the United States.

Sheppard never fully gave up his devoted attitude toward white people, a characteristic shared by many African Americans who grew up in the post–Civil War South. But he showed great sensibility for the deteriorating social and economic conditions of the African population as a consequence of colonial oppression.

William Henry Sheppard's articles and speeches illustrate the important role black missionaries played in the understanding of the changing relationship between African Americans and the continent of their forefathers in the early twentieth century.

Acknowledgments   This essay is part of a larger research project on the influence of African Americans on the relations between the United States and Africa between 1880 and 1930, sponsored by the German Research Foundation (DFG).

Notes

1. Kimpianga Mahaniah, "The Presence of Black Americans in the Lower Congo from 1878 to 1921," in Joseph E. Harris, ed., *Global Dimensions of the African Diaspora* (Washington, D.C.: Howard University Press, 1993), p. 409.

2. Joseph A. Fry, *Henry S. Sanford: Diplomacy and Business in the 19th Century America* (Reno: University of Nevada Press, 1982).

3. John O. Baylen, "Senator John Tyler Morgan, E. D. Morel, and the Congo Reform Association," *Alabama Review*, 15 (1962): 117–132.

4. See Samuel N. Lapsley to John T. Morgan (November 9, 1891), in the John Tyler Morgan Papers, Library of Congress.

5. On the very complex structures within the Kuba Kingdom, see Jan Vansina, *The Children of Woot: A History of the Kuba Peoples* (Madison: University of Wisconsin Press, 1978).

6. Donald F. Roth, "The 'Black Man's Burden': The Racial Background of Afro-American Missionaries and Africa," in Sylvia M. Jacobs, ed., *Black Americans and the Missionary Movement in Africa* (Westport, Conn.: Greenwood Press, 1981), p. 32.

7. David L. Lewis, *W.E.B. Du Bois: Biography of a Race* (New York: Henry Holt, 1993), p. 122.

8. Armstrong, quoted in Lewis, p. 124.

9. William H. Sheppard, "Into the Heart of Africa," *Southern Workman*, 22 (1893): 182–187.

10. William H. Sheppard, *Presbyterian Pioneers in the Congo* (Richmond, Va.: Presbyterian Committee of Publication, 1917), p. 143.

11. Walter L. Williams, *Black Americans and the Evangelization of Africa, 1877–1900* (Madison: University of Wisconsin Press, 1982), p. 124.

12. J. C. Vellut, "La Violence Armée de l'Etat Indépendent de Congo," *Cultures et Devéloppement*, 16 (1984): 671–707.

13. Quoted in William H. Sheppard, "Light in Darkest Africa," *Southern Workman*, 34 (1905): 220.

14. Sheppard, "Light," pp. 220–225.

15. U.S. Senate Committee on Foreign Relations, Memorial Concerning Conditions in the Independent State of the Kongo, 58th Congress, 2nd session, 1904, Document 282.

16. William M. Morrison Papers, Presbyterian Church (U.S.A.), Department of History, Montreat, N.C.

17. Larryetta M. Schall, "William H. Sheppard: Fighter for African Rights," in Keith L. Schall, ed., *Stony the Road: Chapters in the History of Hampton Institute* (Charlottesville: University of Virginia Press, 1977), pp. 105–124.

18. Vass to Hawkins (June 21, 1905), in the Lachlan C. Vass Papers, Presbyterian Church (U.S.A), Department of History, Montreat, N.C.

19. *Kasai Herald*, 1 January 1908: 12–13.

20. Quoted in *Minutes of the Executive Committee of Foreign Missions of the Presbyterian Church* (Nashville, Tenn.: January 4, 1904).

21. See the Lachlan C. Vass Papers, Presbyterian Church (U.S.A), Department of History, Montreat, N.C.

22. While the official reason for Sheppard's retirement was ill health, the real reason was sexual misconduct. Sheppard was forced to resign in 1910 but was reinstated as a minister in 1912. The official sources of the Southern Presbyterian Church remained quiet about Sheppard's inglorious retreat from Africa. The facts were revealed after the evaluation of additional APCM missionaries' correspondence. See Robert Benedetto, ed., *Presbyterian Reformers in Central Africa: A Documentary Account of the American Presbyterian Congo Mission and the Human Rights Struggle in the Congo, 1890–1918*, trans. Winifred K. Vass (New York: E. J. Brill, 1996), p. 423ff.

23. See Sylvia M. Jacobs, *The African Nexus: Black American Perspectives on the European Partition of Africa, 1880–1920* (Westport, Conn.: Greenwood

Press, 1981), and Elliot P. Skinner, *African Americans and the U.S. Policy Toward Africa, 1850–1924* (Washington, D.C.: Howard University Press, 1992).

24. For example, L. H. Gann, Peter Duignan, *The Rulers of Belgian Africa, 1884–1914* (Princeton, N.J.: Princeton University Press, 1979); Jean Stengers, *Congo's Mythes et Réalités: 100 Ans d'Histoire* (Paris: Louvain-la-Neuve, 1989).

18

• • • •

Sexual Violence and the Black Atlantic

On Alice Walker's Possessing the Secret of Joy

M. Giulia Fabi

For what the process of torture does is to split the human being into two, to make emphatic the . . . distinction between a self and a body, between a "me" and "my body." . . . Torture, like any experience of great physical pain, [is] mimetic of death; for in death the body is emphatically present while that more elusive part represented by the voice [i.e., the self] is so alarmingly absent that heavens are created to explain its whereabouts.

Elaine Scarry, *The Body in Pain* (1985)

In *Warrior Marks*, Pratibha Parmar and I are sending a message to our sisters . . . and the message is this: If in fact you survive your mutilation, and the degradation that it imprints on soul and body, you still have a life to live. Live it with passion, live it with fierceness, live it with all the joy and laughter you deserve.

Alice Walker, "Heaven Belongs to You," *Re-Visioning Feminism* (1995)

I think Marge Piercy was right in one way in her review of *Meridian* although in another way she was very humorous. She said that what the book needed to end it was a marriage or a funeral. Marriage is absurd. Meridian is not interested in marriage, but I can see that the expected end of that kind of struggle is death. It's just that in addition to all of her other struggles, her struggle is not to die. That's what she means when she talks about martyrs not permitting themselves to be martyrs, but at some point just before martyrdom they should just go away and do something else.

Alice Walker, interview in *Black Women Writers at Work* (1983)

The awareness of how human bodies can be systematically reduced to the total objectification of captive flesh,[1] the practice of breaking the silence on female-specific experiences of sexual and racial abuse, the insistence that racial violence is always "en-gendered"[2]: these issues characterize the narrative tradition of African American women and dominate the literary works of Alice Walker, who has often focused on "victims of sexual and communal abuse."[3] Indeed, Walker's emphasis on the violence connected with the "private" world of romantic or familial relationships has "engendered" controversies that have in some ways reinforced her role as eloquent literary spokesperson for important feminist issues.[4]

In her 1992 novel, *Possessing the Secret of Joy*, Alice Walker once again courageously addresses a taboo subject. As critic Barbara Christian has noted, in fact, in *Meridian* "she approached . . . the myth of black motherhood and the idea that revolutionary violence should at least be questioned," and six years later in *The Color Purple* she protested incest within the African American community.[5] In *Possessing the Secret of Joy* Walker focuses on the controversial issue of female genital mutilation in Africa, writing a highly effective narrative that takes an uncompromising stance against it. Like other activists opposed to this ritual practice, Walker treats the topic "peremptorily,"[6] in ways that leave her text open to critiques that emphasize the hegemonic potential of many impassioned condemnations of Third World cultural traditions. In this essay I do not intend to underestimate Walker's own awareness, as a cultural critic, of hegemonic intercultural and interracial processes, which she has analyzed in relation to the United States.[7] I will propose, instead, a textual and intertextual analysis of Walker's novel and argue that the complexity (as well as the effectiveness) of *Possessing the Secret of Joy* emerges most clearly when it is contextualized within the African American female literary tradition, as well as within Walker's previous novelistic condemnations of sexual violence against black women in the United States.

In *Possessing the Secret of Joy,* Walker interweaves three major, closely related thematic concerns: the condemnation of genital mutilation as a traditional patriarchal tool to oppress women; the indictment of female complicity in their own mutilation and victimization; and the insistence on the need to break the oppressive silence that surrounds this taboo issue, a silence that represents another, more indirect form of patriarchal domination and culturally enforced female complicity. These themes have a long history in Walker's own previous literary production and in the literary tradition of African American women. Walker's focus on female genital mutilation in Africa is on a continuum both with nineteenth-century condemnations of other practices of sexual violence against black women in America (such as the systematic rape of female slaves and the "*externalized* acts of torture and prostration"[8] that were an integral part of the slave system) and with forms of sexual oppression after the official end of slavery in the persistence of pernicious stereotypes of black womanhood and systematic practices of sexual harassment and violence. Harriet Jacobs's *Incidents in the Life of a Slave Girl* (1861), Frances Harper's *Iola Leroy* (1892), and Pauline Hopkins's *Contending Forces* (1900), to mention but a few of the best-known examples, represent early literary renditions of the intersection of racial and sexual forms of exploitation and violence, a theme characterizing many African American women's novels also in the twentieth century.

The controversial issue of female complicity with patriarchy has often been dealt with in terms of the racism of white against black women, but there are also literary antecedents for Walker's outspoken analysis of female complicity within the black community. Examples include Hopkins's discussion of how black female community emphasis in *Contending Forces* on purity and chastity penalizes survivors of sexual violence like Sappho, Irene and Clare's competitive relationship in Nella Larsen's *Passing* (1929), or Geraldine's preconceived hatred of Pecola in Toni Morrison's *The Bluest Eye* (1970).

The need to break the silence surrounding the public dimensions of violence in the private sphere of the home and of sexuality is closely related to the aforementioned themes, both in Walker's works and, more broadly, in the literary tradition of African American women. Harriet Jacobs's emphasis on the truth of her story, Hopkins's insistence on the importance of remembering abuse, the final cursing aloud of Marita Bonner's Madie in "Drab Rambles" (1927), Audre Lorde's later warning "Your silence will not protect you,"[9] and Morrison's notion of "re-memory" in *Beloved* (1987) manifest the same theme that Tashi expresses in the sign she makes after returning to Africa to kill the *tsunga* who mutilated her: "If you lie to yourself about your own pain, you will be killed by those who will claim you enjoyed it."[10]

Because of these echoes and continuities within the African American female tradition, because of the strong reaction *Possessing the Secret of Joy* stimulates, because of my support for the cause Walker is championing, as well as because of the worldwide significance of this novel, I would like to analyze some incongruities in Walker's representation of the oppression of circumcised African women, women whose culture(s) are not her own. She feels rather self-conscious about their "otherness,"as becomes clear in her appendix "To the Reader" (where she lists the secondary sources she consulted on genital mutilation), as well as in her disclaimers about the vague geographical African location of the novel and about having invented the Olinka language.[11] Such self-consciousness, however, does not necessarily weaken her argument. On the contrary, it reveals her awareness of the hegemonic potential of her impassioned abolitionist stance. Indeed, as Walker "claim[s] the storyteller's prerogative to recast . . . events" or "ma[k]e up" words, she partly preempts the by now standard critiques of her geographical and cultural inaccuracy. My critique focuses instead on the representational incongruities that derive from Walker's construction of Tashi as an exemplary victim. We, as readers, must attentively and self-consciously decodify a book whose potential weakness may paradoxically reside in the very breadth and effectiveness of its appeal.

In Love and Trouble, Walker's first collection of short fiction published in 1973, includes a short story entitled "The Child Who Favoured Daughter" about female mutilation in the United States. In this story, a father finds out that his daughter is in love with a married white man and orders her to leave him. His daughter's simple "no," the only word she utters in the entire story, triggers off a violent response that culminates in her mutilation and finally in her murder: before shooting her, the father cuts off her breasts, leaving "two bleeding craters the size of grapefruits on her bare bronze chest and fling[ing] what he finds in his hands to the yelping dogs."[12] This mutilation of, and contempt for, female flesh clearly anticipates *Possessing the Secret of Joy* and finds an equivalent in the powerful

scene when Tashi remembers how M'Lissa threw her sister Dura's mutilated genital parts to an eager chicken.[13] In both cases, excision emerges
as an extreme attempt to control women's sexuality and as a most obvious symptom of female oppression in patriarchal societies. In both contexts, the mutilated body becomes a "privileged symbolic space that
translates cultural conflicts into a visible representational frame."[14] Also,
in both cases the violence presupposes "a weak, dead, or otherwise absent
or estranged mother who is unable to protect herself or her children," either from the father or from the ritual practice of excision.[15]

The similarities between "The Child Who Favoured Daughter" and
Possessing the Secret of Joy, however, only underscore the differences between them. While the "standing mastectomy" inflicted on the daughter
results from her attempt to resist patriarchal dictates,[16] Tashi's mutilation stems from a desire to belong and become strong through obedience
to what the Olinkans call "our leader," a desire that, in light of its destructive consequences for women, throws into sharp relief the masculinist
bias of nationalist movements. Walker's decision to make Tashi *choose* to
undergo her mutilation foregrounds very effectively also the power of ideological and cultural indoctrination,[17] as well as the related issue of
women's complicity with their own victimization.

Within the economy of the novel, Tashi's original sin of complicity
traps her within an inescapable cycle of victimization that she is initially
unable, and finally unwilling, to break. In fact, the novel presents a pronounced and consistent focus on death and suicide as escapes from what
the protagonist perceives, literally, as a dead-end situation: Tashi's (absent) flesh continues to dominate the novel and parallels the lifelessness
of Tashi's postexcision existence. On the one hand, the novel is framed by
Tashi's descriptions of her own death-in-life. The novel begins: "I did not
realize for a long time that I was dead."[18] The equation of life and death is
maintained in her closing signature: "Tashi Evelyn Johnson. Reborn,
soon to be Deceased."[19] On the other hand, death and suicide structure
the entire plot of the novel. *Possessing the Secret of Joy* opens with Tashi's
panther story, which legitimates a highly lyrical, but nevertheless suicidal, death as a way out.[20] Later on, mutilation is portrayed explicitly as a
metaphorical murder and as a form of enslavement that connotes a living death.[21] Toward the end of the novel, when she seems to have come
out of her metaphorical death and to have reached self-consciousness
through her therapy sessions and Pierre's anthropological explanations
for her nightmares, Tashi commits a suicidal murder, which she does not
try to hide but, on the contrary, confesses. And her confession will speed-
ily lead to her execution.

The unremitting "grimness"[22] of Tashi's story is very effective as a tool to advance the author's indictment of genital mutilation practices, but it creates representational tensions and incongruities for Walker, who has consistently focused on "contrary women"[23] who attempt to fight back, though not necessarily effectively or successfully.[24] In *Possessing the Secret of Joy*, on the contrary, the female protagonist is completely trapped by her (absent) flesh, and even when she recovers full consciousness of what was done to her, and learns to condemn it as part of the larger subjection of women, she does not shift her focus from death or attempt to reappropriate her captive subjectivity, except for a fleeting moment that remains "uncanny": "[J]ust at the end of my life, I am beginning to reinhabit completely the body I long ago left."[25] But she lives only long enough to understand what happened to her and to explain it to the reader. Such an understanding leads to the heightened horror of the spectacle of her death, the self-immolation of a lamb prepared for slaughter.[26] The theatricality of her death, the elaborate and crowded staging of her execution, lend a mythical aura to Tashi's resigned acceptance of death, a death that, though lyrically camouflaged as a rebirth, is actually an act of self-destruction like that of Lara the panther. The double scene with Olivia that frames the novel is in this regard very significant: Tashi chooses both her initial metaphorical death by circumcision[27] and finally her execution,[28] a repetition that epitomizes the inescapability of her initial victimization.

Tashi's conviction that she would never "be able to write a book about [her] life, nor even a pamphlet, but that write *something* [she] could and would"[29] assumes a metanarrative significance that underscores how excision has irrevocably deprived Tashi of control over her story, as well as over her life. Tashi's relationship to writing contrasts most obviously with Walker's characterization of Celie, who "writes herself into being,"[30] but it recalls Walker's previous literary explorations of the "conundrum that the African American literary tradition is, in a sense, founded on the bodies of raped and mutilated ancestors, whose bodies are literally inscribed by the scars of slavery and sexual abuse, or whose illiteracy motivates their offspring to acquire an empowering literacy."[31] With Tashi, Walker expands this conundrum to Africa: the mode of the protagonist's death embues her with a mythical aura that seems to push her back into the past, enacting the symbolic status of a founding mother. Tashi's immolation, in fact, is depicted as inspirational for women of the younger generation like Mbati.

The emphasis on death and the inescapability of the past creates a very moving martyr, but it weakens the portrayal of Tashi's agency and attempt at resistance. The passivity that she sees as resulting from her mutilation seems to constitute part of her consciousness, not just her condition. "Self-possession will always be impossible for us to claim,"[32] she tells Mbati, a declaration that heightens the effectiveness of Walker's indictment of genital mutilation but at the same time creates representational problems in articulating a vision of social change that can include women so completely determined by their condition. These representational problems become particularly evident when *Possessing the Secret of Joy* is read against a "utopian romance" like *The Color Purple*, to which Walker explicitly refers in one of the quotations that precede the novel.[33] In *The Color Purple* Walker decided to liberate Celie "'from her own history' because she 'wanted her to be happy,'"[34] even at the cost of catapulting her outside the generic confines of the realistic novel,[35] but in *Possessing the Secret of Joy* Walker does not let her protagonist entertain the possibility of a deliverance (other than death) from her imprisonment in her (absent) flesh.

To paraphrase one of my opening quotations, Tashi is a martyr who permits herself to be a martyr, as Walker (after her experimentations with closure in *Meridian*, *The Color Purple*, and *The Temple of My Familiar*) permits herself *not* to avoid a typical "suggestion of the older structuring plots": death.[36] The "punitive or transcendent individual death" that, as critic Rachel Blau DuPlessis has argued, in *Meridian* Walker transformed into "a 'communal spirit, togetherness, righteous convergence' which has both a spiritual and a political meaning," takes center stage in *Possessing the Secret of Joy*.[37] In this novel, Walker's difficulties in reconciling her call for social change with the resigned victimization of her protagonist emerge very clearly on at least two occasions. The first is Tashi's last conversation with her spiritual daughter Mbati. The connection between political change and life affirmation that characterized *The Color Purple*[38] is weakened here by Tashi's acceptance of death. Walker betrays an awareness of this fact and addresses it in Tashi's response to Mbati's determination not to have a child because "the world is entirely too treacherous." Tashi replies: "Are you saying we should just let ourselves die out? And the hope of wholeness with us?"[39] In distinguishing between individual and race suicide, Walker makes clear that Tashi is indeed the exemplary victim but that her choice of death must remain unique. Against her individual immolation, the ending opposes the living bodies of the demonstrators (who were also probably circumcised) and the bodies of their baby girls.[40]

These same representational tensions emerge also in the startling contrast between the end of the novel and the subsequent note of "Thanks." The novel closes with an execution and with Tashi's soul's last words: "I am no more. And satisfied."[41] The "Thanks," on the contrary, begins with a hymn to life. Walker writes: "Despite the pain one feels in honestly encountering the reality of life, I find it a wonderful time to be alive,"[42] and she declares herself "reassured . . . that human compassion is equal to human cruelty and that it is up to each of us to tip the balance."[43] Here Walker recuperates, rather abruptly, the sense of hope and the emphasis on agency that she has underplayed in her victimized fictional protagonist. Similarly, the supportive international community Walker evokes in her "Thanks" stands in sharp contrast with the isolation, or the inability to communicate, that characterizes most of Tashi's postexcision fictional existence. It is significant in this sense that Tashi should move beyond such isolation chiefly when she is in prison awaiting her execution: at that point, her mothering of Mbati reestablishes the vision of future cooperation and solidarity among women, albeit without changing Tashi's role as exemplary victim.

I highlight these representational tensions to emphasize the Manichean structure that underlies the text. The complex worlds of "Advancing Luna—and Ida B. Wells" (1981), "The Child Who Favoured Daughter," or *The Third Life of Grange Copeland* (1970) are missing from *Possessing the Secret of Joy*. In those texts, which dealt with African American characters and situations, Walker combined an uncompromising indictment of sexual violence with a particularly insightful analysis of the historical, social, and personal contexts that enabled the reader to understand the characters' reactions. On the contrary, the underlying Manichean structure of *Possessing the Secret of Joy* outlines (and critiques) in broad strokes the power dynamics that inform traditional practices of genital mutilation in Africa, but it does not allow for a deep, multifaceted investigation of the cultural and individual issues surrounding it.

I am not invoking a superficial brand of cultural relativism, whereby all traditional practices are acceptable as long as their origin can be explained. On the contrary, I lament the cultural and historical contextualization that could have grounded the reader's conviction of the need to abolish genital mutilation not only in horror, but in the understanding of the postcolonial situations and the intricacies of the characters' reactions, moving beyond the rather simplistic explanations of the African "animal-like ignorance and acceptance that most angers Tashi,"[44] or of an indoctrination so complete as to inhibit the very possibility of resistance.

Walker does refer to these issues in Tashi's opening conversation with Olivia,[45] but she moves on too quickly to depict the devastating effects of genital mutilation. She focuses on effectively transmitting the full horror of the situation, trying to build as large a coalition as possible. Within this framework, mutilation is broadly portrayed as a strategy to force women into submission, and although undoubtedly true, Walker does not lead us to comprehend the specific practice in question. This very vagueness enables Walker to expand the problem of genital mutilation in Africa to include, metaphorically, widely diverse forms of female oppression (frigidity as a form of psychological mutilation, footbinding in Asia, clitoridectomy in the West), as well as other issues such as animal rights.[46]

The wide basis of the novel's appeal is at once the source of its power and of its weakness, for it glosses over asymmetries of power between different groups of women and their cultural specificities. The "difficulty of preventing identification from becoming appropriation" and therefore betrayal has recently been discussed by feminist critics such as Karen Sanchez-Eppler in relation to nineteenth-century white abolitionist writers' profusely detailed depictions of violence against female slaves.[47] The politics of representation and abolitionism, whether of slavery or of genital mutilation, intersect: then as now the urgency of the situation demands swift and effective action, but it does not benefit from simplifying the process of social change.

I would like to close by returning once again to *Meridian*. Walker's own reflections on the Civil Rights Movement, in fact, reveal important interpretive and critical insights into the larger world of *Possessing the Secret of Joy*, since her reflections focused explicitly on the connection between ends and means; on the complexities of lasting social change, grounded in a multifaceted understanding of the past that goes beyond absolute glorification or absolute refusal; on the need to question alliances that are important and strategic but that do not and should not erase the differences between our subject-positions; and, finally, on the responsibility to question our wholehearted devotion to a cause, even as we remain convinced of its rightness.[48]

Acknowledgments   I would like to thank Michel J. Huysseune for his insightful critical readings of earlier versions of this essay.

Notes

1. See Hortense J. Spillers, "Mama's Baby, Papa's Maybe: An American Grammar Book," *Diacritics* 17.2 (1987): pp. 65–81.

2. Teresa de Lauretis, "The Violence of Rhetoric: Considerations on Representation and Gender," *The Violence of Representation: Literature and the History of Violence*, ed. Nancy Armstrong and Leonard Tennenhouse (London: Routledge, 1989), p. 245.

3. Trudier Harris, "From Victimization to Free Enterprise: Alice Walker's *The Color Purple*," *Studies in American Fiction* 14.1 (1986): pp. 1–17; quotation from p. 1.

4. The most publicized and virulent controversy surrounded the 1982 publication of *The Color Purple*.

5. Barbara Christian, "We Are the Ones that We Have Been Waiting For: Political Content in Alice Walker's Novels," *Women's Studies International Forum* 9.4 (1986): pp. 421–426; quotation from p. 424.

6. Francoise Lionnet, *Postcolonial Representations: Women, Literature, Identity* (Ithaca, N.Y.: Cornell UP, 1995), p. 130.

7. See, for instance, her landmark collection of essays *In Search of Our Mother's Gardens* (1983).

8. Spillers, "Mama's Baby," p. 68.

9. Audre Lorde, *Sister Outsider* (Trumansburg, N.Y.: Crossing P, 1984), p. 41.

10. Walker, *Possessing the Secret of Joy* (1992; New York: Pocket Books, 1993), p. 108.

11. Walker, *Possessing*, pp. 283–285. Such cautionary remarks were probably motivated by similar critiques about the African letters in *The Color Purple*.

12. Alice Walker, "The Child Who Favoured Daughter," *In Love and Trouble* (New York: Harcourt Brace Jovanovich, 1973), pp. 35–46; quotation from p. 45.

13. Walker, *Possessing*, p. 75.

14. Lionnet, p. 127.

15. Harryette Mullen, quoted in Hortense Spillers, "'The Permanent Obliquity of an In(pha)llibly Straight': In the Time of the Daughters and the Fathers," *Changing Our Own Words: Essays on Criticism, Theory, and Writing by Black Women*, ed. Cheryl A. Wall (New Brunswick, N.J.: Rutgers UP, 1989), pp. 127–149; quotation from p. 142.

16. Spillers, "The Permanent Obliquity," p. 140.

17. Walker, *Possessing*, pp. 241–243. The issue of "choice" is a complicated one, especiallly when we think of Walker's emphasis on Tashi's ignorance of what the ritual practice actually involves, though she has heard Dura's screams. Nevertheless, Tashi, unlike her sister, is older and she is not physically compelled to submit to excision: to that degree, she has more freedom of choice.

18. Walker, *Possessing*, p. 3.

19. Walker, *Possessing*, p. 279.

20. Walker, *Possessing*, pp. 3–5.

21. Walker, *Possessing*, pp. 3, 45, 66–67, 77, 155, 229, 278.

22. Walker, *Possessing*, p. 262.

23. Barbara Christian, *Black Feminist Criticism: Perspectives on Black Women Writers* (New York: Pergamon P, 1985), p. 31.

24. In her aforementioned article, Harris discusses the limited effectiveness of Walker's characters' attempts to rebel or resist. While agreeing with her assessment, I do not share her critique of Walker's focus on dead-end situations and characters. The tragic quality of many of her characters' struggles against oppressive circumstances gives them a heroic valence that is not undermined by their eventual defeat. In *Possessing the Secret of Joy*, on the contrary, Tashi stands out as a victimized martyr rather than a defeated rebel. Indeed, her closing acceptance and even glorification of death suggest that

the murder she has committed is not to be read as an attempt, however inef-
fective, to save herself, but rather as a suicide.

25. Walker, *Possessing*, p. 110.

26. Walker, *Possessing*, p. 275.

27. Walker, *Possessing*, pp. 21–24.

28. Walker, *Possessing*, pp. 254–255.

29. Walker, *Possessing*, p. 109.

30. Henry Louis Gates, Jr., *The Signifying Monkey: A Theory of African American Literary Criticism* (New York: Oxford UP, 1988), p. 245. Gates also notes how the epistolary form empowers Celie, who "writes her own story, and writes everyone else's tale in the text except Nettie's" (p. 245). *In Possessing the Secret of Joy*, instead, Tashi's story is refracted through the points of view of a variety of characters, while Tashi's voice itself is fragmented into those of Tashi, Evelyn, Evelyn-Tashi, and Tashi-Evelyn. In her case, the process of narrative "quilting," which Christian sees at work in this novel, seems to confirm her powerlessness also on a narrative level. See Barbara Christian, ed., *Alice Walker, "Everyday Use"* (New Brunswick, N.J.: Rutgers UP, 1994), p. 15.

31. Harryette Mullen, "Runaway Tongue: Resistant Orality in *Uncle Tom's Cabin, Our Nig, Incidents in the Life of a Slave Girl*, and *Beloved*," *The Culture of Sentiment: Race, Gender, and Sentimentality in Nineteenth-Century America*, ed. Shirley Samuels (New York: Oxford UP, 1992), pp. 244–264; quotation from p. 335, n. 40.

32. Walker, *Possessing*, p. 273.

33. Rajeswari Sunder Rajan, "Life after Rape: Narrative, Theory, and Feminism," *Borderwork: Feminist Engagements with Comparative Literature*, ed. Margaret R. Higonnet (Ithaca, N.Y.: Cornell UP, 1994), pp. 61–78; quotation from p. 73.

34. Walker, quoted in Harris, p. 15.

35. See Keith Byerman, "'Dear Everything': Alice Walker's *The Color Purple* as Womanist Utopia," *Utopian Thought in American Literature*, ed. Arno Heller et al. (Tubingen: Gunter Narr Verlag, 1988), pp. 171–183.

36. Rachel Blau DuPlessis, *Writing beyond the Ending: Narrative Strategies of Twentieth-Century Woman Writers* (Bloomington: Indiana UP, 1985), p. 160.

37. DuPlessis, p. 161.

38. See Christian, "We Are the Ones," p. 425.

39. Walker, *Possessing*, p. 273.

40. Walker, *Possessing*, p. 280.

41. Walker, *Possessing* p. 281.

42. Walker, *Possessing*, p. 287.

43. Walker, *Possessing*, p. 288.

44. Walker, *Possessing*, p. 250.

45. Walker, *Possessing*, pp. 21–24.

46. Walker, *Possessing*, pp. 169, 176, 188, 262–66. In an interesting passage, Evelyn-Tashi extends the notion of metaphorical multilation to American culture: "An American, I said, sighing, but understanding my love of my adopted country perhaps for the first time: an American looks like a wounded person whose wound is hidden from others, and sometimes from herself. An American looks like me" (p. 213).

47. Karen Sanchez-Eppler, "Bodily Bonds: The Intersecting Rhetorics of Feminism and Abolition," *The Culture of Sentiment: Race, Gender, and Sentimentality in 19th-Century America,* ed. Shirley Samuels (New York: Oxford UP, 1992), pp. 92–114; quotation from p. 95. For a more extended analysis of these issues, see also Eppler's *Touching Liberty: Abolition, Feminism, and the Politics of the Body* (Berkley: U of California P, 1993).

48. In this respect, I share Walker's conviction that "women and children who suffer genital mutilation will have to stand up for themselves, and, together, put an end to it. But that they need our help is indisputable" (Walker, "Heaven," p. 63).

19

· · · ·

Alice Walker, Activist

Matron of FORWARD

Tobe Levin, Freifrau von Gleichen

In the film *Warrior Marks*, from among a group chanting "We condemn FGM," midwife Comfort I. Ottah tells the camera: "This is not culture. This is torture."

Although the demonstrators, diasporan African women, oppose a Brent councillor's 1992 motion to legalize genital cutting, we know that the majority of African women involved approve "female circumcision"— the "culturally sensitive" and "respectful" word until 1990—when a regional conference of the Inter-African Committee (IAC) in Addis Ababa proposed altering the terminology. In 1991, the UN Seminar on Traditional Practices Affecting the Health of Women and Children, held in Burkina Faso, recommended the term "female genital mutilation," or FGM, which is now codified in World Health Assembly Resolution WHA46.18 and other international instruments, including documents approved during the Fourth World Conference on Women in Beijing, China, September 1995 (WHO J2). Sadly, a footnote appears in the Beijing Platform for Action's chapter on women and health, allowing "the various religious and ethical values and cultural backgrounds" (United Nations, Draft Platform, 43) to influence assessment of implementation risks and potentially undermine FGM eradication efforts.

Addressing this danger, Alice Walker has produced two books, numerous articles, and a video for the abolition movement, explaining her choice of a "'a form (fiction) that would move people to understand the

issue, to feel this assault on a woman's body, not just think about it'"
(Robson 9). *Possessing the Secret of Joy* (1992) also reassures activists that
"a portion [of royalties] will be used to educate . . . about the haz-
ardous effects of genital mutilation, not simply on the health and happiness of individuals, but on the whole society . . . and the world" (283).
Indeed, Walker donated several hundred copies of her work to raise funds
at a December 4, 1997, seminar in London run by FORWARD (Foundation for Women's Health Research and Development)—for she acknowledges: "women and children who suffer . . . mutilation will have to
. . . put an end to it. But that they need our help is indisputable"
("Heaven" 63).

Since disclosure is essential, Walker is key to today's educational effort. Efua Dorkenoo, FORWARD initiator and 1994 recipient of the Order
of the British Empire, lauds Walker's film and books. "After I read *Possessing the Secret of Joy*," Efua told me, "I wrote to Alice. You see, FORWARD
counsels women like Tashi, whose mental anguish at having suffered
mutilation has become unbearable. Tashi is so real that I wanted to let
Alice know and invite her to be patron of FORWARD. Of course, she
agreed if we called her matron" (interview 1994). The June 3, 1995,
board meeting of FORWARD specifically credited Walker: for the welcome
of Dorkenoo's testimony before the U.S. Congress in 1993; for information
that reached Edward Kennedy, propelling him "in[to] the forefront of international advocacy on FGM with UN Specialized Agencies and the US
Missions in Africa" (Rose 82); and for inspiring congresswomen Patricia
Schroeder and Barbara Rose Collin's bill (H.R. 3247) against FGM in the
United States.

Walker has also inspired the rebirth of German initiatives. Verena Stefan, whose *Häutungen* (1975) shaped the contemporary women's movement, devotes a chapter to Tashi in *Rauh, wild und frei: Mädchengestalten in
der Literatur* (1997). And Walker's influence has even reached the Bun-
destag: at a parliamentary hearing on FGM (30 April 1997) MP Angelika
Köster-Lossack called her speech "Warrior Marks: A Feminist Analysis of
Genital Mutilation and its Consequences for Foreign Aid" (Levin, "Pain,"
24). Of greatest significance, however, is the action taken by Christa
Müller, wife of SPD chief Oskar Lafontaine. When the first lady of Benin
asked for German assistance, Müller agreed, leading on January 29,
1996, to the first press conference of (I)NTACT (Internationale Aktion
gegen Beschneidung von Mädchen und Frauen [International Action
against Circumcision of Girls and Women]). The full-page advertisement
for Alice Walker and Pratibha Parmar's *Narben oder Die Beschneidung
der weiblichen Sexualität (Warrior Marks)* subsidized the program for
(I)NTACT's debut colloquium on March 16, 1996, whose theme, "Female

Circumcision: Physical Torture and Spiritual Agony under Cover of Cultural Tradition," takes a firm stand against the paralysis often following appeals to cultural relativism. Comfort Ottah, a featured speaker, told me how she welcomes this opportunity to network close to, if not precisely on, the governmental level. One arm of FORWARD's strategy has been to urge states to commit significant resources to eradication.

For the first time the regional director for Africa of the World Health Organization (WHO) chaired the IAC's triennial conference in Dakar, Senegal, in November 1997, yet most governments remain indifferent—or hostile. Indeed, opposition takes many forms. "After the showing of our film in London," Walker notes, "there were death threats against . . . Dorkenoo" (River 38). Nor has Walker gone unscathed. In *Newsweek* (1993) Dr. Nahid Toubia calls the Pulitzer Prize winner "'a writer whose star is fading . . . trying to sensationalize [a very sensitive issue] in order to get the limelight back'" (Kaplan et al. 124). Walker admits being pained by such reactions, motivated perhaps by her failure to measure up to an Afrocentricity Ann duCille calls "therapeutic essentialism," (duCille 39) and critiques, with Cornel West, for its "'retrograde views on black women, gay men, and lesbians'" (West in duCille 35). Furthermore, in *The Same River Twice*, Walker mourns that "the eye . . . turned on . . . suffering . . . African sisters—not a blind one, fortunately—was marred by its 'colonial gaze'" (38).

Charging Walker with "misunderstanding . . . African culture," Gay Wilentz (1993) regrets her "polemic": "[D]riven by a belief that not only African . . . but all societies actively thwart women's sexuality and control over their bodies, [*Possessing*] tends to efface difference and will be problematic for readers acquainted with African history," because "Western stereotypes of 'Africa'" may be "reinforce[d]" (16). Not without some justification, Wilentz questions Walker's imprecision: no single tribe, let alone the composite Olinka, can legitimately represent a diverse continent with boundaries drawn as colonial conveniences. Nonetheless, Wilentz argues less convincingly when she asserts that use of the "most extreme form of female circumcision" lends "an aspect of voyeurism [to] Walker's approach; her taking such liberties unfortunately puts her in the company of other Western writers before her for whom 'Africa' merely represented the exotic or the grotesque," since "infibulation is practiced extensively *only* in Mali, Somalia and Sudan, and rarely in Kenya and most other black African countries " (16, emphasis mine). Yet, according to UN figures, this practice affects the lives of 9,220,400 women and girls in the Sudan (89%); 3,773,000 in Somalia (98%); thousands of immigrants in Europe, Australia, Canada, and the United States, (UN D-2), and it is spreading: for instance, "the demand for infibulation

. . . is on the increase [in Ethiopia]" ("Ethiopia" 15). True, 85% of mutilations are "mere" excisions, but I would contend, with Walker, that both
severe and milder surgeries take place for similar reasons and that the
drama of Tashi's ordeal elicits empathy, not racist scorn.

Yet, seconding Wilentz, an unpublished statement released on November 19, 1993, by "a group of African women who have . . . worked
. . . to abolish the . . . practice" deplores Walker's portrait of "an
African village, where the women and children are without personality,
shadows . . . dancing and gazing blankly through some stranger's
script of their lives. The respected elder women of the Secret Society in
the Gambian village turn into slit-eyed murderers adorned in blood
money and wielding rusted weapons with which to butcher children"
(Allan 2). Tuzyline Allan (1994) worries that negative views of Walker's
intervention may "inhibit feminist alliance across cultures" (2). And
equally alarming, in a 1993 *New York Times* editorial, African residents in
the United States blame Walker for their distress, reducing to personal
display her attention to "their" issue. The video they fear is "emblematic
of the Western feminist tendency to see female genital mutilation as the
gender oppression to end all oppressions . . . a gauge by which to measure distance between the West and the rest of humanity" (Dawit and
Merkuria A-27). Despite Walker's having made "a deliberate effort to
stand with the mutilated women, not beyond them," (*Warrior* 13) her
African critics contend that, for them at least, she has not succeeded.

Clearly, though, she has tried. A careful reading of *Possessing the Secret
of Joy* reveals Walker's attempt to preclude such charges, as she dramatizes cultural distinction and suggests the inability of anyone born in
America to wholly comprehend her protagonist's pain. To the uninitiated, the Swiss analyst's "exceedingly sharp . . . large razor" (Walker,
Possessing, 36) would suggest shaving or carpentry, but FGM only to the
mutilated. Only Tashi, "out of habit," can recognize "the sliding gait of
the 'proper' Olinkan maiden" (144), while to her therapist, the patient
goes unrecognized as an African, not an American (17). Tashi/Evelyn,
ringing true to Dorkenoo, remains the expert in her own behalf.

Most disarming, however, is a call to break "the harrowing silence of
the bulk of African women who uphold the practice" (Ahmadu 43).
Fuambai Ahmadu, claiming to speak for the mutilated in the West, deplores publicity:

Ten years ago the debate about female circumcision was limited to
health officials, missionaries and others with a particular interest
in Africa. Now, [in] any mainstream women's magazine [you
might] chance upon a blown-up photograph of a young African

girl with her legs spread open to reveal her bare vagina, stitched
closed for the world to see. (43)

This exposure, Ahmadu concludes, induces shame.

Sadly, it does. But Walker is compassionate, for instance, on *The South
Bank Show* (1992), sharing with moderator Julianne Greenwood her concern for the victims. "I anticipate a lot of grief, a lot of pain, disguised as
anger," she said. However, she has answered other critics less patiently. At
Oakland's opening of *Warrior Marks*, she admonished her audience to
"refrain from spending more than ten minutes stoning . . . the messenger. Within those minutes thousands of children will be mutilated" (Revi-
sioning 63) As A. Kluvitse confirms, "FORWARD is not 'mounting a campaign to force millions of women to give up their traditions'. We are
working to ensure that 6,000 children are not held down every day while
essential parts of their genitalia are cut off" (6). Still, African supporters
insist, "It isn't abuse; it's an act of love" (Dorkenoo interview 1995).

"Transcultural *metissage*," Françoise Lionnet's term, may help medi-
ate what is, in part, a war of words. The non-European authors she reads
"de-exoticize the non-West, indicating the centrality of their concerns to
the self-understanding of people everywhere. They insist on the rela-
tional nature of identity and difference, on the productive tensions between the two, and on the intricate and interdependent ways in which
human agents function" (6). Yet Walker, as one "colonized" in white
America, does this as well: Tashi's suffering, Adam realizes, on a "continuum of pain" (Walker, *Possessing* 165), is universalized to trigger sister-
feeling. And in giving Pierre such a pivotal role, Walker joins Lionnet's
authors in dramatizing "mongrelization" or "creolization"—Lionnet's
words—thereby challenging the "cultural relativism," or hands-off attitude, of some of Walker's critics, a stance suspect in a world of constant
change. In fact, in the chapter titled "Dissymmetry Embodied: Nawal El
Saadawi's *Woman at Point Zero* and the Practice of Excision," Lionnet uses
this "specific ritual practice . . . to test . . . cultural relativism" (129),
pointing to "two competing claims: on the one hand, the campaign for
. . . abolition of . . . ritual practices on the basis of a universal ethical
imperative against the physical torture and psychological impairment of
millions of women; on the other hand, the advocacy of respect for the
cultural autonomy of African societies that denounce any feminist intervention as 'acculturation' to Western standards" (131). According to the
"logique" of her métissages, however, this second mode of posing the
issue already distorts it, for we do not have—except cynically when it
comes to affairs of the woman—any so-called postcolonial society *in*

Africa still unaffected by "Western standards." Assitan Diallo has re-
searched the topic:

> [Diallo's thesis] entitled *L'Excision en milieu Bambara* [asks] whether
> excision possesses the same functional value in Mali today as it did
> in the past and whether . . . its initiation significance [remains].
> She . . . discovered from her respondents (. . . women, excised
> some time ago, and men, considering the excision of their children
> today) that these ceremonies have disappeared. The traditional
> songs are no longer taught . . . and not one [girl] . . . had re-
> ceived any instruction concerned with initiation to adulthood. (in
> Dorkenoo, *Rose*, 40)

Although some ritual goes on (in Sierra Leone for example), change is the
rule, in a negative sense: as medicalization increases, the age of intervention decreases. Thus do "traditions" alter.

But the underlying masculinist discourse is constant, and behind the
rhetoric of rights lies a maligned female body. In her *LA Times* review of
Possessing the Secret of Joy (1992), Tina McElroy Ansa shares an anecdote:

> Months ago, [she] heard an African-American male scholar/writer
> say in the manner of a comic throwing away a line. "Hey, did you
> hear that Alice Walker dedicated her latest novel to [']the innocent
> *vulva*[']?" He sort of pursed his lips and looked slowly around the
> room. Then, . . . rais[ing] one eyebrow, [he] . . . chuckled and
> went on to another subject. As if to say, "Nough said." His gesture
> was part amusement, part embarrassment, part incredulity, part
> derision. (32)

And, I would add, exemplary in its trivializing a "feminine sorrow."

Nothing is trivial about the figures: ten thousand at risk in France,
twenty thousand in Great Britain. This year alone two million worldwide
will be knifed. So when Walker dedicates her book "With Tenderness and
Respect To the Blameless Vulva," she clearly does so to draw the world's
attention to an organ abused, misunderstood, and maligned, by women
and men alike. "My own body was a mystery to me [Tashi explains to her
therapist, Raye] as was the female body, beyond the breasts, to almost
everyone I knew" (Walker, *Possessing*, 119). Despite the fact that, as Aud
Talle (1993) informs us, "unmarried girls [in Somalia] often show their
infibulation to each other and compare the neatness of the scar and the
size of the orifice," (96) what they see is the vulva's erasure.

Campaigning in France, GAMS (Groupe femmes pour l'Abolition des

Mutilations Sexuelles), reminds us of precisely what is at stake: lining the labia majora, a bed of smooth, muscular fibers and fatty tissue enjoys a rich supply of blood, including significant veins to enlarge the wings when flushed. The labia minora, opulent in pigment, reveal an extraordinary elasticity, also increasing in size when filled, like the woman's erectile apparatus, the clitoris, its roots, and accompanying muscles. A suspending ligament links it to the pubis, an analogy between female and male morphology reflected in the clitoral system's complexity, the "button" (Celie's term) even more richly endowed with nerve endings than its homologue, the penile gland. So GAMS concludes: "The difference between female and male resides in the fact that the male erection projects outward from the body, while the female fills the space within" (GAMS 54, translation mine).

Possibly the first novel dedicated to female genitalia, *Possessing the Secret of Joy* personalizes the global eviction of women's selves from their bodies, for the clitoris is a metonymic of possession. An unnamed woman visits Tashi-Evelyn in prison, bringing her "photographs of paintings she has discovered among caves and rocks. . . . [In one of the photos appears] the little figure from M'Lissa's hut, smiling broadly, eyes closed, and touching her genitals. If the word 'MINE' were engraved on her finger, her meaning could not be more clear" (Walker, *Possessing*, 196–197). Corporeal integrity means self-esteem. Perhaps utopian, this model of wholeness marks the razor's edge of loss—as autonomy is mutilation's target.

In a remarkably candid analysis, Abdou Sylla of the University of Dakar explains excision—which he favors—in precisely these terms. Clitoridectomy "permits passage from a narcissistic and egotistical pleasure (masturbation) to a heterosexual and social [i.e., male] *jouissance*," which the professor avers "coincides with the African conception of feminine sexuality" (324). He notes that in Africa

clitoridectomy [affects women's integration] according to social criteria. During childhood the little girl has ample opportunity to . . . masturbate . . . [until] the clitoris is severed . . . at an age to procreate. Clitoridectomy thus prepares her for the only sexual role society envisions: motherhood. In traditional African societies, the clitoris is considered the organ of narcissistic pleasure, that is, the joy one gives oneself, in isolation, egotistically. By suppressing it, society redirects female sexuality toward the vagina, the organ of social pleasure. . . . Excision therefore . . . promote[s] passage to a form of sexuality in the service of procreation . . . by reducing the possibility of egotistical, solitary and sterile enjoyment. (324–325, translation mine)

Et voilà! Stopping just short of openly claiming that excision exists for the male—although in the Sudan, *Adlat El Rujal* or reinfibulation literally means "'men's circumcision', and the woman who undergoes it says 'she went in for repair'" (Lightfoot-Klein 35)—the passage betrays a fear that women, if given the chance, would favor their own tools. And if not cynical (for today, where do we find "traditional society"?) it reveals the patriarchy's self-deception, taking for granted the limits it places on "the second sex." Translated into Walker's idiom, "the cock was undeniably overweening, egotistical, puffed up, and it was his diet of submission that had made him so" (Walker, *Possessing*, 78).

Submission is further implied in Dura's "murder." Like Muthoni in *The River Between*, who decides to "become a woman in the tribe," suffers clitoridectomy, and dies as a result, leaving a sister behind,[1] Tashi also assumes the role of witness to her sibling's torture, breaking taboo by hiding in the grasses, and then repressing the memory of Dura's agony. Complicating the picture further, Tashi actually observes an absence: her dear one's nonappearance in the row of older girls tells her to whom the screams belong. In her own mind then, and also in M'Lissa's, the child's inhuman sounds have echoed ever since, forming a collective—yet inarticulate—howl.

Defacing the Jungian therapist's pristine wall with her chromium green fowl—the cock's stain on a virginal surface—releases Tashi's memory, liberating language. "[The] boulder . . . in [her] thoat," the blockage of speech, is finally removed, unearthing "a word; and behind that word [her] earliest emotions. Emotions that had frightened [her] insane" (Walker, *Possessing*, 80–81). Once "death" becomes "murder," an agent is revealed. Before, "no one was responsible. No one was to blame" (Walker, *Possessing*, 81). Now guilt can be projected outward, finally deflected from the self.

These key ideas—the taboo, the hiding, the witness, the repressed, and its release in testimony—can also be found in Holocaust aesthetics and the interpretative schemas applied to literatures of trauma. Lawrence Langer, for one, problematizes an idiom for the unspeakable. "In the Beginning was the Silence," he writes. As Adorno hinted, language itself falls short, incommensurate with the agony to be shared and unable to respect the injured. We find, however, that events, too, impose a hush. For "no apparent reason," they "violate the coherence of childhood" (Langer 21), leading to disorientation that can induce insanity. Shame is also the victim's part, in camp and hut. Note the exciseuse in *Warrior Marks*: even if you put a knife to their throats, the initiates will not tell what was done. What is in the box is secret. The society is secret. The woman's genital is secret. And the secret is shame.

Shame then weaves its own disguise. The excised is forced to take cover, as Tashi perceives when Adam comes: "Nothing runs out of my eyes to greet him . . . my self [in] hiding behind an iron door" (Walker, *Possessing*, 45). And common to descriptions of excised girls are the eyes, "dead," nonreflective, no longer mirrors to the mood—of self or other—but masks instead. Society, too, colludes in this veiling: "No one spoke of the other, the hidden scar, between Tashi's thin legs" (Walker, *Possessing*, 65). Similarly, Shoah's victims' pain often remains underground. Survivors' children suffer a loving parent's emotional frigidity, the young exiled by what cannot be said. In Walker, this unspoken is an oxymoron: for instance, the "ringing silence" following childbirth that Tashi-Evelyn thinks she hears. Or is it the equally inarticulate "screaming of monkeys" (Walker, *Possessing*, 58)?

Elaine Scarry (1985) applies to these relations between speech and *schmerz* in torture another oxymoron: "physical pain has no voice" (3), yet the agony can be appropriated by the torturer. In fact, Scarry's argument in *The Body in Pain*—a "book about the way other persons become visible to us, or cease to be visible to us" (22)—can be fruitfully applied to Walker's tale. In *Warrior Marks* the epigraph says: "'What is the fundamental question one must ask of the world? . . . Why is the child crying'" (Walker, *Possessing*, n.p.) Excerpted from *Possessing the Secret of Joy*, the answer ties Walker's empathy to her own wounded youth. "It's remarkable," she notes, "that the [girls'] suffering . . . is the thing . . . least considered. Children cry in pain and terror . . . yet their elders . . . just assume they will forget" (*Warrior* 349). Walker, however, has never forgotten, nor have the victims in study after study. The FORWARD case files overflow with unforgotten trauma. Thus, Walker asks: "Do we have a responsibility to stop the torture of children . . . or are we like the midwife who said that when she's cutting . . . and the child screams she doesn't hear it? Are we expected to be deaf?" (*Warrior* 350).

Scarry sees this deafness as pain conflated with power, posing the ethical question as follows: "How [can] one person . . . be in the presence of another . . . in pain and not know it—not know it to the point where he himself [sic] inflicts it, and goes on inflicting it?" (12). The answer lies in isolated subjectivity: "To have great pain is to have certainty; to hear that another person has pain is to have doubt" (7). In this formula we read activist literature's fundamental mandate, to induce la nausée. But this explains only in part. Scarry structures torture of three simultaneous phenomena: "(1) the infliction of pain[;] (2) the objectification of the subjective attributes of pain[;] (3) the translation of the objectified attributes of pain into the insignia of power" (50). In other words, "in torture . . . the obsessive display of agency . . . permits one person's body to be translated into another person's voice, [converting] real human pain . . . into a regime's fiction of power"(18).

In little girls whose clitoris and vulval lips are aggressively removed, we see patriarchal power (with which submissive female agents can also be invested), a specific force illuminated by Scarry's theory. "The physical pain [of torture] is so incontestably real," she writes, "that it seems to confer its quality of 'incontestable reality' on that [authority] which has brought it into being" (27). That is, genital annihilation confirms the operator's status. Yet "torture is being used . . . precisely because the reality of that power is so highly contestable, the regime so unstable" (27). Now, to focus for a moment on recent feminist gains, can we not discern a flaw in patriarchy's armor, a hint of its own illegitimacy, a fear about its fragile surface?

Given the tenacity of FGM, I doubt that the system demanding it might collapse any day soon. But the telling of the trauma, as in Walker's novel, brings that moment closer. In *Testimony: Crises of Witnessing in Literature, Psychoanalysis, and History*, Shoshana Felman and Dori Laub record a "rebirth to speech in the testimonial process," an "emergence from the life of silence" (47). When Evelyn, in a sitting with Raye, uses these words, "As for the thing that was done to me . . . or *for* me" (Walker, *Possessing*, 117), she too testifies, but what she affirms is ambivalence, for in the last analysis, the torture has become culture. In Hanny Lighfoot-Klein's work *Prisoners of Ritual* (1989), an informant says, "My parents arranged this for me" (70). Another woman remarked, "[Since I believed that] the continued existence of this small piece of flesh would have made me unclean and impure, and . . . caused [my husband] to be repelled by me[,] I began to be happy the day I recovered from . . . the operation and felt . . . rid of something which had to be removed, . . . clean and pure" (165). Equally contented is the infibulated professor, who remarked, "I live my life in a community where every other woman is like me" (118).

Today, however, the very fact that these women voice their views confirms that métissage is under way, and mutilation has no place. As Dorkenoo says in *Warrior Marks*, African women in diaspora will spearhead the abolition movement, which Tashi does when she slays M'lissa. Tashi also has allies in unexpected quarters. One is the European colonialist Doris Baines, a hidden campaigner on board the ship leaving Africa toward the close of *The Color Purple*. Having sent one of her "wives" to Oxford medical school, Doris tells her grandson, after praising Akwean child-raising methods, "They do a bit of bloody cutting around puberty. But Harry's mother the doctor is going to change all that. Isn't she Harold?" (Walker, *Purple*, 237).

Let us hope Doris is right. Yet despite increasing institutional commitments—in particular FORWARD's allies; the UN with its agencies; the German government whose parliamentary hearing of April 30, 1997, borrowed Alice Walker's words, her "warrior marks" as its slogan—the silence, I have found, grows thick again, moving me to ask why the black girl's agony vanishes when it should be announced most vigorously. For instance, bell hooks, in *Talking Back. Thinking Feminist. Thinking Black* (1989), chose to contradict Barbara Christian's opinion that "'people of color . . . have theorized . . . different[ly] from the Western form of abstract logic'" (39). "Inaccurate," hooks claims, considering "different groups of African people, like the Dogon, who have very abstract logical schemas to support rituals that focus on creating gendered subjects" (39). The Dogon may well illustrate hooks's point, but their logical schema genders subjects by amputating the clitoris, a surgery we know is not physiologically parallel to the circumcision of boys, nor is it abstract. And I also question the reticence of another admired and respected critic. Although Carole Boyce Davies (1994) emphasizes dignity, she leaves her reader to extrapolate abolitionist support. Why? Davies contends that running "any feminist issue . . . up the scale to its most radical possibility, its most clarifying illustration[,] will reveal the experience of Black women" (137). Yes, indeed—but that includes ablation of the clitoris, sealing of the labia, inscription in the patriarchal order enforced by mothers on their girls.

Davies also "speaks to the need for feminists to racialize and historicize their definitions of motherhood" (137). Yet, how can African Americans do this without considering FGM? Lack of knowledge does not explain these omissions. Nuruddin Farah, who deals repeatedly with infibulation in his novels, chose to present Somalia in *Transition* (1995)—a highly influential context that might have been used to profound effect—without one word about infibulation. Why?

Political strategy? Hesitation to privilege sexism over racism? If gender has priority, what becomes of tribal solidarity? African American female critics may also be responding to the virulent attacks on non-Africans who, in the seventies, helped launch the movement. The AAWORD's 1980 UN Mid-Decade for Women conference "Statement on Genital Mutilation" charged that "this new crusade of the West has been led out of the moral and cultural prejudices of Judaeo-Christian Western society: aggressiveness, ignorance or even contempt, paternalism . . . activism . . . sensationalism" (217). Copenhagen's altercations clearly discouraged support, yet, since all discussants actually agree that FGM should cease, what continues to divide us?

Behind much of the rhetoric, failed coalition, and hostility to Walker is homophobia. Assessing opposition to *The Color Purple*, Walker notes that "the group Blacks Against Black Exploitation of Blacks in the Media made it clear that a primary concern . . . was not merely the character of Mister, but a fear of the 'exposure' of lesbianism 'in the black community'" (Closet 546). Johnnetta B. Cole, in her "Afterword" to Beverly Guy-Sheftall's *Words of Fire*, asks why "so many contemporary African American women . . . dread . . . being called feminist" (550), suggesting that they are "certainly not immune to the extensive presence of homophobia in American society" (551). And in Africa, such attitudes are even stronger. Genevieve Pastre, a lesbian whom Awa Thiam had invited to a 1982 CAMS (Commission pour l'abolition des mutilations sexuelles) conference, in Dakar, Senagal, was nearly denied the floor, in part due to heterosexual bias. As Buchi Emecheta tells Thelma Ravell-Pinto, "Western feminists . . . are only concerned with issues . . . related to themselves and transplant these onto Africa. Their own preoccupations—female sexuality, lesbianism and female circumcision—are not [African women's] priorities" (50). Instead, Emecheta contends, Africans care "about infant and child mortality, health problems, food production and hunger, education for their children, and how to make enough money to feed their families" (51)—concerns of the great majority of FGM's opponents as well!

Yet the most poignant reason for African American silence regarding mutilation is voiced by Joanne Braxton, who found in contemporary black women's oeuvre that

> the ancestral figure most common . . . [is] an outraged mother [who] speaks in and through the narrator . . . to 'bear witness' and to break down artificial barriers between [reader and writer]. Not only does [she provide] a 'benevolent, instructive, and protective' presence to the text, she also lends her benign influence to the very act of creation, for the Black woman artist works in the presence of this female ancestor, who passes on her feminine wisdom for the good of the 'tribe', and the survival of all Black people, especially those in the African diaspora created by the Atlantic slave trade" (300).

The dissonance between this mother and her knife-wielding counterpart makes me want to weep.

Instead, I write, join (I)NTACT, support FORWARD, and thank Alice Walker, who has helped move the world somewhat closer to integrity.

Notes

1. Tobe Levin, "Women as Scapegoats of Culture and Cult: An Activist's View of Female Circumcision in Thiong'o's *The River Between*," in *Ngambika:*

Studies of Women in African Literature, ed. Carole Boyce Davies and Anne Adams Graves (Trenton, N.J.: Africa World Press, 1985), pp. 205–221. Choosing to express tribal solidarity by electing to undergo the rite also occurs in Kenyan Muthoni Likimani's *They Shall Be Chastised* (Nairobi: East African Literature Bureau, 1974).

References

AAWORD. "A Statement on Genital Mutilation." *Third World. Second Sex. Women's Struggles and National Liberation.* Ed. Miranda Davies. London: Zed, 1983: 217–220.

Ahmadu, Fuambai. "Rites and Wrongs." *Pride* (April/May 1995): 43–46.

Allan, Tuzyline. "The Textual Politics of Clitoridectomy." Unpublished essay, 1994.

Ansa, Tina McElroy. Review of *Possessing the Secret of Joy* by Alice Walker. *The Los Angeles Times* (5 July 1992). Reprinted in *Alice Walker: Critical Perspectives Past and Present.* Ed. Henry Louis Gates, Jr., and K. A. Appiah. New York: Amistad, 1993: 32–34.

Braun, Ingrid, Angelika Schwarzbauer, and Tobe Levin, eds. *Materialien zur Unterstützung von Aktionsgruppen gegen Klitorisbeschneidung.* Munich: Frauenoffensive, 1979.

Braxton, Joanne M. "Ancestral Presence: The Outraged Mother Figure in Contemporary Afra-American Writing." *Wild Women in the Whirlwind. Afra-American Culture and the Contemporary Literary Renaissance.* Ed. Joanne M. Braxton and Andrée Nicola McLaughlin. New Brunswick, N.J.: Rutgers University Press, 1990: 299–315.

Cole, Johnnetta B. Epilogue to *Words of Fire: An Anthology of African-American Feminist Thought.* Ed. Beverly Guy-Sheftall. New York: New Press, 1995: 549–551.

Davies, Carole Boyce. *Black Women, Writing and Identity: Migrations of the Subject.* New York: Routledge, 1994.

Dawit, Seble, and Salem Mekuria. *The New York Times* (7 December 1993): A-27.

Dorkenoo, Efua. "Cutting the Rose." *Female Genital Mutilation: The Practice and Its Prevention.* London: Minority Rights Group, 1994.

Dorkenoo, Efua. Personal interview, 14 October 1994.

Dorkenoo, Efua. Personal interview, 3 June 1995.

duCille, Ann. "Postcolonialism and Afrocentricity: Discourse and Dat Course." *The Black Columbiad: Defining Moments in African American Literature and Culture.* Ed. Werner Sollors and Maria Diedrich. Cambridge, Mass.: Harvard University Press, 1994: 28–41.

"Ethiopia. Why Should Pretty Flowers Be Destroyed for no Reason at All?" Inter-African Committee on Traditional Practices Affecting the Health of Women and Children. Newsletter no. 17. (April 1995): 15.

Farah, Nuruddin. "Bastards of Empire: Writing and the Politics of Exile." *Transition: An International Review* 65.5.1 (Spring 1995): 26–35.

Felman, Shoshana, and Dori Laub. *Testimony: Crisis of Witnessing in Literature, Psychoanalysis, and History.* New York: Routledge, 1992.

GAMS (Group femmes pour l'Abolition des Mutilations Sexuelles). "Excision et Santé Publique. Étude médicale." *Les mutilations du sexes des femmes aujourd'hui en France.* Paris: Éditions tierce, 1984.

Greenwood, Julianne. Moderator. *The South Bank Show.* BBC 2 (11 October 1992).

Guy-Sheftall, Beverly. *Words of Fire: An Anthology of African-American Feminist Thought.* New York: New Press, 1995.

hooks, bell. *Talking Back. thinking feminist. thinking black.* Boston: South End Press, 1989.

Jama, Zainab Mohamed, and Annette Nielsen. "Female Circumcision—More than a Question of Health." *Tanzania Sunday News* (19 May 1991).

Kaplan, David A., Shawn D. Lewis, and Joshua Hammer. "Is It Torture or Tradition?" *Newsweek* (December 20, 1993): 124.

Kluvitse, A. Letter to *Pride* (June/July 1995): 6.

Langer. Lawrence. *The Holocaust and the Literary Imagination.* New Haven: Yale University Press, 1975.

Levin. Tobe. "A Pain that Knifes the Soul: Parliamentary Hearing against Genital Mutilation of Girls and Women." *WISE Women's News,* vol. 7, 2 (1997): 24.

Levin, Tobe. "Women as Scapegoats of Culture and Cult: An Activist's View of Female Circumcision in Ngugi's *The River Between.*" *Ngambika: Studies of Women in African Literature.* Ed. Carole Boyce Davies and Anne Adams Graves. Trenton, N.J.: Africa World Press. 1986.

Lightfoot-Klein, Hanny. *Prisoners of Ritual: An Odessey into Female Genital Circumcision in Africa.* New York: Harrington Park Press, 1989.

Likimani, Muthoni. *They Shall Be Chastised.* Nairobi: East African Literature Bureau, 1974.

Lionnet, Françoise. *Postcolonial Representations: Women Literature. Identity.* Ithaca, N.Y.: Cornell University Press, 1995.

Ngugi wa Thiong'o. *The River Between.* London: Heinemann, 1965.

Parmar, Pratibha, director. *Warrior Marks.* Prod. Alice Walker. Distr. Women Make Movies, 1993.

Ravell-Pinto, Thelma. "Buchi Emecheta at Spelman College." SAGE: *A Scholarly Journal on Black Women* 2-1 (Spring 1985): 50–51.

Robson, Angela. "'Torture, not Culture'." *Amnesty: Campaign Journal of Amnesty International British Section* 63 (Sept./Oct. 1993): 8–9.

Scarry, Elaine. *The Body in Pain.* Oxford: Oxford University Press, 1985.

Stefan, Verena. *Rauh, wild & frei. Mädchengestalten in der Literatur.* Frankfurt: Fischer, 1997.

Sylla, Abdou. "Pratiques mutilantes et féminité. Questions d' esthétique de la femme africaine." *Bulletin de l'Institut Fondamental d'Afrique noire.* Serie B, Université de Dakar. Sciences Humaines 46 (1986–87): 305–330.

Talle, Aud. "Transforming Women into 'Pure' Agnates: Aspects of Female Infibulation in Somalia." *Carved Flesh. Cast Selves. Gendered Symbols and Social Practices.* Ed. Vigdis Broch-Due, Ingrid Rudie, and Tone Bleie. Providence, R.I.: Berg, 1993: 83–106.

United Nations. Draft Platform for Action Fourth World Conference on Women. A/CONF. 177/L.1. 24 May 1995.

United Nations. World Health Organization. Division of Family Health. "Female Genital Mutilation: Actions for Eradication." *Female genital mutila-*

tion/Mutilations sexuelles féminines. Geneva: WHO/FHE/'94.4 (31 July 1994): G1–G2.

United Nations. World Health Organization. Division of Family Health. "FGM: United Nations Actions." *Female Genital Mutilation. Mutilations sexuelles féminines.* Geneva: WHO/FHE/94.4 (31 July 1994): J1–J2.

United Nations. World Health Organization. Division of Family Health. "FGM: Prevalence and Distribution." *Female Genital Mutilation. Mutilations sexuelles féminines.* Geneva: WHO/FHE/94.4 (31 July 1994): D1–D3.

Walker, Alice. "In the Closet of the Soul." *Words of Fire: An Anthology of African-American Feminist Thought.* Ed. Beverly Guy-Sheftall. New York: New Press, 1995: 538–547.

Walker, Alice. *The Color Purple.* New York: Simon & Schuster, 1982.

Walker, Alice. "Heaven Belongs to You." *Re-visioning Feminism around the World.* New York: Feminist Press, 1995: 62–63.

Walker, Alice. *Possessing the Secret of Joy.* New York: Harcourt, Bruce Jovanovich, 1992.

Walker, Alice. *The Same River Twice: Honoring the Difficult.* New York: Scribner, 1996.

Walker, Alice, and Pratibha Parmar. *Narben oder Die Beschneidung der weiblichen Sexualität.* Trans. Ursula Locke-Groß. Reinbek bei Hamburg: Rowohlt, 1996.

Walker, Alice, and Pratibha Parmar. *Warrior Marks: Female Genital Mutilation and the Sexual Blinding of Women.* New York: Harcourt, Brace, 1993

Wilentz, Gay. "Healing the Wounds of Time." Review of *Possessing the Secret of Joy* by Alice Walker and *Bailey's Café* by Gloria Naylor. *Women's Review of Books,* vol. 10, 5. (February 1993): 15–16.

20

• • • •

Passages to Identity

Re-Membering the Diaspora in Marshall, Phillips, and Cliff

Johanna X. K. Garvey

"It appeared she had brought the memorabilia of a lifetime—and of the time that reached beyond her small life—and dumped it in a confused "heap in the room. . . . It expressed her: the struggle for coherence, the hope and desire for reconciliation of her conflicting parts, the longing to truly know and accept herself" (401). This description of the semi-chaos of Merle Kinbona's room in Paule Marshall's *The Chosen Place, The Timeless People* (New York: Vintage, 1969) echoes the museum-like quality of the fictive Bourne Island where the narrative unfolds—a place "where one not only felt that other time existing intact, still alive, a palpable presence beneath the everyday reality, but saw it as well at every turn, often without realizing it. Bournehills . . . might have been selected as the repository of the history which reached beyond it to include the hemisphere north and south" (402). Written over twenty-five years ago, this novel by an African American woman with familial roots in Barbados explores issues of race, history, and identity that also inform more recent texts about the African diaspora and *its* roots/routes in the Middle Passage and slavery. Like Marshall, Michelle Cliff and Caryl Phillips (among others) attempt to rescript a fragmented and multiple history, to trace the passages of Europeans eastward and of Africans to the "New World," and to imagine the watery paths that have no signposts and that thus resist any return. As the narrator of Phillips's *Crossing the River* (New York: Knopf, 1993) explains at the outset, "the chorus of a common memory began to haunt me," two hundred and fifty years of voices, male and female, black and white, African, British, American. Similarly, in *Free Enterprise* (New York: Penguin, 1993), Cliff envisages U.S. history as inextricably entangled with that of Africa and the Caribbean. Perhaps Marshall's Bourne Island best figures this intersection of places and identities and stories: approaching from the air, a traveler notices its location in the West Indies, off to the right of the other islands, in the Atlantic, the furthest edge (or bourn) of the "New World," facing east to Africa. It is thus both cusp and meeting point, of white and black; of Africa, Europe, and the Americas; of past, present, and future.[1]

All of these novels emphasize the necessity of memory, as they remember the diaspora, retelling its history and listening to its myriad voices scattered and lost. On the Atlantic side of Bourne Island, the water is dangerous, the reefs threatening, "with a sound like that of the combined voices of the drowned raised in a loud unceasing lament—all those, the nine million and more it is said, who in their enforced exile, their Diaspora, had gone down between this point and the homeland lying out of sight to the east. This sea mourned them" (106). Although Marshall repeatedly refers to the Middle Passage, and the concomitant experiences of slavery, she roots the fiction in a single island at a specific moment in contemporary history.[2] Cliff and Phillips, if in different ways, experiment more with time and space, each attempting to transport the reader into a multidimensional confrontation with the slave trade and the transatlantic passages it initiated. I would suggest that all three writers, from varying directions, are ideally situated to perform these crossings: Marshall, born in Brooklyn, raised in a tightly knit Bajan community and making trips "home" to visit relatives; Phillips, born in St. Kitts, transported almost immediately to England, eventually resident not only there but in India, Sweden, the West Indies, and the United States; Cliff, born in Jamaica to a family of mixed heritage, herself light enough to "pass" yet choosing to identify as black, transplanted to the United States and educated in Britain.[3] To examine the African diaspora and the passages that created it may necessitate some fundamental experience of displacement, a questioning of the meaning of "home" and "family."[4]

Marshall's *The Chosen Place, the Timeless People* displays the most concerted attempt to rediscover roots, to ground identity in a place and a history, most clearly evidenced in the story of Cuffee Ned, leader of a slave revolt against the white estate owner My Byram (perhaps a play on words—"buy rum").[5] In this narrative of resistance, repeated throughout the novel and reenacted at Carnival by residents of the poverty-striken Bournehills district, Marshall stresses the importance of memory. As Merle says of those who celebrate Cuffee Ned, "'But we're an odd, half-mad people, I guess. We don't ever forget anything, and yesterday comes like today'" (102). When the current absentee landlord visits the cane factory, we see how history loops in an unending pattern of oppression and inhumanity, illustrated in the descendants of slaves: "the disembodied look to the men at work there, who never failed to call to mind ghosts confined to the dark hold of a ship set on some interminable voyage" (221). In another reference to the Middle Passage, when the Bournehills residents march quietly at Carnival with their float representing Cuffee Ned's attack, their feet make a sound that

> conjured up in the bright afternoon sunshine dark alien images of legions marching bound together over a vast tract, iron fitted into dank stone walls, chains—like those to an anchor—rattling in the deep holds of ships, and exile in an unknown inhospitable land— an exile bitter and irreversible in which all memory of the former life and of the self as it had once been had been destroyed. (282)

This description would seem to be at odds, however, with the emphasis throughout the novel on the importance of re-membering, of using history, all of it, of not forgetting but always looking both backward and forward. Perhaps Marshall, one of the first contemporary writers to try to recreate the slave trade itself, shows us just how difficult that reverse passage proves to be, an example of the "inner anxiety" of the text (Gikandi 177, 179) or the book's double vision (DeLamotte).

Rather than romanticizing Africa and assuming an easy journey back, Marshall captures in the apparent contradiction of her descriptions the paradox that history repeats itself yet memory alone cannot transport those of African descent to the motherland. Cuffee Ned, then, becomes both the one hope, the savior who will come again, and also the perpetually dispossessed, captured and killed by the slave owners.[6] The residents of Bournehills continually recall and call to this near-mythic figure throughout the year, but particularly at Carnival when they pour libation to him as if to a god and celebrate his rebellious acts that transformed the landlord's estate into "Pyre Hill."[7] His resistance becomes theirs, too, "the experience through which any people who find themselves ill-used, dispossessed, at the mercy of the powerful, must pass" (286–287). This "passage" occurs as the group traverses the streets of New Bristol with the replica of Pyre Hill, retelling the story, "all the way back to the beginning" (286). This voicing of history—a story not just of Bourne Island but of the entire diaspora—meets initial resistance not only from the whites observing but also from more "privileged" blacks who do not want to "rock the boat" (or bring back memories of the slave trade). Yet the final image of this crowd suggests that Cuffee Ned's story

gives them—everyone—the power to re-member the past and to challenge its present legacy of oppression and abuse:

> And more than ever now that dark human overflow . . . resem-
> bled a river made turbulent by the spring thaw and rising rapidly—
> a river that if heed wasn't taken and provision made would soon
> burst the walls and levees built to contain it and rushing forth in
> one dark powerful wave bring everything in its path crashing
> down. (289–290)

For the main characters in the novel, both white and black, this "river"
inspired by Cuffee Ned does indeed bring down walls—as Merle sleeps
with (Jewish American) Saul—and create destruction—as Saul's wife
Harriet first experiences racist fear when she is swept along by the crowd
and ultimately commits suicide in the ocean when she realizes she cannot "buy" Merle or dissolve Saul's attachment to her.

If Cuffee Ned is the link to the past and the means of keeping memory
alive, Merle is the present bridge between communities on Bourne Island
and also to its two antagonistic motherlands—Britain and Africa. Like
her jumbled room with its remnants of a collective past, Merle provides a
meeting ground for peoples, nations, eras. A gathering at her home "almost suggested the coming together of the members of a family who had
been scattered to the four corners of the earth and changed almost beyond recognition by their differing circumstances, but the same still"
(110). Just as she manages to connect the poor of Bournehills with the
upper-class blacks of the island, so she links the visiting whites to both
sectors.[8] In thus placing the black woman at the center of the tale, Marshall achieves what Sylvia Wynter discusses as the re-placing or re-
membering of "Caliban's 'Woman,'" who was struck from the story by
both colonizers and colonized. Wynter points to the centuries-long si-
lencing via absence of the female counterpart to Caliban; tellingly, Merle
Kinbona's most salient trait is her incessant *talk*, indeed a coming-to-
voice as well as the defense or therapy it may also represent.[9] Her attire at
the beginning of the novel may (as several have argued) epitomize
Merle's fragmented identity: "She had donned this somewhat bizarre outfit, each item of which stood opposed to, at war even, with the other, to
express rather a diversity and disunity within herself, and her attempt,
unconscious probably, to reconcile these opposing parts, to make of them
a whole"(5). But, in the context of Merle as bridge—and center—it may
be equally useful to interpret her mixed accoutrements as the "mask of
history" in Caribbean identity: "The masked figure merges forms from
Africa with those invented in the diaspora; in the process, new meanings
about self, history, and culture are created" (Gikandi 175). Merle's "outfit"

may be seen as well as a performance of identity available to the "post-colonial migrant" as explored by Abena Busia. I would argue that Merle is more "together" than a surface reading of her clothing or her surroundings seems to suggest and that she is the ideal "twilight consciousness" to illustrate the "limbo" position between cultural traditions and also the ideal instrument to help us re-member the passages that not only separate but also link those opposing sites.[10]

Merle negotiates the divides not only between races and classes but also between generations. In her teaching she passed on the story of Cuffee Ned to schoolchildren, until fired for this radical departure from the text:

> She was teaching history or one of them big subjects. But it seems they didn't like the way she was teaching it. She was telling the children about Cuffee Ned and things that happened on the island in olden times, when the headmaster wanted her to teach the history that was down in the books, that told all about the English. But she refused, saying that way made it look like black people never fought back. (32)

Taking as her next text the tales that have survived the Middle Passage, she instructs the children as she entertains them: "She was recounting another episode in the life of Spider, the wily hero of the Anancy tales told throughout the islands, who, though small and weak, always managed to outwit the larger and stronger creatures in his world, including man, by his wit and cunning" (224). Whereas in her own studies in England she pursued the sweep of "Western" history from the colonizers' angle, Merle is also the historian who offers the companion volume to that story. Her choice of Anancy marks her as both heroic rebel and as maternal repository of an African heritage.[11]

Ultimately, she will become the (temporary) bridge back to Africa, headed to Uganda to find the daughter taken from her by her husband. Having sold the furnishings of her room, including paintings of estate owners, a sketch of a slave ship, her talcum powder, her straightening comb, she looks younger, less scarred. As she says to the American Jew, Saul, "I have the feeling that just being there and seeing the place will be a big help to me, that in some way it will give me the strength I need to get moving again . . . It's more what you said: that sometimes a person has to go back, really back—to have a sense, an understanding of all that's gone to make them—before they can go forward" (468). So she will follow a reverse passage, south to Trinidad, then to Brazil, to the city of Recife, which reaches out into the Atlantic toward Africa "as though yearning to be joined to it as it had surely been in the beginning" (471). Marshall implies that Merle, born at a crossroads between Africa and both Britain and the United States, will succeed in this transatlantic passage and fit the disparate pieces of her self together to form a coherent identity. Yet, in keeping with the novel's "double movement" (Gikandi 173), the very end of the book also undercuts such a simple notion of return and rescue. Pyre Hill appears to burn still, unextinguished over the centuries, and the road swelling with rain threatens to "take a walk" (472), to become an impassable river.[12]

Caryl Phillips dedicates his book to "those who crossed the river." Listening to their voices, he has created a dialogic, interconnected narrative of people whom the narrator calls "my children." Just as Merle sets off to locate the daughter "stolen" from her, Phillips's characters seek to recover familial bonds—the white American "father" and his black African "son"; the former slave and the daughter sold away from her; the English woman and the African American soldier who was her husband and the father of her son. It is more difficult to identify the links between the British slaver and his "cargo" as family connections, yet in this section of the book—written as a journal—Phillips illustrates how, in the act of trading goods for souls, the merchant forged bonds no less solid than those of blood.[13] *Crossing the River* is structured in four parts, set in different sites and historical moments, from nineteenth-century Africa to the western United States in the years surrounding the Civil War, to the Middle Passage from 1752 to 1753, and finally to "somewhere in England" from 1936 to 1963. A patchwork of time, this narrative suggests that any segment of history surrounding the Middle Passage includes in microcosm the story of that core event in modern world history.[14] Though the reader can trace the lines that may branch into a family tree, the joins are never explicitly shown, so each segment stands on its own, its protagonist more lost than found. Whereas Marshall centers her novel and then draws the lines that connect that center outward in space and backward in time, Phillips is "crossing the river" at multiple points to demonstrate both the interlocking quality of diasporan experiences and the irreparable fragmentation that hinders any full re-membering.[15]

Thus, in part I, "The Pagan Coast," the former slave Nash Williams, once freed by his owner, has disappeared in Africa after being repatriated. This "father," Edward, journeys to Africa himself in a fruitless quest to locate his "lost son." Nash's letters from Liberia have indicated his increasing acculturation there and his desire to identify Africa as home: "Liberia," he has claimed, "is the finest country for the colored man. . . . We, the colored man, have been oppressed for long enough. We need to contend for our rights, stand our ground, and feel the love of liberty that can never be found in your America" (61). Nash has also written of the continuing, indeed expanding, slave trade: "Hardly a week passes on this coast of Africa without some report of a sea-bound slaver, and its unfortunate cargo, who have been afforded protection by the unfurling of the Star Spangled Banner" (41). He explains that the U.S. flag means safety *not* for the captured Africans, whom the British would release if seizing these ships, but for those perpetuating the Middle Passage. Meanwhile, the white "father" cannot release his black "son" or loosen the ties of this unnatural family. Edward makes a reverse journey, a voyage marked by illness and discomfort, his own Middle Passage of sorts, to Africa in search of the disappeared family member. Ultimately forced to accept the failure of his "mission," after learning of Nash's death, Edward finds himself alone and abandoned after he crosses a final river and stands before Nash's deserted house; the natives observe the strange old white man "with the pity that one feels for a fellow being who has lost both his way and his sense of purpose" (70). We might say that he resembles in human form a slave ship that errs both literally and metaphorically. Nash's own return has ended in a sort of desolation, the final settlement he established now a site of filth and idleness; the white man's attempt to "discover" or re-member his African son is equally doomed, Phillips suggests—raising the question, who *can* cross the river?

Martha, the central character of part II, "West," may be the sister of Nash—we catch glimpses of each as part of a vignette of three children sold into slavery by their African father—but her story also emphasizes loss and disconnection. Moving in and out of first-person narrative, this section weaves together a present moment when the former slave is left behind by other blacks on the trek west and her memories that take her back eastward, to Kansas, to Virginia, and to the beach in Africa where she stood with her father and brothers as a child, looking at the slave ships offshore: "Her journey had been a long one. But now the sun had set. Her course was run" (73). The focal point of these recollections is the loss of her daughter, Eliza Mae, sold away from her as a "prime purchase." In a repeated scene of loss and dispersal, we see Martha, her husband, and Eliza on the auction block, the family split apart as each one goes to a different "owner," and the young girl utters the word "Moma" as if it is the only one she possesses. Martha's maternal pain at separation echoes the paternal guilt and longing expressed by the initial narrator of the novel, the African father forced by poor crops to sell his children into slavery. Martha continues her journey west when her new owners plan to sell her back "across the river to Hell" (80), as she says—from North to South, that is—and she finds (temporarily) sympathetic blacks to aid her. But similar to those Africans who became ill in the Atlantic and were jettisoned alive, Martha, too, is left behind and spends a final night in Colorado. Imagining that she will make it to California and fantasizing a reunion there with Eliza Mae, Martha falls asleep for the last time: "She would never again head east. . . . She had a westward soul which had found its natural-born home in the bosom of her daughter" (94). Her dead body is discovered by the woman who has offered her shelter in Denver, and Martha becomes the epitome of the dispossessed, unknown and unloved, even her name a mystery to those who will bury her. She continues to inhabit a limbo space, in this case one not of resistance so much as of disconnection. Thus far in Phillips's narrative, neither a return eastward nor a flight to the West succeeds in establishing a true home for those enmeshed in the aftereffects of the Middle Passage.

In part III, "Crossing the River," the experiences Phillips represents demonstrate the sickness at the heart of slavery. Written as the journal of the ship's "master," James Hamilton, these pages follow the repetitious exchange of goods for people, and the increasing illness, deaths, and threats of insurrection as Hamilton attempts to fully "slave" his vessel. In a fictional version closely paralleling actual documents of slavers, Africans become a list of numbers, identified by age, sex, price.[16] Again we catch a glimpse of the sister and brother who may become Nash and Martha, but they appear only briefly, nameless, in the numbing inventory of Hamilton's trade. This is traffic not only in humans as live bodies to sell and exploit but also in dead ones, as the "log" becomes more a list of the ill and dying than of the living. Despite these "losses" and the constant attempts at rebellion, after "crossing the river" one final time, Hamilton finishes his "mission" with 210 new slaves and prepares to leave the coast. He writes of his human cargo, "They huddle together, and sing their melancholy lamentations. We have lost sight of Africa" (124). With sections that repeatedly indicate the impossibility of a reverse passage, in this case seemingly from the moment of departure, Phillips's book delineates the profound loss that colors all experience of the African diaspora.[17]

The fourth part offers no greater hope of reconnection and recovery, but instead extends the family tree into the twentieth century, to an affair between a young English woman and an African American soldier stationed in her village.[18] Perhaps to indicate the increasing work required to piece together the intermingled history spawned by the Middle Passage, this section moves back and forth across time in a disjointed, fitful manner. The reader is forced to pay careful attention to fit together the puzzle picture of characters and events, to grasp how to re-member this branching family tree. We look backward at the narrator Joyce's youth and unhappy marriage to Len, then watch in gradually unveiled stages her acquaintance with the GI Travis, their hasty marriage during leave time, his death off the coast of Italy, and her reunion eighteen years later with the son she was forced to give up. We witness ongoing racism, as Travis is beaten for dancing with a white woman, as Joyce realizes that they could neither be accepted in England nor allowed to live together in the United States. Thus, when the "coffee-colored" son appears on her doorstep, though she welcomes him in, she knows that "he would never call me mother," and she also realizes she cannot tell him he is "home": "I almost said to make yourself at home, but I didn't. At least I avoided that. Sit down. Please, sit down" (232). This son's voyage to identity may have resolved some questions, but his "landing" is temporary, his diasporan experience still one of exile and displacement.

Had the text ended with this scene of recognition and estrangement, this re-membering of the diaspora would imply that there is no community, no place, no return, no home for the displaced. Instead, however, the narrative voice of the African father resumes a dialogue with the "children": "their voices hurt but determined, they will survive the hardships of the far bank. Only if they panic will they break their wrists and ankles against Captain Hamilton's instruments" (235). Though this "guilty father" says there is no reverse passage, "no paths in water," no signposts, he also re-members these "diasporan souls" on the other side of the river, into a space of kinship: "But they arrived on the far bank of the river, loved" (237). The "I" speaks in all of the voices, making of them one family. Similarly, "loved" resonates as both adjective and verb, linking them back to Africa and moving them on into future familial bonds. Disjointed and fragmented, this narrative achieves a unity different from that embodied in Marshall's character Merle and her home on Bourne Island. In juxtaposing and interweaving—if covertly—the disparate lives in Africa, Britain, and the United States, Phillips has found another, equally effective way to convey the enormity of the Middle Passage, its intrusion into and its rearrangement of human relationships.[19]

Michelle Cliff's *Free Enterprise* directly refers in its title to the traffic in African souls and its continuing legacy in the "New World," but it also is itself a "free" undertaking, a collage of U.S. history that reveals or unveils what has been hidden and ignored in fear and myth. A series of overlapping and interlocking vignettes, this narrative often bursts at the seams, "getting ahead of the story, or behind" (4).[20] The opening scene offers an image of the diaspora, in the collection of bottles—"a chaos of residue," "[i]ngredients from here, there, and everywhere" (5)—adorning the trees outside Annie Christmas's house. The water of the Mississippi River that flows past cannot erase the various scents, such as that of the bottle labeled Khus-Khus Original African Scent, which takes Annie "home" to a Caribbean island and to its entire history: "Arawak. Slavery. Cane" (5).[21]

As in *The Chosen Place, The Timeless People*, Cliff's novel looks for a center in the West Indies, but here it is a more diffuse location:

> They inhabited a confused universe, this Caribbean, with no center and no outward edge. Where almost everything was foreign. Language, people, landscape even.
> Tongues collided. Struggled for hegemony. Emerged victorious, or sank into the impossibly blue waters, heavy as gold. (6)

Unlike Marshall's Merle, who grounds the novel and enacts the reverse passage to Africa at its conclusion, Cliff's fictive Annie is only one of a large cast of characters, none of which is *the* protagonist, and none of whom makes the return journey. And unlike Phillips's book, *Free Enterprise* presents no sharply delineated and unified sections but instead resembles Annie's "family tree" of bottles, dangling in the air, their scents intermingling, their stories floating on the air and needing voices to preserve them over time.[22] The text seeks to uncover lost versions of history—the official one is "a cheat"—but it refuses to accept the possibility of going back.[23] One forgotten character Cliff focuses on is Mary Ellen Pleasant, a black woman who played a role in John Brown's attempt to free the slaves.[24] In imagining a conversation between the enterprising Pleasant, who financed Brown's mission, and the white man before his capture and hanging, Cliff appears to reject a return to roots:

> Neither will it do us any good, as some have suggested, as my own, exhausted father did, to take a boat back to Africa in search of home, as if a reverse passage can reverse history. The time has passed for all that. We are no longer African. We are New World people, and we built this blasted country from the ground up. We are part of its future, its fortunes.
> We belong in the here and now. (151)

Nevertheless, even if this novel (unlike Marshall's or Phillips's) refuses to make that voyage, it does travel in time and space to present a patchwork of African American—and U.S.—history and to show its origins in the slave trade.[25] In Marshall's narrative, the sea often serves as the voice for those nine million dispossessed, victims of an enterprise based in capitalism and exchange of "goods"; similarly, water imagery connotes both the Middle Passage and the river that cannot be recrossed in Phillips's work. Cliff also turns to representations of the ocean to re-member the horrific passages, specifically to a painting by Turner titled *Slavers Throwing Overboard the Dead and Dying: Typhoon Coming On*.[26] Displayed at a dinner party as an important acquisition, the depiction is based on a ship, the *Zong*, and a case in which traders threw slaves overboard to collect insurance money—another version of investment.[27] The narrator in this scene, Mary Pleasant, wonders to herself about the financial backing of the venture and then examines the picture itself, showing arms and a leg, disconnected and bearing chains, sinking in the waves alongside bright fish: "I was grateful that the artist had portrayed it thus, indicating the horror of the thing aslant, by these few members, and a reminder of their confinement" (73). Thus, Cliff, too, chooses to retell "aslant," not returning to the Middle Passage itself but to its representations and ramifications in the nineteenth and the twentieth centuries.[28] As Mary Ellen Pleasant, in 1874, muses to herself, the new owner of the painting pens a letter to her: Alice Hooper, a white woman, expresses confusion and regret at not speaking up against the trades both in and of the art work that she has just purchased. Yet, at the thought of her own implication in slavery, she resists guilt: "The whole thing could become a game. For if I cut every link to every enterprise which might have supported the traffic in human souls—sold every piece of stock in every maritime company, for example—I would still have to reckon with the mills, the question of property in and of itself" (78). Indeed, as Cliff—and Marshall, Phillips, Toni Morrison, John Edgar Wideman, Charles Johnson, and more— illustrates, the United States is irrevocably "built" on slavery; once one traces the paths backward, not even as far as Africa but just to the previous century in this country, complicity is rampant, ignorance its support.[29] Cliff's Alice Hooper pronounces beliefs that remain prevalent today, as she writes to Mary Pleasant that her desire to have the latter explain the painting to the assembled white folks was due to "a sense of you as someone all too familiar with the horrors of slavery and the Middle Passage. . . . I was prevailing on you to educate us. To be our authority" (78). As Cliff's re-membering demonstrates, we all need to educate ourselves, to understand who we are and how our identities have been formed by the past.[30]

Illustrating the interrelated nature of past, present, and future, Cliff's "hologrammatical" man appears to Mary Pleasant on several occasions as she voyages by water to Martha's Vineyard. His first manifestation occurs the morning after she has viewed the Turner painting; he stands in uniform in the shadows of the Parker House dining room, "waiting on his time, when he would first be called Homeboy, then Detroit Red, then X." Mary unknowingly tries to locate him in the past—a shade—"not knowing he was an impression of the future." When he sits down across from her, "she could see his beautiful, as yet unborn eyes before her, could see herself reflected in them" (76). This imagined encounter between Mary and Malcolm underscores Cliff's contention that everything is here, and now—that no moment of history must be forgotten and that black Americans are at the center of that history, connected to each other and supporting one another, family. A later exchange between the two characters stresses this necessity of re-membering: "Why didn't I know you? About you? My point exactly" (142). These words are perhaps at the core of the author's own project. As Mary's steamer is about to reach the shore, the hologrammatical man tells the sleeping woman, "'I am with you always'" (153). Mary stands at a juncture of past and present in this extended sequence, thinking back to her mother and her maternal grandmother in the Sea Islands, who watched the traffic from the Guinea coast, and looking ahead almost a century to another leader and revolutionary. She senses everyone behind her, and we perceive those to follow. Yet in this re-membering, it is significant that Cliff never takes us as far back as Africa, only to the horrific waterways that both separate and link that continent and the West, implying even more emphatically than Phillips or Marshall that a reverse passage cannot be accomplished.

A final sequence in *Free Enterprise*, appropriately situated on a boat offshore the eastern seaboard of the United States, interweaves threads from the diasporan experience that Mary Pleasant embodies and calls to memory. As she thinks of those who came before, as well as of those whom she has known, the sea is a constant presence:

> The ocean was impassive.
> There were no ship tracks, no oceanic ruts where they'd plowed, like the ruts across High Plains, High Desert. . . .
> The ocean closed its books, darkness revealing nothing. . . . Underneath, underneath right now the painting came to life. The stunning fish, the brown limbs, the chain. . . . She felt everyone behind her. In the here and now. (209, 210)

Though the ocean may "close its books," the voices of history are still speaking, if only we listen to them. Mary Ellen returns to the site of the Free African School on the Vineyard, now a ruin but the memories of it still present as she walks the bluff. She recalls how the teacher would have the children memorize and then recite a narrative, for "Books are fragile things. . . . We must become talking books; talk it on, like the Africans, children. Talk it on" (211). And the text that comes alive is that of a woman, spoken in the voice of a child, remembered by that poet now grown old, the narrative of "Phillis": "'In the year 1761, a little girl about seven or eight years old, I was stolen from my parents in Africa, and being put on board a ship, a passage I can hardly remember, was brought to Boston, where I was sold for a slave'" (212). As Phillips uses first-person narration to retell the story of the slave trade and its continuing aftermath, Cliff employs layers of "'I'"s to write a palimpsestic passage that remembers the passage that we must all not "pass on" or bypass in our recounting of modern history. The author, a Jamaican light enough to pass but choosing instead to identify with her black roots, meets the African American entrepreneur and rebel Pleasant, who recalls the African-turned-slave Phyllis Wheatley, as they individually and collectively pen the story of the Middle Passage and the "Black Atlantic."

These three texts offer a spectrum of approaches to the African diaspora and the slave trade that initiated it, bringing displacement, exile, and death to millions. The sea itself often serves not only as catalyst but as repository for the memories of the Middle Passage. In *The Chosen Place, the Timeless People*, the narrator speaks of the Atlantic, "its unceasing lament. What, whom did it mourn? Why did it continue the wake all this time, shamelessly filling the air with the indecent wailing of a hired mute? Who were its dead?" (363). Such questions have inspired Marshall, Phillips, and Cliff to explore the roots of African Caribbean and African American experience, and to re-member those who participated, on several sides, in that past. In that process, ghosts are both raised and laid to rest—*Free Enterprise*, for instance, ends at the grave of Mary Ellen Pleasant, in Napa, California. Perhaps these passages perform a cleansing, like that of the sea in Marshall's novel, which undergoes a filtering and purification each year. Afterwards, at least momentarily, "though the sea continued to hurl itself in an excess of grief and mourning onto the shore, sending up the spume like tears, it did so with something less than its usual hysteria" (461). All of these authors show that the Middle Passage, buried and pathless as it may seem in the Atlantic, can never be forgotten, indeed must be re-membered by all of us who are its "heirs and descendants," and perhaps in that retelling its pain may be brought to the surface and the nine million recognized.

Notes

1. On this positioning, see Stelamaris Coser, *Bridging the Americas: The Literature of Paule Marshall, Toni Morrison, and Gayl Jones* (Temple UP, 1994), 3, 34; Melvin Rahming, "Towards a Caribbean Mythology: The Functioning of Africa in Paule Marshall's *The Chosen Place, the Timeless People*," *Studies in the Literary Imagination* 26, 2 (Fall 1993), 79, 86; Eugenia DeLamotte, "Women, Silence, and History in *The Chosen Place, the Timeless People*," *Callaloo* 16, 1 (1993), 227–228, 234.

2. Coser explores the interconnection of time, place, and peoples offered by this choice; see her chapter 2. See also Barbara Christian, *Black Feminist Criticism: Perspectives in Black Women Writers* (Pergamon Press, 1985), 113.

3. In commenting on Marshall's Merle, Rahming points to a movement

that characterizes all the words under discussion: "Since, like Caribbean society, Merle is herself the repository of a cultural diversity, her impulse toward a unified consciousness can be seen as reflecting the sociopolitical impulse of the Caribbean toward the coherence of its disparate parts, the meshing of its varied cultural influences into a distinctly Caribbean cultural identity" (81). Following Paul Gilroy, *The Black Atlantic: Modernity and Double Consciousness* (Harvard UP, 1993), I would argue that these authors also display a *diasporan* cultural identity.

4. In *Small Acts: Thoughts on the Politics of Black Cultures* (Serpent's Tail, 1993), Paul Gilroy comments: "The value of the term 'diaspora' increases as its essentially symbolic character is understood. It points emphatically to the fact that there can be no pure, uncontaminated or essential blackness anchored in an unsullied originary moment. It suggests that a myth of shared origins is neither a talisman which can suspend political antagonisms nor a deity invoked to cement a pastoral view of black life that can answer the multiple pathologies of contemporary racism" (99). For an extended discussion of black aesthetics and the diaspora, see Belinda Edmondson, "Race, Tradition, and the Construction of the Caribbean Aesthetic," *New Literary History* 25, 1 (Winter 1994), 109–120, and her "Race, Privilege, and the Politics of (Re)Writing History: An Analysis of the Novels of Michelle Cliff," *Callaloo* 16, 1 (1993), 180–191. See also Coser, 22–24; Daryl Cumber Dance, "An Interview with Paule Marshall," *Southern Review* 28, 1 (Winter 1992), 14; Susan Willis, *Specifying: Black Women Writing the American Experience* (U Wisconsin P, 1987), 57.

5. On the origins of "Cuffee Ned," see Coser, 38. I thank Julia Petitfrere, herself a native of Barbados, for pointing out to me the likely meaning of Byram's name.

6. For the Christian overtones of this character, see Rahming, 85. Willis argues that this performance turns a multiplicity into a unity, if only for a time (68–69). See also Missy Dehn Kubitschek, *Claiming the Heritage: African-American Women Novelists and History* (UP of Mississippi, 1991), 80, on Cuffee Ned's failure.

7. For further discussion of the Carnival scenes, see Simon Gikandi, *Writing in Limbo: Modernism and Caribbean Literature* (Cornell UP, 1992), 187–190, and Coser, chapter 2.

8. Kubitschek discusses the exchange of stories, especially between Merle and Saul (83–84.)

9. See Sylvia Wynter, "Beyond Miranda's Meanings: Un/silencing the 'Demonic Ground' of Caliban's Woman," in *Out of the Kumbla: Caribbean Women and Literature*, eds. Carole Boyce Davies and Elaine Savory Fido (Africa World Press, 1990), 363, 365. See also Joyce Pettis, "'Talk' as Defensive Artifice: Merle Kinbona in *The Chosen Place, the Timeless People*," *African American Review* 26, 1 (1992), 109–117, for a discussion of the links between diasporan experience, identity, and speech.

10. See Gikandi, 10–14. See also Davies, on Caribbean women's identity, migration and fluidity, as well as the links to Africa (60, 70).

11. On the Anancy stories as link to Africa and to mothers, see Gay Wilentz, *Binding Cultures: Black Women in Africa and the Diaspora* (Indiana UP, 1992), See also Michelle Cliff, "Clare Savage as a Crossroads Character," in

Caribbean Women Writers: Essays from the First International Conference, ed. Selwyn R. Cudjoe (Calaloux Publications, 1990), 287. In "Sea Change: The Middle Passage and the Transatlantic Imagination," Carl Pedersen notes the links between limbo and Anancy, citing Wilson Harris (in *The Black Columbiad: Defining Moments in African American Literature and Culture*, ed. Werner Sollors and Maria Diedrich, Harvard UP, 1994), 45.

12. On the slave trade, see Joyce Pettis, "A MELUS Interview: Paule Marshall," *MELUS* 17, 4 (Winter 1991–1992), 125–126. On romanticizing Africa as opposed to using history and memory to re-member, see "Filming Slavery: A Conversation with Haile Gerima," *Transition* 64 (1994): 90–104. Mary Jane Schenck discusses the text as at odds with itself and Merle's position at the end: "Ceremonies of Reconciliation: Paule Marshall's *The Chosen Place, the Timeless People*," *MELUS* 19, 4 (Winter 1994), 50.

13. For a fascinating discussion of "origins" and lines of descent, see David Chioni Moore, "Routes: Alex Haley's *Roots* and the Rhetoric of Genealogy," *Transition* 64 (1994): 4–21.

14. Gikandi's discussion of modernism and Caribbean writing clearly argues for seeing the slave trade and colonialism as creating a modern consciousness for all involved and later affected. Aldon L. Nielsen makes a similar argument in *Writing between the Lines: Race and Intertextuality* (U Georgia Press, 1994).

15. See Moore, 9–10. It is interesting to note that Phillips's earlier novels have moved from the Caribbean to England (*The Final Passage*), and then followed the reverse trajectory (*Higher Ground, Cambridge*), while in this latest one we see multiple, interlocking passages.

16. See Nielsen, chapter 5, for a discussion of how other writers have incorporated such "logs," based on actual documents, into their texts.

17. For an early, fictional recreation of such events in the slave trade, see Martin R. Delany's novel *Blake, or the Huts of America* (originally published in installments in the mid nineteenth century), especially chapters 49–54.

18. Phillips himself grew up in Yorkshire, and some of the background for this section of the novel seems based on his own experiences and observations. See *The European Tribe* (Faber & Faber, 1987) and "The Other Voice: A Dialogue Between Anita Desai, Caryl Phillips, and Ilan Stavans," *Transition* 64 (1994), especially p. 82.

19. In a discussion of his film *Sankofa*, Haile Gerima says, "I think the only weapon the African race has is history. And history exorcises, history heals, the African people. . . . There is no future without the past" ("Filming Slavery," 100).

20. Cliff comments on Caribbean writing and a Creolism of form: "You can be much more experimental, you can mix styles up, you don't have to be linear, you don't have to be dichotomous, and believe it's either poetry or prose or whatever. You can really mix the media," Judith Raiskin, "The Art of History: An Interview with Michelle Cliff," *The Kenyon Review* 15, 1 (Winter 1993), 58.

21. In one interview, Cliff refers to Annie as a Jamaican in exile, "who is in many ways standing in for me," Renee Hausmann Shea, "Interview with Michelle Cliff," *Belles Letters* 9, 3 (Summer 1994), 32.

22. As Cliff has said of Caribbean "identity," "the Caribbean doesn't exist

as an entity; it exists all over the world. It started in diaspora and it continues in diaspora," Meryl F. Schwartz, "An Interview with Michelle Cliff," *Contemporary Literature* 34, 4 (Winter 1993), 597. The bottles offer a visual image of this scattered collective.

23. See Edmondson, "Race, Privilege" (187) on "Re-Writing History." Cliff notes that she started out doing graduate studies in history: "'I've always been struck by the misrepresentation of history and have tried to correct recieved versions of history, especially the history of resistance. It seems to me that if one does not know that one's people have resisted, then it makes resistance difficult." Opal Palmer Adisa, "Journey into Speech—A Writer between Two Worlds: An Interview with Michelle Cliff," *African American Review* 28, 2 (1994), 280.

24. See Shea, for Cliff's explanation of the choice of Pleasant. See also Raiskin, 665; Adisa, 279–80.

25. As Nielsen notes, "The Middle Passage may be the great repressed signifier of American historical consciousness" (101); "the Middle Passage is everywhere inscribed within the archives of our thought" (102); and it "irrevocably hinges African and American cultural experience" (103).

26. In developing his theory of the "Black Atlantic," Gilroy also points to the centrality of "the image of ships in motion across the spaces between Europe, America, Africa, and the Caribbean. . . . Ships immediately focus attention on the Middle Passage, on the various projects for redemptive return to an African homeland, on the circulation of ideas and activities as well as the movement of key cultural and political artefacts" (4).

27. Cliff has already referred to this incident in her earlier novel *Abeng*. Delany's novel illustrates a similar event; see Gilroy, *The Black Atlantic*, especially 19–29, for a discussion of Delany.

28. For background on Turner's painting and a discussion of its significance in diasporan experience, see Gilroy, *Small Acts*, 81–84.

29. Nielsen and Gilroy, from different angles, make this argument most forcefully. Paule Marshall comments on creating the character Harriet, whose family—the Shippens—made their money originally in the slave trade: "An in-depth study of just how these American families were very directly involved—not only the men, the captains, brokers, and slave owners—but also how the women from respectable families of the North . . . had their side trade in slaves" (Pettis, 125). We can see a link, then, between Harriet and Cliff's recreation of Alice Hooper.

30. Much has been made, of course, of Cliff's own identity. See Edmondson, "Race, Privilege" (especially 182–185). For an insightful examination of the different "readings" of Cliff's identity, see Sally O'Driscoll, "Michelle Cliff and the Authority of Identity." *Journal of the Midwest MLA* (Fall 1995). On "passing" for either white or black, see Adrian Piper's brilliant essay, "Passing for White, Passing for Black," *Transition* 58 (1992): 4–32.

21

. . . .

Return Passages

Maryse Condé Brings Tituba
Back to Barbados

Robert H. McCormick, JR.

Maryse Condé likes large-scale cultural confrontations and the sparks generated by the collision of contending cultures. That is the essential principle of *Segu* (New York: Ballantine, 1987; *Ségou: Les murailles de terre*, Paris: Laffont, 1984). Situated on the Niger River in present-day Mali, Segu was the center of the former Bambara civilization vanquished first by Islam and then the expanding "civilization" of the French colonialists in western Africa.

The essential idea of the novel was to represent the nobility of a late-eighteenth-century African civilization and chart the ensuing conflict between it and Islam. Acknowledging a commercial component in *Segu*'s origin, Condé indicated that a former editor at Laffont had pointed out to her the lack of a great historical novel ("grand roman historique") on Africa.[1] The sequel, *The Children of Segu* (*Ségou: La terre en miette*), plots the French incursion from St. Louis Island down the Senegal River and depicts the fall of a powerless, decadent Segu to the better-armed French colonial forces.

In her first two novels, Condé avoided the colonial period and the paths of its depiction well-traveled by such prominent African writers as Chinua Achebe and Ngũgĩ wa Thiong'o. Condé set her first novel in post-colonial Guinea. Published in French in 1976, *Heremakhonon* (*Hérémakhonon*), whose ironic title means "waiting for happiness" in Malinke (taken from the name of a Guinean department store where there was

nothing to buy except Chinese toys of poor quality),[2] focuses on the illusions of the post-Independence Marxist Guinea as they are progressively
revealed to the confused young Guadeloupan, Veronica Mercier, a Paris-
educated philosophy teacher.

Attempting to discover "Africanness" outside the parameters of European colonialism, Condé sets the beginning of her *Segu* in 1797. The novel
is dedicated to the author's "Bambara ancestress." Although dedicated to
a fictitious woman of the past, *Segu* is clearly conceived as relevant to the
self-image of all blacks of the African diaspora. Condé does not explain
how she knows her ancestors are Bambara, if they are. However, it is important to the conception of her novel that her ancestors are of a princely
family, comfortable, and physically beautiful. Yet—I concur here with
Leah Hewitt[3]—Condé does not idealize her characters, nor the historical
period. Nonetheless, the members of her fictional family have never even
imagined the scourge of slavery, at least not as victims of such an institution. They did have their own slaves, and the precolonialist intra-African
practice of slavery and its justification by *all* civilizations and religions in
the region is discussed in some detail in the novel.

The Bambara civilization was highly civilized. The Scottish explorer of
Africa, Mungo Park, was astounded upon his arrival in Segu in around
1797: "The view of this extensive city, the numerous canoes upon the
river, the crowded population, and the cultivated state of the surrounding countryside, formed altogether a prospect of civilization and magnifi-
cence which I little expected to find in the bosom of Africa."[4] The Bambara civilization is represented in the novel by Dousika Traore's family,
ultimately partially converted to Islam during one of the major phases of
its expansion into black Africa later in the nineteenth century.

The prime areas of cultural difference between the two clashing civilizations, as Condé presents them, are their attitudes toward women and
their conceptions of the nature of God. Condé's Bambara civilization is
characterized by bare-breasted young girls, a generally permissive attitude toward sex, by polygamy, and by polytheistic ancestor worship.
Young male "fetishists" (clansmen worshiped "boli" or clay models of
their ancestors) chaff at Moslem restrictions on their right to drink
"dolo," their indigenous alcoholic beverage. In marked contrast, Moslem
women will be veiled and hidden. Some monotheistic Moslems in the
novel dismiss the "fetish worshippers" by telling them disparagingly to go
sacrifice their chickens! The animist will also be accused of practicing
human sacrifice.

Paralleling later-arriving Christianity, Islam makes inroads on traditional African life through its monotheism and its schools. The young
Tiekoro, Dousika's son by his first wife, will be fascinated by Arabic and

the advantages of learning, especially in understanding and communicating with the outside world. Some animists will see the universal Moslem religion as a possible solution to tribal violence, and many will also be impressed by the Moslems' architectural skill as manifested in their mosques. Tiekoro converts and becomes a sort of saint. He also helps spread Islam by the example of his austere, meditative lifestyle, his learning, his school, and the miracles he allegedly performs in prison. He is ultimately executed, however, as a result of machinations initiated by members of his own family, notably his brother, who continue to support ancestral values. Even in the case of the conversion of a Bambara, often for political reasons, a cultural tension subsists between Islam and the converted Bambara's former animist beliefs. Tiekoro continues to take women after his marriage, and his conception of Islam is contested by fundamentalists.

Especially in *The Children of Segu*, Condé interjects frequent holy sayings and verses from the Koran to illustrate the spiritual force of Islam at that time, although the expansion of Islam is primarily attributed to the "jihad" launched, in 1854, by El-Hadj Omar Saidou Tell. Like Achebe, Condé sympathizes with the threatened traditional way of life. In response to questions about possible bias in her presentation of Islam, however, Condé maintains that she aimed to portray this period of Moslem expansion both accurately and objectively and that she was equally critical of Christianity when its links to colonialism merited such criticism.[5]

The principal protagonists of *Segu* are male. When questioned about this, in 1984, Condé responded, that she was not interested in portraying women brandishing swords and that in Africa then, women were oppressed.[6] In the novel, the female characters have only family-related roles, and they are never consulted in important community matters in either of the two cultures. After Dousika's death, the family council, according to tradition, gave Nya, his first wife, to his younger brother. Women are often depicted as restless, dissatisfied. Two women of Segu, Siga's mother, who is Dousika's slave concubine, and Nadie, Tiekoro's wife, unhappy with their treatment by men or by the clan, commit suicide by throwing themselves, the latter with her child, into wells. Condé insists research support her fictional portrayal,[7] which subverts conventional ideas about the rarity of suicide in traditional African civilization.

A family saga, *Segu* deals with the self-perpetuation of the Traore family—thus, the importance of sexuality. In this novel, as in Condé's work in general, desire is generally satisfied expeditiously without Proustian detours. Before his conversion, Tiekoro, to cite only one example, more or less rapes Nadie in the privy behind a bar when he first sees her.

Later, after having been led on, then spat on and called a "dirty nigger"[8] by Ayisha, the Moslem daughter of his landlord, Tiekoro marries Nadie when he finds out she is pregnant. The female characters are obviously more circumspect, yet they mock the men they like, and send secret letters, for example. In *The Children of Segu*, with the arrival of Islam, men surrendering to such nonspiritual impulses will feel obligated, or be forced, to legitimize them by marriage.

In *The Children of Segu*, Condé depicts the second major cultural confrontation. The threatened Islamicized society of Segu tries to organize a hasty alliance of Moslem communities to protect itself from the French, but the ever-changing semi-Islamic political entities cannot stop their in-fighting, and the chief of Segu, ironically adorned with traditional fetishist ornaments symbolizing his alleged power, is forced to become the unwilling servant, in the wake of the Berlin Conference, of colonialist rifles, canons, and the soon-to-arrive priests.

A best-seller in France, *Segu* sold some 300,000 first-edition copies for Laffont in its first year.[9] Translated into many foreign languages, the set of two volumes has now been published by "Livre de poche" and Penguin. Its commercial success indicates the relevance and originality of the novel's subject matter, especially for its non-African readership. Condé's African readership was less receptive, though. In an interview that dealt with *Segu's* reception, Condé says that, after her Segu novels, she "decided never to write about Africa again because the book was so terribly received by Africans and Africanists. They took the opportunity to write so much nonsense about the West Indians and their so-called intuition of Africa that I was hurt. Tituba came to me or I came to her . . . at a period of my life when really I wanted to turn toward the Caribbean and start writing about the Caribbean."[10]

From Africa then, Condé enacts her own authorial "Transatlantic Passage" to the New World in *I, Tituba, Black Witch of Salem* (*Moi, Tituba, sorcière . . . Noire de Salem*), published in France in 1986, and her more overtly autobiographical *Tree of Life* (*La vie scélérate*), originally published in 1987.

The Guadeloupan writer maintains that *I, Tituba* is not a historical novel like *Segu*,[11] but clearly a major part of its initial impact is its strikingly new historical perspective and highly successful effort to recuperate from obscurity the black Barbadian woman whom previous writers and historians had, for the most part, neglected.

The title is a significant one. "I" is an affirmation: it affirms that Tituba exists[12] and indicates that the focus is more on a women than on the collectivity, as in *Segu*. Tituba is forced to say "I" because as a black female slave from the Caribbean who lived in the seventeenth century, she was invisable. The oft-stated goal of both Tituba's first person narration and the author herself[13] is to resuscitate that existence:

> I felt that I would only be mentioned in passing in these Salem witchcraft trials about which so much would be written later, trials that would arouse the curiosity and pity of generations to come as the greatest testimony of a superstitious and barbaric age. . . . There would be no mention of my age or my personality. I would be ignored. . . . Tituba would be condemned forever! There would never, ever, be a careful, sensitive biography recreating my life and its suffering.[14]

The narration begins on a slave ship crossing the Atlantic; thus, the understood origin of the plot, and of Tituba, is Africa. The novel retraces the slave triangle. However, it has a significant new twist since the narration's geographic focus moves from Africa, to Barbados, to Salem, but then back to Barbados. In the first paragraph Condé makes clear that Tituba's existence is determined by her mother's skin color and the institution of slavery: Tituba's mother, an Ashanti named Abena, is raped by an Englishman in front of his mates on the deck of the slave ship, *Christ the King*. After Abena is sold to a Barbadian plantation owner, she stabs him when he, too, tries to take the young mother by force. As an example to the other slaves, Abena is hanged. Her black lover, Yao, the Ashanti who created Tituba by his "will and imagination"[15]—if not by his seed—and who gave her, as an indication of his love and his creativity, her name, commits suicide by swallowing his tongue upon being sold to another plantation as a punishment.

The title also insists on Tituba's key role as a witch, or "sorcière," even though Condé does note that the words "Black Witch of Salem" were added by her publisher.[16] This function is attributed to Tituba by others against her will, even in the beginning in Barbados. Tituba finds the persistent negative evaluation of her skills unfair, especially since she understood early in her life that she was "born to heal, not to frighten."[17] After the brutal hanging of her mother, Tituba was initiated into the secrets of nature, those of the mountains, the sea and of Barbadian plants, by Yetunde, an old woman of Nago origin, who is called Mama Yaya in Creole. After this initiation, Tituba is occasionally asked to cast spells. She does reluctantly, and only to make things better. In Salem, for example, she refuses Sarah's request to get rid of Goodwife Priscilla Henderson, Sarah's mistress, who beats her slave because of her unhappy marriage. Tituba justifies her nonintervention on behalf of a slave: "The woman who revealed to me her science taught me to heal and console rather than to do evil."[18]

Tituba is visited frequently by her dead mother and Yao, her mother's lover, visits in which Condé links African ancestor worship to new world "voodoo," a theme she also includes in *Tree of Life*. These returning extraterrestrials, predominantly women, are characterized as "life-giving forces."[19] They protect, teach, advise, and support Tituba in her difficult moments: they are the primary facilitators of her regeneration.

In *The Crucible* Arthur Miller renders the essential material of the Salem witch trials from the perspective of the 1950s and McCarthyism. Miller shows that petty interests, relating primarily to the economics of the parish of Rev. Samuel Parris, and adolescent manipulation of the Puritan belief in the devil caused the Puritans' shift from intolerance to murder. He also makes clear that Parris was a merchant in Barbados, where he acquired Tituba, before he entered the ministry, a second profession for which he was little qualified.

A widower in *The Crucible*, Rev. Parris screams, "Out of here!" at Tituba in his very first utterance in the play to get her away from his sick daughter. He is already attributing responsibility for her sickness to Tituba. Thus, Samuel Parris illustrates one of the key themes of Condé's novel: the transferral of the evil in himself and in his Puritan community to the powerless black slave who tries to cure, with some success, both the daughter and Mrs. Parris of their physical ailments.

Like Miller, Condé indicates that Tituba was finally freed by saying she had had contact with the devil and by denouncing, quite unheroically, other women. Thus, she followed the counsel and simulation of her African Caribbean husband, John Indian (the court records, that Condé quotes, indicate her legal name was Tituba Indian[20]), who had become a Christian and gradually abandoned his identity in order to survive. Tituba will ultimately assert her own identity by rejecting both the sin-obsessed Puritans and her all-too-ready-to-assimilate African Caribbean husband.

Although sympathetic with Tituba's status as victim, Miller relegates her to the minor role of an eccentric, mistreated slave. Condé eroticizes her Tituba and gives her more narrative weight. When a naive Tituba meets John Indian for the first time in Barbados, she feels immediate attraction for him. Soon thereafter, she meets him at a local dance and leaves with him in spite of her spiritual mentors' disapproval. This spontaneous sexual arousal and its rapid realization is a pattern already apparent in *Segu*.

Later, even though she is free, Tituba accepts becoming a "slave" in order to remain with John Indian when he is sold to Parris by a jealous Susan Endicott. Throughout the novel, Tituba is a counterpoint to Rev. Parris and his wife, who are embarrassed to undress themselves when they have sex and to undress the girls when the doctor comes to examine them for tangible marks of the devil. Rev. Parris's most significant sexual activity is to participate in the gang rape of Tituba. This attempt to force her to acuse other women reveals again that the real devils are the Puritans.

Both in Barbados and Salem, John Indian, son of an Arawak Indian and a Nago woman, is a good lover. In the spiritual and caloric frigidity of Salem, he keeps Tituba warm. In her later relations with Christopher and even with her younger "son"/lover, Iphigene, Tituba thinks nostalgically of her sexual relation with John Indian. John Indian's function is thus somewhat ambiguous as he "leads" Tituba away from her home in Barbados (i.e., her identity), but he also introduces her to her own sexuality, an important part of her being throughout her life and even after her death!

Tituba knows, though, that John Indian pushed his collaboration too far and that he would accuse even her of being a witch[21] to save his own skin. She later learns that John Indian was as much involved in the denunciations as the Puritan girls, that "John Indian was in the front line of the accusers, that he accompanied the girls . . . shouted when they shouted, had seizures when they had them, and gave names louder and stronger than they did. . . . They even said he had pointed to Satan in the harmless shape of a cloud above the heads of the condemned prisoners."[22] There is even a hint that John Indian was a tacit accomplice in the gang rape of his wife. Later in the narrative, Tituba had a dream in which the three hooded participants were Samuel Parris, Christopher, and John Indian. Despite the sexual pleasure he provides, John Indian is not included as one of the male life-giving forces like Yao and Iphigene. Furthermore, it is his child she aborts.

Justifiably, Condé maintains her novel is a work of imagination.[23] She states she could not possibly have relied solely on the few historical documents about Tituba. She does, however, use extracts from Tituba's trial deposition, a document found in the Essex County Courthouse in Salem. This historical document, lodged in the center of the novel, anchors the narration in 1692 Salem. In her effort to create a complete black Caribbean woman, however, Condé imagines and recreates Tituba's pre-Salem past and her post-Salem future, both situated in the Caribbean, the locus of her identity.

Perhaps in one instance, however, Condé's imagination was too fertile. In jail, Tituba meets, and is consoled by, Hester Prynne, recuperated by Condé from *The Scarlet Letter*. At one point, they embark on a contemporary dialogue about women's issues, and Hester says, "You're too fond of love, Tituba! I'll never make a feminist out of you!" "A feminist? What's that?"[24] Tituba asks.

Condé revealed in an interview that this scene was a joke that constituted one element in a larger pastiche of all the clichés of a heroic novel
with a feminine protagonist.[25] Clearly Hester is part of that "joke," in
that her exaggerated and self-destructive behavior is contrasted with
Tituba's more real cowardice. On the other hand, and despite the author's disclaimers, the prolonged evocation of Hester is significant. Still
another example of "life-destroying" forces determining the destinies of
women, Condé's Hester not only commits suicide even though she is
pregnant, but she also entreats Tituba to do the same, thus provoking
Tituba to reaffirm her desire to live. Hester also vaguely evokes "bodily
pleasure"[26] between women.

Nonetheless, that same Hester becomes one of the "life-giving
forces"—the only white non-African one and the only woman of Tituba's
own generation. Hester's importance to the larger constellation of
Tituba's life is shown later on when Tituba names a Barbadian orchid
after her. In the epilogue, Tituba's spirit knows that Hester's is "pursuing
her dreams of creating a world of women that will be more just and hu-
mane."[27] At that same time, Tituba's disembodied spirit is working for
the independence of all men and women in Barbados. When she is not
satisfying "a bit of leftover desire."[28]

Condé's ending is key to our understanding of her resurrected Tituba.
The basic historical fact (i.e., that Tituba was sold after her release to pay
for her prison fees) is incorporated as Condé's fictional protagonist is sold
and eventually finds her way back to Barbados after being freed by her
new master, a Portuguese Jew. Benjamin Cohen d'Azevedo was himself a
victim of New World intolerance when his house, nine children, and two
ships were burned by those same invidious Salemites. It is also significant to Tituba's psychological well-being that her "sweet, crooked, mis-
shapen" owner/liberator made love to her and that he called her his
"beloved witch"[29] because she brought him into contact with his deceased wife, Abigail, and later with his children.

As a part of her coda, the West Indian author displaces to Barbados
the Jamaican tradition of the "Maroons," a tradition she already introduced in the Segu novels. Back in Barbados, Tituba, albeit older, still has
not lost her sexual identity, but she has not found herself, either. She becomes involved with Christopher, the polygamous leader of the small Maroon community isolated in the mountains of the island. He is interested
in Tituba only so long as he thinks she, as a witch, can make him "invin-
cible." His ego and his illusions—later he thinks he is already immortal-
ized because he heard "field niggers" singing a song about him he had
made up himself—are boundless.

Song is important in the novel as an indicator of Tituba's resurrection.

With respect to the song for him, Tituba asked Christopher if there were not a song for her. He answered that there was not and started to snore. Soon thereafter he starts to take her with his clothes on, like Samuel Parris, and he refuses to talk of the general revolt about which rumors were circulating. Tituba starts to wonder if a man who treats her so negligently can really be a revolutionary leader.

We subsequently discover that Christopher's courage is quite limited. In fact, in keeping with the history of the less-than-heroic last group of Maroons, he enters into an agreement of complicity with the plantation owners stipulating that the remaining Maroons will be left alone in the mountains if they alert authorities to potential plantation uprisings. Although he has fathered Tituba's child, Christopher betrays her and her new young lover, Iphigene, who she nursed back to life after he had received 250 whiplashes. Iphigene is the real leader of the revolt, a revolt that will be squelched before it breaks out. Both Tituba and Iphigene are hanged by the colonists, the young leader first. The last rebel hanged, Tituba surrealistically narrates her own death.

Condé has Tituba return to her native Barbados, but also creates an active last image of her dying at least wanting and preparing to fight slavery. Condé asserts she does not write programmatic feminist novels. Nonetheless, she relates her resuscitated heroine to the legend surrounding Nanny, the most famous female leader of rebel slaves in Jamaica. Furthermore, Condé revealed in an interview that she was deeply moved when she visited Nanny's deserted Jamaican tomb.[30]

To reinforce the positive revalorization of Tituba in the context of Caribbean civilization, Maryse Condé closes with an epilogue in which Tituba reappears as a spirit, just as her parents and spiritual mentors had. On her island, she hears a young Barbadian boy humming a song about her, a song more meaningful than anything she could have hoped for from Christopher. Tituba is so happy that she drops three mangoes onto the ground in front of the young boy. By that action, and by her subsequent affirmations, she demonstrates that she is nourishing the islanders "with dreams of liberty."[31] Thus, in the end, Tituba inscribes herself, in the minds of the islanders, back into history, and she hopes to be part of their future history of freedom.

She also "adopts" the child she never nurtured (she aborted John Indian's child and Christopher's died with her) when her spirit enters into the daughter of Délices, the latter having died in childbirth. Thus, she finally has a child, Samantha, one she chose and one to whom she reveals the secrets of the herbs and animals. Her spirit also menaces Christopher, so much so that he loses his taste for women. The spirit of Iphigene, working together with Tituba's, selected a fine Congo child that the overseers are already keeping an eye on. Perhaps because he, too, started humming Tituba's song.

In conclusion, *Segu* and *I, Tituba* are linked by their reflection on identity and pride and on the forces negating them. In *Segu*, collective Bambara pride is being undermined by the incursion of Islam and French colonialism. In the latter novel, an individual black woman's pride—almost but never quite broken by the unholy trinity of slavery, Puritanism, and masculinocentrism—is reconstructed.

Like her own fictional creation, Maryse Condé is returning home too. The new force the spiritualized Tituba feels must be related to what Condé felt as she moved from her objective historical narrative on her unknown black ancestors to the recreation of the identity of a black Caribbean woman from a contemporary point of view. At one point in Tituba's narrative, Yao says she will return home to Africa. Tituba, who frequently asks Mama Yaya when she will return home, always understands home to be the Caribbean.

Condé's fanciful paradise for Tituba is Barbados, a Barbados inhabited by the spirit of Iphigene, someone she loves. She is in communication with her lover, she "chooses" a daughter, people sing about her, and she continues to soothe suffering slaves and to work for freedom. After having effectuated her "return passage," she understands her maternal and political roles, her role as free "spirit" in the Caribbean.

Unlike Veronica Mercier in *Heremakhonon*, Tituba does not need to look for her identity in Africa. Tituba has found her geopolitical home in the Caribbean. Her journey is over even if she is not at rest. After *I, Tituba*, Condé's next novels, *Tree of Life* and *Crossing the Mangrove*, will also be set in the Caribbean. The latter work can be interpreted as focusing on the Martinican poet, Aimé Césaire, author of the work considered to be the point of origin of French West Indian literature, *Return to My Native Land*.

Notes

1. Françoise Pfaff, *Entretiens avec Maryse Condé* (Paris: Karthala, 1993), p. 74.

2. Pfaff, p. 62.

3. Leah Hewitt, *Autobiographical Tightropes: Simone de Beauvoir, Nathalie Sarraute, Marguerite Duras, Monique Wittig & Maryse Condé* (Lincoln: University of Nebraska Press, 1990), p. 164.

4. Quoted by Basil Davidson, *Africa in History: Themes and Outlines* (London: Weidenfeld and Nicolson, 1968), p. 213.

5. Pfaff, pp. 82–83.

6. Pfaff, p, 80.

7. Pfaff, p. 78.

8. Maryse Condé, *Segu*. Trans. Barbara Bray (New York: Ballantine, 1987 [1st ed., 1984]), p. 91.

9. Pfaff, p. 83.

10. Quoted by Ann Armstrong Scarboro, in afterword to Mayrse Condé, *I, Tituba, Black Witch of Salem* (Charlottesville: University Press of Virginia, 1992), p. 204.

11. Pfaff, pp. 88–89, 96.

12. Kathleen M. Balutansky, "Creating Her Own Image: Female Genesis in 'Mémoire d'une amnésiaque' and 'Moi, Tituba, sorcière.'" *L'Héritage de Caliban.* Ed. Maryse Condé, et al. (Guadeloupe: Editions Jasar, 1992), pp. 29–47.

13. Pfaff, p. 91.

14. Maryse Condé, *I, Tituba, Black Witch of Salem*. Trans. Richard Philcox (Charlottesville: University of Virginia Press, 1992 [1st ed., 1986]), p. 110.

15. Condé, *I, Tituba*, p. 6.

16. Armstrong Scarboro, afterword to *I, Tituba*, p. 205.

17. Condé, *I, Tituba*, p. 12.

18. Condé, *I, Tituba*, p. 68.

19. Condé, *I, Tituba*, p. 85.

20. Condé, *I, Tituba*, p. 104.

21. Condé, *I, Tituba*, pp. 109–110.

22. Condé, *I, Tituba*, p. 119.

23. Pfaff, p. 89.

24. Condé, *I, Tituba*, p. 101.

25. Pfaff, p. 90.

26. Condé, *I, Tituba*, p. 122.

27. Condé, *I, Tituba*, p. 178.

28. Condé, *I, Tituba*, p.178.

29. Condé, *I, Tituba*, p. 131.

30. Pfaff, p, 86.

31. Condé, *I, Tituba*, p. 175.

22

• • • •

Mediterranean Passage

*The Beginnings of an African Italian Literature
and the African American Example*

Alessandro Portelli

Turning White

"I am not ashamed of my parents for having been slaves," says Ralph Ellison's invisible man: "I am only ashamed of myself for having at one time been ashamed."[1] The autobiography of Nassira Chohra—born in Marseilles, France, of Sarawi descent, living in Italy, and writing in Italian—reveals how she reacted to the discovery of her own blackness: "For a week, I was terribly ashamed of my mother and of the color of my skin, and only now do I understand that I shall never be ashamed enough for having been ashamed of her."[2]

The African American character and the African-French-Italian author share the same experience of denial and reconstruction of identity, the same dialectics of shame-pride-shame, self-doubt, and self-discovery. Perhaps, African American history can tell us something of the contemporary emigration experience, and the making of African American literature can teach us how to read the recent writings and narratives of the African, Asian, and Latin American newcomers to Italy—a task for which, so far, we have received hardly any support from established studies of Italian literature.

After discovering that she was black, Chohra recalls:

> I ran home like mad, looking for a mirror. I found one in a drawer: small, with a scratch in the middle. Doesn't matter, I thought; it's

just what I need. I looked at myself a long time, running the index finger of my right hand along my cheek to see whether, by some magic, I could make that color that filled all of me go away.[3]

Once again, this scene takes us back to the very origins of the African experience in Europe and America. Olaudah Equiano writes:

I had often observed that when [Mary's] mother washed her face it looked very rosy, but when she washed mine it did not look so. I therefore tried oftentimes myself if I could not by washing make my face the same color as my little play-mate, Mary, but all in vain; and now I began to be mortified at the difference in our complexions.[4]

Comparison, however, yeilds not only analogies but also illuminating differences. In Equiano's time, the dominant culture uniformly saw blackness as a stigma, the mark of Cain to be "refin'd" away, if not materially, at least spiritually, as Phillis Wheatley suggested. In 1970, when Nassira Chohra tried to wipe the black off her face, and in the 1990s, when she wrote about it, blackness was fraught with more ambiguities. Racism is as pervasive as ever, yet popular culture also feeds us images of blackness as ambiguously desirable: "the lure of the other color," as a major Italian news magazine's cover story put it recently, illustrating the concept with the image of a beautiful, naked black woman.[5] No wonder Italian pop groups flaunt such names as "Vorrei la pelle nera" (I Wish My Skin Was Black, after a 1960s hit) or "Neri per caso" (Just Happen to Be Black).[6]

Thus, while blackness "filled" Nassira Chohra like a disease, it also suggested other roads to visibility. The mirror of her infancy became the movie screen of her adolescence, as she gravitated toward the fashion industry and show business: "[L]ike all the girls, I dreamed of being an actress, I tried desperately to be an actress, took all the screen-tests, and I was never right. Always, the problem of color—it was either too light or too dark, I was never the right color."[7]

Never the right color: a good metaphor for a transitional, uncertain identity in a state of passage. In this web of ambiguities, we discover the obverse to the black wish to be white and to the white wish to be black: the black *nightmare* of becoming white. Whiteness can be a sign of the loss of presence, power, meaning. "Since I've been in Italy, my skin is no longer the same," says a young woman from Somalia; "it is lighter, I don't like it, it keeps getting whiter and whiter. I'm afraid I'm turning white."[8] This nightmare is also not without precedent in African American literature. "Lonesome Ben" is Charles Chesnutt's story about a runaway slave who has left his family behind and feels "all alone in de world." Chesnutt writes:

[H]e went down by de crick in broad daylight, an' kneel down by
de water an' looked at his face. Fus' he didn't reco'nize hisse'f
an' glanshed back ter see ef dey wa'n't somebody lookin' ober is
shoulder - but dey wa'n't. An' w'en he looked back in de water he
seed de same thing—he wa'n't black no mo', but had turnt ter a
light yaller.[9]

Turning white is a metaphor for a broader sense of loss. "My own
family happened to be a family of healers," says Pap Khouma, a Senegalese immigrant, in his autobiography. "And my father is also a healer.
He lost part of his powers after a trip to Europe. I wonder what happened
to him in Paris."[10]

Color Lines

When W.E.B. Du Bois wrote in 1903 that "the problem of the twentieth
century is the problem of the color line," he specified that the line was
drawn "in Asia and Africa, in America and the islands of the sea."[11] Europe seemed to be exempt. The line that was drawn *within* other continents, seemed to run, rather, *between* Europe and Africa: in the Atlantic
Ocean, with the mediation of America; and, more immediately, in the
Mediterranean Sea, which divides and joins southern Europe and northern Africa. Only recently has the color line become visible *inside* European societies, as the African diaspora has spread northward, toward the
former colonial nations.

In Italy, a country that had thought of itself as racially homogeneous
(if regionally divided), and had crossed the Mediterranean southward in
belated colonial conquest, the influx of Third-World population has been
felt as a major cultural shock. On the one hand, against all historical evidence, Italians continued to believe that we were not racists and therefore
need not be concerned about race at all. On the other hand, the brevity
and violence of the Italian colonial experience had prevented the growth
of an Italian-speaking "Talented Tenth" in former Italian colonies and
the creation of an Italophone African literature. There is no Italian
Rushdie, Khureishi, Ben Jalloun; the Somali writer Nuruddin Farah
speaks Italian but, although his characters use an occasional Italian
word, he writes in English. African Italian literature begins in the 1990s,
from scratch.

This "Mediterranean Passage" and its consequences are much less
bloody and dramatic than the Atlantic Passage from Africa to America.
Emigration is one thing, deportation another; the condition of even marginal proletarians is not to be compared to that of slaves. One of the most

immediately visible differences is literacy, in the broadest sense. A large percentage of Third-World (and East Europe) immigrants to Italy are literate, educated, and polyglot—if often speechless. For instance, the narrator of Salah Methnani's *Immigrato,* when he meets his first Italian girl, is so overwhelmed that "the only thing I manage to say, also to make an impression, is that I have a degree in languages: I speak—beside Arabic, of course—French, English, some Russian, and Italian."[12]

Also, immigrants are almost always still in touch with their own families and with their country of origin. The act of writing, therefore, is fraught with less difficulties and implications than in the case of, say, Phillis Wheatley, or Wilhelm Amo, or even Frederick Douglass. These writers have not been forced to display literacy in order to prove that they are human.[13]

On the other hand, perhaps because of the few barriers to written expression, the actual writings of these authors have remained somewhat invisible. Literary critics have dismissed them (often without bothering to read them) on account of their supposed lack of artistry; social scientists have approached them as well as their African American predecessors, only as documents and testimony, if not of the human nature of Africans, at least of immigrant "conditions."

It has taken almost two hundred years for Wheatley's work to be recognized and read as an articulate literary text in its own terms. We need not make the same mistake and wait two centuries before we decipher immigrant literary discourse.

Versions of Two-ness

All of the above means that, rather than make broad generalizations, we should read individual works closely. I would like to begin with another seminal text of African Italian literature: a poem by the Cameroonian author Ndjock Ngana, who also signs himself with the Italian name of Teodoro—"God's gift."[14]

> Living only one life,
>   in one town,
>   in one country,
>   in one universe,
> Living only in one world,
> Is prison.
>
>   .   .   .   .
>
> Knowing only one language,
>   one trade,

one way of life,
one civilization,
Knowing only one logic,
Is prison.

Having only one body,
one thought,
one knowledge,
one essence,
Having only one being,
Is prison.[15]

This poem begs comparison with Du Bois's concept of "double-consciousness" and "two-ness" in African American subjectivity.[16] Du Bois's famous passage is itself twofold in its implications: on the one hand, two-ness endows "the Negro" with "second-sight in this American world"; on the other, it lacerates the subject in "two unreconciled strivings, two warring ideals in one dark body." Ndjock Ngana seems to lean toward the former possibility: two-ness, this double-named poet says in his double-colored, double-titled book, means freedom, second sight.[17]

Like Wheatley's "On Being Brought from Africa to America," this poem is a plea for inclusion. Just as Wheatley reminded her Christian readers that "Negroes black as Cain / May be refin'd and join th'angelic train" in a multicultural spiritual world,[18] Ngana tells his readers that we will all be freer if we include blackness in our material world. Ngana, however, differs from Wheatley because his strategy is not a unilateral "refinement" or assimilation, but mutual syncretism: multiculturalism as possibility. Ostensibly, the message is addressed to white European readers, but on the lower frequencies Ngana also addresses a signifying anti-essentialist message to the black portion of his audience. They, too, would be wrong if they locked themselves into "one" African "essence." For both black and white, prison consists in excluding otherness from one's self.

Ngana projects an ideal while Du Bois describes an experience. Thus, while Ngana sees only liberation in the ideal of multiplicity and syncretism, Du Bois also speaks of pain, of "unreconciled strivings" and "warring ideals" in "one dark body." To read the heavy price, the tragic side of two-ness, the painful rendering of identity and consciousness involved in the contemporary multicultural passage, we must turn to other texts.

Princesa, the narrative of Fernanda Farias de Albuquerque, a Brazilian transvestite, written in prison in Rome, is the story of a person with, literally, two languages, two names, two bodies, and a syncretic ethnic identity.[19] It is the story of how Fernando becomes Fernanda, the story of a female body struggling to emerge from within a male one, under the effects of hormones and the hands of the Brazilian *bombadeiras*, bodymolders:

> Anaciclin, four pills every day. Fernando slowly wears away. The penis grows smaller, the testicles shrink. Body hair grows sparer, hips widen. Fernanda grows. Piece by piece, gesture upon gesture, I descend from sky to earth, a devil—a mirror. My journey.[20]

Transatlantic, transsexual, transvestite, translated—the story of Fernanda is the story of being "torn asunder," of unreconcilable yearnings of being and pain of becoming. She works the streets of several Brazilian cities before she reverses the Atlantic crossing, moving first to Spain and then to Italy, where she winds up in jail—a woman locked in a men's prison, just as her female body had been locked inside her male one.

> On the sidewalks of the great metropolis, Severina a bombadeira displays her masterpieces. Rounded, smooth bodies, injected with silicone. A fantastic twinkling of performances and fantasies. Severina a bombadeira eased my worries. No, no liquid silicone in the face; too risky. I hesitate: I'm afraid, Severina. What do you mean, afraid? If you want to become a woman, you must first go through pain, only after that will you be Fernanda.[21]

Becoming a woman means going through pain, and the narrative is indeed filled with actual physical suffering: beatings, rapes, police brutality, heroin, AIDS, jail. Yet perhaps no passage is more powerful than the combination of the physical and the symbolic in the initial scene of Fernanda's own, peculiar "middle passage," so ironically similar to archetypal scenes of childbirth and abortion, and, indeed, somehow a combination of both: "November, nineteen eighty-five. Severina, in her house, rounds my hips with injections of liquid silicone. Without anaesthesia."

Reading Fernanda's autobiography and Ndjock Ngana's poem together yields more than the explicit difference between a hopeful and painful version of two-ness and multiculturalism. The metaphor and experience of the multiple body, in fact, is an essential commentary on a crucial theme of postmodernism: the fragmentation of the self. Postmodernism represents the end of the unity of the subject as a liberation, a breakthrough into antiauthoritarian possibility. Though the hortatory tone sounds somewhat belatedly romantic, Ndjock Ngana's text stands for the postmodern experience of breaking out of the "prison" of identity and logocentric logic. On the other hand, however, colonial peoples and subordinate classes have already had a long experience of fragmentation as the result of violence and oppression, not liberation. As they shore their fragments against their ruins, the aim is less to explore fragmentation than to seek a plausible oneness. Thus, Fernanda's experience of fragmentation as pain includes both the struggle to deny and destroy an imposed (male) subjectivity and the struggle to create her chosen authenticity. Like the cyborg—a metaphor for transgendered, virtual sexuality and identity in much contemporary fiction and philosophy[22]—Fernanda creates herself out of implants and silicone. She achieves, however, not the virtual reality of her imagined sexuality, but an extended exploration of pain.

Two-ness as Writing

In these two texts, as in most of the literature of the Mediterranean passage, two-ness also becomes an organizing textual principle, primarily in the sphere of language. Ngana's book, like most of the poetry published by immigrants in Italy, is bi-lingual, with the original Basaa text facing the Italian version. In Nassira Chohra's autobiography, there is an almost invisible, but radical, linguistic-geographic shift: the book is all in Italian, but the first chapters take place in France; therefore, the Italian she writes is a monolingual representation of the French she actually spoke. When she moves to Italy, however, the language of experience and the language of the narration coincide. Only at this point do occasional French expressions begin to appear in the text, as markers of her gradual bilingual adaptation.

Princesa also introduces the Portuguese language in the title and in crucial words in the text (bombadeira). Most important, the Italian text of *Princesa* evolved through several languages. Fernanda was encouraged to write by a Sardinian shepherd who was serving life in her prison and who taught her not Italian but Sardinian (so different from standard Italian as to be rightly considered an autonomous language). She filled a number of notebooks in a wild mixture of highly vernacular Portuguese, oral Sardinian, and street Italian before her text was finally shaped in the brilliant Italian of another prisoner, former Red-Brigade member Maurizio Jannelli. Sadly, the cultural environment is not ready for the publication of Fernanda's original manuscript, which is probably closer to the language actually spoken by immigrants than any published text so far.[23]

Like early African American literature, immigrant writing in Italy must in fact adapt itself to the standard language. Black English had to

wait a long time (and go through the ambiguous phase of dialect literature) before it was recognized as a powerful medium.[24] The waiting period for the Italian Africanized by the immigrants may be shorter but is
ongoing. At this time, isolated words appear in the texts to designate objects for which there is no Italian expression. Arabic and African terms
are always explained in the text or in footnotes, indicating an implied Italian audience; immigrant variations on Italian are duly explicated (when
Khouma says that African immigrants use the Italian words for "uncle"
to designate the police, he explains: "Uncles are those who want to rule
your life").

Language is frequently thematized: as a difficulty to be overcome; as a
mask of feigned ignorance or signifying irony ("I gave the police a false
name. . . . False names are easily found in the *Wolof* language: just any
word meaning *shoes*, or *turtle*");[25] as a deliberate wearing of the stereotype ("Since I have realized that my acceptable knowledge of Italian
makes things more difficult rather than easier, I have begun to talk as one
would expect a *vu cumpra'* ");[26] as a form of empowerment for those who
become cultural mediators and interpreters between their community
and the European environment ("The police have realized that I speak
Italian fast and ask me to interpret for a Senegalese who doesn't speak a
word of Italian. A step forward. I become court interpreter in Senigal-
lia").[27] The main drift is, however, toward correctness; thus, the beginning and end of Salah Methnani's *Immigrato* are framed by the narrator's
initial failure and final success in pronouncing correctly the Italian word
dieci, ten. Functional concerns tend to prevail over expressive ones. The
Eritrean writer Ribka Sibhatu, who was a student in my department,
asked me to revise her manuscript; when I spotted a few minor irregularities in her Italian, I suggested she keep them in as a sign of her effort in
performing literature in another language, but she insisted on correcting
them because, she said, the book would be read by immigrant Eritrean
children, and it was of paramount importance that they learn to speak
Italian properly.

The bilingual form or background of the texts is also the outward
manifestation of another form of two-ness: multiple authorship. Just as
the case for early African American authors, behind each text there is an
editor, an interviewer, a translator, and a transcriber. It was a while before African American texts began to carry the label "written by himself
or herself"; even those carried paratextual apparatuses written by white
sponsors.[28] Many texts of the Mediterranean passage carry two names—
an immigrant and an Italian one—on the cover. In some cases, they indicate joint authorship (Fernanda Farias de Albuquerque and Maurizio
Jannelli for *Princesa*; Mario Fortunato and Salah Methnani for *Immi*-

grato); more often, they designate an author and an editor (Nassira Chohra and Alessandra Atti Di Sarro for *Volevo essere bianca*). In a number of cases, the editor is the actual writer in the material sense, the person who transcribes an oral narrative and gives it literary shape (Oreste Pivetta for Pap Khouma's *Io, venditore di elefanti*; Laura Maritano for Salwa Salem's *Con il vento nei capelli*). And even when author, writer, translator, and editor are the same person, two names may appear as in the Ndjock Ngana/Teodoro case.

While recognizing the claims of the Italian collaborators, this explicit declaration of joint authorship also draws attention to the dialogic construction of the text. In this, African Italian literature differs from the African American precedents, in which the names of white collaborators figured less prominently, possibly in order to enhance the sense of authenticity of those first-person narratives. If anything, these immigrant texts look more like those early Native American autobiographies discussed by Arnold Krupat, in which (perhaps also because of the linguistic transition) the white interviewer-editor-writer was as prominent as the Native American author-narrator.[29] Immigrant writers, however, often had as difficult a time with their coauthors as African American authors did with their editors and amanuenses. Thus, linguistic and literary "correctness" may be not only a chosen objective but also a forced normalization of identity and style. Nassira Chohra explains:

> I wrote in Italian because it was the thing to do, although I spoke the language very little. . . . I wrote in Italian also because I had to submit it in Italian to publishers. But it wasn't good enough, it had to be perfect. I found a young journalist . . . and she edited it, she corrected to make it presentable. But I must admit that there have been problems between us, because I absolutely refused to let her change anything in the story . . . and because the first part of the book is told by a seven-year-old child, I tried to stick to that, so she had a problem with that, too.[30]

Sometimes, this collaboration leaves visible signs in the forms of linguistic contradictions in the text. Thus, when I asked Arabic-speaking Salah Methnani why he used "arabesque" for "meaningless," he explained that that particular passage had been written by his Italian coauthor.[31]

Complex authorship, in fact, also stands for split authority. The purpose of the paratextual material accompanying African American texts was to authenticate them as *documents*, and the same purpose prevails in the presentation of contemporary African Italian texts. Both the "Notice to the Reader" in the narrative of Briton Hammon (1760) and the dust jacket to Salah Methnani's *Immigrato* insist that the language is "artless" and "unadorned" in the former and "limpid and straight" in the latter. The ostensible artlessness of the style is supposed to guarantee the factual veracity of the tale, which is therefore to be read not as a literary text but as a social document. Yet, the text often bears the marks of literary intention: for instance, many autobiographies are narrated not in the past but in the historical present tense, an easy way to invite empathy and identification but very unlikely to be used in extensive oral narration.

The problems apparently arise also when author and translator belong to the same culture. Moshen Melliti, the author of an early immigrant novel, wrote in what he described as the vernacular, hybrid Arabic spoken by the multinational immigrant community (as opposed to literary Arabic) and claims that this was lost when his translators (one of whom was a Palestinian immigrant himself) turned the book into a rather stilted Italian "poetic" prose.[32] True or not (the sentimental tone prevails also independently from the language), Methnani's claim can be seen at least as a sign of the problems inherent in the literary representation of the speech of non-canonic subjects by unauthorized writers.

Immigrant writing is generally accepted only as documentary; this fact imposes restrictions in terms of the available literary genres and linguistic registers. For instance, the language of Melliti's novel is often stilted, betraying an effort to prove the immigrant author's control of respectable, literary Italian. As he explained, he had intended to write a work of fiction, based on his own experiences, on stories he had been told, on things he had witnessed while researching a magazine piece he wrote on immigration. The fictional nature of the text was reinforced by contributions from his coauthor, Mario Fortunato. The two authors, however, were unable to interest a publisher in a work of fiction signed by an unknown immigrant. Any book by an immigrant had to represent experience and testimony, not expression and creativity. The immigrant, like the slave, is to be an object of either research or pity, not a subject of writing and language.

The most complex case of dual authorship and authority is *Princesa*. Rather than merely setting Fernanda's manuscript into publishable order, Maurizio Jannelli used it as the raw material of his own imaginative journey from within a prison cell:

> Once I collected the story, the dream began. I entered a sort of personal hallucination. . . . [D]evils, the devil began to come into my cell. I didn't realize how important the devil was. It was there, pervasively, in every page Fernanda had written. . . . The most difficult journey was the one into the body. Writing an autobiography in collaboration implies a short circuit. One of the two must

wear the clothes of the other. And I found myself playing the role of the transsexual, somewhat. I must admit that this was the most rewarding part of the experience, which literally hurled me into the reasons of the Other.[33]

In other words, as Jannelli explains, "Fernanda" is one thing, and "Princesa" is another—one the subject of an autobiography, the other the character in a book. Fernanda's autobiography and Maurizio's imaginative creation are, however, indissolubly merged in the same book, in the layers and levels of the same words. Whether Jannelli used Fernanda's words as raw material for his own discourse, and molded her text like the bombadeira moulded her body—or whether he extracted and liberated the inner meaning of her story like her female body emerged from her male flesh, is hard to determine. Fernanda did not seem to mind and allowed Maurizio to speak with, and for, her in the public appearances they made together after the book was published, when they were both out on parole and she was working as a secretary for the cooperative of political convicts that published her book. Neither her coworkers, nor the media, nor those intellectuals who, like me, promoted the book, really understood how severe this new fragmentation was. Everyone expected Fernanda to *be* Princesa, but she was still only Fernanda. When she could take it no longer, she broke parole and disappeared. She was found working the streets of a small town in central Italy and taken back to jail. Only much later was she extradited back to Brazil, where she was last reported to be living in her hometown.

Scenes of Writing: The Prison and the Street

Prison is another image that Fernanda Farias de Albuquerque shares with Ndjock Ngana. Once again, Ngana makes a metaphor out of what is physical experience for Fernanda. Indeed, prison is both a common experience and a handy metaphor in much immigrant writing. On the experiential plane, it is an inevitable consequence of the marginal, often illegal condition of immigrants ("All go to jail. For an hour, for a day, for a week. . . . The charge is always the same: undocumented on board")[34] and a memory of repression for political exiles. On the metaphoric plane, on the other hand, prison represents the condition of frustration, marginality, invisibility of both exiles and immigrants.

Hassan Itab, a Palestinian guerrilla who carried out a terrorist action in Rome after the Sabra and Chatila massacres, combines both perspectives, writing in and about the Italian jail in which he was detained after his arrest, where he thought he was awaiting execution ("Locked in a cell 24 hours a day. Locked in silence. Locked in waiting for a decision to be taken").[35] Ribka Sibhatu, an Eritrean exile, also tells of the time she spent in jail in her home country, waiting for death:

> [E]very night, each time we heard those feet coming, we thought they were coming to take—there was no trial, we didn't know how things went, so for ten months, every day your life is in tension, because they take away one by one. . . . And then, when we heard the shackles, and the feet—"it's my turn." And at night we're not afraid for our neighbor, only for ourselves. It is in the morning that we weep for the girl who was taken.[36]

In *The Victim as Criminal and Artist*, H. Bruce Franklin identifies the penitentiary and its variant, the plantation, as the sources of important genres in American literature, from slave narratives to chain gang songs.[37] Franklin emphasizes the symbolic role of jail as the scene of writing, and therefore of writing as an act of resistance. The prisoner creates in language a freedom physically negated by his or her surroundings. This is also true for much Third-World writing in Italy: for Fernanda Farias de Albuquerque, writing was not only an alternative to suicide but also a way of denying jail. Written in prison, her book ends with the memory of a comrade who died in it, and with her refusal to write about it:

> One arrives in Europe, in the arms of the devil, effortlessly, speaking low, in silence. In your country, people do not die noisily. Shot or knifed, among screams and scissors blows. Here, people disappear quietly, in an undertone, Silently. Alone and desperate. From aids or heroin. Or inside a prison cell, hanging from a water pipe. Like Celma, whom I wish to remember. She slept in the cell next to mine, in this other hell where I now live and which I decided not to narrate.[38]

Ribka Sibhatu also tells about a comrade who died in jail and links her death to the pervasiveness of silence. The dots that split the poem in two, she explained, are both a mark of the silence that accompanies death, and an icon for the bullets that killed her comrade:

> For the world to understand,
> While they were digging her grave,
> Wrapped in mysterious death,
> She wove an aghelghel
> And sent it with no hmbascià.

> In an intense night,
> In shackles they took her from me!
> . . . .
> Every day she is absent,
> But in the dark she is omnipresent!
> Because she will not be parted from me,
> Bring me my Abebà's aghelghel:
> Maybe in it is the answer,
> The key to her shackles
> that are now holding me.[39.]

Abebà's shackles of silence and absence hold Sibhatu's wrists; Hassan Itab is "locked in silence"; Fernanda de Albuquerque is unable to write about her time in prison. Jail, then, is both a place and a state of mind, a sphere of silence as a scene of writing. This is a familiar process in African American literature: "my cell became my chapel," wrote John Marrant as early as 1770. Similarly, the space of seven-year confinement becomes for Harriet Jacobs the space from which she writes letters that deceive and manipulate her master. A narrow space in which images of jail merge with images of the underground ("alone / in my small / and narrow room upstairs") becomes the place of writing and memory for Haim Rady, an undocumented Moroccan poet living underground in Sicily. The poem is called "Clandestine," which in Italian has a strong connotation of "stowaway," of being confined in a narrow ship's hold.

> I am now living
> In the small room upstairs
> But it is too narrow
> For my future
> And my dreams become confused.
> They keep telling me, "Let yourself go and forget"
>
> But how can I do that?
> How can I forget
> And send away that voice
> That keeps calling me?[40.]

While prison stands for social invisibility and enforced silence and immobility, another space—the street—dominates both African American and African Italian writing as the social and imaginative correlative of displacement and marginality, on the one hand, and of ambiguous visibility, displacement, and vulnerability on the other. In the streets of New York, Frederick Douglass felt a "sense of loneliness and insecurity"; Richard Wright was "depressed and dismayed" by "the flat black stretches of Chicago."[41] Salah Methnani, from Tunisia, writes:

We meet in the morning, for breakfast, at the [Welcome] Center at Piazza Bologna, then at Colle Oppio for lunch, a shower in the afternoon in via Marsala, and so on. . . . In the evening, everybody gathers around the big TV screen in the railroad station.

Slowly, I have learned to recognize meeting places according to ethnic group and place of origin. There is an alternative map of Rome, other than the one you find in the yellow pages. . . . A true second-level topography, a sort of underground circuit in the open air.[42]

The two relevant metaphors in this passage are the alternative map and the reversal of space. The figure of the alternative map returns when the narrator reaches Turin: "I buy a map of the city and set to studying it. Strange: laid out on paper, Turin seems to make even less sense. Rather than unwinding in a possible reading, the lines of the streets twist and tangle into a web, a meaningless arabesque. I drop the map in a dust bin."[43] Space makes no sense to these new-time explorers; the throwing away of the map inevitably reminds readers of American literature of parallel gestures by Melville's Ahab and Faulkner's Ike McCaslin. The heroes are literally treading uncharted space, a nonworld that is also an underworld.

The vertical reversal of space, implied in Methnani's metaphor of the "underground . . . in the open air," is developed in a poem by Thamir Birawi, an exiled poet from Palestine:

> In Rome at night the graves open up
> In Rome at night the dead rise
> they walk around
> hands on their heads
> in the rain
> shoeless
> toothless
> without a ticket
> undocumented[44]

"The street is where black children get their education," wrote H. Rap Brown: the street is a place of marginality and homelessness but also a space of verbal virtuosity and social creativity.[45] The street is where immigrants spend most of their time, because they have no place to stay and because that is where they often ply their trade. Being in the streets so much (the peddler has become a stereotype for all immigrants) makes them more visible, giving the impression that there are many more in Italy than is actually the case and contributing to racist fears and hysteria. Pop Khouma was an "elephant peddler," Fernanda Farias de Albuquerque a prostitute, Methnani a dope pusher in the mean streets of Florence.

Moshen Melliti's *Pantanella. Canto lungo la strada*, combines in its very title the canonic space of the street ("road song") with another space of the immigrant experience, an abandoned building (the Pantanella, which was the most significant multiethnic immigrant aggregation in Rome until its population was evicted and scattered by the police, was an abandoned pasta factory). As in many African American narratives, there is much of the picaresque in these stories of wanderers and marginal men, about flophouses and abandoned buildings, street corners and beaches, police stations, subway stations, train stations: "the train, which North Africans call *el fajaa* (which means fear, danger), is the last alternative to cheap hotels and homeless centers."[46]

The train represents both homelessness, with its accompanying agony and fear, and mobility, possibility, freedom. These books are filled with trains, airplanes, automobiles. Each section in the autobiography of the Palestinian exile Salwa Salem is named after the countries in which she has lived: her native town of Nablus, then "Kuwait 1959–1966," "Vienna 1966–1970," "Italy 1970—1992."[47] The chapters of Salah Methnani's narrative also bear the names of towns, tracing Italy's geography from the deep South of "Mazara del Vallo" to the North of "Milan"—framed by "Tunis" and "Kairouan," departure and (temporary) return.

The picaresque element combines enforced mobility with a subjective desire to see the world. The first African American narrative, that of Briton Hammon, begins when, "with the leave of my master, I went from Marshfield, with an Intention to go a voyage to sea"—a voyage that takes the narrator to Florida Indian villages, Cuban Spanish jails, and the streets of London. The wish to "go a voyage" is sublimated in later slave narratives into the desire to escape from slavery but remains a distinct motive in immigrant texts. On leaving his father's house, Pap Khouma discovers "the happiness of feeling independent"; Salwa Salem experiences her life abroad as the realization of a woman's right to live "with the wind in her hair"; Salah Methnani's narrative persona is moved less by economic need than by visions of Italy as "an enchanted, happy land." And Ribka Sibhatu says that she became an exile both "to save [her] life" and to pursue " the search for [her]self"—two impulses that she combines in one word: freedom.

The slaves' Atlantic passage was entirely a matter of force; the Mediterranean passage of many immigrants is a shifting balance between (much) necessity and (some) choice. The narrator of Salah Methnani's book expected that in the West he would find "not only work, but liberty as well." As he sets upon his journey, he asks himself a classic question: "Am I leaving as a North African emigrant, or as another young man bent on seeing the world?"[48]

Narratives of Disappointment

"I step out of the plane with the right foot, as the fortune-teller had prescribed. In fact, I go through passport control without any problems. We go on to the customs sign. They glance at our things, our documents, our bags. That's all. We're really in. This is Italy. I am out of the airport, in the street, in the open and in the sun."[49] Like many African American autobiographies, these texts can be described as narratives of "emersion": the movement is the same, from south to north, from warm to cold, from a "suffocating" (Methnani) or "limiting" (Salem) environment to the open spaces of the metropolis.[50] However, whereas in classic African American autobiographies the emersion is usually the end of the tale, in most immigrant narratives it is the beginning. The emphasis is less on what the protagonists have escaped or left behind than on what they discover once they emerge into the new environment. Narrative beginnings tend to be strong, with a sharp element of separation and a lively note of hope; endings—often, second departures after temporary returns—are often tentative and somewhat inconclusive.

We may tentatively identify two basic structures, depending on whether the "passage" is placed at the beginning or in the middle of the narrative. I call the former "immigration narratives," entirely devoted to the experience in the new country: two typical examples are the books of Pap Khouma and Salah Methnani. The other type, which devotes much space also to the narrator's preemigration experience and native culture, is closer to a standard autobiographical model, more concerned with outlining the story of a life than with emigration per se. The most outstanding examples of this type are *Princesa* and the autobiographical narratives of Nassira Chohra and Salwa Salem.

"Immigration narratives" are most frequently written by men, whereas autobiographies proper are more often the work of women. One cannot definitively generalize this difference in terms of gender, (e.g., Ribka Sibhatu's book of stories and poems devotes two sections to her native land and culture). Social identity may also be a factor: Salem, Sibhatu, Chohra—an intellectual, a student, and an actress—rank high in the immigrant social scale, while Khouma and Methnani are identified with the standard immigrant trade, peddling, an almost entirely male occupation (although by the time they published they had become a union organizer and a journalist, respectively). There are so far no significant

narratives by women employed in the most representative and numeri-
cally significant female occupation: domestic work. There is no African
Italian *Our Nig* as yet: access to public speech for immigrants seems to be
so far predicated on access to the public space of education or of the
street.

In other words, just as the authors of slave narratives differentiated
themselves from their fellow slaves by their escape to tell their tale (and,
in some cases, by the ability to write it), these authors are not "common"
immigrants, and their work cannot be taken as direct, unmediated expression of the average experience. The titles attempt to suggest as much:
in *Io, venditore di elefanti* or *Immigrato* the protagonists are representatives
of a social group, just like the tags "an American slave" in African American autobiographies. Their representative quality, however, lies primarily
in their imaginative ability to gather many stories into their own (as is
consciously the case in *Immigrato*). They are representative not as socio-
logical documents, in other words, but as literary works.

Aside from their internal differences, most immigrant autobiographies and narratives share the attitude that Salwa Salem labels "Western
disappointment": "I was going to live the dream that had accompanied
me for two years," she writes; "I would see 'the merry nights of Vienna,' I
would go to the opera and the Philharmonic to listen to Beethoven and
Mozart, I would study child psychology." But her impact with the Aus-
trian metropolis is not what she had anticipated: "We went through
a dark, almost deserted city, full of huge, somber palaces." In this
dark place, she encounters not culture but racism, isolation, loneliness:
"I spent most of my time alone in our horrible apartment, or took
long walks in the parks, under a grey sky, with an umbrella in my hand.
. . . I was disappointed, betrayed by a reality that I had imagined
differently."[51]

The umbrella is an important symbolic element in this passage, because the weather—rain, snow, cold—is a pervasive metaphor in these
narratives. While Austria may actually be cold and rainy, Italy prides itself on its warm sunny climate, yet immigrant narratives describe it as
a cold, rainy, foggy, nocturnal, hostile land. As he lands in Rome at the beginning of his narrative, Pap Khouma steps "into the sun," but the last
page leaves us with the sense of "the cold of this place, to which I'll never
get used." The cold in Methnani's Rome is both physical and psychological: "It's getting cold. The town is harder, the people more intolerant."[52]
And Thamir Birazi writes: "I am an immigrant, I work at night, and I suffer from the cold—I ride my motorbike home each night to a cold water
flat on a seventh floor; there is also an inner cold, not physical, but one of
the things I dislike about Rome is the cold weather."[53] From warmth to

cold, from light to dark, from family and community to loneliness is the trajectory of immigrant disappointment about the West.

In the narrative of Salah Methnani, the dialectic of Western disappointment is articulated in the shifting balance of his identity between the "North African emigrant" and the "young man bent on seeing the world" I have already mentioned:

> Without a job, of any kind, and with money getting lower and lower, I feel suddenly pushed back toward a reality that I can't, that I don't want to accept. I am forced to see myself no longer as a young man bent on traveling and learning. No: suddenly, I discover that I am in every way a North African immigrant, jobless, homeless, undocumented.[54]

He had heard so much about Rome and its monuments that he feels "as if at home" when he arrives with plans much like Salem's in Vienna: "I might go to the Sistine Chapel and the Vatican Museums. I might take a stroll in the Forum. I will no longer be dominated by the image of the undocumented migrant to whom pleasures and desires are denied." But the next sentence declares "Then, like all the other immigrants in the capital city, I hang around the railroad station." In foggy Turin, he goes into the Egyptian museum, but gives up after the first room. The story of emersion changes into one of disillusion and degradation: "Around me, talk of drugs and jail. Violence, marginality, loneliness: I fear that the circle may close, that I, too, may become a small point in its circumference." The downward spiral culminates in a brush with prostitution and a brief experience as drug user and pusher: "I walk with the typical gait of addicts: small, nervous, skipping steps. I, too, am an addict now. An undocumented addict. I have an identity, at last."[55]

Immigrato resembles a combination of *The Autobiography of Malcolm X* (with its themes of hustling and degradation) and Richard Wright's *American Hunger*. Like the second part of Wright's autobiographical narrative, *Immigrato* is structured around a dual emersion: arrival and discovery, disappointment, new emersion into identity. Like Wright, Methnani finds this new identity in the space of writing:

> In the last few days, I have started a diary of sorts, where I jot down the most meaningless, insignificant events and details. I tell myself that at least this way time, people, gestures, shall not pass in vain. In a few months, I shall be able to open my notebook and ask a page: "Do you remember when . . .," or, "what was that girl's name in Mazara?" The notebook, in silence, will answer: it will point out the names, the outlines, and then the bodies. Solitude,

I deceive myself, will be peopled here and there, by a presence, a distant shadow. For a moment, I will be my own traveling companion.[56]

The theme of writing, to which the text returns several times, indicates the self-conscious literary intention of the authors. The last chapter is the most elaborate in compositional terms and also culminates with writing. Methnani's persona is on his way back to Rome, with the hope of a job; the chapter ends, and the narrative resumes in his father's house in Kairouan. He has returned home on vacation, with some money, carrying presents, to tell his story to the father from whom he had been estranged since childhood. Just as Douglass skips the mechanics of his escape from slavery, Methnani skips the details of how he escaped the streets; both elide the mechanics of deliverance and concentrate on its inner consequences. And, just as Douglass ends his narrative with the recovery of his voice and the beginning of his antislavery work, Methnani ends with the completion of writing, the mastery of language, and a new beginning as a writer:

The bus took the main road to El Fahs and Tunis. I searched my suitcase, under the seat in front of me, for my yellow notebook. I wrote a few words. There was only one page, then no more white sheets left. On that page, diagonally across, I wrote in Italian the word "ciao." I thought the journey was just beginning.[57]

Notes

1. Ralph Ellison, *Invisable Man* (Harmondsworth, England: Penguin, 1965), p. 17.

2. Nassira Chohra, *Volevo diventare bianca*, with the assisitance of Alessandra Atti Di Sarro (Rome: E/O, 1993), p. 13. The English translation of all passages quoted in this essay is mine.

3. Chohra, p. 11.

4. Olaudah Equiano. *The Interesting Narrative of the Life of Olaudah Equiano, or Gustavus Vassa, the African.* (1789), in Arna Bontemps, ed., *Great Slave Narratives* (Boston: Beacon, (1969), p. 27.

5. *Panorama*, "Il fascino dell'altro colore," cover page, Feb. 18, 1995. The black model Naomi Campbell is covered only with splotches of gold paint; her left hand is buried somewhere between her thigh and her lower abdomen.

6. On blackness as glamour and desirability in Italian popular culture and advertising, see Robert Orsi, "Forte, nera, potente. Il discorso razzista nella cultura di massa italiana," *I Giorni Cantati* 1, (January–March 1987), pp. 27–30; also in the same issue, Alessandro Portelli, "Faccetta nera is beautiful," pp. 31–32. See also my "Su alcune forme e articolazioni del discorso razzista nella cultura di massa in Italia," *La critica sociologica*, 89 (Spring 1989),pp. 94–97.

7. Nassira Chohra, seminar "Toward an African Italian Literature?" Rome, July 9, 1993. After playing bit parts in movies for a couple of years, Chohra gave up her acting career when she came to Italy and got married.

8. Quoted in Nicoletta Diasio, "La paura di diventare bianco. Malattia e riformulazione dell'identità in un contesto migratorio: una ricerca della Caritas di Roma," *AC—Rivista di Antropologia Culturale*, 5 (1992), pp. 30–35.

9. Charles Chestnutt, "Lonesome Ben," in Sylvia Lyons Render, ed., *The Short Fiction of Charles Chestnutt*, (Washington, D.C.: Howard University Press, 1981), p. 113.

10. Pap Khouma, *Io, venditore di elefanti*, with the assistance of Oreste Pivetta (Milan: Garzanti, 1990), p. 21

11. W.E.B. Du Bois, "Of the Dawn of Freedom," in *The Souls of Black Folk* in *Writings* (New York: Library of America, 1987), p. 372.

12. Mario Fortunato and Salah Methnani, *Immigrato* (Rome-Naples: Theoria, 1990), p. 95.

13. Henry Louis Gates, Jr., "Phillis Wheatley and the 'Nature of the Negro'," in *Figures in Black* (New York: Oxford University Press, 1987), pp. 61–79.

14. Ndjock Ngana was born in Iklanga (Cameroon) in 1952; he began writing socially engaged poetry when he attended the university at Yaoundé in the 1970s. He is married to an Italian woman and lives and works in Rome. His most recent book of poems is *ÑindôÑerô* (Rome: Edizioni Ricerca, 1994), a collection of poems in Basaa translated into Italian by the author. The title means "black" in Basaa and Italian.

15. Ndjock Ngana, "Prigione," in *ÑindôÑerô*, pp. 134–135. The English translation in the text is mine.

Vivere una sola vita,	U niñik ndigi niñ yada,
in una sola città,	nkoñ wada,
in un solo paese,	loñ yada,
in un solo universo,	mbok yada,
vivere in un solo mondo,	u niñik ndigi i mbai
yada	
è prigione	wee u yé i mok.
. . . .	. . . .
Conoscere una sola lingua,	U yik ndigi hop wada,
un solo lavoro,	bôlô yada,
un solo costume,	ngobok yada,
una sola civiltà,	ntén ni wada,
conoscere una sola logica,	u honlak ndigi ka
yada,	
è prigione.	wee u yé i mok.
Avere un solo corpo,	U banga ndigi nyu yada.
un solo pensiero,	mahoñol mada,
una sola conoscenza,	i yada,
una sola essenza,	iu hiada,
avere un solo essere,	u banga ndigi libak yada,
è prigione.	wee u yé i mok.

16. Du Bois, "Of Our Spiritual Strivings," in *Writings*, pp. 364–365.

17. The African Ñindô on the cover is printd in white, while the Italian *Nero* is printed in black. The image is a two-faced mask, with a black face and a white one.

18. Phillis Wheatley, "On Being Brought from Africa to America," in William M. Robinson, ed., *Early Black American Poets* (Dubuque, Iowa: William C. Brown, 1969), p. 100.

19. Dark-skinned Fernanda de Albuquerque would not be classed as black in either Italy or Brazil. On the other hand, her mixed ancestry was evident. As Massimo Canevacci writes, in Brazil "every person is a one-person micro-ethnic group": *Sincretismi. Una esplorazione sulle ibridazioni culturali* (Genoa: Costa & Nolan, 1995), p. 12. The story of her fear and hatred of blacks in Rio de Janeiro, and her love for one black man in the same city, creates a complex subtext of color in this text of gender.

20. Fernanda Farias de Albuquerque and Maurizio Jannelli, *Princesa* (Rome: Sensibili alle Foglie, 1994), p. 57.

21. Farias de Albuquerque and Jannelli, *Princesa*, pp. 58–59.

22. Mario Perniola, *Il sex appeal dell'inorganico* (Turin: Einaudi, 1994), pp. 36–46; William Gibson, *Neuromancer* (New York: Ace, 1984); Donna J. Haraway, *Simians, Cyborgs, and Women: The Reinvention of Nature* (New York: Routledge, 1991).

23. A sample of the manuscript, face to face with Iannelli's revisions, was published in *Caffé*, a magazine "for a multi-ethnic literature in Italy," 1 (September 1994), pp. 4–5.

24. Sylvia Holton, *Down Home and Uptown: The Representation of Black Speech in American Fiction* (Rutherford, N.J.: Farleigh University Press, 1984); Henry Louis Gates, Jr., "Dis and Dat: Dialect and the Descent," in Dexter Fisher and Robert B. Stepto, eds., *Afro-American Literature: The Reconstruction of Instruction* (New York: Modern Language Association of America, 1979), pp. 88–119.

25. Khouma, *Io, venditore di elefanti*, p. 84.

26. Fortunato-Methnani, *Immigrato*, p. 58 *Vu' cumpra'* ("wannabuy") is the racist slur invented to sterotype all immigrants as pidgin-speaking peddlers.

27. Khouma, *Io, venditore di elefanti*, p. 102.

28. See Robert B. Stepto, *From behind the Veil* (Urbana: University of Illinois Press, 1979).

29. Arnold Krupat, *For Those Who Come After: A Study of Native American Autobiography* (Berkeley: University of California Press, 1985).

30. See note 7.

31. Interview with Salah Methnani, Rome, February 17, 1995.

32. Moshen Melliti, *Pantanella. Canto lungo la strada* (Rome: Edizioni Lavoro, 1992).

33. "La figura di una donna," *Caffé* 1 (September 1994), pp. 4–5 (based on interviews with Fernanda Farias de Albuquerque and Maurizio Jannelli, Rome, May 1994 and March 1995).

34. Khouma, *Io, venditore di elefanti*, p. 63.

35. Hassan Itab, *La tana della iena* (Rome: Sensibili alle Foglie, 1991), p. 15.

36. Interview with Ribka Sibhatu, Rome, January 24, 1991.

37. H. Bruce Franklin, *The Victim as Criminal and Artist* (New York: Oxford University Press, 1978), chapters 1 and 3.

38. Farias de Albuquerque and Jannelli, *Princesa,* p. 103. In the interview quoted above (note 33), Maurizio Jannelli also says that writing was "therapeutic" for him when he was in jail.

39. Ribka Sibhatu, "La mia Abebà," in *Aulò. Canto-poesia dall'Eritrea* (Rome: Sinnos, 1993), pp. 70–73. The *aghelghel* is a palm leaf basket used to carry a festive bread called *hmbascià.* Sibhatu described the meaning of the dots in the interview quoted above (note 36), and explained that the *aghelghel* is her Eritrean version of Keat's Grecian urn, a metaphor of beauty beyond death. The English translation is mine.

> Perché il mondo comprendesse,
> mentre scavavano la sua fossa,
> avvolta nella morte misteriosa,
> intrecciò un aghelghel
> e lo mandò senza hmbascià.
> In un'intensa notte,
> me la rapirono con le manette!
> . . . .
> Ogni giorno è assente,
> ma nel buio è onnipresente!
> Perché non vuole separarsi da me,
> portatemi l'aghelghel della mia Abebà:
> forse è lì la risposta,
> la chiave delle sue manette,
> che ora stringono me. . . .

40. Haim Rady, "Il clandestino," *Caffé* 2 (December 1994), p. 1.

> Adesso io abito
> nella piccola stanza di sopra
> ma è troppo stretta
> per il mio futuro,
> e i miei sogni si sono confusi.
> Mi dicono sempre: "Lasciati andare e dimentica."
>
> Ma come posso farlo?
> Come posso dimenticarmi
> e cacciare quella voce
> che non cessa mai di chiamarmi?

41. Frederick Douglass, *Life and Times of Frederick Douglass* (New York: Collier's, 1962), p. 203; Richard Wright, *Black Boy [American Hunger]* in *Works* (New York: Library of America, 1991), vol. 2, p. 249.

42. Fortunato and Methnani, *Immigrato,* p. 37.

43. Fortunato and Methnani, *Immigrato,* p. 102. On the orgin and use of the word "arabesque" in this context, see above, section 3.

44. Thamir Birawi, "Portoghesi" (stowaways, undocumented), manuscript supplied by the author.

45. H. Rap Brown, *Die, Nigger, Die* (London: Allison & Busby, 1970), p. 27.

46. Fortunato and Methnani, *Immigrato, p. 55.*

47. Salwa Salem, *Con il vento nei capelli. Vita di una donna palestinese,* with the assistance of Laura Maritano (Florence: Giunti, 1993).

48. Khouma, *Io, venditore di elefanti,* p. 20; Salem, *Con il vento nei capelli;* Sibhatu, interview; Fortunato and Methnani, *Immigrato,* pp.10, 14.

49. Khouma, *Io, venditore di elefanti,* p, 26.

50. Fortunato and Methnani, *Immigrato,* p. 14; Salem, *Con il vento nei capelli,* p. 157. On narratives of emersion, see Stepto, *From Behind the Veil.*

51. Salem, *Con il vento nei capelli,* pp. 105, 114.

52. Khouma, *Io, venditore di elefanti,* p. 143; Fortunato and Methnani, *Immigrato,* p. 65.

53. Thamir Birawi, interview, Rome, February 15, 1992.

54. Fortunato and Methnani, *Immigrato,* pp. 25–26.

55. Fortunato and Methnani, *Immigrato,* pp. 43, 80, 52, 102.

56. Fortunato and Methnani, *Immigrato,* p. 52.

57. Fortunato and Methnani, *Immograto,* pp. 129–130.

Epilogue

Transatlantic Passages Revisited, Tenerife

Melba Joyce Boyd

gypsy fortunetellers
revealed the fate
of the undiscovered
country charted
in the black glimmer
of obsidian crystals—
the agony of Africa
inside the unmaking
of America,
the transatlantic cemetery
where history grieves
for the crevices
in our soul,
in the echoes
of clanging chains,
of aching flesh
in the ship's tomb,
the lament
of blues poems
still believing
the rendering light
has meaning beyond
talk—
the touch of thought
as succulent
as a desert blossom

in the arid
climate
of reckoning,
unable to resolve
blood clots
and the imprint
of shame
in paradise.

perhaps,
the gods gathered
on the edge
of Volcano Teide,
above the
sea of clouds,
to bless and
to curse us,
regarding the
contradictions of
earthly evidence
and this choir of
writers, scholars,
myth makers, librarians,
and teachers of texts,
commiserating for courage
to greet ghosts and
to deliver cryptic messages
here, in the Isles Canaries,
the scene of the crime,
where Columbus
traded Black Gold
and stole
nautical mythology
and encoded it onto
maps and an ocean grave
we retrace
with swollen fingers
and jagged hope
empowered by
the anger of
a volcano
and the reverberation
of a turbulent age
haunting human
pursuits to
be of some value.

Index

slave ship dance, 33–44
  as limbo dance, 7, 18–19, 41–42, 43,
    65–66
slave ships, 41
slave system
  in Africa, 19, 48, 272
  chattel status, 117, 118
  Christian converts, 52, 53
  deceit modes under, 40
  economics and, 54–55, 117–19,
    128
  gender and race under, 117–25
  ideological defenses, 5, 6–7, 47–48,
    49, 53, 100–101, 127–34, 219
  loss of self under, 167
  revolts, 37, 38, 41, 279
  U.S. expansionists, 128, 130, 131,
    134
  U.S. original arrivals, 30–31
  violence against women and,
    112–13, 230, 236
  in Virginia, 194–95
  whip's coercion, 36–37
  See also abolitionism; transatlantic
    slave trade
slave trade. *See* transatlantic slave
  trade
"Slave Trade, The" (Major), 83n.2
Smith, Bessie, 125
Smith, Seba, 201n.14
Smith, Venture, 108, 109–10
Snelgrave, William, 47–48, 49
Snitow, Ann, 83n.4
social criticism, 105–6, 108
Somalia, 242, 245, 250
Some Historical Account of Guinea
  (Benezet), 48
Some Memoirs of the Life of Job (Bluett),
  107–8
Song of Solomon (Morrison), 99, 178,
  184–85, 188
Songye, 218, 220, 221
"Sorrow of Yomba, The" (poem), 37
South America, 26, 27, 28, 29, 30
South Carolina
  Fields as missionary in, 144–51
  revival of African slave trade,
    100–101, 128–37
  slave origins, 22

See also Sea Islands
Southern Methodist Episcopal Church,
  132
Southern Presbyterian Church, 216,
  218, 219, 222
Soveraignty and Goodness of God, The
  (Rowlandson), 107
space in-between, 7, 6
"Speaking in Tongues: Dialogics,
  Dialectics, and the Black Woman
  Writer's Literary Tradition"
  (Henderson), 101–2,
  154
spider, 42, 259
Spillers, Hortense, 72, 119, 124, 156
Spratt, Leonidas, 128, 129, 130
Sprigg, Nancy, 199
Stanley, Henry Morton, 217
"stealing away," 42
Stefan, Verena, 241
Steiner, George, 58
Stepan, Nancy Leys, 204, 211
Stillman College, 219
stilt dancing, 43
storytelling, 10, 40, 42, 156, 160, 161,
  162
street imagery, 295–96
Sudan, 242, 247
suicide, 38
Sula (Morrison), 85n.26
Sundquist, Eric J., 205
Sun Poem (Brathwaite), 67
supernatural, 211–12, 276. *See also*
  fantastic
Surinam, 29
Sylla, Abdou, 246
syncretism, 102, 153, 158–62, 286

Takaki, Ronald, 127
*Talking Back. Thinking Feminist. Think-
  ing Black* (hooks), 250
"talking drums," 39
Talle, Aud, 245
Tate, Claudia, 206
Teage, Colin, 196
Temple of My Familiar, The (Walker),
  147, 234
Tenerife, 11
Testimony: Crises of Witnessing in Lit-

ADZ-0135